THE BOOK AT WAR

HOW READING SHAPED CONFLICT AND CONFLICT SHAPED READING

ANDREW PETTEGREE

BASIC BOOKS

New York

Basic Books
Hachette Book Group
1290 Avenue of the Americas, New York, NY 10104
www.basicbooks.com

Printed in Canada
Originally published in Great Britain in 2023 by Profile Books Ltd
First U.S. Edition: December 2023

Published by Basic Books, an imprint of Hachette Book Group, Inc. The Basic
Books name and logo is a registered trademark of the Hachette Book Group.

The Hachette Speakers Bureau provides a wide range of authors for
speaking events. To find out more, go to hachettespeakersbureau.com
or email HachetteSpeakers@hbgusa.com.

Basic books may be purchased in bulk for business, educational, or promotional
use. For more information, please contact your local bookseller or the Hachette
Book Group Special Markets Department at special.markets@hbgusa.com.

The publisher is not responsible for websites (or their content)
that are not owned by the publisher.

Typeset in Garamond by MacGuru Ltd

Library of Congress Control Number: 2023940521

ISBNs: 9781541604346 (hardcover), 9781541604353 (ebook)

MRQ

Printing 1, 2023

CONTENTS

BOOKS AS WEAPONS IN
THE WAR OF IDEAS

The seed of the idea that became this book was planted, appropriately enough, during a visit to the Imperial War Museum in London in 2017. I had dropped by to see an exhibition on the preservation of art, including the museum's own collection, at the beginning of the Second World War, when it was moved out of reach of the anticipated bombing. As a historian of media and communication, this set me thinking: what happened to their books? In the seventy-five years since the war, there has been a lot more attention given to the preservation, looting and restoration of art than to books.[1] There are good reasons for this: while works of art are individual, recognisable and often extremely valuable, the book collections displaced by the war contained much that was mundane, often copies of works published in many thousands of copies. Even where the owner can be identified, by a bookplate, signature or library stamp, books often have little more than sentimental value.

Yet, in the twentieth century, the book stock of Europe and many Asian countries went through a period of turbulence unlike anything previously experienced in world history. Libraries were destroyed, along with tens of thousands of private collections, and even where stock survived it was often appropriated by the victors. Much has never been returned. Berlin, Warsaw, Minsk, Munich, Kassel: the libraries in these cities, with their unique surviving copies of early printed books, musical scores and manuscripts, will never be the same again. This is the story of libraries at war that has often been told: wanton destruction, ameliorated by plucky attempts to keep the show on the road. Famously, libraries were set up in London Underground stations for those sheltering; everywhere, brave librarians worked tirelessly to save their collections from bombing or the depredations of the occupying power.

With these images emblazoned on the memory, many would sympathise with an account that presents the destruction of libraries as a human and cultural tragedy. Anyone reading these words already values books; we are bookish people. We tend to assume books and literary culture have a positive impact on the world, informing, enlightening, assisting the cause of progress. The burning of the Jewish libraries in Poland by the Nazis was an attempt to obliterate their entire cultural heritage and indeed carried off many irreplaceable works. For those who care about literary culture, this deliberate humiliation by the Germans, themselves a people who revered books, was a dagger to the heart. This book acknowledges and revisits these atrocities. But it also asks, was the bombing of libraries, the destruction of books, always a tragedy?

In 1931, the decision was taken to build a new library for Oxford University to provide storage for its growing collection. When war broke out in 1939, it was almost complete, but not yet filled with books. The New Bodleian was immediately made available for a variety of war work. It housed the Admiralty's photographical library, which liaised with the headquarters of the Inter-Services Topographical Division, intended to co-ordinate cartographical activities between the services and housed in the School of Geography. The New Bodleian took in the Royal Observer Corps and the Educational Books Section of the Red Cross, with its essential service providing books for Allied Prisoners of War (POWs). Many college libraries and collections outside Oxford made use of its deep vaults to house their greatest treasures, but then so did the Blood Transfusion Service, stockpiling plasma for the Normandy landings. It is hard not to concede that with this array of war work, the New Bodleian was a legitimate war target. The same could be said of the peerless map collection of the Royal Geographical Society in London, or the scientific collections of the Berlin Technical University in Charlottenburg, crucial resources in the battle of science. Its 250,000 volumes would indeed all be lost to

A legitimate war target? Between 1939 and 1945 the New Bodleian (now the Weston Library) housed both vulnerable treasures from other collections and important war departments. Oxford colleges were also given over to vital war work. Why Hitler never bombed Oxford, also home to the Cowley automobile works, is much debated.

bombing in 1943. And while we continue to mourn the attack in Coventry that destroyed much of the city, it also carried off the public library's important collection of technical literature, a critical resource for war industries in the West Midlands.

Neither are all books good books. Should we lament the loss of the 9 million copies of Hitler's *Mein Kampf* circulating in Germany by 1945, or the 100 million copies of Mao's Little Red Book destroyed when his cult receded? What of Clausewitz, whose clear-eyed pursuit of crushing victory banished the last vestiges of chivalrous respect for the enemy, and opened the way to warfare that made little distinction between combatants and civilians? The very qualities that are often celebrated in literature – its universality, accessibility, the ability to touch multiple lives with an idea or an inspiring narrative – also allowed for the spread of hateful ideologies, as books were twisted for propaganda or exploited to cause harm to enormous swathes of an opponent's population. As well as destroying the Jewish libraries, the Nazis also ascribed great value to them, creating new, vast collections in order to understand their enemies. This bizarre project is indeed the reason why so many Jewish books eventually survived.[2]

When writing this book, I drew on three main sources: books about war, the books generated by war, and archival material consisting of contemporary letters, memoranda and diaries relevant to the experience of reading in wartime, the administration of wartime publishing and the displacement of libraries. This encompasses many hundreds of historical studies and other sorts of contemporary print. For I should make clear that when we talk about books in this text, we range far beyond hardback books and the new paperbacks that transformed wartime reading from the 1930s. The warring nations employed the whole panoply of print: books, pamphlets, scientific periodicals, magazines, newspapers, leaflets and broadsheet notices. The attempt to undermine the morale of enemy troops by firing shells filled with leaflets urging them to surrender may seem hapless and comical, but leaflet dropping was an important part of aerial warfare. Leaflets warning French and German citizens of an impending bombing or artillery barrage allowed some to flee and save their lives. Without print, hierarchies dissolved. When, in April 1945, citizens living in the ruins of Berlin were confronted with two cardboard placards, neatly penned by hand and signed 'Hitler' and 'Goebbels', the dire penalties threatened were brushed aside. Without the authority of print, the handwriting looked pathetic and inconsequential. One onlooker summed up the general disdain: 'Well, just look what those two have come to.'[3]

All of these various print media are explored in this book, not least because they were so interconnected. Many books first appeared as a serial in a literary magazine (John Buchan's *Thirty-Nine Steps* is an excellent example from 1915). The book world and journalism were also closely interwoven. Authors wrote for the newspapers, and newspapers in return promoted the authors' books. Published writers were also in high demand for writing propaganda during times of conflict. This sort of war work was often welcomed by authors, as pressure on paper supplies led to

War is cruel and tragic, but it also allows unexpected talents to blossom. Here a young naval rating takes time off from his duties to sketch a cartoon for a forces newspaper on Orkney.

the closure of the magazines and journals that had provided so much of their income. It is also the case that readers often made no distinction between books and the magazines from which they received much of their news and entertainment. Phyllis Walther was a graduate of London University who in 1939 returned to the family home in Dorset with her young son, leaving her husband to his war work in London. Here Phyllis is responding to a survey circulated to the diarists of Mass Observation about her reading habits:

> The only books I read regularly are *Picture Post*, which I send to my sister in Australia for her birthday and Christmas presents, the *New Statesman*, which she gives me for my present, and *Reader's Digest*, which my father takes in.[4]

None of these three titles named were books in our sense of the word, though _Life_ and _Picture Post_ were, thanks to their extraordinary front-line photography, some of the important publications of the war.

I have read (and bought) many hundreds of books, pamphlets and printed ephemera in the course of researching this text, but if I had to nominate one favourite war book it would be the diary of Nella Last.[5] In 1939, Nella was a housewife in Barrow-in-Furness, a shipbuilding port on the Cumbrian coast. Nella was not formally educated, but she was a natural diarist. Her shrewd, astringent and sometimes ungenerous observations make for a classic account of life under siege from the new horror of war, bombing.

Nella was a devoted reader in her youth, but seems to have read very little during the war. Queuing for food, her voluntary war work and her diary and market garden left her little time for more than a brief glance at the evening paper. This was not at all unusual. Some barely opened a book in wartime, while others experienced the opposite, relying on books as a healing balm in troubled times, with husbands, sons or daughters away from home, and bombers overhead. Many discovered books for the first time, either manning a lonely post away from the front line, or in the forced isolation of a prisoner-of-war camp. So, despite the fact that books and printed matter all too often functioned as vectors of the poisonous ideologies which brought soldiers to commit terrible deeds beyond the imagination of their previous civilian selves, we will also look at books as sources of comfort and solace in turbulent times.

It cannot be a coincidence that the major wars of the nineteenth and twentieth centuries were fought between the world's most bookish nations (which arrived at this position on a tide of mass literacy from the nineteenth century onwards). Germany was the first to adopt wholeheartedly the science of war, with the United States its most adept pupil. The Great War of 1914–18 locked in combat the old world's most respected literary culture, France, and its two greatest publishing giants, England and Germany. This war also gave new energy to the publishing industry in the United States, while the revolution of 1917 initiated a drive towards universal literacy in the new Soviet Union that transformed Russian society. War also radically altered both the terms of the international book trade and the workings of the publishing industry. Former friends and partners could no longer work with each other, as imports from enemy nations were banned. For the defeated, there was the humiliation of having your publishing industry put to use by the conqueror, if not dismantled altogether. Bombing destroyed millions of books, in libraries and private homes, but also in the warehouses of publishers and wholesalers. Publishers could see their entire backlist go up in flames as the result of a single bomb. For all combatant nations there were inevitably new regulations, most obviously paper rationing and censorship.

Censorship plays a more subtle role in this story than one might expect. Nazi Germany made its intentions clear from the first with a total ban on the works of Jewish and 'decadent' authors. Yet it was not clear who fell into the latter category, and it was left largely to librarians to determine what should become of the purged books, if they even recognised them. In Soviet Russia fear of the Gulag was normally enough to effect compliance among authors. In the democracies censorship was more subtle, though German books were withdrawn from libraries in the United States in 1917 (and sometimes burned) and the Cold War cull of books in American libraries impacted many widely read authors, not least Dashiell Hammett and Howard Fast. Ten years previously, the US Army and Navy had been distributing Fast's books to the troops in their Armed Services Editions. In Britain, paper shortages had the most profound impact, making it difficult for literary authors to get a hearing, while the public was crying out for first-hand accounts of the war. Censorship here relied mostly on publishers' discretion, sometimes reinforced by a quiet official word in the ear. This almost cost us one of the great works of the twentieth century, George Orwell's *Animal Farm*, rejected by a string of publishers on the intervention of the intelligence services, reluctant to see its implied criticism of a vital wartime ally, the Soviet Union, reach the public – though ironically the Ministry of Information official whose whispered advice caused publishers to steer clear was later revealed as a Soviet agent.[6]

Despite backstairs lobbying of this character, there was a real difference between the publishing culture in the democracies and the totalitarian states. While public libraries in Germany filled their shelves with copies of books by members of the Nazi elite, in Britain the Moberly Committee, charged with the allocation of extra paper to titles of national importance, rather magnificently refused to grant an allocation for a new edition of a life of the Duke of Marlborough, written by his descendant, the prime minister and hero of the hour, Winston Churchill. And while Churchill's books were firmly banned from prisoner-of-war camps in Germany, *Mein Kampf* was available in British public libraries and a recommended text for the libraries supplied to each army camp. Presumably, the authorities believed that exposure to Hitler's raging could only stiffen their resolve to fight on.

This uneven exchange brings us to one other notable feature of this conflict. It is seldom remarked that the Second World War pitted in opposition war leaders who were also bestselling authors. For Winston Churchill, writing was in his blood, from his first essays in journalism in India and the Boer War, adventures distilled into his first autobiography, *My Early Life* (1930). In the wilderness years before the second war, writing and journalism helped keep him ahead of his mounting debts. In 1953, he would win the Nobel Prize for Literature, for his oratory and historical writing. His adversary, Adolf Hitler, achieved no such recognition, but he did produce the most notorious text of the twentieth century, *Mein Kampf*, in which he laid out in remarkable detail his programme for Germany and the fate that would await its enemies. Published in two volumes in 1925 and 1926, it received a tepid reaction, and sales only took off as his National Socialist party came closer to government. Hitler was also a discerning reader and collector, particularly of architectural and history books, as can be confirmed from the books in his private library at Berchtesgaden, appropriated by American soldiers in 1945 and now in the Library of Congress.[7]

Belying his reputation as crude and uneducated, Joseph Stalin was a deeply literate and thoughtful reader and lover of books. School in a small Georgian town on the fringe of the Russian empire provided a welcome refuge from a dysfunctional family,

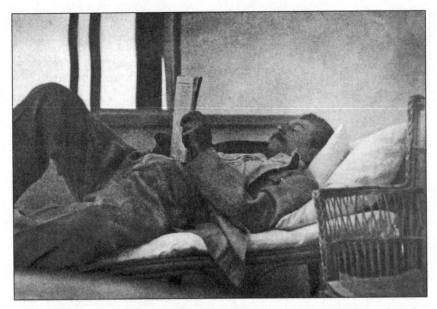

Stalin rose to capture the heights of Soviet power largely through allowing himself to be underestimated. Even today, the image of the bestial mass murderer disguises another side to one of the best-read political leaders of the twentieth century.

and Stalin's intelligence was recognised early. At the local Jesuit college, he courted disapprobation by accessing forbidden literature from a local circulating library. Revolutionary politics would disrupt his ambition to go to university and become a professor, but he continued to read, assembling in his apartment at the Kremlin and his dachas a carefully curated library of 15,000 books.[8] This was not a show collection: a good proportion of the books that have survived are covered in his detailed and sometimes caustic annotations. Stalin would carry this editorial flair into a deep involvement with some of the major writing projects of the Soviet state, including the *Short Course History of the Communist Party and the Soviet Union* and school history texts. Stalin wrote far more than he is given credit for: his *The Foundations of Leninism*, *Marxism and the National and Colonial Question*, *Problems of Leninism* and *Dialectical and Historical Materialism* circulated in millions of copies during his lifetime. The war of ideas would be fought by men who had staked their career on the power of words.

It is also worth recalling that Charles de Gaulle, during the war the lonely symbol of French defiance, first came to prominence as an author of a widely admired text on armoured warfare, *Vers l'Armée de métier* (*Towards a Professional Army*). The audience for such a book crossed national boundaries: within a year, it had been translated into both German and Russian.[9] A lifelong and discerning reader, as president de Gaulle would take a deep interest in the affairs of the Académie Française. During the war, he certainly played the weakest hand to great effect, ensuring that France emerged as one of the victorious combatant nations despite the humiliation of 1940 and the shame of the Vichy Republic.

All of these warrior authors would eventually be outpaced by Chairman Mao Zedong, founding leader of the People's Republic of China. A billion copies were printed of the *Quotations of Chairman Mao*, universally known as the Little Red Book, and it was translated into more than fifty languages. Mao also has the rare distinction of having served as a librarian. As a penniless boy from the provinces with no connections, he was lucky to be found a position as an assistant in the Beijing University library, but this mundane work only increased his sense of alienation:

> My office was so low that people avoided me. One of my tasks was to register the names of people who came to read newspapers, but to most of them I didn't exist as a human being ... I tried to begin conversations with them on political and cultural subjects, but they were very busy men. They had no time to listen to an assistant librarian speaking southern dialect.[10]

His attempts to take what scraps he could from the university led only to humiliation. When he tried after a lecture to initiate conversation with the well-known leftist intellectual Hu Shih, then completing his seminal *Outline of the History of Chinese Philosophy*, and a man only two years older than Mao, Hu brushed him aside when he discovered he was not a student but an assistant librarian.

For all this, Mao was a persistent and devoted reader: he arrived in Beijing having already read in translation Rousseau's *Social*

Contract, Montesquieu's *L'Esprit des lois* and Adam Smith's *Wealth of Nations*, which he found in the provincial library at home. Yet he never forgot these early slights. Having carefully nurtured connections with the professional classes when the Communist Party first seized power, the memory of youthful rebuffs came home to roost in the brutal treatment of intellectuals in the Cultural Revolution.

It is therefore no wonder that belief in the power of the written word to shape the destiny of nations became so widespread in the twentieth century. As Stalin told a writer's congress in 1934: 'We need engineers of the human soul, writer-engineers building the human spirit.'[11] In the words of the German communist intellectual Friedrich Wolf, literature was already thoroughly weaponised: 'The material of our age lies in front of us, hard as iron. Poets are working to forge it into a weapon. The worker has to pick up this weapon.'[12] In the post-war communist bloc, belief in the power of the word was unshakable. Even the dour and austere East German leader Walter Ulbricht would exhort his writers 'pick up the quill, comrade', while simultaneously instituting a system of censorship and control that would survive through to 1989.

The Western democracies were less overt in their appropriation of libraries for political purpose, but the underlying ideologies of imperialism and national destiny were well represented on their shelves. In all nations, once war broke out, writers and libraries were expected to play a full role in forging victory. Once that victory was achieved, after the Second World War the Allies would face the problems of how to sanitise, or exploit, the collections of the defeated. Self-interest played its part in these decisions, as did the continuing importance of libraries as ideological bastions in the front line of post-war ideological conflict, now fought out on a global scale.

Let us leave the last word to the most prominent of the major war leaders who cannot be credited as a major author, Franklin D. Roosevelt. President Roosevelt certainly appreciated the value of books, though more as a collector: already in 1938, he was able to give to the nation a library of 15,000 books, pamphlets and maps, along with a lovingly assembled collection of historical naval charts. And he easily recognised that the wave of horror that swept the United States at the German book burnings could be put to good use. In 1942, he declared:

> We all know that books burn, yet we have the greater knowledge that books cannot be killed by fire. People die, but books never die. No man and no force can put thought in a concentration camp forever. No man and no force can take from the world the books that embody man's eternal fight against tyranny of every kind.[13]

This became a famous poster, with a monumental book behind miniature storm troopers throwing books into the fire, and the tagline 'Books are weapons in the war of ideas'. Roosevelt was an accomplished rhetorician, and like most great orators, he used words carefully. When he and other political leaders identified books and authors, poets and publishers as key resources in the business of war, we must take them seriously. This book shows how this came to be.

PART I

BUILDING THE FIGHTING NATION

1

A CALL TO ARMS

In the Introduction to this book, I hope I have challenged the assumption that literature is inherently peaceful, either a non-combatant or a tragic victim of conflict. Indeed, books and publishing have deep roots in the history of warfare: wars set people against people, nation against nation, and tested the power of competing ideologies. Libraries, as the seeding grounds of these ideologies, were often deliberately targeted for destruction. For libraries, from the time of ancient Greece and Rome to the public library movement of the nineteenth century, had never simply been collections of books. They were also a public demonstration of a society's values, occupying prestige space in the city centre, often the gift of a community's leading citizens. Destroying these institutions was a thrust at the heart of an enemy society.

Libraries would also be destroyed as part of the symbolic humiliation of the defeated. The obliteration of your most precious objects, of the stored cultural heritage of a civilisation, was a means of putting the contest of competing ideologies beyond repair. For the Aztec and Mayan empires, the destruction of their books by Spanish conquistadores was not just a demonstration of power: it was also ritual denigration of their system of beliefs, a sign that their gods could not protect them. The Nazi troops who in conquered Poland burned the sacred books of Jewish communities orchestrated a similar ritual, insisting that the local Jewish population were forced to witness the defiling of their most sacred texts. In the brutal battle for Sarajevo in 1992, Serbian troops deliberately aimed their artillery at the National and University Library of Bosnia-Herzegovina, in the same way that in 1981, a Sinhalese mob had laid waste the library of Jaffna, the central

On *Kristallnacht*, the night of broken glass (1938), the Nazis looted and
burned Jewish shops and destroyed 1,400 synagogues. Their holy books
were a natural target, as they would be again in the conquered territories,
beginning with Poland, after the beginning of the Second World War.

repository of Tamil literary culture. Both the victims and the perpetrators knew just how much cultural meaning was bound up in
these collections.

From the Roman general Sulla, parading through Rome with
the looted library of Aristotle, to the author Stendhal's tour of
German libraries searching out books for the new National Library
of France on behalf of the all-conquering Napoleon, victorious
generals have always seen books, like works of art, as legitimate
plunder. For the Swedish armies of the Thirty Years' War (1618–
48), such cultural appropriation served a double purpose: to stock
the libraries of their universities and towns, while at the same time
depriving their religious opponents of the texts vital to building the
Catholic faith. The Swedish ransacking of the libraries of central
Europe was organised with all the precision of a military campaign.
On accepting the surrender of a town, the Swedes would seek out
local dignitaries who could lead them to the principal archives and
libraries. The contents would be carefully guarded until they could
be packed and shipped back to Sweden, before distribution to the
royal library, the university of Uppsala or grammar schools. Some
were lost in a disastrous fire at the royal library, but the rest are still

in Sweden; surprisingly, there has never been the same clamour for the return of looted books as misappropriated art.[1]

So, the historical roots of themes pursued in this book, the birth of military strategy, the war of intelligence or the importance of accurate mapmaking, are deep. Yet for all that, there is also clear evidence of a quantum shift in warfare, and its implications for the library world, in the last two centuries: that is, from the middle of the nineteenth century onwards. This transformation of war-making had three main elements: the professionalisation of the military, especially of the officer class; the industrialisation of weaponry; and the mobilisation of the civilian population, eliding the distinction between combatant and non-combatant. This had enormous impact on the role of the book in wartime, and the impact of warfare on library stock.

This era was also a time of transformational change in the Western world, to this point the main incubator of the library movement. Between 1800 and 1914, the population of Europe increased from 180 to 460 million. In the United States, growth was even more spectacular, from 5 to 106 million. Much of this population growth went to provide a workforce for the new industrial economy. Integrating these new citizens into the social fabric required, above all, a vast increase in educational provision. This fuelled a concerted drive towards compulsory education in both Europe and America. By the early twentieth century, Western societies were approaching universal literacy in both the female and male populations. This permitted a parallel impetus towards a network of public libraries, free to all, catering to the reading needs of the broad mass of the population. The wars of the late nineteenth and twentieth century, therefore, are the first in which the majority of both combatants and civilians were able to consume and respond first-hand to the literature of the time, from newspapers to information leaflets to cheap thrillers and serious works of fiction. This is why, although I refer to earlier histori-cal eras, this book will focus on the period that begins with the American Civil War and continues through the end of the Cold War, in which books played an important role as both persuaders and provocation. The CIA flying balloons over the Iron Curtain with Bibles attached was not likely to achieve much, but it made a point.

The century after 1850 was the historical era when nations discovered both the power of books to shape conflicts, and the deficiencies in their own collections. Archibald MacLeish was one of the most influential librarians of the twentieth century: as the Librarian of Congress in 1939, he would play a major role in shaping American policy during the Second World War. MacLeish was quick to realise that if the United States were to prevail in the great global struggle, all the resources of the nation would need to be mobilised for the fight – and that included books and libraries. In 1945, he would reflect that

> War, modern war at least, cannot be fought without the most complete library resources. No library resources can ever be too complete for the necessities of a great industrial state engaged in a war which involves all its facilities, all its man-power, and all its knowledge. We know now, whatever we may have thought we knew before, that no island in any ocean on earth is too remote or too small or too inconspicuous to be of vital concern to the planning and operating staffs in a war fought with modern air power and modern sea power, to say nothing of modern power on the land. The Library of Congress knows to its cost what its failure to collect over the last century and a half every scrap of printed and manuscript material on the islands of the Pacific has meant to its service to the government of the United States.[2]

MacLeish was right: when Japan attacked Pearl Harbor in December 1941, America found itself fighting a war in a part of the world about which it knew very little. The character of the enemy, the conditions its troops would face, even the names of the islands and atolls that would inscribe themselves on the American psyche in the next three years: all these were a mystery. When, in February 1942, President Franklin D. Roosevelt sat down for his weekly radio address, he suggested to his listeners that it would help if they had a map or globe to hand as he spoke. The next day, bookshop shelves were swept bare of maps and atlases as Americans hastened to follow his advice.

What was true of America was true of belligerent powers throughout the twentieth century. When war broke out in Europe in 1914 and again in 1939, the resources which had been taken for granted, well-stocked libraries and archives, proved to be sadly wanting. Sometimes the gaps were almost comically extreme: when in 1940 Winston Churchill was planning the pre-emptive attack on Norway intended to deprive the rampant German army of Norway's harbours and coastline, the best resource to hand was an old copy of the Baedeker guide to Scandinavia. Yet this was a war of science, strategy and intelligence, of new weapons to be developed and brought into service: all of this required access to the best scientific literature as well as research and analysis. It was just as important to prevent this same information falling into the hands of the enemy. Never were books and periodicals more urgently required, more essential to national survival.

Books played an equally important role on the home front. Deprived of other entertainments, bereft of husbands and wives, sons and daughters, many of those left behind, or shivering in uncomfortable digs far from home, turned to books. Public libraries, to this point rather underappreciated, came into their own, and publishers, despite constraints on the supply of paper, enjoyed a golden age. All the belligerents put enormous efforts into supplying books to their troops, stimulating some of the most innovative publishing initiatives of the century. Nowhere were books more appreciated than in prisoner-of-war camps.

Books also played a role in inculcating the ideologies that led formerly friendly nations to turn on each other with such savagery. Books were the seedbeds of ideology, nurturing hatreds, justifying aggression, mobilising public opinion. When we ask why ordinary men were inspired to fight for a cause, we must not forget the role of literature in bringing this about, and when war came, librarians, like any other public officials, threw themselves into the struggle, eager to play their part in a patriotic cause.

When war broke out, the entire physical, industrial and intellectual capital of a nation had to be mobilised for the war effort, and libraries were critical strategic assets. Few resources were more precious than the extended runs of scientific periodicals stored in university libraries; conserving and protecting what had to this point been knowledge shared around the worldwide scientific community became a critical war aim. University and national libraries also became crucial resources in the war of intelligence, which grew from a limited attempt to round up enemy spies and infiltrate governments abroad into an enormous apparatus of information gathering and analysis, occupying many of the nation's best minds. Once warfare turned from defence to attack, having accurate maps was the difference between a well-planned operation and chaos: libraries as well as geographers would play a critical role in the development of war cartography.

Public libraries also had their role in the national cause: as offices for the numerous new bureaucracies of wartime, selling war bonds, handing out ration books. Their book stock was transformed by the deluge of government printing informing shopkeepers and householders of the numerous new regulations they were obliged to follow, as well as books making the case for war and charting its progress. Libraries also became a critical element of the infrastructure of support for troops and civilians far from home and deprived of their usual home comforts. Some opened up their newsrooms to military personnel at the weekend. Public libraries played a major role in supplying the military installations in their vicinity, and co-ordinating donations for the new camp libraries. Books were also collected to send to troops abroad, and, given the chronic shortage of paper, for pulping and reuse: indeed, although when we think of books destroyed in wartime our minds might turn to the dome of St Paul's illuminated by the blazes consuming the publishing houses of London, or the battered shell of the Berlin State Library in 1945, in Britain the donation of books for pulping accounted for as many books destroyed in the Second World War as bombing.

This huge network of libraries had been a long time in the making. In the United States, the densely settled New England states led the way. In Britain, the critical moment was the passage in 1850 of the Public Libraries Act, empowering local authorities to establish libraries in their town or borough. By 1914, there were more than 5,000 library authorities established in Britain under the terms of the 1850 Act, collectively circulating between 30 and 40 million volumes a year. By 1903, the United States boasted at least 4,500 public libraries, with a total book stock of some 55 million volumes. This growth would continue: by 1933, Germany had more than 9,000 public libraries, while the collective book stock of American libraries now exceeded 140 million books.

The potentialities of this new library system were not lost on governments bent on ideological renewal, or waging war. Hitler and Lenin were both great friends of the library. As dawn broke after the storming of the Winter Palace in 1917, Lenin impressed on the newly appointed Commissar for Education that libraries would be a key weapon in the fight for hearts and minds:

> Try to pay attention to libraries in the first instance. We must borrow from progressive bourgeois countries all those methods they have developed for making library books widely available. We must make books accessible to the masses as soon as possible. We must try to make our books available all over Russia, in as large a quantity as possible.

Despite the devastation of the old tsarist libraries in the civil war that followed, Lenin's objectives were largely realised, accompanied by a huge increase in literacy across the Russian population. Lenin's passionate commitment to libraries was very personal. In the long years of exile, he seems to have planned out his travels around Europe to have access to the world's great libraries, and settled in London, Munich, Kraków and finally Zurich. In the years before his return to Russia he kept office hours in the Zurich Public Library, nine till twelve in the morning, one till six in the afternoon. Library records confirm that he read or consulted 148 books and 232 articles in English, French and German.[3] By January 1916, he had drafted *Imperialism: The Highest State of Capitalism* sitting in his favourite seat in the Zurich library. Having been created by a published book, *The Communist Manifesto*, Bolshevism was an inherently bookish movement, and along with Lenin, who assembled his own library only when finally settled in Russia, the major Russian revolutionary figures, Kamenev, Zinoviev and Bukharin, all collected books. Vyacheslav Molotov had 10,000 books and Marshal Georgy Zhukov, the hero of the campaigns against Hitler's army, assembled a collection of 20,000.[4]

This book explores this weaponisation of book culture under six main headings: building a fighting nation; libraries as munitions of war; books on the home front; providing books for troops; book plunder and destruction in wartime; reconstruction of book stocks and the war for ideological supremacy in the Cold War. This brings us to the cusp of the digital age and cyber warfare. It ends with a reflection on what will be the continuing role of libraries in an age where print is increasingly challenged by other means of communication, but societies still make massive provision for war. Meanwhile, the Global South is embracing the library at the same time as Western nations look elsewhere for sources of information and entertainment: the library is far from dead, and its contents will continue to be a subject of profound social and political importance.

There are also three themes that flow through the whole book rather than being addressed in their own chapters: patriotism, poetry and propaganda. Though not so obvious as the technical advances of the nineteenth and twentieth centuries, patriotism was an essential element in modern warfare. In medieval times, soldiers fought for their lord, with or against the king dependent on the loyalties of their local magnate. Town-dwellers identified with their local community more than their nominal prince, who, thanks to the complexities of dynastic succession, might be a foreign ruler who did not speak the language and sometimes never even set foot in his more far-flung territories. The coalescence of nation states into discrete blocks of territory following relatively clear geographical boundaries began first with the emergence of England (then Britain), France and Spain, but Italy and Germany, core centres of European trade, culture and technical innovation, only became nation states in the nineteenth century.

Thus, it was only in wars of the twentieth century that patriotism could be systematically deployed in the battery of ideological weaponry. Soviet troops were urged forward to the defence of Mother Russia; German conscripts fought for the defence of the Fatherland. But the focus of this patriotic energy was by no means clear if you were a resident of Ukraine, Alsace, Latvia or French Canada. In the First World War, peoples of many nationalities – Poles, Ruthenians, Finns, Czechs, Irish and Bosnians – were compelled to fight for countries to which they felt little national allegiance. In the case of Poland, divided between its larger neighbours in the eighteenth century, Poles fought in the armies of three great powers, Russia, Germany and Austro-Hungary, many against family and friends, separated by unhappy accidents of geography: for Poles, the First World War was a civil war.[5] Because claims to nationhood were based on the existence of ethnic language communities, vernacular poetry and literature were essential vectors of both national historical grievances and the courageous claim to autonomy. These were memories and aspirations that would never die, as the tragic fratricidal conflicts for the splintered segments of Yugoslavia would demonstrate in the last decades of the twentieth century.[6]

It was easy to envy Britain or Spain for the geographical clarity that defined the nation state: in the heartlands of Central Europe there was no such luxury. For much of European history it was more accurate to talk of borderlands than frontiers. Between France and the Low Countries or within the complex tapestry of the Holy Roman Empire in the sixteenth and seventeenth centuries, it was easy to undertake a journey without realising where you had passed from one jurisdiction to another. By the nineteenth century, advances in surveying and cartography had effected a radical change in both the concept of frontiers and the capacity for conflict. It was no coincidence that it was in Germany that geography first became a university discipline, and its professors were among the most virulently nationalist proponents of a greater Germany. Hitler was by no means the first to trumpet the concept of *Lebensraum*.

Throughout the history of warfare, poetry had served as a means of articulating sentiments and emotions often dangerous to express in prose. In the first era of print, pamphleteers would be out on the streets with their narratives of their king's latest triumphs in the field; it was left to the poets to digest more discreetly the pain of defeat. Poetry took on an equally potent role in the globalised conflicts of the modern age, as a rallying cry for national unity, stiffening resistance in times of adversity, or as an ideological teaching tool. The outbreak of war in 1914 was greeted by an outpouring of verse throughout the continent. According to one authority, in Germany alone, 50,000 poems a day were being written in the first month of the war, and Germany's hymns of praise to martial values were echoed around the continent. The sense that war provided a means to escape an age of decadence and vapid consumerism was common to many of the belligerent nations. As early as 1910, the German Georg Heym was confiding to his diary: 'If only someone would start a war, even if there's no good reason. This peace is greasy and grimy as wax on old furniture.' With hostilities begun, poets welcomed war as a force of renewal: according to the Italian Gabriele D'Annunzio, 'It is only through war that those people who have degenerated can stop their decline, for war unfailingly gives them either glory or death.' His compatriot Filippo Tommaso Marinetti, the son of a professor of literature, concurred: 'We will glorify war – the world's only hygiene – militarism, patriotism, the destructive gesture of freedom-bringers, beautiful ideas worth dying for.'[7]

This willingness to shed the blood of the nation's young may be distasteful, but it offers an important corrective to our common perception that poetry was an inherently anti-war medium. In Britain, the poems of war are best known to us as a post-traumatic literature of bitterness and regret. The archetype of the British war poet is a young officer who turned from patriotic enthusiasm (Rupert Brooke) to disillusionment (Wilfred Owen). But in fact most British war poets were civilians and a quarter were women. Through long service as the literary epitome of the pity of war, the poems of the British public-school officers have achieved far greater resonance than was the case on their first publication. In their own day they were easily drowned out by the self-confident sense of mission of the imperialist verse so successfully disseminated by

Rudyard Kipling and his heirs, poems that articulated the patriotic pride of a generation, and helped motivate the rush to the recruiting offices in 1914.

It bears emphasis that at the beginning of the twentieth century poetry had a far greater social presence than in our own era. Poetry was central to the education system, and many newspapers routinely printed readers' poems. In the emerging powers to the east, the role of poetry was if anything even more important. Mao's poems set out his approach to war and ideological struggle. Stalin, like Mao a passionate devotee of the medium, first published poetry in a Georgian journal at the age of seventeen, romantic verses that were of sufficient quality to find a place in highly respected anthologies.[8] Poetry was particularly important because, despite the drive towards greater literacy, the peasant oral tradition of these societies was still very strong. The ease with which poetry could be learned and regurgitated amplified its impact far beyond reading. This insight helped ensure the success of the collection of aphorisms that became Mao's Little Red Book, one of the greatest publishing phenomena of all times, and a major propaganda tool both within China and throughout the world. In the battle of competing ideologies, poets could insert their ideas where soldiers and weapons could not reach. Those who succeeded were feted and rewarded, as when the Soviet leader Nikolai Bukharin rhapsodised on the work of Vladimir Mayakovsky: 'The poetry of Maykovsky is poetry in action . . . It is a hailstorm of sharp arrows shot against the enemy. It is devastating, fire-belching lava. It is a trumpet call that summons to battle.'[9]

The ambiguity of poetic expression also set challenges that the ubiquitous censors were not always able to meet, whether this was in communist Eastern Europe or occupied France. In 1942, the poet Max-Pol Fouchet persuaded the censor that Paul Éluard's 'Une seule pensée' was a love poem, rather than a passionate cry for freedom. It was widely distributed, not least in the miniaturised magazines dropped on France by the RAF.[10] In the post-war period of communist rule, the East German security service, the Stasi, went so far as to establish its own poetry circle. This was placed under the custodianship of a well-published comrade who would report back to his superiors on the ideological reliability of the work shared.[11]

Propaganda as a tool of war was alive and thriving from the invention of printing in the fifteenth century, given impetus by the tragic religious conflicts of the sixteenth century. In the era of the Reformation, when Europe was divided into warring Protestant and Catholic camps, books were perceived as instruments of evangelisation. Nowhere was this more forcefully demonstrated than in Paris in the second half of the sixteenth century. Paris was a resolutely Catholic city, deeply resentful of the insolence of Protestants parading through the streets, singing their psalms and defacing roadside shrines. This provoked a devastating print campaign of denigration, comparing Protestants with the heretics and despised groups of medieval society: when in 1572 the citizens of Paris got the chance to turn on their Protestant neighbours, they did so with a ferocity that left several thousand dead on the streets in the famous massacre of St Bartholomew's Day.[12] And it worked. In the years that followed many thousands who had joined the Huguenot churches would quietly abandon their faith and be reconciled with Catholicism. As the Paris printer Nicolas Chesneau would remark in a preface to one of these works: 'pamphlets were weapons in a spiritual war'. The pamphlet barrage had played a major role in saving France for Catholicism.[13]

The new technologies of the twentieth century not only transformed warfare, they also opened up new opportunities for propaganda. In the First World War, aeroplanes were used not only for aerial reconnaissance but also for dropping leaflets. The French leafleted Freiburg, as well as dropping a few bombs; on the Eastern Front German planes dropped leaflets explaining to the Russian soldiers that they were shivering in the trenches to advance the interests of British capitalism. Given the low rate of literacy among the Russian conscripts, it is unlikely these carefully crafted messages had much impact. In the Second World War, Britain devoted an extraordinary amount of resources to air propaganda despite acute shortages of paper, to the delight of French school pupils who by 1942 had apparently given up stamp collecting in favour of tracts dropped by the RAF. In Germany, where possession of such material was punishable by death, they had little discernible impact.

If the leaflet war may look like a lavish expenditure of money for little perceptible gain, then the best sort of influencing often came from books that were not written as propaganda at all. One of the most unexpected publishing successes of the Second World War was a book with the catchy title *Social Insurance and Allied Services*.[14] This was the Beveridge Report on post-war social provision, and quickly sold a million copies, more when a summary version was published as a pamphlet priced at threepence. It was also translated into French and German, and dropped with other airborne literature to convince friends and enemies alike of Britain's good intent. At the end of the war a transcription of two German reports about the Beveridge Report was found in Hitler's bunker. They described Beveridge's plan as 'a plutocratic fraud on the English people' while simultaneously claiming that it was 'an especially obvious proof that our enemies are taking over national-socialistic ideas'.[15]

Authors suffered in wartime, often torn between their vocation and war service, while outlets for their work inevitably shrank as magazines were closed and publishers husbanded their paper ration. Writers seldom did their best work when writing for the government, a particularly daunting assignment in Moscow where comrade Stalin was an avid and critical reader. Of books conceived as propaganda, the most successful was probably John Steinbeck's portrait of life in occupied Europe, *The Moon Is Down* (1942), though this was criticised in America for making the occupying troops too human.[16] Arthur Koestler's *Darkness at Noon* (1940) certainly shook the faith in Soviet Russia of many on the political left, a task then pursued with peerless wit and imagination by George Orwell in *Animal Farm* and *1984*. Published after the cessation of European hostilities in 1945, *Animal Farm* became a worldwide bestseller, Orwell having kept it to 30,000 words to facilitate the sale of translation rights. More insidious was the Cold War popularity of James Bond, whose adventures infiltrated the Iron Curtain with the insouciant glamour of the novels' hero. Worried Russian officials commissioned a damning putdown in a leading Soviet publication: 'Who is Mr Ian Fleming, the creator of this – to put it mildly – rubbish?'[17] Attempts to create a more ideologically compatible alternative, such as East German television's Iron Feliks, did not have quite the same resonance.[18]

Books probably secured their most lasting success with the ideological formation of the nation's youth. The author John Le Carré, a schoolboy during the Second World War, was subjected to the full imperial menu: Henrietta Marshall's *Our Island Story* in the classroom, and for recreations, the adventure stories of Percy F. Westerman, Sapper and Henty, and the heroic deeds of Biggles, Bulldog Drummond and Domford Yates's Berry.[19] The unshakable sense of British superiority that seemed to survive any level of battlefield catastrophe and irritated their American allies was nurtured in this pre-teen and adolescent reading. But it was only Germany that attempted the complete militarisation of its youth, with a tragic level of success. Membership of the Hitler Youth and the League of German Girls was compulsory from the age of ten. The emphasis on party discipline and physical activity did little for education, but suited many children, happy to be out of the classroom. Drafted into service at an increasingly young age, many remained convinced of victory right up to the last days of the war. It ended with Allied soldiers having to mow down soldiers as young as twelve as these children enthusiastically manned artillery positions which their elders had abandoned.

Propaganda obviously had more chance of success when it bore some resemblance to observable reality. It was important to Allied credibility that their news services acknowledged setbacks: in this Churchill's frequent speeches to Parliament and the nation set a good example. It had been very different in the First World War, when the patriotic obfuscations of war correspondents had greatly angered the troops in the trenches. In Russia, the established policy of covering bad news in a blanket of silence meant that for much of 1941, most citizens had no idea which cities had fallen to the Germans. In Germany, propaganda was scarcely necessary in the first years of the war, as the home front basked in an uninterrupted sequence of brilliant victories. But the retreat in the east from 1943 required the full repertoire of Nazi circumlocution. Action had been taken to 'straighten the front'; troops had withdrawn to prepared positions. Germans by this point had a good sense of eastern geography from the triumphant maps of Germany's new territories published in the newspapers or atlases. The scale of the casualties, impacting almost every home, also defeated any hope of concealment. Journalists would have known all this; the mixture of false optimism and stern admonition that filled the dwindling pages of the newspapers was designed more to protect journalists from retribution than persuade their readers.

One thing was clear: whether the literature drove young men forward to their deaths, or strengthened the spirit of a country under occupation, literature mattered. The urgent sense of the importance of books as tools of war, whether it be fiction, poetry, history, atlases or books of current political analysis, was shared by all combatant nations and insurgency movements, even those, as in the post-colonial conflicts of the second half of the twentieth century, who were deliberately starved of access to the printing press.

At the turn of the nineteenth century, many commentators, politicians and authors saw warfare as a means of cleansing societies that had become decadent and soft. Books, poems and public rhetoric did a great deal to spread this insidious doctrine, and young men yearned to establish their manhood through valorous deeds. There were brave voices raised against this cult of death, by religious dissenters, conscientious objectors and pacifists, but until recent times they have remained a small minority.[20] In Germany, the well of patriotism following the crushing Prussian victories of mid-century and the subsequent proclamation of the German Empire in 1871 overwhelmed even the Mennonites, whose tradition of non-violence reached back to the sixteenth century.[21] Those who could not accommodate the new militarism joined the wave of emigration to Russia or the United States.

With hundreds of thousands flocking to the recruitment centres, the First World War was a difficult time not to be in uniform. In Britain, after conscription was introduced in 1916, pacifism faced a crossroads: only 16,000 would declare themselves conscientious objectors and most accepted some sort of civilian service. Literary London was well represented in this number, though the offhand performance of Lytton Strachey and Duncan Grant at their tribunal went down badly with other conscientious objectors, aware that these Bloomsbury luminaries could rely on their eminent connections to secure them a safe berth to live out the war. Much of Bloomsbury reconvened at the Garsington estate of Philip and Ottoline Morrell, where desultory labour in the garden and farm was generously interpreted as work of essential national importance.[22]

A far more tragic case was that of Stephen Hobhouse, son of a former MP, who refused to bend and was sentenced to imprisonment and hard labour. This provoked one of the most remarkable tracts of the war, published by Stanley Unwin, himself a conscientious objector, under the name of Stephen's mother.[23] Much of the book trade refused to stock *I Appeal unto Caesar*, but it eventually sold 18,000 copies, sparking a debate in Parliament about the unnecessary brutality of the treatment of conscientious objectors in prison. What Unwin did not mention, though he must have been aware, was that though the book was published as the work of Mrs Henry Hobhouse, its actual author was the pacifist philosopher Bertrand Russell.[24]

Between the wars, pacifism benefited from the revulsion against the waste of human life in the first war, especially evident in literature and memoirs published from 1928 onwards such as Robert Graves's *Goodbye to All That*. Isolationism in the United States, and in Britain the hope for international solutions to European tensions, gave peace campaigners important allies in the political mainstream. In the 1930s, literary figures of established reputation, including Beverley Nichols, Storm Jameson and A. A. Milne, wrote passionate and effective polemics. In the case of Milne, moving a long way from Pooh Bear, the earnest *Peace with Honour: An Inquiry into the War Convention* (1934) went through five editions in just over a year.[25] It is interesting that in these changed circumstances, none of these books struggled to find mainstream publishers. The Peace Pledge Union, committed to the rejection of war in any circumstances, gathered more than 100,000 adherents.

In these years, Gandhi's creed of non-violence was attracting increasing attention, not least in the United States, though his particular interpretation of Hindu teaching did not go unchallenged. In a shrewd move, in 1939 the British authorities in India sponsored the publication of *The Bhagavad-Gita Philosophy of War*. The Bhagavad Gita was one of the most revered of Hindu texts, and surprisingly warlike. Robert Oppenheimer, witnessing the first detonation of the atomic bomb his genius had done so much to create, was quoting the Bhagavad Gita when he reflected 'Now I am become death, the destroyer of worlds.' The British purpose in stiffening Indian support for the war was hardly disguised: *The Bhagavad-Gita Philosophy of War* was a special publication of the *Civil and Military Gazette* of Lahore (the newspaper in which between 1883 and 1889 the young Rudyard Kipling cut his journalistic teeth).

As hope of avoiding war faded, pacifists faced a difficult choice. The Peace Pledge Union was forced almost to a comical extent to downplay the thuggery and violence of the Hitler regime, inviting readers of *Peace News* not to be too 'unctuous' in their condemnation of the violent attacks on Jewish shops in the *Kristallnacht*. Arguing that 'totalitarianism has come to stay', *Peace News* suggested that we should take from it 'what is necessary and good', after the conquest of France musing that Nazism was the 'defined instrument' of European unification.[26] Despite or perhaps because of these pronouncements, by the time of Dunkirk, many writers had abandoned their pacifism, including Nichols, Jameson and Milne, Rose Macaulay and, most surprisingly, Bertrand Russell. It took Jameson three months to write *The End of this War*, the pamphlet that explained this change of mind.[27] Those who held out included Frances Partridge, an associate of Leonard and Virginia Woolf in the Hogarth Press, and her husband Ralph. Their house in Wiltshire became a far less dissolute version of Garsington, a place of respite from the Blitz for their literary friends.[28]

In the Second World War, the government also played a canny hand, widening access to alternative service and avoiding sending even the most determined conscientious objectors to prison. Even

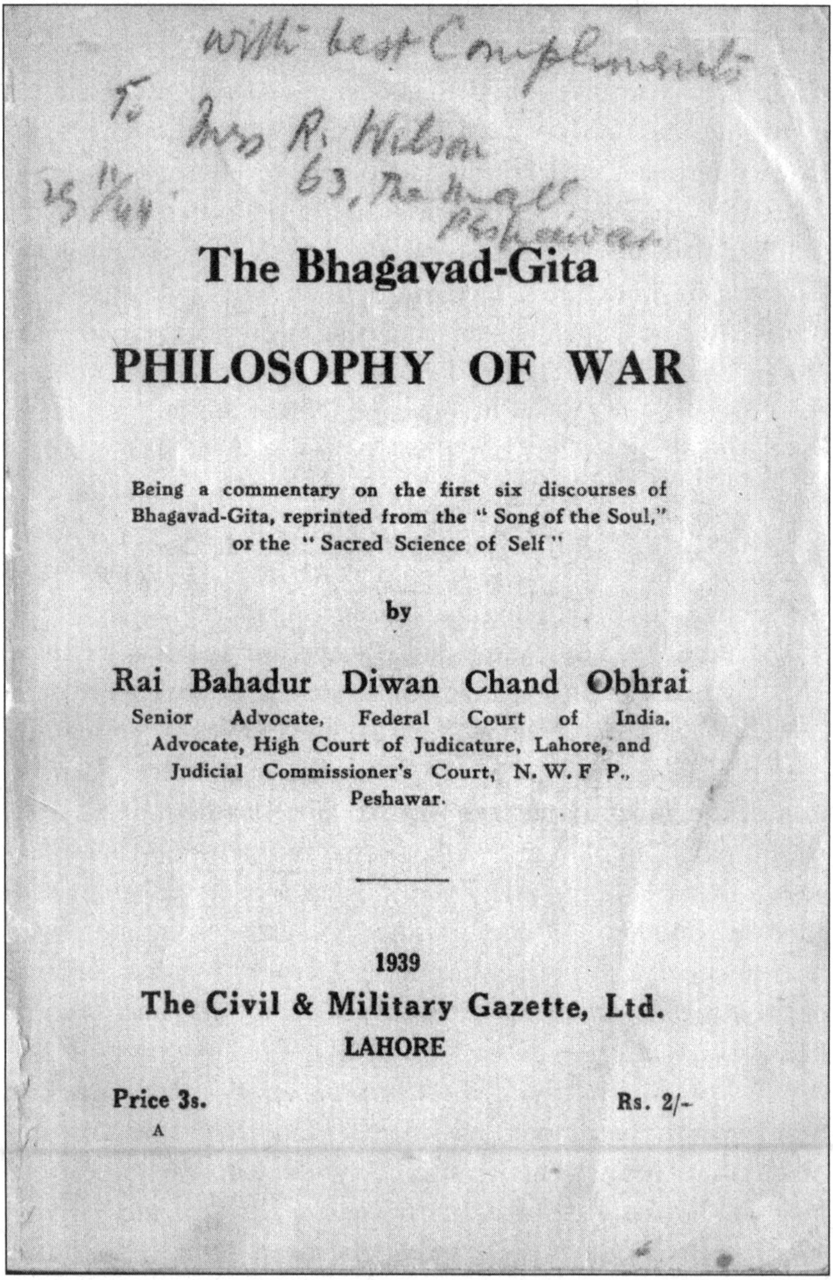

with best Compliments
To
Mrs R. Wilson
63, The Mall
Peshawar
25/11/44

The Bhagavad-Gita

PHILOSOPHY OF WAR

Being a commentary on the first six discourses of
Bhagavad-Gita, reprinted from the " Song of the Soul,"
or the " Sacred Science of Self "

by

Rai Bahadur Diwan Chand Obhrai

Senior Advocate, Federal Court of India,
Advocate, High Court of Judicature, Lahore, and
Judicial Commissioner's Court, N. W. F P.,
Peshawar.

———

1939

The Civil & Military Gazette, Ltd.
LAHORE

Price 3s.   Rs. 2/-

A

The Bhagavad-Gita Philosophy of War (1939) was a perhaps belated attempt
to woo Indians away from the pacifism of Mahatma Gandhi. Gandhi
would continue to be a thorn in the side of the British administration
throughout the Second World War, though without following some
other leading Indian politicians into open support of Japan.

the lifelong pacifist and Labour Party leader George Lansbury would acknowledge that 'we possess rights and privileges such as no other nation allows pacifists in wartime'.[29] By the end of the war, only two of every thousand conscripts sought exemptions, and many of those who accepted non-combatant roles, such as the diarist Denis Argent, later asked to be transferred to active service, in his case bomb disposal.[30] For many conscientious objectors it was important to demonstrate that their religious or political objections to war did not emanate from cowardice.

All of these arguments would be played out again after the Second World War, though in a very different political and strategic context. The horrors of potential nuclear annihilation, along with graphic television coverage of brutal, unwinnable conflicts in the Global South, tested to the limit the popular consensus that had underpinned the two world wars, for better or worse. The Ban the Bomb demonstrations of the nuclear age, and the 'peace dividend' that followed the collapse of the Soviet bloc in 1989, gave pacifism a new salience, challenging the assumptions that underpinned great power military doctrine. Until then, the literature of wartime would reflect the attitudes of the time: sometimes questioning and critical, but just as frequently valorising, enabling or otherwise active in the process of waging war.

2

THE ART OF WAR

In 2032, we will be marking the two hundredth anniversary of one of the most influential books ever written on warfare: *On War* by Carl von Clausewitz. This evergreen classic of military theory still figures prominently on the syllabus of military schools and training academies as the starting point on any serious discussion on strategy and the waging of war.[1] Yet it was not the book that Clausewitz intended to write. When he died in 1831, *On War* was still a jumble of semi-revised drafts; it was left to his wife and literary helpmate, Marie von Brühl, to turn these disparate manuscripts into a publishable form. For a literary classic it is a difficult read, with inconsistencies and unclarity that no doubt would have been resolved had Clausewitz lived to correct it. It remains an imperfect guide to one of the most agile military minds of the nineteenth century. With so much unresolved, the recent discovery of a catalogue of the personal library jointly owned by Carl and Marie seemed to offer a promising line of enquiry into Clausewitz's working method and the key influences shaping his thought. Yet instead, we have another conundrum, because this personal library comprised a mere 380 books: this in an age when a scholar might easily have assembled a library of several thousand works (Marie von Brühl's grandfather, Heinrich, prime minister of Saxony, assembled a famous collection of 62,000 books).[2]

Perhaps the explanation lies in the fact that Clausewitz was not a rich man, but he did have one further advantage that other scholars did not enjoy, in that he lived literally down the corridor from one of the great military libraries of the age, the 15,000 volumes of the Prussian Military Academy (Kriegsakademie), of which Clausewitz was the superintendent. He most likely also had

Carl von Clausewitz. His landmark strategic text owed much to the superb library of the Prussian Military Academy, and to his wife, Marie von Brühl, who prepared the unfinished drafts of *On War* for publication.

access to the Royal Library: a letter survives from Clausewitz to the royal librarian in 1824 asking if a lieutenant could borrow a book from this fine collection, so he no doubt had the same privilege.[3] The duties of the superintendent of the Kriegsakademie were not heavy; indeed, Clausewitz may had resented the appointment as a means of side-lining him in the military command structure. Having attended his office each morning, mostly to authorise advances on their stipends for impecunious cadets, he retired to his wife's sitting room to write, taking whatever books were necessary for him.

If we ask why *On War* has enjoyed such an enduring reputation, historical context is important. *On War* was published in 1832, at a time when European states were still recovering from the obliteration of their armies by Napoleon, by general agreement the greatest battlefield general of the age. Lest anyone forget, Napoleon's reputation was constantly burnished by Antoine Henri, Baron de Jomini, Clauswitz's chief contemporary rival for supremacy in the military academies of Europe.[4] This was also the time when Europe's great powers, to which one should add the emerging military powers of the non-European world, Japan and the United States, recognised that the greater complexities of warfare, and the new power of weaponry, called for a more systematic approach to military education.

Between 1820 and 1890 all the major global powers built on the more fragmentary eighteenth-century initiatives with schools of officer training. Some, such as the United States, embraced the need for a technical, mathematical education more willingly than, for instance, Britain, where the traditions of the gentleman officer were maintained deep into the nineteenth century. But all established their military schools first and foremost for the technical disciplines of artillery and the engineers (traditionally less aristocratic). All of these institutions required instructors and libraries.

Out of these hesitant attempts to imitate the most successful battlefield victors, first France and then Prussia, the cornerstone of the new German Empire proclaimed in 1871, there eventually emerged a threefold structure of military education: cadet schools for the young, officer academies and staff colleges for strategic training. Yet as the graduates of these various institutions died in their thousands in the gallant yet murderous assaults of the First World War, one is left to reflect whether much had been achieved in this education revolution. How important was book learning in the making of warriors, when set alongside other factors such as good breeding, the habit of command, genius, luck, raw courage and superior armament? The extent to which ordinary troops shared in the pedagogical revolution of the officer class is also highly

uncertain. Military memoirs – another enormous genre of literature generated by warfare – seldom dwell on time spent poring over
books as the most critical element in the making of a soldier. Yet
for all that, books and desk time had by the end of the nineteenth
century become an essential part in the making of a fighting force.

As long as there has been writing, men have written about war. Sun
Tzu's *The Art of War*, written in the sixth century BC, offers a cool-
eyed dissection of the contemporary struggles for supremacy in
the Chinese kingdoms. It is presented as a series of terse nostrums
on military tactics, field craft and spying, and has enjoyed a high
reputation in the Western world since its rediscovery by European
writers in the nineteenth century.[5] The sacred texts of Judaism,
canonised as the Old Testament, are suffused with the clash of
civilisations, as the people of Israel fought to establish their claim
to a domicile in Palestine. Sieges, massacres, brave warriors and
pitched battles punctuate the narrative; certainly, no one could
come away from a reading of the historical books of the Bible, or
the psalms, believing that waging war was inherently immoral.[6]

> For the Lord takes delight in his people; he crowns the humble
>   with victory . . .
> May the praise of God be in their mouths; and a double-
>   edged sword in their hands,
> to inflict vengeance on the nations; and punishment on the
>   peoples,
> to bind their kings with fetters; their nobles with shackles of
>   iron,
> to carry out the sentence written against them; this is the glory
>   of all his faithful people.[7]

The ubiquity of war in Christianity's sacred texts would cast a long
shadow over the debate on the legitimacy of war in the Christian
world. Certainly, for most of the twentieth century, few Christian clergymen found any difficulty in offering their enthusiastic
support for their country in wartime.

Still in the ancient world, the Romans, a highly literary as well as a military people, contributed greatly to the literature of war. Julius Caesar's accounts of his military campaign in Gaul played a large role in establishing his claim for supremacy in the ruthless battle to rule Rome. The mix of history and strategy in this book would offer a prototype for generations of military history writing, as victorious generals sought to burnish their reputations, either through their own writings or those of eager proxies. All the Roman historians, from Livy to Plutarch, were almost by definition military historians, since this was an empire established and defended by relentless war, either against other nations or within itself. It is one of the great ironies of the history of literature that after the collapse of the Roman Empire in the west, these histories survived for the best part of a millennium buried among the collections of Christian texts in decidedly unwarlike monastic libraries, to be rediscovered by the eager scholars of the Italian Renaissance in the fourteenth and fifteenth centuries.

The advent of the art of printing in the fifteenth century led to a rapid increase in the number of books in circulation, and greatly expanded the social profile of those who could afford to buy them. Military handbooks formed a popular element of this market. These could vary from earnest textbooks on drill formation to pamphlet descriptions of the latest engagements in the extended conflicts of the period: the Dutch Revolt, the French Wars of Religion, the Thirty Years' War. The war memoirs of Blaise de Monluc and François de la Noue (one Catholic, one Protestant) were reissued regularly, and the best of the military manuals were rapidly translated into a range of different languages.[8] Despatches from the front were a particularly favoured form of publication, and middle-ranking commanders could build both reputation and a useful side income by acting as part-time correspondents.[9] This was partly because military news also made up a large part of the copy of the first newspapers, published in Germany, France, Britain and the Netherlands from the first decades of the seventeenth century. Since most governments frowned on newspaper coverage of domestic politics, the movement of troops and diplomats necessarily dominated the copy in these first news-sheets.

The seventeenth century brought further important developments, thanks largely to Louis XIV and his incessant war-making. The building of fortifications to defend the vulnerable northern borders of his expanding kingdom was the responsibility of his chief military engineer, Sébastien le Prestre de Vauban, and generated a series of texts on military architecture that would remain required reading into the nineteenth century. So great had the demand become for military textbooks that in 1637, Gabriel Naudé, one of the first professional librarians and a shrewd judge of the evolving book market, issued a catalogue of recommended reading on warfare, *Syntagma de Studio Militari*.[10] This was a market skewed towards the practical rather than the theoretical, which is why Niccolò Machiavelli's reflection on *The Art of War* stood out. From its publication in 1521, *The Art of War* went through more than twenty editions in the next 150 years. It owed its success partly to the fact that Machiavelli challenged the prevailing wisdom of Italian warfare in the late Middle Ages, which had mostly relied on contracting mercenary generals to fight the battles of the city states. In contrast, Machiavelli urged his Florentine masters to train a citizen militia to be always available to defend the republic in danger. The battle won, the troops would revert to civilian life.

This was bold, but not necessarily innovative: Machiavelli had cribbed most of his ideas from the ancient Roman military strategist Vegetius. Indeed, this cult of antiquity was perhaps the most unexpected aspect of military writing in this period. The invention of printing is generally seen, quite correctly, as a breakthrough technology, and a building block of modernity. This, however, disguises the fact that in their choice of texts the first generation of publishers were extremely conservative. Whether it was science, geography, medicine or military tactics, the authority of the ancient Greeks and Romans reigned supreme. In science and medicine this was a considerable barrier to empirical research; at least in the field of military tactics the Romans had a solid record of success to recommend them. So although Machiavelli sold well, Vegetius sold better.[11] Julius Caesar's texts, most notably his account of his victories in Gaul (France), went through a staggering 200 editions in the first two centuries of print. The popularity of the ancients does suggest that few were read exclusively for practical military guidance: the generals of the seventeenth and eighteenth centuries would have had little use for descriptions of tortoise shield formations when faced by field guns and mortars.

Given the longevity of these classical authors, the emergence in the nineteenth century of the duelling authorities of Jomini and Clausewitz at least offered a fresh beginning for the science of war. Their struggle for supremacy also took place in a wholly new context: the progressive professionalisation of military education. At the end of the eighteenth century, even the concept of a national army was relatively new: the American War of Independence was fought largely between citizen militias on the one side and German mercenaries on the other. Thanks to the creation of a standing army under Louis XIV and the ability of Napoleon to vanquish any combination of forces sent against him, France led the way. Jomini's writings took their authority from his place at Napoleon's side, observing the battlefield genius at work. Yet even in this glorious passage of French arms, there was the beginning of an alternative German school, reaching back to the establishment of the Prussian Military Academy by Frederick the Great in 1765. Both this and the establishment of the French Military School of Saint-Cyr took for granted that the landed nobility would provide the backbone of the officer corps, as would be the case with the later and less impressive British establishments. But the existence of these academies, and a second tier of training schools for the artillery and military engineers, at least recognised that leading troops required something more than noble breeding, courage and good horsemanship.

The United States was not encumbered with an aristocratic officer class, but it still modelled its military institutions very largely on these European prototypes. The United States Military Academy was established at West Point, in New York State, in 1802. The new college did not flourish until the War of 1812 (when English troops sacked Washington, DC) demonstrated the urgent need for a more dynamic programme of officer education. Galvanising West Point was very largely the achievement of Sylvanus

Class of 1914

The West Point Class of 1914 pose in front of the library. Not all of these light-hearted young men would have given a high priority to book-learning, but the library certainly provided an outstanding resource for a military education.

Thayer, who between 1817 and 1837 established a curriculum closely modelled on that of the École Polytechnique, the military academy in Paris. The new curriculum focused on mathematics, infantry tactics, gunnery and military science, with a strong tilt towards engineering.[12] Thayer had spent two years in France before taking up his post, touring its military schools and scooping up thousands of maps, charts and pamphlets, along with the key texts of military science. This laid the basis of what would become one of the best technical libraries in America.[13] Reinforcing the French connection, the newly appointed professor of engineering was Claude Crozet, a veteran of Napoleon's army who had served as the emperor's bridge engineer and studied at both the École Polytechnique and the School of Engineering and Artillery at Metz. Another key influence in these years was Dennis Mahan, who also spent two years at French military academies before returning to West Point as professor of civil and military engineering, a post he occupied for the next thirty years. A prolific author, Mahan wrote a number of key texts on military architecture, as well as translating critical French works into English.[14]

In 1853 the Military Academy advertised the strength of its library with a published catalogue. It was indeed an impressive collection: 6,259 titles divided into seventy-nine categories, leading with the most pertinent technical disciplines, military engineering and artillery.[15] The French influence is clear: Vauban, Thiébault, Rocquancourt and Vaudoncourt, the mathematical texts of Le Blond and Legendre and the astronomical texts of Lalande all feature in multiple titles. Jomini's works are a prominent feature, including the fifteen-volume *Histoire critique et militaire des guerres*; there is no sign of Clausewitz. Not surprisingly, students were expected to be proficient in French, to the embarrassment of Stonewall Jackson, one of the great instinctive strategists of the American Civil War, a country boy who arrived at West Point with little formal education. After heroic struggles to master the curriculum, and subsequent service in the Mexican–American War, Jackson rather incongruously returned to college as professor of physics at the Virginia Military College, the first state military college in the republic. His lectures, learned by heart and delivered without evident passion or variation in intonation, were not popular with students.[16]

The engineers who passed out from West Point played an important role in the building of America. About a quarter of those graduating in the first half of the century went to work for railway companies or on other civil engineering projects. West Point was also seen as an important instrument of nation-building. In the words of one cadet, James Dalliba in 1822:

> They come together with all the sectional prejudices, habits and knowledge . . . Their former habits, manners and prejudices soon become extinct. They form a new character, a national character, which is nowhere else formed in the country . . . They separate and scatter to every part of the country, but their feelings are not separated, and their interests are not divided, and generally never will be.[17]

This optimistic prognosis was to be shredded by the Civil War of 1861–5, when West Point graduates fought, with varying degrees of distinction, on both sides. European military observers were not on the whole impressed by the tradecraft on display in the battles they witnessed. To the Prussian military attachés, the campaigns they followed seemed like nothing more than 'armed mobs chasing each other'. This dismissive aphorism was more damaging for being attributed to the great Prussian strategist von Moltke. The condescending self-confidence of the German military went down very badly with the victorious Union generals, but it was beyond dispute that in the three great victories of its mid-century ascendancy, Prussia had accomplished the sort of decisive battlefield engagements that had eluded the American armies in four years of bloody fighting.

Americans were not oblivious to the steady build-up of the Prussian military: for the 105 American officers who crossed the Atlantic between 1812 and 1860, Berlin became an obligatory stop.[18] The American Civil War coincided with the first of Prussia's lightning victories in Denmark and ended shortly before the annihilation of the Austrian army at Königsgratz. But it was the humiliation of France (1870–71) that signalled the unambiguous emergence of a new world power, and led to the total reorientation of military science. With France's defeat, Jomini's glorification of Napoleon lost its lustre and Clausewitz merited a second look, especially when von Moltke named *On War* as the book from which he had most profited. It was precisely at this point that Clausewitz's seminal text was first made available to an English-speaking audience.[19] Military theorists would spend the next two generations probing the secrets of Prussian success.

It is hard to overestimate the shock to the European ecosystem of the Prussian victories in the wars of 1864–71. It was as if a new great power had suddenly erupted in the Central European landmass: the events of the next fifty years would prove that this was largely true. If it had ever been the case that Prussia was, as Mirabeau had quipped, an army with a country attached, the spectacular growth of the German economy and population, its intellectual and scientific prowess and national self-confidence, would prove after 1871 that this was a gross understatement. With an ample supply of critical raw materials such as coal and iron ore, and the best-developed railway network in Europe, Germany was well equipped for a rush towards modernity. By 1914 it had developed world-leading chemical and engineering industries, bolstered by a superb network of universities and technical institutes. This scientific and intellectual infrastructure would be a potent resource in the wars of the twentieth century.[20]

Even so, and despite the sophistication of its culture and scholarship, Germany remained to an unusual extent a militarised nation. In 1871, Bismarck had been able to use the prestige of victory to establish a constitution that largely freed the military from civilian control, apart from intermittent wrangles about its budget. The German emperor, as supreme commander-in-chief, was also the final arbiter of foreign policy. This caused remarkably little public disquiet because the army was hugely respected as, in effect, the creator of the nation. The new German Empire profited militarily from two further legacies from the Prussian state: an established system of conscription, which ensured access to deep reserves of trained soldiers in the event of future conflict, and the institutional structures of military training and education, built up steadily in the century since the era of Frederick the Great.

These structures, which in the eyes of foreign observers were the most potent vehicle of German military exceptionalism, took their modern shape in the reconstruction of the German army after the humiliating capitulation of Prussia at the battle of Jena in 1806, which demonstrated comprehensively that the military infrastructure designed by Frederick the Great had run its course. In the years that followed, Frederick's Académie des Nobles was re-founded as the Kriegsakademie, now in principle open to those of non-noble birth, though the Prussian Junker class would prove surprisingly resilient in retaining their dominant place in the military hierarchy. The Kriegsakademie rapidly became an advanced training school of Prussian officers; attendance was a prerequisite for appointment to the Prussian general staff.

As the system was developed during the course of the nineteenth century, the Kriegsakademie became the apex of a hierarchy of institutions that trained successive generations of officers for both service and leadership, with young boys enrolled in the cadet preparatory schools at the age of ten, from where they would hope to move on to the Hauptkadettenanstalt (HKA) in Berlin at fifteen.[21] Graduates of the HKA would then hope for a place on the elite Selecta class of the Kriegsakademie, which guaranteed them a commission and the prospect of a rotation through the General Staff. The preparatory schools followed the curriculum of a German *Realschule*, with its emphasis on science and modern languages: there was no specific military training until cadets reached Berlin. There was a strong emphasis on sport and outdoor exercise, and particularly gymnastics, which was thought to breed self-confidence, endurance and agility. This offers an interesting contrast to the British military academy at Sandhurst, where the original plan to build a gymnasium was abandoned on the grounds that gymnastics would make cadets 'too active and nimble and not stiff enough for the ranks'.[22]

The spartan atmosphere, insufficient food, freezing cold and rampant bullying of the German schools would have been familiar to any denizen of the Victorian public schools in England, but the cadet schools took the cult of brutality to extreme lengths. Endurance of pain, accepted without demur, was the foundation stone of cadet training, mostly inflicted by fellow cadets. This was so universally accepted that cadets voluntarily added to the pain with self-inflicted torments:

> Twenty-five strokes of the cane on the muscles before breakfast; why, that's nothing, no one turns a hair at that anymore, even when it hurts so much and one's arms are streaming with blood – fifty with the whip, that's laughed to scorn.
>
> With good nature, thick skin and some cunning, we found the heavy yoke becoming lighter with each day that passed, and with each day we felt more plainly that we had taken the steel within us . . . [By the end of the year] no one can deny that the little man has truly turned into steel . . . His muscles are firm, his body is toughened, he has a lively sense of honour and he is ready to die for his comrades.[23]

These quotations come from the cadet school stories of Johannes van Dewall, drawing on his experiences of the preparatory school at Bensberg in the 1840s, one of several such celebrations of the cadet school ethos. Both the cadets and their parents knew what they could expect.

The cadet schools were regarded as so important to the cult of German militarism that the Versailles settlement insisted on their closure. In 1933, Hitler would revive cadet education in a series of boarding schools modelled on the English public schools, where boys would be raised in the military arts for service in the SS and Wehrmacht. More than half of those who graduated, some as young as sixteen, died in the service of the Reich.[24]

Given the importance of the cadet schools to the creation of a German military elite, it is all the more remarkable that the greatest of all military strategists, Helmuth von Moltke, largely bypassed this educational system. Von Moltke was the son of a German officer in the service of the Danish crown and attended cadet school in Copenhagen. His first experience of German military education was studying at the Kriegsakademie as a commissioned officer, where he subsequently claimed he had read little but the required texts, preferring to occupy his leisure hours with literature and pursuing his own writing projects. He devoted eighteen months to a translation into German of Edward Gibbon's *Decline and Fall of the Roman Empire* and published extensively throughout his career. A gifted linguist, he learned Turkish in the course of an extended detachment advising on the modernisation of the Ottoman army. A published volume of letters written during his time in Turkey became something of a literary sensation. In 1857, he would be appointed chief of the Prussian general staff, guiding the Prussian army to its great mid-century triumphs.

It is difficult to encapsulate the genius of von Moltke since, unlike Jomini, he peddled no fixed strategic nostrums.[25] Rather one can point to his speedy grasp of the importance of technical innovation (the breech-loading rifle, the railways), his emphasis on flexibility and his understanding that modern armies were simply too large to be directed by a single commander. Germany would secure its greatest triumphs bringing disparate forces to a single point of concentration for a hammer-blow victory. This required that the habit of command was established throughout the hierarchy, as set out in his milestone *Instructions for Large Unit Commanders* (1869), the first such handbook of its kind. Other characteristic Prussian institutions were regular war games, and the annual 'ridings', where the whole general staff rode out together on an extended open field exercise. One of von Moltke's first acts in command was to reorganise the general staff, establishing a mobilisation section, a geographical section and a military history section, demonstrating the importance he attached to the practicalities of modern warfare, education and intelligence, qualities not necessarily ubiquitous in the Prussian Junker class.

In the wake of the Prussian victories, other nations, with the exception of Britain, would hurry to establish their own general staff. But it was not the institution itself so much as von Moltke's longevity as its director (1857–88) that held the key to German success. Von Moltke was a sophisticated, cultured and cosmopolitan figure, but his reinvention of the art of war also had its dark side. His emphasis on independent thought made clear that the commander should explain the mission, then leave the officer in the field to determine the means of execution. 'Strategy', he warned, 'was a system of expedients.' 'No plan survives contact with the enemy's main body.'[26] The combat manual of 1900 explicitly specified that:

> In every situation, even the most extraordinary, each officer should apply his entire personality, without shrinking from responsibility, to fulfil his mission, even without waiting for orders concerning all the details.[27]

This doctrine of subordinate control would have its final tragic manifestation in 1941 with the genocide on the Eastern Front, where the Wehrmacht was a willing agent of murder. No specific orders were necessary, when the outline of the mission was clear.[28]

Equally pungent was the law of necessity, the idea that the military mission trumped all moral considerations. This directed the harsh treatment of civilians, exemplified in the execution of

civilians in the Franco-Prussian War and carried to extremes in
the brutal colonial conflict in South-West Africa (1904–7).Once
again, the combat manual gave a clear steer towards harsh measures:

> Mild treatment of enemy civilians is usually the most useful
> method. However, harshness appropriate to the earnestness
> of the situation should not be omitted regarding hostile
> inhabitants. Mildness and leniency in the wrong place can
> become harshness towards one's own troops.[29]

The other clear manifestation of disregard for the accepted laws of
war was the Schlieffen Plan, which depended on the violation of
Belgian neutrality in the course of a German attack on France. As
executed in 1914, this put Germany on the back foot with world
opinion from the opening days of the First World War. Ruthless-
ness had its price.

Military education in Britain developed in a very different context
from that of Germany. Despite its ultimately decisive intervention
in the Napoleonic wars, Britain was essentially a naval rather than
a military power. While its navy was of sufficient strength to take
on those of any two other major nations (as it frequently had in the
eighteenth century), there was a clear understanding that for most
of the nineteenth century the British army was too small to make
a significant contribution to a major European conflagration. It
was only in 1906 that war with Germany, in alliance with France,
became central to British military planning.

  Great Britain emerged from the long conflict of the Napoleonic Wars victorious but mired in debt. Pressing domestic
problems would take precedence over the next half century, while
the military budget was drastically pared back. This had serious
consequences for the Royal Military College, established in 1802
on the prompting of one of Wellington's most distinguished staff
officers from the Peninsular War, John Le Marchant. In 1812 it was
settled at Sandhurst.[30] The initial plan envisaged 400 students,
with a quarter of the places reserved for the sons of officers killed in
battle. These high-minded ideals were swiftly eroded by the general

conservatism of army culture, and a lack of visionary leadership after Le Marchant's death at Salamanca in 1812. The entrance examination of 1834, at which point candidates would have been aged between thirteen and fifteen, required students to have mastered the four rules of arithmetic and several antique authors, Cornelius Nepos or Caesar in prose and Virgil or Ovid in verse; regurgitation of the classics still trumped practical talents. The examination for a commission required a close knowledge of Vauban's seventeenth-century systems of fortification.

Sandhurst, in contrast to the training colleges in the United States or on the continent, had no military library. Students were expected to supply their own textbooks, and discursive reading was out of the question. In 1864, a reading room was created along with a billiard room, as a response to complaints about a lack of recreational facilities. Given the prevailing culture, the billiard room would certainly have been the more frequented. Even in 1893, Winston Churchill was obliged to order from his father's bookseller his own copies of Hamley's *Operations of War*, Prince Kraft's *Letters on Infantry, Cavalry and Artillery* and Maine's *Infantry Tactics*, along with histories of the American Civil War, the Franco-Prussian War and the Crimean War.[31]

In 1854, all the students at Sandhurst over the age of sixteen were hurriedly given commissions and shipped off to the Crimea. The poor performance of British troops in this campaign led to a new wave of scrutiny and proposed reforms. One consequence was the creation of a staff college for officer education (also on the Sandhurst campus), another a drive towards the provision of military libraries. The staff college was provided with what became an excellent library and another was built at the British army camp in Aldershot. This was the gift of the Prince Consort, Albert, enthusiastically supported by his wife, Queen Victoria. When it opened shortly before Albert's death in 1861, the library boasted a carefully chosen selection of some 600 books on military science and military history. While the evidence of a Latin education was still apparent in a large range of books on the Peloponnesian Wars, Albert's gift also included more contemporary French and German authorities, including several volumes of Clausewitz. It is interesting that to obtain his position, the first librarian, Sergeant Gilmour, first had to demonstrate his proficiency in these languages.[32] This was an officers' library, with a gracious reading room and an upstairs smoking room. Even so, it was poorly frequented; only when it was merged with the novels and lighter fare from the garrison library did it attract more than a handful of users daily.

The staff college, teaching the skills of leadership to commissioned junior officers, fared better, though even here the library may have been used more by the teaching staff than the officer students.[33] The teaching staff were often men of some distinction, like Patrick MacDougall, author of *The Theory of War* (1857), Edward Hamley, who wrote *Operations of War* (1866), and later George Henderson, responsible for the posthumously published *The Science of War* (1910). The curriculum also reflected the modernising urge, with more concentration on artillery, topography, strategy and geology. Even so, the working environment seems to have been anything but intense. One late-century student devoted most of his time to writing a lengthy history of the American Civil War and still passed out top of the class; another equally talented contemporary spent most of his time in London qualifying as a barrister. And there were drawbacks to being lectured by the authors of the class textbook. Hamley insisted that *The Operations of War* be the sole text covered in the military history examinations, and woe betide a student who ranged more widely in his papers. The recipe for success was straightforward: in the words of one natural diplomat, to 'serve up Hamley, Hamley nothing but Hamley – that always gets full marks'.[34]

Graduation from the staff college was by no means necessary for a staff position, and the most talented would not necessarily apply. According to Ian Hamilton, a dashing and distinguished officer, it was the proud boast of his regiment, the Gordons, that they never sent anyone to the staff college. Other regiments used the staff college as a dumping ground for subalterns they wanted to be rid of for a couple of years. Britain also ducked the general continental trend by refusing to establish a general staff on the Prussian model, despite the recommendations of the Hartington Commission in 1890 in favour of such an innovation. The publication of Spenser

Wilkinson's portrait of the Prussian general staff, *The Brain of an Army*, in this same year brought the issue into the public domain, but the proposal was blocked by a combination of radicals and liberals, who feared the power such an institution would place in the hands of the military. The case was also weakened by an insouciant assumption that a major European war was a thing of the past; or, as Sir William Beresford expressed it to Winston Churchill, that 'there would never be another war between civilised peoples'.[35]

The British army's engagements in the second half of the nineteenth century seemed to give weight to this sentiment. The army found itself fighting in a series of small wars against non-European opponents. These were wars in which the overwhelming supremacy of European firepower could compensate for any amount of tactical ineptitude and provided reams of copy for the London newspapers. The colonial wars in Africa, India and Afghanistan also bore no relation to the syllabus of the military schools, which remained wholly focused on European wars. The deficiencies of this system were only fully exposed in the Boer War of 1899–1902, when the army faced irregular troops of European origin fighting with up-to-date weaponry.

Thus far, all the military training programmes we have discussed were intended for the officer class. Educational opportunities for troops and non-commissioned officers were far more sparse. In the United States, where most white males were participants in the American version of democracy, there was at least no positive opposition to soldiers reading; but in early nineteenth-century Britain a different temper prevailed. The Duke of Wellington had denounced his own troops as the 'scum of the earth', but he seemed in no hurry to improve their morals or level of education. At a time when Britain seemed to totter on the edge of revolution, Wellington believed education to be the problem, not the solution: 'If there is mutiny in the Army – and in all probability we shall see one – you'll see that all of these new-fangled school masters are at the bottom of it.'[36] Colonel Le Marchand's plan for troops' education had been rejected out of hand in 1800, on the grounds that 'it was inconsistent with the habits of the country to raise private soldiers to so close an equality with their officers, as well as from the apprehension that the measure might prove injurious to the service at large by leading to frequent promotions from the ranks'.[37]

While this adamantine obscurantism prevailed in the highest echelons of the British army, it was left to the East India Company, the rulers of British India, to lead the way. India presented particular problems for garrison life: isolated communities far from home with few friends outside the compound; blistering heat, constraining outdoor recreations; and unsafe water. It was no wonder that the Company believed that their soldiers would take refuge in drink. But instead of the normal army remedy, the fear of flogging if caught drunk, the East India Company put their faith in the power of education, recommending, in the words of the commander-in-chief in Bengal in 1823,

> the use of a set of well selected books, as while they would afford rational amusement to the soldiers in their leisure hours, they would likewise tend to improve their minds and to lessen licentious propensities often induced by mere mischief and want of something to occupy their attention.[38]

This swiftly became the template for the generous provision of both books and educational facilities. The regimental muster made provision for a schoolmaster and two assistants, a schoolmistress for the solders' children and a librarian. The library facilities were placed under the supervision of regimental chaplains, and to their credit, they were the first to caution against filling the reading rooms with pious tracts. The soldiers wanted up-to-date novels and also to be allowed to take the books with them back to their barracks; this too was conceded. The encouragement of reading aloud also helped spread the value of the library to the less literate (almost 40 per cent of the troops in the British army were reckoned to be illiterate still in the late 1850s) and to offer some form of civilised diversion to the women of the regiment. Generally the provision of library facilities in British India was thought to have been a great success, notwithstanding the difficulty of preventing the books from being eaten by ants.

The impetus for the foundation of libraries in home bases came from the unlikely source of the 1838 Royal Commission on Military Punishments, later reinforced by the persuasive skills of the redoubtable Florence Nightingale. The 1838 commission, building on the experience of the East India Company, sought to substitute education for flogging, and in 1840 the Queen's Regulations would include an instruction for the provision of barrack libraries and reading rooms. An allocation of £2,000 was provided; soldiers were permitted to borrow books in return for a subscription of one penny a month. By 1844, thirty-eight libraries had been established at home, and forty abroad. By 1853, the army could account for 117,000 volumes in 150 libraries, with 16,000 soldier subscribers.[39]

This represented substantial progress, and more would follow, building on the experience of Florence Nightingale in the Crimean War. Having addressed the principal deficiencies in medical provision, Nightingale also established a reading room at Scutari, supplied with books, newspapers and games donated by her own family.[40] A substantial number of books were despatched to the Crimean peninsula on the personal initiative of the queen; at the end of the war, the 2,112 books still serviceable were divided between the garrisons of Dublin and Aldershot, where a new Victoria Soldiers' Library was opened in 1859.[41] Nightingale, meanwhile, was lobbying for a more comprehensive settlement. Here she found a willing ally in Colonel John Lefroy, an adviser to the secretary of war, who in 1859 recommended both the supply of newspapers to the army reading rooms and more generous library provision.[42] The civilising impact of these measures should not be exaggerated. Even at the time of the First World War, general levels of literacy among the troops were often low, as the young officers sent out from the English public schools would discover when censoring their men's letters, or even helping them write them.[43] Only in the Second World War was the army dealing with something close to universal literacy in the ranks of the conscript armies, motivating a push towards political education classes undertaken, sometimes unwillingly, by junior regimental officers.[44]

In 1905, bowing to the exigencies of modern warfare, the British army finally conceded the establishment of a general staff. This was still not universally popular, particularly with the troops condemned to the endless trench warfare of 1914–18. It is one of the enduring myths of the First World War that the general staff enjoyed a cosy war, safely removed from the front. This was almost the opposite of the truth. In 1914, far too many staff officers were permitted to volunteer for front-line service, depriving the War Office of experienced staff and stripping the staff college of instructors. So many died in the first year of fighting that experienced staff officers became a virtually extinct species.[45] The same was true of the graduates of Sandhurst who joined the British Expeditionary Force as regimental officers, where the rate of attrition was particularly severe. Soon experienced officers were being replaced by raw teenagers straight out of public school. Their training in the school cadet corps served the army well, if usually all too briefly. Machine guns, it turned out, had little respect for the quality of Latin learning; the Western Front was an equal-opportunity killer.

Here – in the experience of the war, in its raw brutality and massive sustained casualties – may be one key to the extraordinary durability of Clausewitz's *On War*. The difficulty with military education, even in its reformed manifestation at the end of the nineteenth century, was that it risked always fighting the last war, or, in the case of military history's obsession with Napoleon, the last war but five. Clausewitz drew a different lesson from Napoleon's victories, the real possibility of wars of oblivion. With the carnage on the Western Front, the pulverising of Germany in 1945 and the subsequent threat of nuclear destruction, Clausewitz seemed ever more relevant to each succeeding generation. Military strategists could not plot a route map to inevitable victory; any textbook plan inevitably disintegrates under the pressure of events, or in Clausewitz's words: 'War is the realm of uncertainty; three quarters of the factors on which action in war is based are wrapped in a fog of greater or lesser uncertainty.'[46] He, more than anyone, recognised that the reality of wars is that they are brutal, confusing struggles that leave most plans abandoned as soon as the fighting begins. But they could warn of the terrible price to be paid, when advanced weaponry was combined with the cult of the warrior, powered by ideologies of national supremacy. That, ultimately, was the poisonous legacy of military writing to the twentieth century.

3

FROM *UNCLE TOM'S CABIN* TO STALINGRAD: WHY MEN FIGHT

When Harriet Beecher Stowe went to Washington in 1862 to meet the president of the United States, it would be hard to say which of the two was the more famous. Stowe was the author of the runaway bestseller of the nineteenth century, *Uncle Tom's Cabin*, a vivid, deeply moving tale of life in the slave society of the American South. After serialisation in the *National Era* in 1851–2, *Uncle Tom's Cabin* would sell 300,000 copies in the United States in its first year of publication, before going on to take Europe by storm.[1] By the time the author came to London, then the literary capital of the world, *Uncle Tom's Cabin* had sold a million copies worldwide, and Stowe received a rapturous welcome, somewhat to the chagrin of Charles Dickens, forced to make a gracious speech at a banquet in her honour.[2]

Her host at the White House reception, Abraham Lincoln, was by this time in the second year of a war to save the United States, after eleven Southern states had left the Union, determined to preserve the right to retain the institution of slavery. Legend has it that Lincoln greeted his guest thus: 'Is this the little woman who made this great war?' With this homely scene we have, it appears, the clearest evidence of the influence that literature could exert over war-making. Although not all its characterisation of Black characters has stood the test of time well, and encoded some negative stereotypes still in play today, it is undeniable Stowe's dissection of the cruelties of slavery cut through in a way that fifty years of debate over the morality of enslaved labour could not. The abolitionist icon Frederick Douglass wrote generously of *Uncle Tom's Cabin* that 'nothing could have better suited the moral and

humane requirements of the hour. Its effect was amazing, instantaneous, and universal.'[3]

The same could be said of Douglass's own *Narrative of the Life*
(1845) and *My Bondage and My Freedom* (1855), and *Twelve Years
a Slave* (1853) by Solomon Northup. These books provided a more
powerful distillation of the great moral issue dividing America
than the myriad pamphlets and shifty legal compromises that
had characterised this unsettled period of American history. The
ambiguity and caution of Northern policymakers in this period
also has its echo in the antebellum publishing industry, where the
reputable Boston firm that was first offered *Uncle Tom's Cabin*
turned it down, on the grounds that they had no wish to antago-
nise their Southern customers. This reluctance to be associated
with anti-slavery tracts meant that a high proportion of such work
was published at the author's cost, or with the help of anti-slavery
associations.[4] *Uncle Tom* was different, a bestseller across the ages.
It was speedily translated into French but banned in tsarist Russia,
though apparently *Uncle Tom's Cabin* was Lenin's favourite book
as a youth. In 1934, Alexey Feodosievich Wangenheim, the former
head of the USSR's Hydrometeorological Centre in Moscow,
found a copy in French to read in the Solovetsky camp library, one
of the first settlements of what became the Gulag.[5]

Here, then, we seem to have texts that matter: books that have
the power to move opinion and shape attitudes. So it is all the
more frustrating that the famous exchange between Stowe and
Lincoln probably never took place. Stowe certainly visited the
White House and took tea with the First Lady, but it was only in
the year of Stowe's death, thirty-four years later, that that apoc-
ryphal greeting crops up in an article by her biographer and friend,
Annie Fields.[6] Was it even a true statement of the case: is this what
made men fight? Was this a text that turned the menfolk of the
Northern states into confirmed abolitionists? If so, it is unclear
whether Abraham Lincoln would have viewed this as a good
thing: he was initially a reluctant abolitionist at best, and fought
the election of 1860 on a very different platform. In fact, slavery
seldom featured when Union soldiers articulated their reasons for
joining up and fighting the South. In an extensive sample of the

surviving correspondence of Union soldiers, only one in ten mentioned emancipation as an important motivation for fighting.[7] Lincoln's Emancipation Proclamation in 1863 proved bitterly divisive in the Union army. Their detestation of Southerners emanated more from outrage at secession, the need to defend the Union and the constitution, and the principles of fair play and justice: the results of elections, however unwelcome, should be observed. If the Union did not prevail, the United States would be exposed as a failure, with consequences that would resonate around the world. Samuel Storrow, who interrupted his college studies in Massachusetts to join up, put it more eloquently than most: 'If our country and our nationality is to perish, better that we should all perish and not survive to see it a laughing stock for all posterity, to be pointed at as the unsuccessful trial of republicanism.'[8]

The most profound impact of *Uncle Tom's Cabin* was to reinforce the paranoia of the Southern states. The Southern planter class prided themselves on their honour and Christian principles and felt both had been besmirched by Stowe's polemic. Publication inspired a glut of 'anti-Tom' novels and defences of the Southern way of life. But most Southern booksellers simply refused to sell it. Copies of the book were publicly burned in Athens, Georgia, and in 1856, a bookseller was run out of Mobile, Alabama for stocking it. His plaintive defence that he had only ordered fifty copies because 'so many of our planters and other customers begged me to procure for them a copy' cut little ice with his neighbours.[9]

The overseas reaction must also not be misread. Many English readers enjoyed *Uncle Tom* not just for its gut-wrenching portrait of the ill-treatment of the enslaved, but for its wholly unflattering revelations of the cruelty and hypocrisy of America. It was enjoyed for exactly the same reasons that Charles Dickens would later be welcomed in the public libraries of Nazi Germany and Soviet Russia, his graphic descriptions of the poverty and degradation of Victorian London puncturing the smug superiority of imperial Britain. And for all the enthusiasm for *Uncle Tom*, when war broke out many in England favoured the South, partly for pragmatic economic reasons. The loss of access to Southern cotton through the Union blockade led to real hardship in the English industrial towns.

Sales figures, in other words, cannot be equated with influence: people read things precisely *because* they disagree with them powerfully, or wish to understand the workings of their opponent's mind. Otherwise, we should be distinctly worried that Hitler's *Mein Kampf* remained on the bestseller list in Britain for the best part of two years between 1938 and 1940, boosted by the publication of the first unabridged English edition shortly before the outbreak of the Second World War. Yet this success was greeted with such insouciance in Britain that *Mein Kampf* was generously stocked by the public libraries and included on the titles recommended for inclusion in army camp libraries.

It is seldom possible to trace a movement in public opinion to the influence of a particular text at a particular moment. Climates of opinion, still more the underlying attitudes and assumptions of particular nations or social groups, are built up over a large space of time, and where war is concerned, events influence books as much as the reverse. Ideas first present in a book may seep out into the broader culture over decades, making it hard to put a finger on the moment they became influential or accepted. Nevertheless, print undoubtedly plays its role in shaping policy and in lighting the powder trail that leads to war. Perhaps of even more importance is the role of books, newspapers, pamphlets and magazines in sustaining the will to fight once battle is joined. Although we can trace the roots of war literature to the first centuries of print, this is ever more the case with the emergence of mass literacy in the nineteenth and twentieth centuries. This posed a challenge to the small circles dominating decision-making, requiring a far larger measure of consent, passive or active, than in earlier eras. The cheering crowds waving their men away to the front, and the soldiers willing to endure almost unimaginable privations, mutilation and death, all had their reasons for doing so: and often what they had read played a critical role.

Before the eighteenth century, for those who made up the armies of the major European powers, service as a soldier was relatively uncomplicated, if often arduous and unpleasant. Men left their fields and went to war because their local magnate demanded it.

Others enlisted in mercenary armies as an alternative to prison or destitution, or to escape a suffocating home life. The officer class continued to be drawn mostly from the ranks of the nobility, fulfilling their hereditary duty of service to the sovereign. The growth of industrial cities in the nineteenth century brought a complete change to the constitution of armies, and to the terms of service. Working men now had alternative avenues to a decent living, at a time when standards of education were transformed. Women too had more opportunities to contribute to the household income, and expected to play a larger role in shaping family decision-making. By the twentieth century, they would come to represent an important part of public opinion which had to be cultivated: men would not fight if the home front had lost confidence in the cause.

So warfare now required larger armies and more sophisticated weaponry; it also required a more intensive engagement with those who fought. The men who were expected to flock to the colours were now exhibiting a much closer personal interest in politics and had much more to lose. This did not mean that the formation of policy became a democratic process: the decision for war continued to be made in relatively restricted circles. But those who made these decisions were increasing aware of the need to carry with them the men who they expected to fight; and sometimes they might even find themselves pushed into conflicts that they had not themselves favoured.

The Boer War of 1899–1902 provides an interesting case study of this new political environment, not least because the government, epitomised by the colonial secretary, Joseph Chamberlain, was at first extremely reluctant to confront the Boers – South Africans of Dutch origin – who had settled in the Transvaal and Orange Free State to escape British rule in the Cape Province. And yet the war was fought, propelled by a fury of patriotic enthusiasm, cunningly aroused by its exponents carefully cultivating every layer of the radiating circles of opinion-formers that made up the British establishment.[10] The humiliation which British forces would endure when war broke out demonstrated that Chamberlain's reservations were fully justified.

For Sir Alfred Milner, governor of the Cape Province and

Patriotism could take many forms, not least choosing the correct brand of tobacco. This publicity book associating each of the British generals active in the Boer War with a particular brand of cigarette or pipe tobacco was published by WD and HO Wills. Field Marshal Lord Roberts, 'the most powerful and popular personality in the British Army', was awarded the 'mild and fragrant' Three Castles.

principal proponent of the South African War, success seemed elusive when he returned to England to lobby for action.[11] As had been the case throughout the course of history, having 'the king's ear', personal contact with the inner circle of policymakers, was essential to success. Milner pursued his assault in a series of country house weekends, where he met and lobbied most of the major parliamentary protagonists. Although not born into the charmed circle, Milner was well known and respected in the inner corridors of government, not least as the author of *England and Egypt* (1892), an authoritative account of British rule based on two years of service in the Egyptian financial administration. A book of another sort, Percy Fitzgerald's *The Transvaal from Within*, now greatly assisted his cause in London.[12] Fitzgerald's account of

recent events presented the Boer administration of the Transvaal
as aggressive and oppressive, particularly in their disenfranchise-
ment of their English-speaking minority. Fitzgerald's book was the
sensation of the season, going through nine impressions before the
end of 1899; it helpfully characterised the quarrel with the Boers
as an attempt to secure justice for oppressed English inhabitants.

This was a cause that would more likely appeal to public
opinion, and to those circles of influencers who might shape that
opinion. Here discreet access to the corridors of power and the
universities, especially the University of Oxford, played an important role. This was another environment in which Milner, who
had won a string of university prizes in a glittering undergraduate
career, was effortlessly at home. The dinner given to wish him well
on his way to South Africa was an elite affair attended by sixteen
former presidents of the Oxford Union and the rising stars of
both political parties, George Curzon and H. H. Asquith. Oxford
offered a conveyor belt of talent to parliament, the Bar and the
imperial administration, including fifteen viceroys and governor
generals of India.

By May 1897, the Cabinet was persuaded, and Chamberlain
grudgingly conceded that President Kruger must be confronted.
But this was not yet the war of annexation that Milner favoured:
this required mobilising the third circle of influence, the small
number of men who owned or edited the London newspapers.
As a former assistant editor on the *Pall Mall Gazette*, Milner had
many old colleagues now in places of influence, and they took
up the drumbeat of war. Ten thousand troops were embarked for
South Africa, prompting the Boers into a pre-emptive mobilisation: and Milner had his war, on terms the man in the street could
understand. The press would play an important role in maintaining
support through the unexpected early defeats at the hands of the
Boer irregulars, concentrating instead on the determined defence
and relief of Ladysmith and Mafeking, along with individual acts of
heroism. A major contributor was the young Winston Churchill,
already an experienced war correspondent, with two well-received
books to his name on his early war service, *The Malakand Field
Force*, about an engagement on the Indian North-West Frontier,

and an account of the Omdurman campaign in Sudan, *The River War*.[13] Following the Boer War as principal war correspondent of the *Morning Post*, Churchill admitted having put the best gloss on defeats.[14] He also made his own contribution to the drama by escaping from a Boer prisoner-of-war camp, a daring escapade that attracted huge popularity at home and helped launch his parliamentary career. Never letting anything go to waste, Churchill published his war reports in two well-received volumes, which together with the royalties from *The River War* and his salary from the *Morning Post* left Churchill with a princely £4,000 in the bank, over half a million pounds in today's values. This would be doubled by the proceeds of an extended lecture tour, milking his new celebrity.

In his earlier years of governance, Milner had cherry-picked much of his South African staff from Oxford, and after leaving South African service they would become the core of an influential imperial pressure group, 'the Round Table'.[15] This was one of many such ad hoc committees and dining clubs that exercised considerable influence in political debate. Critically, the universities offered a pathway to eminence and influence for those who, like Milner, had not been born into the political elite. John Buchan, the son of a Free Church clergyman in Scotland, made his way to Oxford via Glasgow University, and flourished through sheer talent and an astonishing work ethic. He soon fell in with Milner, leading to service in South Africa, and the writing of a widely admired study of reconstruction after the end of the Boer War.[16] A partner in the publishing firm Nelson, Buchan maintained a frenetic writing schedule, climaxing in publication of *The Thirty-Nine Steps* (1915), a gripping tale of espionage and the indomitable courage of his Empire hero, Richard Hannay. It went on to sell 1.5 million copies. Buchan, the son of the manse, would end his career as Lord Tweedsmuir and governor general of Canada.[17]

What is most striking in the literature of this period is the cross-fertilisation and synergy between newspapers, periodicals and the long-form book, as we have seen in the nimble opportunism of Churchill's Boer War takings. Books were developed from articles in the newspapers or serialised in magazines; authors wrote articles for the papers; newspapers in return promoted authors through reviews and commissions. This lucrative exchange would continue in the febrile period leading up to the First World War, when newspapers played an ever more influential role in shaping public opinion.

The Boer War was a wake-up call for the military but did little to chasten the imperial spirit of the newspaper and magazine readership; nor did it dent the sense of effortless supremacy that so irritated continental rivals, epitomised in the languid aphorism, variously attributed, that 'to be born English is to win first prize in the lottery of life'. Nevertheless, this self-confidence was accompanied by an undertow of anxiety, fuelled by the justified concern that Britain was in fact ill equipped for the European war thought for much of the second half of the nineteenth century to be an impossibility. If war was to come then only the British navy stood between the British people and the likelihood of a humiliating defeat. These fears found their public airing in a new literature of paranoia, beginning immediately in the wake of the Franco-Prussian War with *The Battle of Dorking* (1871). In this book the British navy is destroyed by a mysterious miracle weapon and an unnamed Germanic power invades, defeating the ramshackle British army in a decisive battle outside Dorking, Surrey. This leads to the conquest of Britain and the destruction of the British Empire: the author, George Tomkyns Chesney, was not one for half measures.[18]

The Battle of Dorking could be laughed off as an example of the sensational literature that made up the lower tiers of imaginative fiction in the mid-Victorian period. Yet by the end of the century, invasion literature was beginning to have a real impact on public opinion. By far the most influential of these texts was *The Riddle of the Sands* (1903) by Erskine Childers. The Irish-born Childers was another young man of talent making his way in London society, with the help of his equally ambitious friends. Childers had been a clerk of the House of Commons alongside John Buchan's flatmate Austin Smythe, and all three were members of the Sunday Tramps, a rambling club. In *The Riddle of the Sands*, two amiable young men on a sailing holiday off the north German coast chance upon advanced preparations for an invasion of England. Relations with Germany were in fact good when Childers's novel was published: in 1894, it was a Franco-Russian coalition that had brought Cossacks to Birmingham in William Le Queux's *The Great War of 1897*. Here the Germans rode to the rescue of their British allies, rather like at Waterloo. Childers successfully anticipated the change in the political landscape, and *The Riddle of the Sands* made a deep impact, not least on Winston Churchill. When war broke out in 1914, the director of naval intelligence was immediately instructed to find Childers and recruit him.[19]

Deprived of his Franco-Russian war in 1897, and recognising a shift in the strategic balance, the irrepressible William Le Queux returned to the fray in 1906 with *The Invasion of 1910*, now with the Germans as the enemy. It is easy to underrate Le Queux, the author of 200 novels and an inveterate fantasist who credited himself with considerable success around the capitals of Europe as a gentleman spy.[20] But his books had an extraordinarily broad appeal: Le Queux was the favourite author of Queen Alexandra, wife of Edward VII, while also being popular among the workers of northern industrial towns. He was among the authors most frequently stocked by public libraries, with a survey of 1907 finding an average of twenty-eight of his books in each.[21] Even the erudite refuge of literary London, the London Library, possesses fifty of his titles, several rebound after repeat borrowing.

The Invasion of 1910 was commissioned by Alfred Harmsworth, the newly ennobled Lord Northcliffe, for serialisation in the *Daily Mail*. When Le Queux first presented the text, Northcliffe insisted on changes to ensure that the fictional German troops proceeded through larger towns with more *Daily Mail* readers. It would be published in twenty-seven languages and sell a million copies. To Le Queux's fury, in the German edition the ending was changed so that the Germans triumphed, and London was sacked. The most intriguing feature of the book is the involvement of Lord Roberts, hero of the Boer War and until recently commander-in-chief of the British army. Not only had Roberts helped Le Queux with the plotting, he also provided

A fantasist and social climber, William Le Queux was nevertheless a hugely popular and influential writer of thrillers and espionage novels. Although Le Queux greatly exaggerated his social cachet and associations with European royalty, he was also a shrewd observer of technological change and an early exponent of both airpower and wireless.

a recommendation, inserted in the preface as a facsimile of his original handwritten letter:

> The catastrophe that may happen if we still remain in our present state of unpreparedness is vividly and forcibly illustrated in Mr Le Queux's new book, which I recommend to the perusal of everyone who has the welfare of the British Empire at heart.

A further significant feature of this martial literature was the bleed-through into boys' story papers. These weekly illustrated magazines formed the core of recreational reading for the whole social spectrum of boys between the mid-nineteenth century and the Second World War. Their tales of adventure and science fiction, school stories and detective thrillers shaped the worldview of precisely those generations that would fight to defend the Empire in two world wars. This was a highly competitive market, and editors were necessarily closely attuned to their readers' preferences. These preferences were, on the whole, highly conservative: they were intended for young readers who wanted to fit in, not change the world. And they believed in Britain and its imperial mission.

The boys' papers played an important role in building the newspaper empire of Lord Northcliffe, and almost every Northcliffe boys' paper carried a serial describing the invasion of England by Germans, French or Russians. In the *Boys' Friend*, *Boys' Herald* and *Marvel* around 1900, the greater fear was of France and Russia. It was left to Sexton Blake in *Union Jack* to uncover a German invasion plan. In Aldine's *Boys' Own Library* in 1907, 'The Aerial War' was a clash between scientifically armed Germany and a Great Britain lagging behind. Five huge monster aeroplanes attempted to kidnap the king by hovering above the royal bedroom at Windsor. In 1908, the *Boys' Herald* solemnly warned its readers that one day there would be war. 'It is no secret that the Britisher is hated abroad ... Why? Because of our huge possessions and colonies, because of our prosperity as a nation, because of our enterprise and grit.'[22] The intensity of the war scares accelerated in the years before 1914. In 1912, 'Britain Invaded' in the *Marvel* had Germans occupying north London.

That same year, Northcliffe made a striking declaration of the contribution he believed his boys' papers made in building martial spirit:

> These journals aimed from the first at the encouragement of physical strength, of patriotism, of interest in travel and exploration and of pride in our empire. It has been said that the boys' papers of the Amalgamated Press have done more to provide recruits for our Navy and Army and to keep up the esteem of our sister services than anything else.[23]

With apologies to Lord Northcliffe, who would have brooked no such contradiction in his own lifetime, the most significant presence in the market in boys' magazines was the *Boy's Own Paper*, established by the Religious Tract Society in 1879. As this rather unlikely publisher might suggest, this was another attempt to wean the nation's youth off low-grade, gory thrillers, especially the 'poor slum children' who were particularly susceptible to 'vice easily acquired from the example of their elders and by reading the penny dreadfuls issued by the guttersnipe press'.[24] The *Boy's Own Paper* succeeded because it manage to square the circle of securing the approval of headmasters and parents without repelling its intended audience of boys. Crucially, it was also thought appropriate for the public library, securing a new audience of aspirant boys without the funds for their own copy. The venturesome combination of serial fiction and true-life adventures together with articles on hobbies, sport and outdoor pursuits captivated an audience of boys that extended far beyond the public schoolboys of the putative officer class. From 1880 the *BOP* had its companion in the *Girl's Own Paper*, which brought in more substantial profits thanks to its wider range of advertising: this was before the era where young men could be enticed to indulge in a wide range of beauty products. A cold bath was the recommended treatment of most predicaments, physical or moral, and the surest route to manliness.[25]

The *Boy's Own Paper* was originally launched in two formats: a weekly Saturday issue at 1*d*, and a monthly bound version at 6*d*, featuring all four weekly issues with the intermittent addition of a large illustrated plate for hanging; this was often the version favoured by genteel families. From the beginning the *BOP* succeeded in attracting writers of quality, including household names like Jules Verne and Arthur Conan Doyle; in a later generation, W. E. Johns would provide his Biggles stories and C. S. Forester an early outing for Hornblower. The *BOP* also established a close relationship with Major-General Robert Baden-Powell (a regular contributor) and his scouting movement. At Baden-Powell's insistence, among the newspapers brought by the column relieving the epic siege of Mafeking were twenty copies of each issue of the *BOP* the cadets in the garrison would have missed during the siege.[26]

The stories carried by the *BOP* returned again and again to imperial themes: sea stories, jungle adventures, pioneering in India, gallant soldiers facing fearful odds. The predominance of sea stories is a reminder of the continuing prestige of the navy (the Senior Service) as an honourable calling. The violence of some of these adventures on occasions sparked concern in the committee of oversight established by the Religious Tract Society, but the *BOP* avoided the excesses of the penny dreadfuls, eschewed roguish heroes and did everything in its power to ensure that boys became strong but generous examples of the imperial ideal. In the words of regular contributor Talbot Reed, in a message to a newly established Manchester boys' club, 'The strong fellows should look after the weak, the active must look after the lazy, the merry must cheer up the dull, the sharp must lend a helping hand to the duffer.'[27]

With the coming of war in 1914, the *BOP* would offer itself wholeheartedly to the cause, with songs, poems and stories of heroism, including a story of the naval officer whose vessel was torpedoed, only to find himself standing on the barely submerged hull of the enemy submarine responsible. When the conning tower opened, the quick-witted officer was able to shoot the first man through and prevent the U-Boat submerging until it could be handed over to an advancing British destroyer.[28] Fact or fiction? The exemplary quality of the tale suggests it hardly mattered for a generation eager to take the place of their elder brothers in the front line. The *BOP* would live on to inspire new readers in the Second World War, with at least one POW beguiling the endless hours in German captivity with ten years' worth of back issues. It would publish its last issue in February 1967.

In Germany and the Soviet Union, the context in which their citizens were induced to fight was very different. This was less a matter of persuasion than of mobilising a nation under arms, Germany in seeking to fulfil the expansionist destiny of Europe's new superpower, Russia engaged in a desperate battle to save the motherland with a recalcitrant population only partially reconciled to the policies, or even the existence, of the Soviet Union.[29] In Germany, many of the factors we associate with the twentieth-century marshalling of public opinion were in place long before the Nazi takeover. In the German Empire after the unification of 1871, the army was almost universally admired, not least as the creators of the nation. This was a thoroughly militarised society, and with peacetime conscription, more of the population would have had experience of military training than elsewhere in Europe.[30] This was also a sophisticated, bookish nation, with admired educational regimes both at the school and university level. Its publishing industry was second only to that of Great Britain in terms of its size and reputation. The high degree of political engagement placed at least some brakes on the ability of the governmental and military elite to wage war. Even General Ludendorff, who in the last two years of the Great War would, with Paul von Hindenburg, exercise quasi-dictatorial powers, had recognised in 1912 the necessity of 'so formulating the *casus belli* that the nation will take up arms enthusiastically and with one accord'.[31]

The demand for a forceful foreign policy and the build-up of Germany's already powerful armed forces could rely on strong support among a generally conservative intelligentsia and the higher bourgeoisie. When the elder von Moltke argued that 'without war, the world would deteriorate into materialism', this struck a chord among many unsettled by the growing wealth generated by German industrial power. According to Heinrich von

Treitschke, professor of history in Berlin, and a leading public exponent of German nationalism, 'The grandeur of history lies in the perpetual conflict of nations, and it is simply foolish to desire the suppression of their rivalry.' This echoed another of von Moltke's aphorisms:

> Permanent peace is a dream and not even a beautiful one, and war is a law of God's order in the world, by which the noblest virtues of man, courage and self-denial, loyalty and self-sacrifice, even to the point of death, are developed.[32]

In fairness, it should be noted that evocations of war as a cleansing spirit in decadent societies could also be found in the works of many contemporary English writers, not least Rudyard Kipling, the most influential of all the imperialist writers of the age.[33]

The working men who would have to pay the price of these effusions were generally more cautious when it came to war, though examinations of working-class reading in the pre-war years offer indications of why, when war came in 1914, the recruiting offices were swiftly overwhelmed with volunteers. Leipzig was a stronghold of the Social Democratic Party, but its working-class population consumed travel literature and colonial adventure stories as avidly as elsewhere in Germany. Henry Morton Stanley's *In Darkest Africa*, and the home-grown classic of Hermann Wissmann, *Across Africa under a German Flag*, were both eagerly devoured, along with the runaway bestseller, *Unter Menschenfressern (With the Cannibals)*.[34] Kaiser Wilhelm II's frustration that the success of the British Empire inhibited German colonial ambitions thus found its echo in wider society, as was reflected in the reactions of the German press to the Boer War. The British army's tribulation at the hands of the Boers caused a great deal of gleeful *Schadenfreude*. European opinion universally supported the Boers, as we can see in a much-undervalued and seldom-studied mode of print communication, the postcard. French and German postcards concentrated exclusively on Boer victories, Afrikaner heroes and British missteps. The eventual British victory engendered little celebration abroad.[35]

O Vaterherz erbebe nicht
Vor Schmerz und bittrem Weh!
Der Kaiser ruft! Das Vaterland!
Soldat! Kopf in die Höh!

Postcard hero. A wounded solider is urged back to duty by invocation
of the Kaiser and his duty to the Fatherland. This was the heyday
of the picture postcard, not just views of the seaside to send to
relatives, but highly charged political images such as this.

Tensions over naval competition, frustration at exclusion from
colonial territories and fear of encirclement led, in the decade
before 1914, to an increasing sense that war was inevitable, though,
as in Britain, it was by no means certain who would be the opponent – here Germany's grievances provided a generous range of
choices. General Friedrich von Bernhardi's *Germany and the Next
War*, published in 1911 and widely acclaimed in the press, had a
considerable impact, arguing 'there is no way in which we can
avoid going to war for the sake of our position as a world power,
and we should not be concerned with postponing it'. The right-
wing press talked of the 'sooner or later unavoidable clash between
the Germanic and Slavonic peoples'.[36] Hitler's obsession with the
danger from the east had deep roots.

Germany emerged from the Great War bruised, bewildered
and resentful. Detestation of the 'Carthaginian' Peace of Versailles
crossed all political and social barriers. The cultural renaissance
in Berlin we now associate with the Weimar Republic epitomised
to many Germans the moral degradation that would inevitably

overcome a demilitarised society. So when Hitler seized power in 1933, the professional classes and prosperous bourgeoisie were on the whole amenable to a re-disciplining of society. This particularly applied to teachers and university professors, who raised little objection to the reorganisation of their professions around Nazi ideological objectives.[37] This was one reason so much progress could be made with the indoctrination of the German fighting man in the twelve years of Nazi rule.

As so frequently, Hitler set out his plans for education with a grandiose scheme, intended to dominate the lives of young Germans inside and outside the classroom from the age of ten into adulthood, so that 'they will never again be free throughout their entire lives'; instead they would become 'fleet as greyhounds, tough as leather, and hard as Krupp-steel'.[38] Membership of the Hitler Youth was compulsory from 1936, but heavily encouraged by school teachers before then. Pupils would then graduate to six months working on the land, followed by two years in the military. Conscription provided the opportunity to politicise an entire age cohort, a process in which the officer corps was expected to play a full role, alongside the ubiquitous newspapers and magazines produced exclusively for distribution to the troops.

Two themes were especially emphasised in these publications: the denigration and dehumanisation of enemies of the Nazi project on political and racial grounds, and the near deification of the Führer as the Germany's sole hope of salvation. Soldiers' correspondence demonstrates that many who fought internalised these key messages. Thus, one soldier welcoming the attack on the Soviet Union, until that day Germany's sworn ally: 'This morning, thank God, it began against our deadly enemy, Bolshevism. It was a great relief to me.'[39] One young officer was impervious even to the delights of newly occupied France, regarded by many Wehrmacht soldiers as a soft billet:

> Later my soldiers and I went to a 'bookstore' in Versailles. You can't imagine what junk and pornography we saw! ... You can truly see that in the areas of cleanliness and morality, the French people have skidded to a new low.[40]

The victories of 1940, so unexpected that the German High Command had no plan for the occupation of all of France, produced a torrent of celebratory literature, much of it published by the Wehrmacht itself. It found a huge audience in both the army and the civilian population, not least among the adolescent boys who would soon be joining the armed forces. The combination of this swaggering sense of German military superiority, combined with racial theory, meant that the Germans consistently underestimated the fighting qualities of the Russians, something on which they could reflect at length as their Panzers came to a grinding halt thirty miles short of Moscow in November 1941. Now they turned to *With Napoleon in Russia*, a memoir of this ill-fated campaign by Napoleon's Master of Horse, Armand-Augustin-Louis de Caulaincourt, providentially published in 1933:

> All the commanders were now asking: 'When are we going to stop'? They remembered what had happened to Napoleon's army. Many of them began to re-read Caulaincourt's grim account of 1812. That book had a weighty influence at this critical time in 1941. I can still see von Kluge trudging through the mud from his sleeping quarters to his office, and there standing before the map with Caulaincourt's book in his hand. That went on day after day.[41]

Günther von Kluge was a contemplative officer with great responsibilities, but in Hitler's scheme of military education the man of action played a greater role than the thinker. The Hitler Youth emphasis on sport and outdoor activities inevitably encroached on attention to school work, much to the delight of many of its members. Youths contributing to a collection of reminiscences of Silesians ejected from their homes at the end of the war had only happy memories of the Hitler Youth. These were farm boys, fit and strong, so very much used to the active life.[42]

The members of the Hitler Youth consumed a variety of martial literature: tales of Stuka pilots, U-Boat commanders and Panzer units; they also enjoyed the memoirs of First World War veterans and the historical novels of Will Vesper (one of the rare convinced followers of National Socialism who was also a good writer).The books and periodicals produced by the Hitler Youth, in contrast, struggled to win a following. Boys preferred *Die Wehrmacht* and the Luftwaffe magazine *Der Adler*. The so-called Hitler Youth Catechism was reckoned so indigestible that copies were often simply not distributed. Many that were shared out were instantly donated to the waste-paper collections conducted by the Hitler Youth and the parallel girls' organisation, the Bund Deutscher Mädel (League of German Girls).[43] Far more to the boys' taste was Erwin Rommel's *Infantry Attacks*, a revised version of lectures given in the Dresden Military School between 1929 and 1933. Published in 1937, it must have received some careful rewriting by the Wehrmacht propaganda unit; it is hard to imagine other circumstances in which the great commander would have expressed the view that 'today the Italian army is one of the best in the world'.[44]

The pinnacle of this new structure of schooling was the Napoli, a series of boarding schools set up in imitation of the English public schools to train the new Nazi elite.[45] Often established on the premises of the old Prussian cadet schools closed by the Versailles treaty, they offered the normal school curriculum along with firearms training, riding, sailing and flying. Unlike the Prussian cadet schools, this was a truly classless structure, with highly competitive entry standards. The schools were generously resourced, and all supplied with an excellent library. Again, the emphasis was on physical prowess: any boy wearing spectacles was disqualified from entry. The graduates of the Napoli were greatly in demand in all the armed forces, leading to unseemly wrangles between the Luftwaffe, the Wehrmacht and the SS. Many who left school to join the forces would not survive the war.

The former Russian Empire, it must be said, was an extremely challenging environment for successful propaganda. This was a vast country, with many settlements very widely spread, and an uncomfortable amalgamation of many different nationalities. In 1937, newspapers were published in the Soviet Union in seventy-one different languages.[46] Outside the great cities, levels of education and book ownership were low. Although on the eve of the Second

World War, 80 per cent of the population were able to read and write (a considerable achievement of the Soviet era), only 9 per cent had received a secondary education. After the beginning of the war, newspapers became so scarce that there were not enough even to supply public library reading rooms. The problem was compounded by the low level of radio ownership: only 1 million sets in private hands in 1940, compared to 56 million in the United States. In a characteristic example of Soviet paranoia, in 1941 private owners were instructed to surrender these radios to prevent their exploitation by 'hostile elements'.[47] Instead, the regime relied on a network of public wireless loudspeakers, where citizens could gather to hear the news. There were 5 million such radio points throughout the USSR, 630,000 of them in Moscow.

The structural difficulties of distributing news and shaping public opinion were compounded by policy. Strict censorship made the newspapers dull and unappealing; newspaper staff were too terrified of retribution to take risks with their reporting. Comrade Stalin spent all too much of his time in the first months of the war revising news reports to obfuscate the rapid German advance and the serial catastrophes enveloping Russian forces in the field. The consequence was that citizens were more likely to believe gossip and rumour than the Soviet press. Journalist knew their reports were dull and uninformative, as one radio editor acknowledged: 'Our propaganda is stupid and bland.' An inquiry into wireless news in 1942 noted that citizens would listen attentively at the wireless points, then walk away saying 'We knew that already.'[48] In contrast to Hitler, Roosevelt or Churchill, Stalin seldom addressed the Russian people directly, a reticence shared by most of the Politburo. If wireless was thus a wasted resource, newspapers were as much valued for their secondary purpose as cigarette or toilet paper as for any news content.

Many of these difficulties dated back to the Great Terror (1936–8), which had hollowed out the professional groups necessary for leadership in war. University professors, scientists, doctors, journalists, artists and writers all suffered, along with the members of the old nobility and bourgeoisie, who were distrusted on principle. Nothing exhibited better the contradictions of the Soviet approach to education: a commitment to the expansion of education and literacy that spawned an impressive network of public libraries, while harbouring an unmoveable suspicion of the traditional intelligentsia. The consequence was vividly displayed at the first of the Gulag camps in the Solovetsky Islands in Russia's Arctic north, which gathered not only a glittering array of intellectual talent, but also a library of some 30,000 volumes, including several thousand in French, German and English, assembled from books brought by the prisoners or taken from other confiscated bourgeois libraries.[49] The Gulag of the later Stalinist period would be much less lavishly equipped.

The purge of writers and artists meant that the Soviet literature of the war was, with limited exceptions, largely in the hand of dull plodders, looking over their shoulders in constant fear of denunciation. Correspondents at the front, inspired by those they had met and whose hardships they had shared, sometimes wrote with a passionate honesty, but there were layers of censorship to be negotiated before these words appeared in print.

Most dangerous of all, Stalin had taken advantage of the Great Terror to eviscerate the army's officer corps. If the army performed particularly badly in 1941, this was partly Stalin's failure to act on the intelligence reports of the impending assault, but also the incapacity of such officers that remained to provide leadership. The Communist Party had its vision of the ideal soldier: preferably factory workers, party members or those with an experience of higher education. But these were, come the war, precisely the groups most likely to receive deferment from service as essential workers. The recruitment in 1941 of millions of new soldiers to stem the German advance also led to a considerable dilution of the quality of the troops; the reduction of the age of conscription to nineteen in 1939 meant that many of the recruits were scarcely trained. By the end of 1941, 3.8 million of these neophyte soldiers had passed into a brutal German captivity from which few would emerge alive.

The German invasion exposed many of the unhealed divisions in Soviet society, not least the ambiguous loyalties in the western territories swiftly engulfed by the German advance, Belarus,

Ukraine and the Baltic states.[50] Neither the peasants of Ukraine nor the citizens of the Baltics had any love for Stalin. The irony of the catastrophe of 1941 was that this most ideological of societies suffered from a deficit of ideological preparation. The decisive stiffening of resistance in the autumn of 1941 occurred when the front line was pushed back to the heart of Russia: the defence of the motherland provided a much more reliable basis for defiant courage than loyalty to the Soviet regime. In the words of one female survivor of the epic siege of Leningrad, 'We did not fight for Stalin. We fought for our families, for our city.'[51] Despite twenty years of communist indoctrination, this sort of local patriotism still counted for a lot.

Before we close this chapter, it is necessary to address one further issue. It is one thing to observe what impelled men to follow the flag, join the colours and sign up. Innocence, optimism and patriotism count for a great deal. This is where the pre-war conditioning of books, newspapers and magazines is most influential. It is more difficult to fathom why soldiers kept at it, faced with the terrible conditions, the imminence of death, the awful mutilating injuries that befell their friends and comrades – this even when the war was self-evidently lost. Why did so many men (and in Russia at least, also women) persevere, and endure, even to their own death? First, it must be said, not all did. In the American Civil War, it often only took one battle to persuade many of these volunteer soldiers that they had no wish to sample its dangers and excitements again. It was a generally accepted truth that half the troops did most of the fighting: others sought a safe berth in the rear echelons or made themselves invisible when the regiment was engaging. During the course of the Second World War, the Soviet army charged 4 million men with desertion, evading conscription or trying to evade the front through self-inflicted wounds.[52] The war on the Eastern Front had a particular brutality, fuelled by racial disdain on the German side, and in the Russian ranks, a hatred born of knowledge of the terrible atrocities committed against their people by the invaders. This hatred was carefully cultivated by the Soviet press, on Stalin's express instructions. He truly believed, as he said in his May

Day speech of 1942, that 'you cannot conquer the enemy without learning to hate him with all the power of your soul'.[53] This, indeed, was one of the most successful aspects of Soviet propaganda. The Germans knew they could expect no mercy; their ferocious defence of their eastern borders was powered by the knowledge of what they and their families could expect if the Russians prevailed. War had a hardening effect, narrowing the frame of emotional reference to a single trench, or village, or building. Men fought on with their comrades, until these died and they fought with new comrades.[54] To the author Guy Sajer, in his autobiographical account of service on the Russian front, comradeship was the only true reason men were able to keep fighting.[55]

It might have been expected that after the Allies had broken out of the beachhead in Normandy in 1944, German resistance in the west would have been less intense. The Allied armies were not keen to take more casualties than absolutely necessary, hence the continued reliance on air strikes. Yet the Germans fought on. This was partly because they continued to believe, against what appears to us to be overwhelming evidence to the contrary, that they might win. According to various surveys conducted with German prisoners of war, belief in victory only began to seep away in the first months of 1945. Among the most determined to hold out were the boys of the Hitler Youth and Napoli schools propelled into the front line at the age of fourteen or younger. When the teachers of Rügen Napoli told their boys that the war was lost, some were so furious that they demanded the key to the weapon store so they could continue the battle on their own. In the famous last picture taken of Hitler decorating members of the Hitler Youth in Berlin, the boys are as young as twelve. American tank units edging forward in the Ruhr were frequently ambushed by child soldiers. Colonel Roland Robb remembered one case when they were stalled by an artillery unit manned by children of twelve and younger. They refused to surrender and all were killed. This incident, and others like it, was deeply traumatic for the Allied troops forced to shoot these children for their own protection.[56] It is a final, macabre testimony to the success of ideological conditioning in the wars of the twentieth century.

PART II

THE MOBILISATION OF KNOWLEDGE

4

THE BATTLE OF SCIENCE

Ernest van Someren was not an obvious diarist. A public school-educated son of a religious enthusiast father and a bohemian journalist mother, he had found refuge from a challenging upbringing in excellence at university and in a secure marriage. But he was an unusual recruit for the British Mass Observation diaries project. Emotionally restrained, not inclined to confidences, he was not above a certain sanctimonious self-righteousness in his interactions with other prosperous suburban professional families. There was also a certain contradiction, which he was honest enough to recognise, that as a Quaker, pacifist and registered conscientious objector, he was happily employed as a research chemist performing vital war work. One of the key projects on which he was engaged would produce the huge steel spools used to lay the Pluto oil pipeline across the Channel, absolutely critical to the success of the D-Day landings.[1]

In his conflicted response to warfare, Van Someren was not unusual in the scientific community. The principle that science was a collective enterprise that recognised no boundaries of creed, politics or ideological system was deeply engrained. Many scientists preferred to hold themselves aloof from all political engagement, and there was a strong pacifist strain that went beyond the widely shared detestation of war. In 1934, a letter objecting to the use of scientific research for military purposes, circulated by the Cambridge Scientists Anti-War Group, was signed by 40 per cent of the members of the Cavendish Laboratory, home to some of the most advanced research in physics in the world. Yet when war came, the scientific communities of all combatant nations committed themselves, with whatever amount of reluctance, to the national cause. Physicists, chemists and engineers would be at the heart of the crucial developments in armaments, systems of defence and communication, as well as weapons that expanded the moral frontiers of war-making in quite terrifying ways. Many of them, like Ernest van Someren, loved their work, preserving a perhaps necessary detachment between problem solving and the human cost of their ingenuity. Experimental science is inherently optimistic, but depends for its success on the dogged brilliance of laboratory-based and theoretical scientists whose working lives are in normal circumstances rather shielded from the harsh realities of how scientific discovery is translated into lethal weaponry. The First World War, and even more the Second World War, would to some extent strip away this emotional subterfuge.

Ernest van Someren's war involved a short commute to Waltham Cross, with occasional trips up to London to consult necessary scientific literature. On Friday 8 November 1940, his diary records a day in the library of the Royal Chemical Society (along with the purchase of some French mustard at Fortnum and Mason). On 4 December he was back in the library abstracting two long German articles, the last references to be collected before publication of the latest of his volumes of spectrochemical abstracts.[2] A more frustrating day was 27 March 1941, when he was trying to trace an elusive German publication. In February, Van Someren had been in the Patent Office Library, one of the most important scientific libraries in the country, though the patents themselves were also an important source of experimental data and military intelligence. If anyone wanted to have concrete evidence of how quickly German industry began abusing the terms of the Versailles treaty, they needed only to have inspected the patents registered by the Krupp armaments firm in 1921, to know that their civilian products were largely a smokescreen.[3]

In 1942, an outburst of frustration shared with Mass Observation by Van Someren would reveal that war or no war, science was still an international business:

Was very busy at work, am trying to get some results on a line which has been thoroughly worked out in Germany and dropped as impossible, and in the USA has been side-stepped by a neat device using a material we can't get here. Shall be very surprised if we get any success at all, ever, but it would be a good thing if we managed it. In the evening I went to a meeting of the local Peace Group.[4]

May 1943 brought better news:

Cycled, did a lot of reading and abstracting work and came across a discovery in a German periodical which I promptly tried on our apparatus and find it will save us a good deal of trouble. It is a simple stunt with an old gramophone needle.[5]

At one level this is all very mundane, but for this present study precious, as few war scientists offer us this sort of window onto their everyday work (Van Someren, very properly, confided none of the specifics of his research to his diary). After the conclusion of the hostilities, war science generated a blizzard of publications, on the radar war, Germany's miracle weapons, the contribution of science to the intelligence war and the race for the atomic bomb. But if you relied only on reading these heroic narratives, you would think these crucial discoveries were made without any of the protagonists ever setting foot in a library. R. V. Jones, in his bestselling *Most Secret War*, does make one reference to a discovery in a Russian technical publication, but perhaps only because of the exotic nature of the source. In the myriad memoirs of Bletchley Park, one hears less about research collections than the recreational library created by Jimmy Thirsk (a former librarian) for this very bookish group of analysts.[6] The necessity for books of reference and analysis goes largely unremarked.

Perhaps this is because access to scholarly publications is too mundane and everyday an experience to merit comment. Indeed, as we will see here, the availability of scientific literature was as essential a part of scientific research as the access to equipment, chemicals or a laboratory. For concrete evidence of this dependence, we need to turn to one of the most fascinating of wartime subplots: the struggle to maintain access to scholarly periodicals published abroad, and the importance of preventing the scientific communities of enemy nations having access to your own scholarly discoveries. This rupture of the normal courtesies of scientific exchange was extremely painful to the scientific community: it was nevertheless a critical part of the wartime arms race.

At first view, the First World War could be seen as a twentieth-century war fought with nineteenth-century weapons and nineteenth-century minds. The most significant military innovations, the tank and the aeroplane, were still in their experimental state and would not impact significantly on the outcome. The tank arrived late in the war when the course of the battle was set, and the aeroplane would make more impact as a tool of reconnaissance than a fighting machine. This was an investment for the future. The major task of science and industry was refining weaponry, firearms and artillery that, along with trench and camp maladies, accounted for the vast proportion of casualties.[7] The most significant technological advance, and one that might truly have changed the course of the war, was the weaponisation of the submarine; again, its significance was only truly understood when the industrial resources were no longer sufficient to build the number required to destroy enough enemy shipping and force the protagonists to the negotiating table.

Innovation was not encouraged by the steadfast refusal of much of the military to accept help from those not working in military institutions. The Cambridge physicist J. D. Bernal recalled a colleague who offered to organise a meteorological service for the military, only to be told that soldiers fought in all weathers.[8] H. G. Wells, the great populariser of science through his novels, was even moved to write to *The Times*, complaining of the government's lack of attention to science. It took the use of gas at Ypres in April 1915 to alert army strategists to the true dangers of ignoring the battle in the laboratory. The German use of gas was partly a recognition that the plan for a lightning victory in the west had failed. That they resorted to gas, in defiance of the established rules of war, reflected the long-established German conviction that military necessity trumped all other considerations. It was also based on the conviction that the Allied nations would not be able to respond in kind. Fritz Haber, the scientist in charge of what was in truth a hurried and improvised programme, told the supreme commander of the German army that the British could not develop a poison gas, because they lacked the scientific capacity. This proved to be a costly misjudgement. Soon both sides had developed lethal gases, and the prevailing westerly winds of Flanders mean that those of the Allied armies were likely to be more effective. By the end of the war, gas had claimed almost 1 million casualties on the combined Western and Eastern fronts.[9]

If Haber had been wrong about the gas, the underlying assumption that Germany entered the war with a marked superiority in terms of its technological and scientific resources was widely shared on both sides. In 1909, 45 per cent of the articles indexed in US Chemical Abstracts had appeared in German journals. In the first fourteen years after the introduction of Nobel Prizes in 1901, Germany had won fourteen of the forty-eight scientific awards, and France eleven. Britain and the United States had won seven between them. In the nineteenth century, Germany was well known for privileging technical and practical knowledge in its system of higher education. But the superiority of its armaments owed every bit as much to its equally luminous reputation in the field of precision engineering. In the First World War, Gustav Krupp, director of the huge armaments complex in Essen, had as much influence as the civilian government, and almost as much as the German High Command. When, in the pre-war period, Admiral Tirpitz had the impertinence to suggest that a profit margin of 100 per cent on supplies to the German armed forces could possibly be subject to a patriotic discount, he was quickly warned off by the direct intervention of the Kaiser. It was no surprise that, after Germany's surrender, the dismantlement of the Krupp factory complex was a specific requirement of the Peace of Versailles.[10]

There is no doubt that appreciation of laboratory research was greatly enhanced by the experience of the Great War. If nothing else, the deadly potential of gas warfare had seen to that. In 1916, the British government established a committee to investigate the neglect of science, prompted in part by a letter signed by thirty-six leading scientists published in *The Times*. This pointed out that Sandhurst was the only major military academy where scientific education was neither an entry requirement nor a compulsory part of the curriculum: perhaps not surprising in a context where of the thirty-five leading public schools that provided most of the officers for the armed forces, thirty-four were headed by a classicist. Science needed advocates in the higher echelons of government: to this point in the whole history of cabinet government, only one senior British minister had been a trained scientist (Lord Playfair, educated at St Andrews, postmaster general in Gladstone's Liberal government in 1873–4).The creation in 1916 of a Department of Scientific and Industrial Research was seen as a first step in providing a degree of national coordination for the building of an enhanced scientific infrastructure. But if British scientists hoped that this would result in a surge of new funding for science in the universities, they would be disappointed.

The leaders of the British military establishment saw things rather differently, focusing instead on the role of their own research establishments (such as the Royal Military Academy at Woolwich or the Royal Aircraft Factory at Farnborough in Hampshire) in securing victory. This reliance on their own facilities may partly reflect a suspicion of intellectuals, but it is also the case that the chain of command in military organisations did not easily allow for taking instruction from civilian scientists.[11] This would be a continuing problem at the beginning of the Second World War, before the scale of the nation's danger forced a partial abandonment of more rigid principles. The fact that prime minister Winston Churchill was fascinated by the role science could play in warfare helped speed this process.

The generals also recognised that in providing the ordnance to hurl back at the German trenches they owed a great debt to the energy and adaptability of Britain's own heavy industries, now that they were deprived of imports from the German armaments giant Krupp (in peacetime Krupp cheerfully equipped the armies and navies of anyone who could afford their products). The development of the tank had been a co-operative effort between the director of naval construction and two private companies, William Foster (a manufacturer of agricultural machinery in Lincolnshire) and the Metropolitan Railway Carriage and Wagon Company of Birmingham. After the war the government provided grants to thirty industrial research associations, each of which maintained a library. These libraries, of the Wool Industry Research Association, the British Rubber Manufacturers and so on, acted a clearing houses for technical information for their members.[12] In this they were following the highly successful German model where the major engineering and chemical giants all maintained their own research departments. The library of Krupp in Essen, established in 1873, consisted by 1937 of some 100,000 volumes and subscriptions to 750 journals.[13] IG Farben, the conglomerate of chemical firms brought together in 1925, maintained a vast statistical unit at its headquarters in Berlin, which functioned almost as a national scientific reference library, an invaluable resource used by many German government departments during the Second World War.

The recognition of the need for more efficient co-ordination of documentation and the exchange of scientific information was a common theme in the inter-war years. In Britain, the Royal Society had played a crucial role in promoting research and invention since the foundation of its *Transactions* in 1665. In 1925–7 it published its first *World List of Scientific Periodicals*, recording the location of some 25,000 scholarly periodicals in 150 libraries worldwide. This would remain a crucial finding list into the 1950s. The foundation in 1924 of ASLIB, the Association of Special Libraries and Information Bureaux, was another crucial step in the promotion of an integrated scientific community.[14]

In Germany, the immediate post-war period was inevitably a time of retrenchment and austerity. The impact of hyper-inflation made the purchase of foreign periodicals well-nigh impossible: of 6,000 foreign periodicals held by publicly funded German libraries in 1914, only 1,700 were still being accessioned in 1921. The State Library in Berlin, Germany's largest, was able subscribe to only 150 of the 2,300 scientific periodicals it had taken before the war. The de-commissioning of the factories of the major German armaments manufacturers was a further major threat to technological development. Yet the scientific infrastructure in Germany was sufficiently robust to ride out the storm, not least because of the intrinsic strengths of the scientific tradition in Germany's universities. The foundation of the Emergency Association of German Science, dedicated to the acquisition of foreign publications for Germany's research libraries with the help of philanthropic donations, also helped turn the tide. By 1929, German libraries were subscribing to 15,000 foreign journals. These periodicals were circulated to interested research institutions by the creation in 1924 of a national inter-library loan service. Here the famous German technological universities, much admired abroad, played an important role as intermediaries between the traditional universities and industry.

The Nazi takeover impacted science as it did every other aspect of German life.[15] The expulsion of Jewish scientists from university posts was vastly wasteful of talent in physics, chemistry and mathematics. Asked by the German education minister how his discipline was faring in the university of Göttingen now that it was 'freed of Jewish influence', Professor David Hilbert risked a curt and dismissive reply: 'Mathematics in Göttingen? There is really none any more.'[16] Jewish influence in foreign scientific publications was also a matter of concern to the Nazis; from 1937, all orders for foreign publications by publicly funded bodies had to be approved by the Gestapo.[17] But for those prepared to accommodate themselves to these new working conditions, in truth almost the entire non-Jewish faculty, the Nazi approach to scientific and technical research brought significant compensations. Looking back from the perspective of November 1945, the Heidelberg chemist Karl Freudenberg admitted that if they could retain one thing from the Nazi period, it would be 'the copious financial means'.[18] It required the systematic attention of the Allied air forces to derail the German scientific juggernaut. In 1943, the bombing of the Berlin Technical University in Charlottenburg consumed its entire library of 250,000 volumes. In December of that same year, an RAF raid on Leipzig destroyed most of the nation's publishing industry, resulting in the closure of critical publications such as the *Chemisches Zentralblatt*, the oldest and highly respected journal of chemical abstracts. Germany was left with its miracle weapons, ground-breaking rocket research conducted in conditions of secrecy somewhat detached from the main scientific community. At war's end it would be this work that the victorious Allies would be most determined to purloin, along with the close-knit team of scientists who had achieved these extraordinary results under war conditions.[19]

Towards the end of 1941, the young Russian physicist Georgy Flyorov went into the local university library at Voronezh, to check the latest English-language journals for recent articles on his own field, nuclear fission. He was surprised to find that from the second half of the year there were none: a radical change indeed, since between January and June 1939 there had been more than fifty such articles published in British, German and American journals.[20] From this he inferred that fission research was now a classified military secret. If this was the case, Hitler must have wished that Germany had shown similar foresight, for the publication of an article in 1939 announcing the splitting of the uranium atom by Otto Hahn's laboratory had been a key factor in alerting the Allies to the possibility that Germany would be first to the bomb. But for this, and a second article in the same year, in the opinion of American scientists writing in 1945, 'Germany might have remained for a certain time in exclusive possession of a fundamental secret of atomic power.'[21] From May 1940, no further articles on nuclear fission appeared in German periodicals, but the horse had already bolted.

Given Germany's extraordinary ingenuity in developing new weapons, and the country's inherent strength in theoretical physics, the commitment of Nazi science to atomic research seems to have been curiously half-hearted: they seem very quickly to have decided that the development of an atomic bomb would have been prohibitively expensive. Already by 1941, Rudolph Peierls, an émigré physicist working on the Allied atomic project, was able to discern that Germany had not committed the financial or human resources necessary to develop a nuclear weapon. This he learned from scrutiny of the *Physikalische Zeitschrift*, which every semester published a list of lecture courses in physics at the German universities. It was clear that most physicists were working in their normal institutional homes, lecturing to no doubt greatly diminished classes, rather than, as in Britain or the United States, seconded to the research teams that created the sort of intellectual critical mass necessary to solve the myriad problems of building the bomb.[22] Here, more than perhaps in any other branch of science, Germany suffered from the heedless dismissal of so much talent when Jews were excluded from the professions. Max Planck, doyen of German physicists, was bold enough to tell Hitler to his face the damage this would do, but Hitler was unmoved: 'If the dismissal of Jewish scientists means the annihilation of contemporary German science, then we shall do without science for a few years.'[23] The cull of Jewish academics had deprived the German universities of 15 per cent of their teachers and researchers, including twenty Nobel Prize winners. This included 20 per cent of the mathematicians and more than a quarter of the physicists. The loss to Germany was an extraordinary boost to British science, but especially to the United States, not least in the development of the nuclear bomb. In the nuclear field the Germans were also badly undone by the arrogant assumption that if German physics could not master nuclear technology, then degenerate Western science posed no challenge. This led to the otherwise incomprehensible declassification of research on atomic fission, with eleven separate articles published in the *Zeitschrift für Physik* or *Die Naturwissenschaften* in 1942 and 1943. These were an unexpected bonanza for the members of the Manhattan Project, appreciably accelerating progress in building the bomb by 1945.

Despite these odd lapses, the opening of hostilities had significantly interrupted the smooth flow of scientific information across national borders. Once again, private industry came to the rescue on the German side, using subsidiaries in neutral companies to purchase the required periodicals. When the United States entered the war in 1941, IG Farben transferred its New York operation to Bayer's subsidiary in Portugal.[24] They also had the opportunity to exploit the scientific infrastructure of the occupied countries. In Denmark, Niels Bohr refused to co-operate, but the Nazis hoped for better in France. The universities and their libraries were treated very leniently. A project led by Dr Ernst Wermke, director of the municipal library in Breslau (now Wrocław in Poland, then part of Germany), was established to search out materials useful to German science, but these were then photocopied rather than simply appropriated. Wermke boasted that his team 'had not taken a single book or page from a French public library or transported it to Germany'.[25] The most successful collaboration was that engineered by Jean Gérard, secretary-general of the Maison de Chemie in Paris. This institution owned one of the best collections of scientific periodicals in the world, which Gérard was able to exploit when developing his indexing and abstracting service, to which he now added a major microfilming operation. After the war he would serve a six-month prison service for his friendly co-operation with the occupying powers. The contrast with the treatment of libraries in the east could not have been greater. Here a host of libraries in Russia, Poland and Czechoslovakia were systematically denuded of their books and periodicals by the German invaders. The Soviet delegation at the Nuremberg trials after the war would assert that the Germans had destroyed 334 institutions of higher education and 605 scientific research institutes. The plunder was so comprehensive that it was impossible to integrate the booty into German scientific libraries before the end of the war.[26]

All the efforts made in Britain to ensure the effective dissemination of scientific knowledge seemed likely to be undone by the renewal of hostilities in 1939. Some lessons had been learned. In 1939, when Oxford and Cambridge students turned out in droves to enlist, the scientists were gently directed back to their labs. There would be no waste of scientific talent to match the loss of H. G. J. Moseley, who had settled the periodical table, killed at Gallipoli, or indeed Bertram Hopkinson, professor of mechanism and applied mechanics at Cambridge, commissioned into the Royal Engineers in 1914 and killed on a solo flight in 1918.[27] But the restriction of access to German periodicals, particularly after the occupation of the Netherlands in May 1940, was a major blow. A survey of 310 significant science libraries in England soon revealed that most had not received any German periodicals after this date.

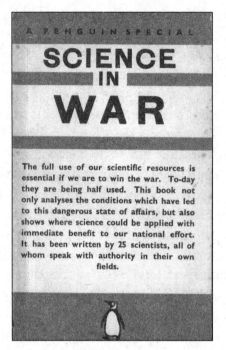

Science in War (1940) was perhaps the most influential of all
Penguin Specials. Conceived at a meeting of Solly Zuckerman's
'Tots and Quots' dining club, this wide-ranging and sometimes
eccentric miscellany of suggestions how better use could be
made of scientific talent found a ready reception, not least from
a prime minister fascinated by science, Winston Churchill.

The first imperative was to make better use of existing resources.
The Science Museum in London, which possessed by far the biggest
library of scientific periodicals, expanded its service to encompass
more than one thousand borrowing institutions. ASLIB began to
compile a series of wartime guides, listing where publications on
critical research areas could be found. At a time when the invasion
and occupation of Britain was more than a remote possibility, plans
were forged for the most important British research (particularly
in the atomic field) to be shared with the United States.[28] Once
this danger receded, attention switched to ensuring that when
foreign periodicals did arrive, they would be microfilmed at His
Majesty's Stationery Office before being sent on to the purchas-
ing institution. This was the genesis of a vast filming operation,

first based at the Science Museum, then at the Victoria and Albert, soon assisted by five state-of-the-art Kodak cameras supplied by American intelligence.

Soon the Americans had their own microfilming service, based in Ann Arbor, Michigan, under the auspices of the Interdepartmental Committee for the Acquisition of Foreign Publications (IDC). This inspired an operation for the systematic reprinting of crucial continental periodicals under licence of the US Alien Property Custodian, which took control of the copyrights of enemy nationals. In the course of the next four years, this authority licensed the copying of 116 separate titles which were distributed to 900 subscribers, almost all involved in war work.[29] The Second World War was in many respects a long-overdue coming of age for the American scientific community, to this point very much under the shadow of the revered German science. As the US government poured federal funds into research, the expertise and scholarly libraries of the universities were much in demand. By 1945, American science had developed the world-leading reputation that it has never subsequently relinquished, a role dramatically announced to the world by the explosion of two atomic bombs over the Japanese cities of Hiroshima and Nagasaki in August 1945.

The Soviet Union provides the most singular case of the development and impediment of science of the major wartime protagonists. No nation invested more in the support of science in the 1920s and 1930s than the communist Russian regime. The building of a public library network and the expansion of literacy was one of the great achievements of Lenin's new society, creating a pathway to excellence through school and university towards one of the myriad research institutes established in the interwar years. The peak of this pyramid of excellence was the Soviet Academy of Sciences. Membership of this internationally admired body came with tangible privileges, including additional food rations, superior accommodation and opportunities to represent the Soviet Union abroad. The vitality of Soviet science found its outlet in a wave of new periodical publications, as each new field or research institute sought to announce itself and share its new insights through

The Pelican abridged version (1942) of J. G. Crowther's *Soviet
Science*, first published in 1936. Crowther had travelled extensively
in Russia between 1929 and 1936, and made no secret of his
admiration for the Soviet achievement in physics, chemistry and
engineering. In 1942, this admiration was widely shared.

publication. Free of the historical bias towards a humanist education that held back Western countries, Soviet physics, chemistry
and engineering were seen as the vanguard of a modernising agenda
that would unleash the huge potential of the new workers' state.

Though a highly privileged cadre, scientists were of course not
protected from the paranoia that enveloped Soviet society in the
interwar years. In this environment, periodicals became not only
instruments of scientific discovery, but also the means by which
enemies of the people could be unmasked and rivals destroyed.
Alexey Wangenheim, head of the Moscow weather bureau, who
we met in the last chapter reading *Uncle Tom's Cabin* in the Gulag,
was brought down largely by a periodical dispute between two
ambitious subordinates. Wangenheim had helped popularise a new
understanding of cyclone theory, prompting one of his colleagues

to write an article on 'New Ideas in Meteorology and their Philo-sophical Implications'. Whatever the merits of the science, the young man had carelessly omitted any mention of Lenin, or Sta-lin's works. These lacunae were ruthlessly exposed in a series of poisonous articles by another young subordinate. When one of Wangenheim's colleagues was interrogated, it was easily believed that the director was 'of authoritarian and careerist temperament, politically hostile to the party'. Within months he was arrested, condemned, and on his way to the Solovetsky Islands in the Arctic Circle, from which he would never return.[30]

The paranoid years of the 1930s were exceptionally difficult for science. Where membership of international bodies had been a marker of prestige, now it became a sign of susceptibility to bourgeois, anti-Soviet influences. In 1934, Russian scientists were banned from exchanging offprints of their articles with foreign scholars without prior permission. The same went for articles sub-mitted for publication abroad. The Main Directorate on Literature and Presses took on the arduous task of inspecting imported scien-tific books and periodicals for harmful content. No more foreign members were admitted to the Academy of Sciences. As the doors to the wider world of science closed, Soviet research lost some of its cutting edge. The Great Purge of 1936–8 would take a heavy toll of scientific talent. More than a hundred physicists were arrested in Leningrad, many the victims of the dangerous practice of mutual denunciation. Of the eight-man delegation to the Second Inter-national Congress of Science in London in 1931, all but one were subsequently purged.[31]

Soviet science was always destined to take a rather different road, given Russia's size, history and social make-up. In the chaotic years after the revolution, millions died of starvation, including seven out of forty-four members of the Academy of Sciences.[32] Simply feeding this vast nation became an intractable problem, exacerbated by the collectivisation of farms and the subsequent deportation or execution of the more prosperous 'kulak' peasant farmers. For this reason, applied biology was the most relevant and politically charged of the sciences, and it also provided Soviet science with its most resonant and deadly scandal.

Trofim Lysenko, the peasant savant who, with Stalin's
support, ravaged the science of genetics and did much to
harm the international reputation of Soviet science.

Trofim Lysenko emerged onto the scene as a protégé of the
respected agronomist Nikolai Vavilov. Lysenko, the son of Ukrainian peasant parents and a practical rather than institutionally
trained biologist, claimed to have achieved extraordinary results
through vernalisation, a process by which the germination of wheat
could be accelerated by exposure to extreme cold. These results were
widely publicised, speeding Lysenko's progress to the heart of the
scientific establishment as a sort of peasant savant. It did not help
that Comrade Stalin was himself deeply interested in plant biology:
pruning the plants and shrubs in his Moscow dacha garden was
his only form of relaxation. Stalin was also a profound believer in

Lamarckism, which challenged conventional genetics by positing that organisms can pass on characteristics acquired during their lifetime. This was to become a cornerstone of Lysenko's pseudo-science.

Lysenko promoted his theories and announced his experimental results in his own periodical, *Agrobiology*, but also through articles in the press. In many respects, *Pravda* was now the most important scientific journal. With clear evidence of Stalin's personal support, critics kept silent, and Lysenko pressed home his advantage, comparing his opponents to the kulaks who had resisted collectivisation. This was deadly: among the geneticists and biologists subsequently condemned was Vavilov, Lysenko's first protector. The names of the purged were scored through in scientific publications, reviving a practice of the sixteenth-century Catholic Inquisition. The statistical work that might have revealed the failure of vernalisation was impossible because the directors of collective farms vastly inflated crop yields to protect themselves. Freed from any peer criticism, Academician Lysenko reported ever more sensational triumphs, turning wheat into rye, cabbages into swedes, pines into firs.[33] It would require the death of Stalin before the scourge of Lysenkoism could be erased from Soviet agriculture.

In July 1945, Luther Evans, Archibald MacLeish's successor as Librarian of Congress, reflected on the contribution of science to the war effort:

> I am allowing myself no poetic license whatsoever when I say that matters of large importance – battles lost or won, programs of action misdirected or well directed – are affected by the presence or the absence in the libraries of the nation of books, government documents, scientific periodicals and the other forms of publication.[34]

A lecturer at the technological university in Berlin in 1941 speaking on 'Science in the Struggle for the Reich and Living Space' offered much the same conclusion in the more robust phraseology of totalitarianism:

War is and always was the historical test of peoples. This is
also true for science and scientists. Their value to their own
people, and their ranking within their own people, is determined in an uncompromising way only by war. For them as
well, war is the only judge.[35]

These two statements, in their different ways, reflected an
undoubted truth about modern warfare: that science, in its many
diverse disciplines, played an essential role in creating new weapons,
enhancing defences and ensuring that the resources of combatant
nations were effectively employed. The accelerated rate of wartime
scientific innovation owed a great deal to the recognition of the
need for more generous resourcing of basic scientific research; it
also relied on preserving the international exchange of scientific
findings on which the incremental development of knowledge
had depended since the seventeenth century. The decision to
inhibit the flow of Western publications was only one of the many
examples of self-harming inspired by the paranoia of Joseph Stalin,
but certainly, in terms of the contribution the formidable Russian
scientific establishment could have made to the war effort, one of
the most serious. In both Germany and the Soviet Union, the fact
that science operated within an ideological framework inimical
to freedom of enquiry was damaging to its eventual effectiveness,
despite the technical achievements of scientists in both nations.

 This was, after all, the first conflict in which it seemed plausible that the invention of a wonder weapon might emerge to
change the whole course of the war. In the event, the unveiling
of the atomic bomb only accelerated an Allied victory already by
this point inevitable, though its consequences for the future were
profound.[36] Centuries of scientific ingenuity had finally arrived
at a weapon that had changed the world forever and could even
destroy it. All future policy and war-making would be conducted
under its dark shadow. And yet this potent culmination of wartime
science was in many respects a classic manifestation of a process
fundamental to scientific research: the pooling of knowledge across
geographical boundaries, the combing of scientific research published in numerous periodicals, and the assembling of a remarkable

array of international talent. It is ironic that the defeated enemy, Germany, inadvertently made its own large contribution, through both the expulsion of scientists and the careless publication of articles on nuclear fission after its own atomic programme had been wound up. Soviet science would also ultimately become privy to these secrets, thanks both to scientific papers salvaged in post-war Germany, and data illicitly shared by communist sympathisers in the West. It is to this intelligence war that we should now turn.

5

THE SPOOKS OF ACADEME

Joseph Toy Curtiss was an unlikely spy, but then so much of what academics contributed to the war effort was distinctly improbable. In the summer of 1942, Curtiss was ensconced in Yale, a historian unhappily teaching English literature in the additional summer semester introduced during the war. So the invitation to meet a man with a cigarette (which he would instantly extinguish) at the Yale Club was a welcome if unnecessarily melodramatic diversion. Curtiss was to become a central figure in the Yale Library Project: an initiative intended, under the cover of gathering material for Yale's already impressive War Literature Collection, to hoover up much needed reference works for intelligence. Yale's librarian was a willing accomplice in this scheme, though there were soon howls of outrage from other major libraries, abetted by the American Library Association, affronted that a rare permit for overseas travel should have been granted to Yale alone. A scheme of sharing the spoils was hurriedly agreed, though by this time the German occupation of Vichy France made Switzerland, the neutral location best stocked with German material, inaccessible. So it was only in July 1943, eleven months after his first contact, that Curtiss arrived in Istanbul.[1]

Istanbul in wartime was a place immersed in clandestine activity. Meetings with the emissaries of other belligerent powers were unavoidable. Curtiss was not helped by the persistent indiscretions of the local head of US intelligence, Lanning 'Packy' Macfarland, a genial Chicago banker. Macfarland's cover was so comprehensively blown that when he entered the local casino, the band would strike up 'Boo Boo Baby, I'm a Spy'. Various staff members working for the Americans reported directly to Russian or Turkish intelligence, while the British ambassador's personal valet was spying for the Germans. By way of balance, several of the local personnel of the German military intelligence, the Abwehr, defected to the Allies. Curtiss ploughed on, gathering up maps, travel books and German texts in the Grand Bazaar, along with telephone directories and old newspapers. Where possible he collected one copy for the intelligence organisations, and one for the universities whose greedy determination not to be outdone had almost capsized the whole operation.

This was the new face of intelligence, no longer, as it had been since the dawn of time, exclusively a matter of spies and scouts, ciphers and prisoner interrogations, all of which featured in the literary culture of spy stories, voraciously consumed by the reading public without regard for their crude exaggerations and improbabilities. Dorothy L. Sayers's Lord Peter Wimsey becomes an intelligence officer in the Great War in *Whose Body?* (1923), and *The Nine Tailors* (1934) revolves around ciphers. Perhaps it surprised even the scholars recruited for intelligence that the tomes accumulated for their daily work would prove essential to modern war-making; but that is what transpired, as voracious information gathering, research and analysis became the core of intelligence work.

The Second World War was a true global war, and the Allies found themselves engaged in conflict in parts of the world where they had little knowledge of the economy, climate or topography, or indeed the attitudes or preoccupations of the peoples they sought to liberate or engage as allies. They also needed to know more, much more, about the military resources of the enemies against whom they were ranged before they entrusted their conscript armies to conflicts in largely unknown territories; and they needed to accumulate this information very rapidly. This pivot towards research and analysis would lay the foundations of a Cold War intelligence establishment of unprecedented size, again with its wildly popular literary outriders. Indeed, in the paranoid world of the Soviet Union and its subject peoples, the fictional agents of John Le Carré, Graham Greene and Ian Fleming's James Bond, as we will see in a later chapter, seemed in the Kremlin more of a threat to the communist way of life than their human equivalents.

That this vast information gathering operation could be created required the human and physical resources of universities working side by side with fighting men and the wartime industries. While their colleagues in science departments adjusted their work to the exigencies of the war industries, intelligence work was also an opportunity for those in the humanities to prove their worth, and one that they eagerly embraced. Historians, classicists, linguists and philosophers could all see their niche in intelligence, and several played an important role in the unfolding struggle. Academics could be wayward, suspiciously left-wing and prone to flights of imagination, but their analytical skills, honed through years of work in archives, could not easily be taught to those not steeped in the academic disciplines. Most of all, they knew how to use a library. Intelligence work had taken a decisive turn, and one from which there could be no retreat when the fight against Germany and Japan turned into the clash of ideologies of the second half of the twentieth century.

In 1415, before King Henry V set off on the French expedition that would be redeemed by the unlikely victory at Agincourt, according to William Shakespeare he had one more item of business to conduct. On the quayside, he unmasked the traitorous courtiers who had betrayed his plans to the French king:

> The King hath note of all that they intend
> By interception which they dream not of.[2]

The guilty courtiers, after suitably repentant speeches, were hustled off to execution. None of the audience at the London theatres would have found this implausible: spies and spying had played a part in war and politics since at least biblical times, when Moses was instructed to send agents 'to spy out the land of Canaan'.[3] And it had not changed so very much between the time of Moses and the outbreak of the First World War. Spies sold secrets, and letters were transmitted in code. It was murky, exciting and sometimes deadly. Whether it contributed decisively to contests generally settled on the field of battle, or wars of attrition pitching one nation state against the other, was more difficult to determine.

During the 300 years between the mid-sixteenth century and the Victorian era, spying and ciphers – secret writing – became the cornerstone of intelligence.[4] The interest in enciphered messages grew with the development of a European diplomatic network in the sixteenth century. As ambassadorial despatches flowed back and forth between the courts of Paris, Madrid, Vienna, Brussels and London, host nations had little scruple in opening the diplomatic bag and removing seals to copy the contents. The use of ciphers to disguise meaning became common, though they could be as troublesome to their intended recipients as to the intercepting party. The great conflicts of the sixteenth and seventeenth centuries revealed all the problems that would bedevil cipher traffic down to the wireless age: the infrequency with which ciphers were changed; the danger that despatches were intercepted or went missing; and the delays before replies could be received. Philip II of Spain, administering his vast empire from his palace of El Escorial near Madrid, insisted that all diplomatic correspondence be sent in triplicate. This improved the chances of reports arriving but multiplied the risk of interception.

When armies took to the field, a whole new apparatus of messengers and scouts had to be created; the dangers of something going astray inevitably increased. Even the most disciplined army struggled with the limitations imposed by topography and horsepower. Scouts could ride out ahead of the main force, but in an advance through hostile territory, the intelligence horizon was little more than a hundred miles.[5] By the mid-eighteenth century most of the major powers had a 'great cipher', with several thousand critical words, places and military terms each represented by a character or character group. Publicly available books, such as John Davys's *The Art of Decyphering* (1737), gave tips on unravelling enciphered messages, but this was a laborious process without the key. In the Peninsular War of 1807–14, Wellington had his own cipher specialist, George Scovell, piecing together the individual elements to create his own copy of the French great cipher. In this he was better served than the Spanish king, Napoleon's brother Joseph, who, bizarrely, had not been entrusted with a copy of the French cipher. Scovell himself put his trust in a 'two-book system', communication between two parties who could decipher a message by reference to a particular agreed book. This had the advantage that the book could be frequently changed, whereas the complexities of revising the great cipher militated against security.[6]

The introduction of wireless at the beginning of the twentieth century brought a sea-change in communication, removing the geographical restraints of communication relying on horse-borne messengers. For intelligence, this brought both new opportunities and new dangers, to which the belligerent powers were not always quick to adapt. The First World War was not notable for the role played by intelligence: Richard Hannay and his brave band of adventurers achieved great things in thwarting German spy rings, but these were fictional characters in John Buchan's hugely popular novels. Real-life spies had a more difficult time.[7] The German attack through Belgium was hardly a surprise, though confected shock and genuine outrage proved a potent weapon with public opinion at home and around the world. Once the conflict had settled into the interminable stalemate of the trenches, where each major offensive was announced by a huge artillery barrage, there was little that intelligence could do to tip the scales.

Unlike the second war, it is hard to point to an intelligence coup that impacted significantly on the course of the war, with the solitary exception of the Zimmermann telegram, a remarkable triumph of the Admiralty codebreakers in the famous room 40.[8] Naval intelligence had intercepted an encrypted telegram from the German Foreign Office offering Mexico a treaty of alliance. As their share of the spoils, Mexico would be allocated the lost territories of Texas, New Mexico and Arizona. A subtle scheme was constructed that would simultaneously allow Britain to convince the Americans that the telegram was genuine (it was), without revealing that naval intelligence was reading German cables. Although the decision to join the war had already been taken by President Wilson before the Zimmermann telegram was made public, the outrage it created undoubtedly helped cement solidary for the Allied cause.

WESTERN UNION TELEGRAM

NEWCOMB CARLTON, PRESIDENT

Send the following telegram, subject to the terms
on back hereof, which are hereby agreed to

via Galveston

JAN 19 1917

GERMAN LEGATION

MEXICO CITY

```
130    13042  13401  8501   115    3528   416    17214  6491   11310
18147  18222  21560  10247  11518  23677  13605  3494   14936
98092  5905   11311  10392  10371  0302   21290  5161   39695
23571  17504  11269  18276  18101  0317   0228   17694  4473
22284  22200  19452  21589  67893  5569   13918  8958   12137
1333   4725   4458   5905   17166  13851  4458   17149  14471  6706
13850  12224  6929   14991  7382   15857  67893  14218  36477
5870   17553  67893  5870   5454   16102  15217  22801  17138
21001  17388  7446   23638  18222  6719   14331  15021  23845
3156   23552  22096  21604  4797   9497   22464  20855  4377
23610  18140  22260  5905   13347  20420  39689  13732  20667
6929   5275   18507  52262  1340   22049  13339  11265  22295
10439  14814  4178   6992   8784   7632   7357   6926   52262  11267
21100  21272  9346   9559   22464  15874  18502  18500  15857
2188   5376   7381   98092  16127  13486  9350   9220   76036  14219
5144   2831   17920  11347  17142  11264  7667   7762   15099  9110
10482  97556  3569   3670
```

BERNSTORFF.

Charge German Embassy.

The Zimmermann telegram, announcing the beginning of
unrestricted submarine warfare, and promising Mexico a
share of the spoils in the event of an Allied defeat.

The supremacy of British naval intelligence in the wireless intelligence war had been established early, when a series of felicitous
events had brought them the three main German naval ciphers by
the end of 1914. At the beginning of September, a German light
cruiser was wrecked in the Baltic, from which a ship of the Russian
navy managed to extract the Imperial German Navy's codebook.
One month earlier, an Australian naval ship had boarded a

freighter whose crew were unaware that the war had begun. This yielded a copy of the German merchant navy code book. Finally, in the second week of October, a skirmish in the Channel led to the sinking of a German destroyer, and a few weeks later an English trawler dredged up a chest containing the codebook used by flag officers, which permitted English intelligence to eavesdrop on conversations between German naval attachés around the world.[9] Yet this command of German radio traffic brought no dramatic consequences. Both the main imperial fleets played a cautious game, aware that a catastrophic engagement could tip the balance of the whole war. The poisonous legacy of this success was that the British navy entered the Second World War reluctant to concede the value of any intelligence not delivered in a naval uniform, and was initially highly sceptical of the rich seam of intelligence emanating from Bletchley Park. From Norway to the Atlantic, British sailors and merchant seamen paid a high price.

US intelligence was woefully underprepared for the Second World War. This was partly by design. In the 1920s the US Army had build a formidable reputation in cryptography, only in 1929 for secretary of state Henry L. Stimson to close it down, on the grounds that 'gentlemen don't read other people's mail'. So deficient were intelligence resources when the US joined the conflict in 1941 that a panicked appeal went out to US citizens to send in their postcards and holiday snaps of foreign destinations, This produced a deluge of mail of little operational use, consisting largely of 'equestrian monuments and seagulls'.[10]

Yet from these unpromising beginnings emerged one of the truly outstanding achievements of the intelligence war, the Research and Analysis Division of the Office of Strategic Studies (OSS), the forerunner of the CIA. The OSS was established in June 1942 on the personal initiative of President Roosevelt; its organisation was entrusted to William 'Wild Bill' Donovan, who brought to this task the whirlwind energy necessary if the US was to make up for lost time in the intelligence war. Certainly, he was not short of eager volunteers from within the academic community. Most of the senior Ivy League professors were strong anglophiles, and had supported early intervention in the European conflict. Now they recommended for service their own talented postgraduates and non-tenured lecturers. To reinforce this plethora of talent, the political scientist Franz Neumann, himself a refugee from Nazism and now employed by the Frankfurt Institute of Social Research in its new home at Columbia University in New York, supplied a list of experts on Germany from among the refugee community. He also provided access to the institute's rich and up-to-date collection of National Socialist literature. In this way was conceived the library of the R&A Division, which would become a formidable resource. By the autumn of 1942, R&A was contracting out significant research projects to Stanford, Berkeley, Denver, Columbia, Princeton and Yale.[11] By the end of 1944, R&A had amassed a library of more than 100,000 items. The OSS also made full use of the major university collections, as well as the Library of Congress and the New York Public Library.

For the academics recruited, adapting their working practice to the new protocols of intelligence work was sometimes uncomfortable. The production of timely reports, pruned of the stylistic embellishments so beloved of academe, was difficult: crisp memos were circulated reminding staff members that 'sobriety is imperative'. 'All parading of erudition which might have been spared without inconvenience is odious.'[12] The security need to dispense with footnotes came close to heresy, but was nevertheless enforced.

The young men of R&A buckled down, producing in the course of the war something in the region of 2,000 reports and a series of country-by-country handbooks and regional surveys. These were, in the main, well received by the military, particularly after the R&A had won its spurs, producing a guide to Morocco to accompany Operation Torch, the American assault on North Africa, in the space of fifty hours: the war's most famous essay crisis. Guides to Algeria and Tunisia followed in the next three weeks.

In the first days of R&A, historians set the tone, but it was ultimately the economists who produced the reports with the most urgent military application. A massive study of the German supply problem on the Eastern Front was all the more impressive because its conclusion went against the established consensus, arguing that

Red Army resistance was more important in stalling German progress than the logistics of supply. In 1942, the economists switched attention to German tank production and the combat effectiveness of the Luftwaffe. The OSS was reasonably effective in defending their young experts against call-up, claiming that middle-aged academics, whom tenure had relieved of the burdens of scholarship, 'cannot be used effectively in our work [for] they have lost both the aptitude for research and the flexibility to change to new habits of work'.[13] R&A also absorbed German refugees more readily than was the case in scientific disciplines, where security concerns, particularly in the atomic programme, were more acute. Many of the OSS academics, especially in the USSR division, were left-leaning, and sometimes inclined to look on Russia more favourably than on their British allies.

In Britain, too, the established intelligence agencies took their pick of the best academic talent. The unit charged with analysing German radio traffic consisted of Hugh Trevor-Roper, later Regius Professor of History at Oxford, his friend Charles Stuart, and two philosophers, Stuart Hampshire and Gilbert Ryle: in the words of one observer, 'a team of brilliance unparalleled anywhere in the intelligence machine'.[14] Perhaps this was unnecessary for the relatively mundane tasks involved. Dick White, later head of MI5, recognised 'a massive intake of brain and abilities from the universities which set entirely new standards of intellectual achievement', but after the war admitted to J. C. Masterman, 'I think that we appropriated too much talent. The demand for men of ability in other departments was enormous and perhaps we were a bit greedy.'[15]

None of the young lions of Oxbridge thought much of the leaders of the intelligence agencies, holdovers from the fallow inter-war years. When Major T. Robbins joined the School of Military Intelligence as instructor in the German army and POW interrogation, he found no materials on the German army available from the War Office and the Staff College Library scanty and out of date. Early in 1940, on his own initiative he travelled to Brussels, where he combed the bookshops for military textbooks in German. As the Yale initiative had demonstrated, some of the material gathered up was extremely mundane: but for the academics now in intelligence it was almost an article of faith that the careful perusal of published materials would provide more fruit than could be hoped for by conventional spying. As Hugh Trevor-Roper, a talented if wayward officer, put it, 'More can be deduced from an intelligent study of public sources than by any number of "reliable" but unintelligent "agents" listening at keyholes or swapping drinks at bars.'[16]

Human intelligence did have its successes. While few captured officers would offer up much in the course of conventional interrogation, some of the best human intelligence of the war would come from monitoring the conversations of German POWs on listening devices planted in their accommodation.[17] And while spies seem to have featured more as double agents, having been turned by their captors, the agent Richard Sorge in Tokyo, ostensibly a German journalist, provided the Russians with a detailed account of Japanese strategic thinking. Russia also benefited from the allegiance of many left-wing intellectuals in Germany, Britain and the United States who served the Soviet cause out of ideological conviction. Whether this high-grade intelligence would be believed in the USSR would be another matter altogether.

As this suggests, the intelligence environment in the totalitarian regimes, Germany and Russia, was very different. The technical achievements of the German telegraphic listening service were very considerable, if not so dramatically vital as the British decryption of Enigma traffic. One of the conditions of the Versailles treaty was that the German intelligence service should be wound up as part of the general process of demilitarisation. So it was somewhat remarkable that when war broke out in 1939, Germany should have not one single integrated service, but ten separate organisations charged with electronic surveillance.[18] The army, navy and Luftwaffe all had their own cadres, along with separate listening organisations for the SS, the High Command and the Foreign Office. The Post Office offered its services intercepting sensitive telegrams and tapping phones. This blossoming of surveillance reflected both the advanced technical competence of

Walter Schellenberg, one of the most talented and imaginative German
intelligence officers of the war, though too much of his energy was spent in
negotiating the tensions between competing agencies and warring bosses.

German engineers and cryptographers, and the febrile insecurities
of the Nazi elite, locked, as Hitler intended, in a complex web of
overlapping jurisdictions and mutual competition. At one point
four separate agencies were all engaged on a single cryptographic
problem, deciphering the diplomatic cables of a neutral nation,
Switzerland.

For all this enervating organisational competition, German
cryptographers achieved a great deal of real worth. Reading British
signals traffic provided warning of the Anglo-French plans to send
troops to Norway in 1940, prompting Hitler to pre-empt this attack

by occupying Denmark and Norway. A dreadful security breach in the chaotic British withdrawal from this campaign resulted in the abandonment of a cache of signals material in Bergen. When discovered in May 1941, this gave the Germans access to the British administrative code, the Foreign Office cipher and the merchant shipping code, crucial to allowing the German U-Boats to find British convoys in the unfolding Battle of the Atlantic.[19] Analysing RAF radio traffic was greatly assisted by the purchase of copies of the *Air Force List*, freely available in London bookshops, which gave the names and registration numbers of the aircraft in the RAF fleet. They provided a mass of 'cribs' for attacking the RAF code. Open-source publications of this type turned out to be extremely valuable on both sides of the intelligence battle. Before the war, French newspapers regularly published information from the French embassy in Berlin, which turned out to be much the same as the intelligence gathered from decrypted cables, once the Germans broke the French diplomatic code. By 1940, the Germans were reading British naval codes, the French military cipher and parts of the British and Romanian diplomatic codes. (Although a non-belligerent at this point, Romania was particularly important to German strategy, because of Germany's reliance on supplies from the rich Ploiești oilfield.)[20]

The Germans also enjoyed considerable success breaking Russian code traffic. The Red Army five-figure code book had been broken during the Winter War of 1939–40, with much help from the embattled Finns. Although the Germans captured a copy of the book during the first days of Operation Barbarossa, the Russians were still using it in 1942. Another lucky break led to the unravelling of the Russian naval codes, which relied on a daily reference point (page 142, line 12, fourth letter) from a book of which both the encoder and recipient had a copy. This had to be a freely available text, but which? The solution was revealed when a Russian military attaché returning to Moscow left a pile of books in a house where a member of the German naval signals intelligence, the B-Dienst, also lodged. The abandoned books included the key text: *The History of the Communist Party*, in an edition not available in Germany. From that point, the B-Dienst had access to all

Russian naval traffic. By August 1941, two months into Barbarossa, the Germans signal staff had broken sixty-nine different cipher mechanisms, including the code used by the Russian general staff.

Conventional human intelligence continued to play its part, much to the delight of Hitler, who was an avid reader of Rudyard Kipling and the spy stories of John Buchan.[21] From France, agents in the cement factories of Nancy and Metz provided precise details of the fortifications of the Maginot Line, and personnel of German–Norwegian fish processing firms furnished intelligence on Norwegian port installations. A long-term sleeper agent in Kirkwall, Orkney, alerted German intelligence to the insufficiency of the anti-submarine nets at the naval base at Scapa Flow. This resulted in one of the most audacious feats of the first year of the war, when a U-Boat made its way into the anchorage and torpedoed the aircraft carrier *Oak Royal*.[22] That apart, British security made a good job of identifying and rounding up German assets in the UK, many of whom were then turned and used as double agents. This would play an important role in the preparation for the climactic intelligence event of the war, Operation Overlord, the Allied invasion of northern France.

The Germans secured one other early triumph by spiriting two British agents away from a rendezvous in the Dutch border town of Venlo, having convinced them they were meeting members of the German opposition. The architect of this audacious plan was Walter Schellenberg, a young man rising through the ranks of the SS security service, the Sicherheitsdienst (SD). Highly intelligent and a shrewd institutional politician, Schellenberg managed to ingratiate himself with Admiral Canaris, a neighbour with whom he used to go riding, as well as Reinhard Heydrich, his boss in the SD, and Heinrich Himmler. Heydrich shared Hitler's exaggerated respect for the British Secret Service, sometimes styling himself 'C' in imitation of the head of MI6.[23]

Schellenberg's work in intelligence is well known to us from the memoir he compiled after the war, and published posthumously. When reading this extremely detailed narrative we must be aware of its context. Schellenberg wrote it in British captivity, awaiting trial for war crimes. He was keen to minimise his responsibility for the brutality, executions and atrocities that were part of everyday life in Heidrich's SD. He has little to say, for instance, of his part in the compilation of the *Informationsheft Grossbritannien*, a manual prepared for the German occupying forces after the anticipated conquest of Britain, nor its sinister supplement, the *Sonderfahndungsliste GB* (Special Search List), enumerating the 2,820 named persons who were to be arrested immediately. The two documents included cultural figures as well as leading politicians and trade union leaders. Virginia Woolf, Stephen Spender, Rose Macaulay, E. M. Forster, J. B. Priestley, H. G. Wells and Aldous Huxley were among the authors marked out for immediate detention: an impressive albeit macabre statement of Hitler's understanding of the power of literature to shape opinion. Having seen the use to which the equivalent list for Poland had been put, Schellenberg would have been under no illusions of the anticipated consequences for those included. As the author Rebecca West put it to Noël Coward, when learning that they had both been on this list, 'My dear, the people we should have been seen dead with!'[24] Twenty thousand copies of this booklet were printed in anticipation of the invasion. When Hitler postponed and then abandoned Operation Sealion, the entire print run was placed in a Berlin warehouse, where it perished in an air raid. Today only two copies survive, in the Imperial War Museum in London, and in the Hoover Institution at Stanford University, one of the fruits of the gathering of Nazi material by American institutional libraries at the end of the war.[25]

Over the course of the war, the Reich Security Main Office and the Gestapo both accumulated enormous libraries. The library of the Wannsee Institute, a specialist collection of materials on Russia, played an important role in providing information on the Russian economy and transport infrastructure in advance of Barbarossa, and Schellenberg kept a small private research library in his office.[26] But the reflective work required for research and analysis always took second place to crisis management. Schellenberg was drowning in files, and his attempts at reorganisation, not least to bring together all the duelling intelligence agencies into one manageable structure, foundered on the insecurities of the Nazi barons. The enormous libraries built from rapacious plunder of Europe's collections were rendered useless by the speed of their growth. A rapidly assembled collection of half a million books requires both cataloguing and curation before it can be useful as a research resource. From 1943, in any case, librarians were being called to the front, and all the major Nazi collections began their peripatetic search for a safe haven out of range of Allied bombers. Many looted books were still in their original crates when Russian, American and British troops overran their places of safety.[27]

What became the most famous intelligence operation of the war began with the purchase, in 1938, of a small Buckinghamshire country house, Bletchley Park. This was intended as a safe haven from the anticipated bombing of London, and the head of the Secret Intelligence Service (SIS, now commonly known as MI6), Admiral Sir Hugh Sinclair, paid the £6,000 purchase price out of his own pocket. In the early years it preserved something of the atmosphere of the Oxford and Cambridge colleges from which its early denizens were mostly recruited, a predictable mix of classicists and chess champions, crossword specialists, linguists and historians. Perhaps surprisingly, in view of its ultimate role in cracking the secrets of Germany's encoded communications, it was only in 1939 that Bletchley recruited its first mathematician, Peter Twinn. He later claimed that he was told that mathematicians were almost blackballed because they were regarded as 'strange fellows, notoriously impractical'. If having the odd scientist was truly necessary, 'it might be better to look for a physicist on the grounds that they might have at least some appreciation of the real world'. He was soon joined at Bletchley by Alan Turing, the mathematical genius who would play such a large part in its story.[28]

Early denizens remember excellent meals in the Hall Dining Room, and games of rounders on the lawn. But the house-party atmosphere was soon dissipated by the deadly seriousness of the task. By 1944, Bletchley was a sprawling encampment which, together with its outstations, employed 10,000 staff, at Bletchley housed in concrete and wooden huts or lodged in villages for miles around. Significantly, in view of what we have learned of

Germany's competing baronries of intelligence, all three services sent large detachments of staff to Bletchley. Women made up 70 per cent of the personnel, another contrast with Germany where women were largely absent from wireless interception until late in the war.

For the years between 1940 and 1945, Bletchley was the focal point and fulcrum of the British intelligence operation. At critical points in the war, the desperate efforts of its mechanical engineers, codebreakers and analysts were all that lay between Britain and the prospect of defeat or starvation. This was an old-style intelligence war: codebreaking with a modern twist, attacking a mechanical electrical encryption machine, Enigma, that permitted near-instant transmission and decoding, but only to the intended recipient who had the required settings.

The key to British success with Enigma was that once the code was broken, this was successfully concealed throughout the war. Before the most significant intelligence was released to field commanders, the source was disguised as the product of high-grade human intelligence. The navy in particular was sceptical of unknown spies, and sometimes failed to act on what they believed to be deliberate misinformation. The Germans conducted frequent reviews, always confirming the impregnability of Enigma traffic; this was a huge stroke of luck for British intelligence. When in 1943 the cautious Admiral Dönitz ordered the addition of an extra rotor in naval Enigma, this led to an eight-month intelligence blackout, and a bloodbath in the duel between German submarines and Allied convoy traffic in the Atlantic.

Even when decryption had been accomplished, it still needed considerable work to make the plain-text messages intelligible. Raw intelligence traffic was an impenetrable jumble of registration numbers, abbreviations and military slang: this needed more than a dictionary to untangle. All messages were passed after decryption to the specialists charged with research and analysis; here, too, the resources had to be created from scratch. This does not seem to have involved the creation of a conventional research library. There are references in Bletchley memoirs to the paucity of reference materials in the early days. In the words of the first office

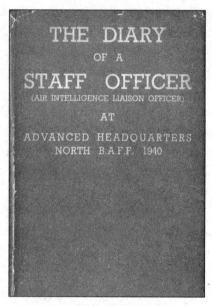

The Diary of a Staff Officer found a ready audience as readers struggled
to understand the unexpected calamity of the campaign in France,
but was withdrawn when censors feared it might alert German
intelligence that Enigma was compromised. With so many copies
in circulation, this seems a futile gesture, but does demonstrate
how carefully the secrets of Bletchley Park were guarded.

manager, Edmund Green, there was 'no furniture, books of reference, maps, atlases, dictionaries or any tools with which we might
be expected to finish the job'.[29] The only library we know of was a
collection of recreational reading in the main house; a second off-
duty facility was built later in the war on the RAF camp. Bletchley
operated a twenty-four-hour working day in three eight-hour
shifts: for the highly educated staff, reading was a necessary refuge
from the intellectual intensity of poring over intractable pages of
figures. According to Asa Briggs, a young recruit who would go on
to a distinguished future in academic work, 'To be with people for
whom books, music, art, history, everything like that was a daily
part of our lives, it was an absolute blossoming.' On off-duty trips
to Blackwell's bookshop in Oxford or Heffers in Cambridge, you
would inevitably bump into other Bletchley staff.[30] The library in
the main house was curated by Jimmy Thirsk, a librarian in civilian

life before the war. He would return to this vocation when demo-
bilised, along with his new wife Joan, a fellow Bletchleyite, who
would go on to be one of Britain's leading agricultural historians.[31]

The recreational library kept the staff happy, but Trollope and
Jane Austen could do little to help penetrate German wireless
traffic. The major analytical tools at Bletchley were not the library,
but a vast dictionary/glossary of German military terms, and an
expanding card index of military organisations and personnel.
Early in the war, office manager Edmund Green claimed to have
obtained a large and priceless card index in exchange for a 'small
and incompetent typist'.[32] This quintessential piece of library kit
played a major role in all the major intelligence organisations that
flourished during the Second World War. In compiling the list of
Britons to be arrested after the German conquest, Schellenberg was
able to turn to the Gestapo's electronically powered card index: the
touch of a button could bring up any one of the 500,000 cards
in the system. The Research and Analysis department of the OSS
earned many plaudits for the speed that it could solve abstruse
problems of military nomenclature almost instantly.[33] But only
disappointment came to the Belgian Paul Otlet, who had created
the most compendious card index of them all, the *Répertoire Bib-
liographique Universel*, an ambitious attempt to capture the world's
knowledge on an Alexandrian scale. Alas, like the great library of
Alexandria, this was not destined to succeed. When Belgium fell
to the Germans in 1940, Otlet's premises were immediately visited
by a high-ranking German military delegation. They swiftly concluded that his eclectic collection, including the 15 million entries
on his card index, had little immediate military use. On his death
in 1944, what remained of the archive was shuttered and forgotten, until interest in Otlet was revived by the advent of the World
Wide Web.[34] Still, in intelligence work card indexes proved to be
every bit as important as a research library, reflecting the mass of
new material that had to be compiled and sorted on a daily basis.
Operational research also made considerable use of IBM punch
cards, another tentative step towards the birth of computing and
one with deadly consequences for those who found themselves in
the grip of the Nazi war machine.[35]

No nation embraced the potential of IBM tabulators more eagerly than Nazi Germany. The 1933 census, which provided detailed and precise information on the location and occupation of Jews, was a triumph for IBM technology, which was eagerly adopted by German industry and government departments. Thomas Watson, IBM's hard-driving chief executive, seems to have been oblivious to the implications of the company's close co-operation with the Nazi state, which he much admired. On a visit to Berlin in 1937 he accepted Hitler's Order of the German Eagle, a select company in which he would soon be joined by Henry Ford and the aviator Charles Lindbergh, champions of American isolationism.[36]

During the war, the Hollerith machines leased to IBM's German subsidiary played an essential role in both the organisation of slave labour and the Holocaust. The Hollerith number helped identify and track prisoners in the concentration camps. There were two dozen Hollerith machines at Dachau and many more at Auschwitz and Buchenwald. IBM's role in supplying German industry, the post office, the military and the railways (critical to the planning and execution of the Holocaust) was well known to US government agencies, but the company was too important to the American war industry to face sanction. By 1943, two-thirds of its factory space had been turned over to manufacturing munitions, and IBM was involved in ninety-nine strategic projects. In the technological battles of science and intelligence, utility would sometimes trump morality.

Every element of intelligence gathering we have discussed in this chapter was employed in Operation Overlord, the Allied invasion of France in 1944. Intelligence was essential to provide a comprehensive understanding of German defences and details of the location of German units; complex counter-intelligence measures helped keep the timing and location of the landing secret. RAF aerial photography units flew many thousands of sorties, filming and re-filming every yard of the coastline between Cherbourg and Calais. The French resistance played a vital part in providing detailed descriptions of the Atlantic Wall fortifications.

Meanwhile, the Political Warfare Executive turned its attention to northern France, beaming radio programmes to German troops, with discouraging news of what their wives were getting up to on the home front, and preparing leaflets to be dropped to be read both by German troops and leaflets warning French civilians of forthcoming attacks on transportation hubs. By D-Day, 3 million leaflets had been distributed by airdrop, and 1 million copies a day were being printed of an Allied daily newspaper for German troops, *Nachrichten für die Truppen*. Issues after the invasion kept German troops informed of the progress of the Allied breakout. An estimated 75–80 per cent of the prisoners netted in the D-Day campaign were found to have Allied leaflets in their possession.

Bletchley played its part, not least in providing the Allied High Command with the complete German order of battle: this provided reassurance that the German High Command still expected the landing to occur in Calais. This was the result of the war's most elaborate deception scheme, which required the creation of a shadow army in Kent, under the command of General Patton, apparently poised to make the shortest Channel crossing

The geology as well as the geography of the coastal areas would also have to be researched, to ensure that the landing craft and tanks did not get stuck on the beaches. Samples of sand were obtained by a midget submarine, and scale relief models of the beaches constructed.[37] The Inter-Service Topographical unit produced a mass of booklets detailing the physical features of the coastline, all printed in great secrecy by Oxford University Press, along with the myriad operational code books.

On 6 June, the invasion fleet set sail. Speeding towards Normandy, it gave the impression of overwhelming force: 100,000 men, supported by a huge armada and command of the air. In truth, it faced daunting problems of supply, a German army five times this size, and an array of beach defences designed by Rommel, German's most celebrated general. That it succeeded, and with a fraction of the anticipated casualties, owed a great deal to the quality of the preparation, and to the raw valour of the fighting men. But it also owed much to the success of the intelligence operation, and the catastrophic failure of intelligence on the German side.

By this point German intelligence capacity was much degraded, not least by the wearying persistence of inter-service rivalries and the increased attention to suppressing domestic dissent: 'Their faith in machines and experts continued to be matched by their suspicion of men, and especially their own countrymen.'[38] Curiously, this suspicion did not extend to the German agents turned by their British captors, pouring disinformation into the ears of their handlers at home. Hitler, who had initially predicted correctly that the invasion would be in Normandy, now had second thoughts and ordered a crucial Panzer formation back to Calais. By the time the deception was revealed, the Allied bridgehead was established, and the Allies poised for the breakout that would sweep them through France.

In 1941, John Godfrey, the director of naval intelligence who had done so much to smooth rivalries between the services, assessed the role of the research and analysis that he would champion throughout the war: 'Intelligence is only rarely dramatic; its true basis is research, and the best results are usually obtained from the continuous study of insignificant details which, though singly of little value, are collectively of great importance.'[39]

How should we assess the role of intelligence in the war as a whole? Perhaps we only see the value of intelligence when it fails. The three great intelligence misses of the war – the German confidence that the Allies could not crack Enigma, their failure to anticipate the Allied landing in Normandy, and the American failure to anticipate the Japanese attack on Pearl Harbor – were all vital to the course of the war. Yet although German intelligence successes against their wartime opponents were comparatively modest, for three years their armies triumphed in virtually every sphere. Both Germany and the USSR were handicapped by the difficulty in presenting bad news to dictators, most notably when Stalin refused to heed the warnings of the German attack in 1941, but also when Hitler gradually retreated into a fantasy world of his own, manoeuvring phantom armies around his grand strategic maps. He ended the war with a troglodyte existence, huddled in his bunker, having Goebbels read aloud to him from Thomas

Carlyle's *History of Germany* – a reminder of happier times. On the other side, intelligence was a science of marginal gains. It gave the Allies a toehold when the tide of war was wholly adverse, most notably in the Battle of the Atlantic. When tables turned after D-Day, a remarkable intelligence triumph, eventual victory was the product of military muscle: brute force, rather than wit and ingenuity, characterised the final Allied effort.[40] In the end, the spoils would be shared between the world's economic powerhouse, the United States, and the belligerent most heedless of the cost of victory, the USSR.

6

LINES ON A MAP

War is good for cartography. Troops, navies and airmen need detailed maps of the theatre of action. On the home front, the civilians of both combatant and neutral nations are introduced to a mass of previously unknown locations: Anzio, Iwo Jima, Pearl Harbor, the Solomon Islands, Narvik. Provision of a good map, atlas or globe was an early priority for many households. The beginning of the European war in 1939 brought such a run on maps and atlases in the Unites States that the stocks of bookshops were soon cleared out, a process repeated with the attack on Pearl Harbor.[1] Even military calamity could be turned to good account. As the British mapmaking specialists Bartholomew cheerfully suggested in an advertisement placed in the *Bookseller* of February 1941:

> Roll up the Map of Europe. It is out of date unless it is the new edition of Bartholomew's *Europe and Mediterranean*, which shows the extent of German Occupied Territory at January 1941, as well as the new frontiers of Rumania. Prices as before: Paper 2*s*; Cloth 3*s* 6*d*.

The same issue offered Bartholomew's *Graphic World Atlas* for 7*s* 6*d* and a perhaps over-hasty 'Libyan Victory Map' in braille. This was distributed free with the Institute for the Blind's weekly newspaper or sold separately for one penny.[2]

Detailed maps were also crucial to military planners plotting campaigns on enemy territory, or indeed enemy spies. These two markets were clearly on the minds of the British government when they introduced the Control of Maps Order in 1940. This made it illegal to sell or dispose of any map on a scale greater than 1 inch to the mile without a licence from the Chief Constable. Public libraries were forbidden to loan such a map to anyone without the appropriate licence. Non-citizens were not allowed to possess maps with a scale greater than 12 miles per inch: librarians should check ID cards if necessary when such maps were asked for. This did not cause any great outcry, though it did almost lead to the incarceration of a senior official of the Scottish air defence, when he was spotted consulting a map on a visit to Arbroath, and reported to the police by a concerned citizen.[3] Librarians reported public pressure to remove all maps from walls in public libraries and generally complied; certain maps were simply taken off the market.[4] Maps were carefully husbanded and collected to help plot the route to victory. When in 1943 the British government embarked on its greatest salvage drive, local committees were enjoined to preserve foreign maps and street guides along with trade handbooks and financial directories to be sent on to the Ministry of Economic Warfare.[5]

Cartography became a part of everyday life. Edward Stebbing, a wry observer of English newspapers and no admirer of the British government's propaganda effort, noted the proliferation of maps in newspapers when it seemed in the summer of 1942 that the tide might at last be turning in the Allies' favour:

> The newspapers are in ecstasies. There are more maps than ever, showing arrows pointing in all directions, arrows inside arrows, arrows straight and arrows coiled and curving like snakes, and various other wonderful symbols. It is a military map-maker's paradise.[6]

The importance of cartography had been clearly understood since before the establishment of the first staff colleges. The Duke of Wellington travelled with a mass of maps and almanacs, and his adversary Napoleon was equally devoted to cartography. And yet with each new conflict, the general staff in each combatant nation always seemed to be caught short. The success of Stonewall Jackson's campaign in the Shenandoah Valley, stalling the Union armies for long enough to prevent the attack on the Confederate

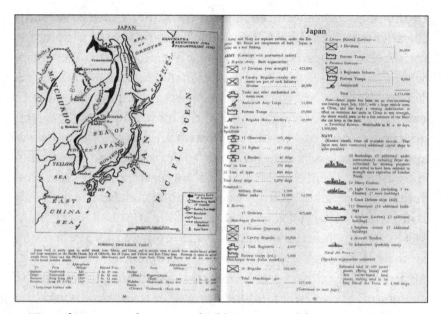

This informative and attractive double-page spread from Ernest Dupuy's study in military geography *World in Arms* (1940) helps explain how maps and atlases became one of the most appreciated genres of wartime publishing. Here, the rather modest statement of Japanese forces did little to prepare British readers for the coming onslaught in the East.

capital Richmond, was a masterpiece of improvised warfare which owed a great deal to superior knowledge of the terrain rather than map-reading. Even in the midst of the Second World War, after huge (and successful) efforts to provide maps for the Allied armies, local commanders could still be caught short. Such a case occurred when Allied troops massed for the assault on the fortress monastery of Monte Cassino: Major General Francis Tuker, who led the 4th Indian Division and was charged to send his troops on a frontal assault, was aghast to discover that II Corps and the 5th Army HQ had no geographical information on the immediate locality. He despatched a subaltern to Naples to search bookshops and libraries for relevant literature. The subaltern returned with two key books, one of which was Baedeker's *Guide to Central Italy* (1879).[7]

This was the danger of unpredictable events, and unknown fronts. Before the launch of the second front in 1944, the

Normandy beaches were mapped, photographed and surveyed in minute detail, but the speed of the advance between Falaise and Paris rendered detailed cartographical preparation for this stage of the campaign redundant. The complexity of the cartographical demands of warfare, the difficulties of planning for remote contingencies, made this the second major front, after intelligence, for the application of academic expertise and the deployment of the resources of research libraries.

'Frontiers are the razor's edge on which hang suspended the issue of war or peace and the life of nations.'[8] This pithy epithet from Lord Curzon, imperial grandee and, in a younger life, celebrated explorer, may have expressed the truth in the late nineteenth century, when Curzon made his own contribution to the literature of exploration. But it certainly does not describe the reality of the situation in an earlier era, the fifteenth to seventeenth centuries, when mapmaking was taking its first tentative steps towards maturity.[9] Borderlands were a morass of conflicting authorities, policed (if at all) by a local noble, rather than the lord to whom he acknowledged obedience: the technical capacity to establish borders as exact lines did not yet exist. Seas and rivers provide the most recognisable borders, but did not necessarily represent boundaries between different authorities. They were generally also far more diligently mapped, not least as coastlines and rivers were so essential to the conduct of trade. Even as late as the nineteenth century, in a sophisticated society such as the United States, much more energy had been directed towards the mapping of coastal features and waterways than the intimidating landmass of the interior.

European explorers were dependent on maps, but also inspired and deluded by their errors. They knew that the Earth was round, but not how far you would have to sail westwards in order to reach the spice kingdoms of the East Indies, hitherto largely reached by the laborious and dangerous landward passage through Asia. European exploration of the Caribbean islands and the great continents of the Americas was largely a consequence of this cartographic innocence. But from the return of Columbus's first voyage, the westward explorations vied in the European public imagination, and for investment, with the well-trodden spice road, and its new competitor, the ocean route round the continent of Africa.

In the next two centuries, marine cartography would advance very rapidly, though discoveries were not willingly shared between the competing powers. The Spanish and Portuguese authorities treated the charts of their own returning vessels as state secrets, a policy that would subsequently also be adopted by the Dutch East India Company. Arriving back in Amsterdam, the first duty of East India captains would be to surrender their logbook and any new charts at East India House. Information, though, leaked out: it was not only the ship's captain who could share information at voyage's end. Thanks to these indiscretions, and the increasing sophistication of the book industry following the invention of printing, cartography made giant leaps in the two centuries after the first European ocean explorations. Whereas medieval Europe had inherited a view of the Mediterranean or Jerusalem as the centre of the known world, the maps of the seventeenth century offer a relatively accurate view of the coasts of five continents. Mapping interior space continued to be a more difficult problem, and one that would endure into the nineteenth century. The famous Blaeu world map of 1635 offered a view of the known world transformed since the first trans-oceanic explorations, but India was still only a fraction of its true size.

In the seventeenth century, maps also became an essential part of the commercial news industry. This took advantage of a growing public appetite for published news, and an intense interest in events, both in the European theatre and abroad. Amsterdam generated a specialist sub-branch of the book industry, creating and selling engraved maps and city views. Views of cities under siege were in particularly high demand, precisely because, as Nicholas van Gelkerken advertised one of his maps, 'you will not repent the money you'll spend, because you can see the army without danger of being shot'.[10] If the siege was protracted, cartographic entrepreneurs would often update their maps to show the progress of the siege works. Maps also became popular features of pamphlets, chronicles and almanacs: all of this helped expand the cartographical imagination of Europe's peoples.

The mapping of the great continents now opened up to European view was, however, a far more difficult task. Explorers and surveyors looked first to the great waterways, the Amazon, Mississippi, Hudson and Indus, to unlock the secrets of these huge landmasses. The progressive expansion of America would depend for two centuries on explorations inland along its great rivers. Remarkably, when the United States descended into civil war in the 1860s, there existed no comprehensive survey of the original thirteen states in any way comparable with the landmark British Ordnance Survey project, conceived to provide reliable maps of Scotland in the wake of the Jacobite rising in 1745 and extended to England in 1791. The energies of American surveyors had been largely engaged with charting the full extent of the massive continent of which they gradually secured control: its boundless potential was far more alluring than the precise dimensions of lands already appropriated by the European colonists.

The nineteenth century was in many ways the golden age of cartography, as the European imperial powers spread their tentacles across the globe, and the United States accelerated its march to the Pacific. British governments wanted to know their Empire more intimately, and jealous competitors turned their eyes towards parts of the map as yet uncolonised. For much of the nineteenth century, competition with Russia in Central Asia was intermittently the most urgent priority of the British government. 'The Great Game', as this was known, was a struggle for influence and territory in which cartography played a crucial role.[11]

When the nineteenth century began, Russian territory was separated by 2,000 miles from British imperial territory, across the deserts and mountains of Turkestan; this nevertheless remained a crucial trade route, and a possible back door into India, the jewel of the imperial crown. British policymakers began to debate the advisability of a cordon sanitaire of compliant local rulers, or even annexation. But more needed to be known: was the Khyber Pass impregnable, and was there an alternative route through the Himalayas? Alerted by the growing activity of Russian traders, successive British governments opted for a dual-track strategy: a series of friendly missions, which would also provide the cover for some

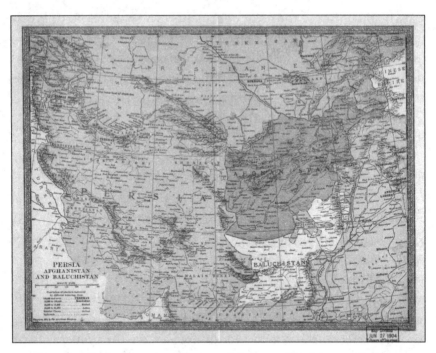

The struggle for supremacy in central Asia was the ultimate challenge
for cartography: remote land-locked mountain ranges, extremes of
heat and cold, suspicious and uncooperative inhabitants. Encouraged
along by the Royal Geographical Society and other learned bodies, each
expedition provided a greater clarity to successive generations of maps.

covert surveying, to be accompanied by a full topographical survey
of the Indian subcontinent. Only in extreme circumstances would
military action be contemplated. Over the course of the century,
this produced mixed results: two Afghan wars, and the annexation
of Sind and Punjab (modern Pakistan) while the Russians crept
ever closer. Against this one must set the triumphant accomplishment of the Topographical Survey of India, the most ambitious
mapping programme ever attempted.

While the Topographical Survey of India was a government
venture, occupying many decades, the exploration of the frontier
was the work of a small number of adventurers, travelling with
some degree of government blessing. Usually led by relatively
young men with an army background and a fascination for the East,
these pioneering journeys were part trade mission, part spying and

part geographical description. Not all lived to tell the tale, falling victim to the prudent Afghan maxim: 'First comes one Englishman for *shikar* (hunting), then come two to draw a map, and then comes an army to take your land. So, it is best to kill the first Englishman.'[12] Those who did return could be sure of a hero's welcome, a public eager for the published version of their adventures and an alert audience at the Royal Geographical Society. Founded in 1830 to promote the advancement of geographical science, the Royal Geographical Society was one of the great institutions of the age of empire, its fabulous map collection 'the Mecca for all true geographers, the home port of every traveller'.[13] This map collection became the cornerstone of a library that by 1893 had expanded to some 30,000 volumes, probably the most comprehensive specialist collection of travel and exploration literature (in many languages) anywhere in the world.[14] In the wars of the twentieth century, this library would be an invaluable resource for the British military.

The Society also greatly enhanced the prestige of exploration and surveying through the annual award of its gold medals: most of the major British cartographers and explorers in the Indian subcontinent won this coveted award at some stage of their careers. The same recognition was not accorded to their local-born colleagues, who played crucial roles in the surveying work. This was particularly important in the surveying of the northern Himalayas, where the presence of English scientists would have been unwelcome. The Topographical Survey of India also relied heavily on the skills of Indian-born staff, without whom it could not have been pursued to a conclusion. As for the Great Game, both sides could rest content: the British in their control of India, the Russians as they gradually absorbed the kingdoms of the Turkestan region, an accretion of territory the size of the western United States.

Civil wars have a peculiar ugliness, because loyalties are so complex. The American Civil War was unusual in that the military dividing line was not class or religious creed but geographical: North against South. Once the loyalties of the border states had been resolved, the issue could only be settled by one side, the Union, carrying the fight to the other. This was asymmetrical warfare in several respects. The North had the numbers, the finance and the power to regenerate its armaments in the forges and factories of the industrial states. But victory required military conquest: to end the conflict, federal forces had to subjugate a vast territory of mountains, swamps, rolling hills and deep impenetrable forests.

Victory for the Union required the mustering of large armies and marching them, with their stores, horses, mules, wagon trains, artillery and ammunition, across unfamiliar terrain on atrocious roads, fording unbridged rivers, skirting impassable mountains. Keeping these armies together and retaining forward momentum was a military art in itself. No wonder that the Civil War armies that received the greatest acclaim were admired as much for their marching as their fighting prowess: Stonewall Jackson's foot cavalry, Sherman's march through Georgia. But an army, advancing into well-defended hostile territory, was blind without maps, and in most of the contested territories maps of the detail required for battlefield manoeuvres were virtually non-existent.

This was the ultimate topographer's war, and here the sides were well matched.[15] The Union could call on most of the US Army Corps of Engineers and its military cartographers; but most of the fighting would be on rebel territory, and here the defenders had the benefit of local knowledge. Stonewall Jackson's campaign in the Shenandoah Valley in 1862, a masterpiece of improvised defence, owed much to his superior grasp of topographical opportunity and danger.[16] Jackson, despite his reliance on instinct, was very close to his chief topographical aide Jed Hotchkiss, whose field map sketches were based on direct observation, often undertaken at great risk, riding out in advance of the army's forward positions with his sketchbooks. The need was to provide maps of immediate utility, identifying critical topographical features such as potential strong points and obstacles. Military topographers were accomplished draughtsmen, and often produced field maps of great beauty, executed with delicate watercolours. The Union topographer David Hunter Struther almost suffered a major catastrophe when his ultramarine went missing. This was an expensive pigment made from lapis lazuli, a semi-precious stone mined in Afghanistan that delivered a luminous blue; if he had not fortuitously retrieved the package it would have been irreplaceable.[17]

The war began, as ever, with a frantic search for maps. This was not an unmapped wilderness: serviceable maps existed down to the county level in most states. But the level of detail was seldom sufficient for marching armies, never mind battlefield encounters. Maps showed roads, but not their quality, and a road that could be navigated by a single man on horseback was not necessarily serviceable for a marching column, especially its wagon train and artillery. Cartographers developed their own separate symbols for 'stone turnpike' (a firm and reliable surface), 'road impracticable' or 'roads very bad'. In the Shenandoah Valley Jackson despatched Hotchkiss to find not just a road, but a road suitable for artillery.

Military mapping, identifying fords shallow enough for ammunition wagons, or inclines up which field artillery could be hauled (gradients of less than 10 per cent), was the primary science of the war. American military education recognised the importance of mapping, to the extent that those who passed out highest at West Point were allocated to the Corps of Engineers. But the most celebrated topographers of the war were often civilians in uniform who did not progress beyond the nominal rank of private. Once maps were made, it was extremely difficult to produce sufficient quantities in battlefield conditions. In any case, in a fluid fast-moving front, the value of a particular map could often be measured in days. Sherman's march to the sea was accompanied by two highly trained mapmakers of the US Coastal Survey; but Sherman made such rapid progress that, as they acknowledged, 'our services have only been required at rare intervals'.[18] As the wars of the twentieth century would demonstrate repeatedly, while a new front could be surveyed in minute detail, armies could easily find themselves in positions – the dense *bocage* hedges of Normandy, the forests of Belarus, the coastal landscape of Iwo Jima – for which there were no simple topographical solutions.

The irony of the First World War was that the most famous of all applications of strategic geography, the Schlieffen Plan, led to four years of virtual immobility. The employment of modern technology,

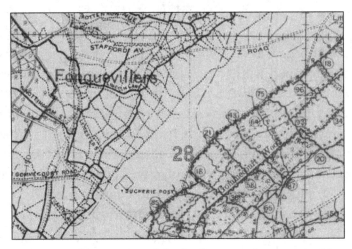

A First World War map of the duelling trench networks. The
orderly parallel network led back to reserve trenches and
ultimately the rest and recuperation facilities where soldiers
might be able to open a book. The introduction of aircraft
improved the accuracy of representation of opposition positions,
though this was an exceedingly perilous form of surveying.

notably railways, to move large bodies of troops rapidly to the front
was intended to have solved problems that had plagued offensive
warfare from the seventeenth to the nineteenth centuries. But
when the French defences held, just, modern armies settled to four
years of troglodyte life, duelling over acres of mud, with extraordinary loss of life. Trench warfare generated a new form of map,
charting the increasingly elaborate spider's web of reserve trenches,
supply trenches, linking trenches between formations, dugouts and
strong points. The elaborate naming rituals for these labyrinthine
structures (Petticoat Lane, Newfoundland Avenue, Tattenham
Corner, a sharp bend on Epsom Racecourse) added an element of
macabre domesticity, masking the grim reality of trench life that
would be incomprehensible to those who had not experienced it.[19]
During the course of the war, the Ordnance Survey published over
32 million copies of large-scale battlefields sheets.

Although the duelling pilots of First World War dogfights have
captured the imagination, the primary use of air power was for
observation, overflying the enemy positions to obtain intelligence

and plan future operations. Though still fairly primitive, this showed the way towards a new form of mapping and military intelligence that would play a critical role in strategic planning during the 1940s. This was also, despite the immobility of the Western Front, to a large extent a global war, with significant fighting in Italy, Eastern Europe, Africa and the Middle East. These more distant theatres in particular engaged the energies of the Royal Geographical Society, which before the outbreak of hostilities had offered its services to the government, in the first instance to prepare an index of the 'horribly unpronounceable' place names of France and Belgium on behalf of the geographical section of the General Staff. This was completed with remarkable speed by September 1914, thanks to the recruitment of dozens of female volunteers from London University and Cheltenham Ladies College.[20]

This triumph strengthened the society's claim to manage the most ambitious cartographical project of the First World War, a complete series of maps of Europe, North Africa and the Middle East, on a scale of 1:1 million. By the middle of 1915, ten sheets had been completed, though government enthusiasm ebbed and flowed as frustration grew at the lack of progress on the Western Front. A strong body of opinion now pressed for an alternative eastern strategy, making hay with the possessions of the decaying Ottoman Empire. Given the absence of accurate maps of the region, the expertise of the Royal Geographical Society was much in demand, leading to considerable tension between the 'easterners' and those who favoured completion of the 'million'. By October 1915, twenty academics attached to the Naval Intelligence Department were squeezed into four large rooms at the society's premises, and the map room had been mysteriously relabelled the 'Arabia Room'. From their efforts emerged twenty-seven handbooks outlining the topography and character of potential theatres of war, from *The River Danube* to *German East Africa*. The unsigned volumes were published under the general editorial supervision of Henry Dickson, professor of geography at the University of Reading. In 1921, the published volumes were released for general sale to the reading public.[21]

In the event, the more ambitious schemes of the easterners

came to nothing, undermined by the disaster of Gallipoli. Attention switched back to the 'million', and a specially commissioned thematic series of maps of language and ethnicity in the Balkans and Austro-Hungarian Empire. As this suggests, the Society's activities were very much focused on post-war planning, and they would receive their reward when the Versailles peace conference formally adopted the British 1:1 million sheets as the basis for discussion of future political realignments. For all that, leading figures in the Royal Geographical Society were left with a bitter sense of opportunities lost. Douglas Freshfield, president 1914–15, mused defiantly whether 'it is an extravagant hope that a lesson had been learned, and that in future the uses of geography both in war and politics may be more fully recognised at Westminster and Whitehall'. In the opinion of Sir Harry Johnston, explorer of Africa and colonial administrator, 'Ignorance of geography in high quarters has tripled the length of the war, tripled its cost, and endangered its victorious issue for the British Empire.'[22]

In cartographical terms, the Second World War began in the Palace of Versailles in 1919. The German political leadership, already in some disarray, was caught unawares by the decision to exclude them from the negotiations. Defeated in battle, they were now heavily outgunned in the framing of Europe's new boundaries, completing the dissolution of the Ottoman and Austro-Hungarian empires. The absence of a German voice (and German cartographers) from the process would have serious consequences. President Woodrow Wilson, enjoying his moment as the world's cartographer in chief, was learning that boundaries were not all about mountain ranges and rivers. He was surprised to be told, rather late in the process, that Bohemia, the heart of the new Czechoslovakia, contained a significant German minority. 'Why', he was reported to have said, 'Mazaryk [the Czech nationalist leader] never told me that.'[23]

The exclusion of German cartographers at Versailles was especially egregious, because in Germany geography was an academic discipline that had reached an unusual level of technical accomplishment and public recognition. The establishment of

The Geography Lesson or *The Black Spot* (1887). A class of French
boys is introduced to the cartographical humiliation of Germany's
annexation of Alsace-Lorraine. The artist, Albert Bettannier, who was
born in Lorraine, would live to see its return to France at Versailles.

the German Empire in 1871 was swiftly followed by the foundation of chairs of geography in eighteen of Germany's universities.
Given the long road to German nationhood, this recognition of
the importance of cartography was well merited. Maps were the
most public manifestation of the creation of this new superpower
at the heart of Europe, in the same way that the dappled jigsaw
of the Holy Roman Empire, with its hundreds of independent jurisdictions, had been a reminder of Germany's humiliating
weakness in the face of France or Russia. The Treaty of Versailles
left many millions of ethnic Germans outside the new borders of
Germany. The strength of the academic discipline of geography
in German universities meant that the perceived unfairness of
the separation of the German peoples could be kept constantly
in the public eye.

In the difficult years of post-war readjustment, Germany's geographers were quick to lay out the case for cartographic revisionism.

In 1921, they in effect proposed that the new boundaries should not be recognised in the German school system:

> The convention of German geographers proclaims that it is a national necessity and duty that the link to Germandom of the areas which were torn from the German Empire in the Treaty of Versailles, including the colonies, remain clearly visible in atlases and maps, and advocates that only those works for which this is the case be used for instruction in all school grades.[24]

These were not mere words. For the next twenty years geographers kept up a ceaseless barrage, advocating the return of territory lost in 1919 and making the case for further eastward expansion. This occurred long before the Nazi takeover: this was one class of professionals who needed no converting to the nationalist cause. Geographers pressed hard for the Germanisation of atlases, especially with respect to place names, always a difficult issue in the ethnically diverse Central European landmass. The ideas of territorial unity of the German ethnic and cultural sphere opened the way for more expansive claims. Professional geographers meeting in 1934 adopted unanimously a motion that publishers should be urged to include a map of German *Volks- und Kulturboden* in all school atlases. Publishers were happy to co-operate. In 1931, the foreword to the new fiftieth edition of Putzger's atlas expressed the hope that it would 'help form a historical awareness in our people and thus contribute to the renewed ascent of our fatherland'.[25]

Academic geographers also played a role in the development of propaganda maps, strengthening claims to territory presently occupied by Poland, while demonstrating German vulnerability to bombing from, for instance, Czechoslovakia: 'a minor state threatens Germany!' In this discipline, the subservience of science to politics was evident, if only fully acknowledged after the Nazi takeover. In 1938, a series of meetings was called to prepare a map of the distribution of Germans 'on which all scientists agreed and . . . which was in our interest'. One of these maps was entrusted to Walter Geisler, professor of geography at the University of

Breslau. Its intention, he told his audience, was to make a cartographic representation that could be defended with scientific arguments, hewing as close to reality as possible while leaving space for claims beyond present national boundaries. A neater encapsulation of Nazi science could hardly be imagined.[26]

Academic geographers caused problems to the Nazi regime only when an abundance of enthusiasm offered a potential source of embarrassment. Shortly after the Nazi takeover, the authorities moved to suppress a 1932 text that delineated a desirable frontier deep into French territory. In 1936 the regime briefly prohibited dissemination of Emil Meynen's *Deutschland und deutsches Reich* because it feared the book might alert people abroad to Germany's expansionist ambitions. Later, when the wind changed, many copies of Meynen's text were purchased to support the campaign for unification with Austria (a Holy Grail for German geographers since 1918).

In the event, the deeds of the Wehrmacht would render much of this academic work redundant, since German conquests had by 1942 extended beyond even the most extravagant hopes of German cartography. Of course, it was armies that would ultimately determine boundaries; scroll forward another five years, and much the same cast of academic geographers would be working with Germany's conquerors to reconcile a new generation of German schoolchildren to the shrunken boundaries of 1945.[27]

For those charged with orchestrating this reversal of fortunes in the Allied High Command, while simultaneously defeating the Japanese in Asia, cartography would again play a critical role. In the first instance, the Allied powers reached out to their own major institutional collections of maps: in the United States the Library of Congress, the New York Public Library and the American Geographical Society, in London to the British Museum library and Royal Geographical Society. In Oxford, the Bodleian Library's new building (now the Weston Library) took in the Admiralty's Photographic Library, while the School of Geography became the headquarters of the Inter-Services Topographical Division, intended to co-ordinate cartographical activities between the services, and avoid duplication of effort. This was a response to the near fiasco of the 1940 Norway campaign, where an absence of up-to-date maps had led to a reliance on the 1912 edition of Baedeker's guide to Scandinavia.

Alice Hudson, until 2009 the librarian in the map division of the New York Public Library, presents the relationship with the military as largely harmonious.[28] The New York Public Library had a collection of more than 100,000 maps, though this was dwarfed by the 1.4 million of the Library of Congress. Unfortunately, the foreign maps in the Library of Congress Collection were largely uncatalogued, impeding quick retrieval for the various war departments clamouring for information. There was a predictable clash of cultures over lending rights. After initially responding rather coolly to a request for loans from its reference collections, the New York Public Library quickly recognised that the normal protocols could not be maintained. It would respond to requests for information on North Africa, Indonesia, Ceylon and the Soviet Union, as well as lending detailed street maps of European cities and a range of overseas telephone dictionaries. From 1942, the Library of Congress would rein in circulation of their own holdings, an example followed by the Army Map Service, which refused to lend maps except when requested through official liaison channels.[29]

It would not be long before the needs of global warfare outgrew the resources of existing institutions. Government departments began to recruit their own geographers and charge them with new tasks. The head of the map division in the New York Public Library was granted a partial secondment to head the geography section of the War Department's New York office of military intelligence. Combining these two responsibilities can have been no easy task.

The most reliable source of new employment was the Research and Analysis division of the Office of Strategic Studies: at the height of the war, this employed 129 geographers.[30] Established titans of the profession, such as Richard Hartshorne, author of *The Nature of Geography*, were joined by junior faculty and graduate students, often their own. The library created to service the needs of these scholars would ultimately accumulate 2 million maps, many obtained through a radio appeal to the public from William

1. Books Are Weapons In The War Of Ideas (US Government Printing Office, 1942). Published soon after the United States entered the Second World War, this iconic image evoking Franklin D. Roosevelt's powerful denunciation of the totalitarian war on free thought placed books at the centre of the conflict between different value systems.

2. For junior officers in the Second World War British army, no duty was more unwelcome than conducting the obligatory sessions in political education. *Current Affairs* and *News-Facts for Fighting Men* were intended to keep them one step ahead of the well-educated and politically engaged members of their company, though it did not always work.

PART 334.] WITH SPLENDID R.A. COLOURED PLATE: "IN CROMWELL'S TIME," by M. CRABTREE. [Price 6d.

THE BOY'S OWN PAPER

BOP

DECEMBER 1906

LONDON, 4 BOUVERIE STREET, EC.

3. *The Boy's Own Paper* did more than any other printed material to send boys and young men flocking to the recruiting centres. Ironically, it was published by the Religious Tract Society, though its pious intent in no way diminished its commitment to the British imperial mission.

WITH KITCHENER TO KHARTUM

STEEVENS

4. G. W. Steevens was one of the most famous war correspondents of his day, and this celebrated account of Kitchener's Sudan campaign in 1898, climaxing in the battle of Omdurman, was an instant bestseller. This copy, published in 1900, was part of the twenty-second edition. This was one of Steevens's last works, as he died of typhoid during the siege of Ladysmith while reporting the Boer War for the *Daily Mail*.

Дорогая моя звездочка Элека! Ты написала мне, что не получила черно-серебристой лисы. Посылаю вторично ее портрет.

5. The meteorologist Alexei Wangeheim tried to make the best of his fall from grace, haunting the Gulag library and making elegant sketches of the local fauna and flora. Despite bombarding Stalin and unpurged friends for clemency, in 1937 he was condemned to death when his camp was required to provide an arbitrary quota of victims for the Great Terror. He was posthumously rehabilitated in 1956.

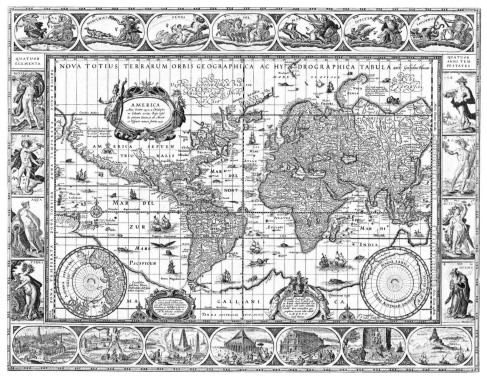

6. This brilliant map, by the Amsterdam publisher Willem Blaeu, shows how much perceptions of geography had changed in the first 150 years of European exploration. The coastlines of five continents are quite accurately delineated, though large landmasses in China, India and the Americas would puzzle cartographers for centuries to come.

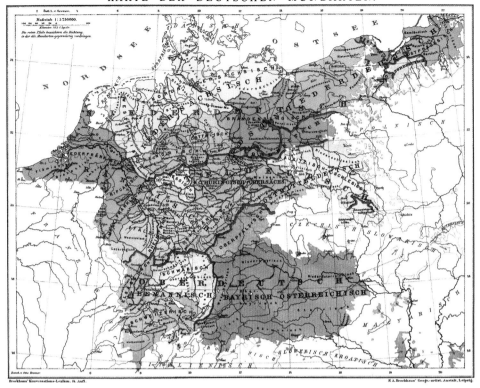

7. Hitler did not create the concept of Lebensraum. Germany's powerful academic geographers had been promoting Pan-Germanism since the turn of the century. The Versailles Treaty only intensified this sense of grievance and demands for consolidation of the German-speaking territories.

8. Cook for Victory. This jaunty cover by Fougasse of Careless Talk Costs Lives fame, cannot disguise the dreary simplicity of the recipes. Rhubarb Surprise Pie, anyone? Sadly, the fact that it was made up almost entirely of rhubarb and cold porridge would have surprised no one.

9. Are We the Barbarians? German professionals in particular were hard hit by the outpouring of condemnation at the conduct of their army in Belgium, particularly the destruction of the library at Louvain. This poster hit back hard, showcasing German social service provision, literacy, investment in schools, book production, Nobel prizes and patents, when compared to France and England.

10. The Second World War was testing for British publishers, but ultimately profitable. Paper rationing ensured that virtually everything they printed would sell, while compulsory war insurance meant that they received compensation for books lost to bombing, much of it slow moving or unsaleable stock.

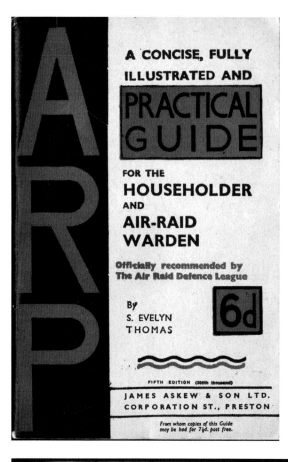

11. Practical Guide to ARP. This comprehensive eighty-five page guide covered every aspect of coping with attacks from the air, from gas to incendiary bombs, shelters, protective clothing, decontamination and the protection of animals and food. It was clearly in demand: this fifth edition took the number of copies published to 300,000.

12. Journalists and publishers spent much of 1941 wrestling with the consequences of the wholly unexpected capitulation of France in 1940. Not all were sympathetic to the former ally.

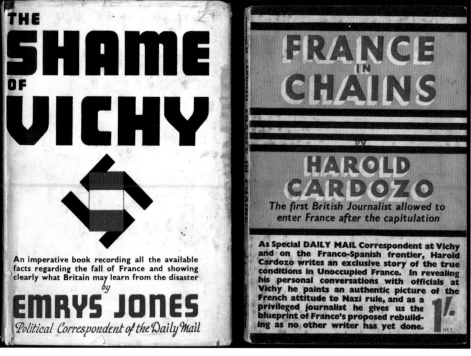

13. Heinz Medefind was a German journalist who spent five years reporting from England before leaving in 1939. This inside account stressed the English reluctance to fight, their arrogance, sense of superiority and hypocrisy, a society mired in the past and ill served by its newspapers. Nothing here would suggest that Britain would prove a resolute opponent.

14. No one had expected His Majesty's Stationary Office to emerge as one of the most important publishers of the war, but the astonishing success of the official account of the Battle of Britain demonstrated the huge appetite for any British successes against the Germans. The Ministry of Information embraced the opportunity both to boost Home Front morale and make propaganda abroad, as witnessed by these French and German translations.

15. Commercial publishers were often frustrated by the success of the HMSO publications, which by 1942 included glossy and heavily illustrated productions such as these. *Combined Operations* was the publication the Reverend Arthur Hopkins found in the hands of all five of his fellow travellers when on a train to Lincoln in May 1943.

16. American public opinion vociferously condemned the Nazi book burnings of 1933, perhaps forgetting that when the United States joined the First World War in 1917, German books were purged from American public libraries, and often incinerated. This image shows German textbooks from the local high school in Baraboo, Wisconsin being burned on the streets.

Donovan, director of the OSS. The Army War Department went one step further, placing an advertisement in popular magazines:

> The War Department, Army Map Service is seeking maps, city plans, port plans, place name lexicons, gazetteers, guide-books, geographic journals, and geological bulletins covering all foreign areas outside the continental limits of the United States and Canada. Of particular interest are maps and guide books purchased within the last ten years, including maps issued by the US government and the National Geographic Society.[31]

During the course of the war, the geographers of the OSS would draw 8,000 new maps, fulfil more than 50,000 requests for information and distribute 5 million intelligence maps. An additional 200,000 maps were obtained by the systematic microfilming of the collections of Harvard and the universities of Michigan and Chicago, along with other repositories. Map offices were established in a number of OSS stations overseas, in Cairo, Algiers, New Delhi, Paris, Bari and Bern, as the war fronts advanced.[32] This work would continue in the post-war period, as OSS agents assisted in the accumulation of valuable topographical materials in Germany.[33]

The Army Map Service, meanwhile, built a whole new infrastructure, having established a mapmaking programme in fifty-seven colleges and universities, including leading women's colleges such as Smith, Wellesley and Bryn Mawr. Edith Putnam Parker, geography professor at the University of Chicago, became educational director of the programme. By the end of the war, 200 women had completed the course, and some moved on to positions of considerable responsibility in the Army Map Service. From 1943 to 1945, women constituted a majority of its 3,000 civilian employees.[34] All told, the United States produced more than 500 million maps between 1941 and 1945, as opposed to 9 million during the First World War.[35] This was the cartographical echo of America's giant leap to great power status.

*

In Britain, too, the achievements of applied geography, after a rocky start, must be reckoned as one of the major successes of the war, a model of co-operation between the services and between academics and the military. In the gloom of 1940 and the tribulation of Norway, two major geographical institutions gave ground for hope: the hydrology department of the Admiralty and the Ordnance Survey. In 1939, as a civilian institution, the Ordnance Survey was well staffed, with 3,000 employees, many of them former officers of the Royal Engineers. It continued to provide an outstanding service throughout the war, turning out some 300 million maps, despite the destruction in 1940 of its Southampton headquarters. The hydrology department was responsible for providing both the Royal Navy and merchant marine with charts and navigational aids. During the course of the war it issued 300 million charts, a tenfold increase over the average for a similar period in peacetime.[36] The smooth running of this essential service may help explain why the new Inter-Service Topographical Department was entrusted to Rear-Admiral Godfrey, director of naval intelligence, who was responsible for two significant institutional developments: NID6, responsible for the preparation of detailed topographical information for all operations, and the Admiralty geographical handbooks.

The geographical handbooks, building on the tradition of the First World War volumes, emerged from a felicitous co-operation between the universities of Oxford and Cambridge. Each volume laid out the relief features and coasts, history, population and transportation geography of a country in a set order. Editorial responsibility was entrusted to either Oxford or Cambridge, though each enlisted the help of the wider community of academic geographers, especially the colleges of London University. The result, by 1945, was a remarkable thirty-one titles in fifty-eight volumes, ranging from Albania and Algeria to Western Arabia and Yugoslavia. The Oxford team enlisted the help of seventy outside experts, while sixty specialist contributors are represented in the Cambridge volumes; indeed, there were few academic geographers in Britain who were not involved in the project at some point.[37]

Elsewhere, major strategic breakthroughs were the responsibility of gifted individuals. Michael Spender developed new techniques for the interpretation of reconnaissance photographs taken from high altitude, drastically reducing the casualty rate of the aircraft undertaking these missions. The Cambridge geographer W. W. Williams devised a technique for measuring the gradient of beaches from aerial photographs, vital for heavily laden troops disembarking from troop carriers. By 1944, the entire coast of northern Europe from Vlissingen to Saint-Nazaire had been charted in minute detail. We should also recognise the contribution of academic geologists, who prepared specialist maps of all the Normandy embarkation beaches, identifying hazards to transportation, sources of drinking water and likely sites for temporary airfields.[38]

One of the most extraordinary and heart-warming cartographical projects of the war was the programme of escape maps, shipped to Allied prisoners of war in the POW camps in Germany. These were printed on silk so that they could be easily concealed, and then smuggled into the camps, hidden in board games, playing cards or gramophone records (these had to be smashed to retrieve the map).[39] To facilitate the construction of these intricate hiding places, the contract for supplying the maps was awarded to the Leeds firm of Waddingtons, a manufacturer of playing cards and board games rather than a specialist mapmaker, though Bartholomew's of Edinburgh supplied the maps to be copied (and waived their copyright). More than 1.5 million copies of 205 separate maps were produced on light fabrics, which suggests that they were intended for operational use as well as for POWs – certainly they were issued to British and American aircrew overflying hostile territory, part of the optimistically titled 'escape packs'.

Despite the care and expense lavished on these maps, it is striking that not one of the accounts of POW escapes that I have read makes mention of them. The author of the most detailed study of these maps suggests gallantly that the POW recipients were sworn to secrecy and respected this obligation even fifty years after the event. It seems more likely that the maps, necessarily small scale, were not much use in plotting a route over unfamiliar territory.

Their principal purpose was psychological, to improve morale, rather like the airmen's escape kits. (I can testify to that from being shown my father's escape photo, intended to make him look like a Frenchman, but self-evidently a RAF officer in a cravat.) The maps, and the ingenuity that had gone into them, persuaded the POWs that they had not been forgotten, and that everything possible would be done to support them. In the camps, they helped reduce the feelings of abandonment and spatial disorientation. To those in the military, cartographical blindness is a particularly severe form of disempowerment, reinforcing feelings of helplessness and impotence in otherwise talented and vigorous young men.

This disorientation was felt wherever armies were separated from their maps. On 25 April 1945, Field Marshal Wilhelm Keitel, chief of the Wehrmacht High Command, was despatched from Hitler's bunker to try to make sense of the collapsing front around Berlin. In normal times, he seldom strayed from Hitler's side. In photographs he can be seen hovering over Hitler's shoulder, as the Führer stands over his map table, deploying his divisions, while his commanders look on with admiration. It was the ultimate expression of the all-powerful conquering leader. Now these divisions were phantom paper formations, and Keitel, too, was a man without moorings.

> Early on the morning of 25.4, I went back to the front and first sought out Gen. Holste at his command post . . . Gen. Wench and his attack personnel had fought their way through to the lakes south of Potsdam, although on a very narrow front that looked like a pointed wedge. But he lacked reserves and additional impact, because stronger parts of his army were involved in intensified fighting around the Elbe crossings (I lack a map to identify the locations more precisely) north of Wittenberg . . . Towards midday, when I wanted to drive through the small town of X (I can't remember the name without a map) . . .[40]

Keitel was writing this in confinement at the end of the war, and his reminiscence captures both the chaos of the last days of the fighting and the vulnerability of the powerful general shorn of his maps.

Through 2,000 years of history, maps have shaped nations and defined battlefields. By the time we reach the twentieth century, an army without maps is scarcely more effective than guns without ammunition. For troops in the front line, the pains lavished on cartography in the campaigns of the twentieth century often made the difference between survival and annihilation. But the need for maps was emotional as well as practical, and one that had deep historical roots. Put simply, it is hard to define a nation without geographic representation. Maps are expressions of power, and as such inherently rhetorical. The choice of what to include (battlefields), and what to exclude (nuclear waste dumps), is deeply political. Maps are not simply representations of physical geography; they are also mirrors of the societies that made them, their social priorities, their self-image and their ambitions. They played an essential role in modern warfare; and they could not have been made without the wholehearted collaboration of a nation's scholars, and the exploitation of their libraries.

PART III

THE HOME FRONT

7

PRINT FOR VICTORY

In the great wars of the twentieth century, books and libraries were not only important as resources of information, for science, intelligence and mapmaking: they also expressed the essence of the societies the warring nations were attempting to build. For Winston Churchill, the war was to be fought 'to establish, on impregnable rocks, the rights of the individual, and it is a war to establish and revive the stature of man'. This built on themes developed during the 1930s, when Churchill warned in vain of the danger of the European dictatorships:

> Arms – instrumentalities, as President Wilson called them – are not sufficient by themselves. We must add to them the power of ideas. It is this very conflict of spiritual and moral ideas which gives the free countries a great part of their strength. [Dictators] are afraid of words and thoughts; words spoken abroad, thoughts stirring at home – all the more powerful because forbidden – terrify them.[1]

Franklin D. Roosevelt, channelling the horror of the American people at the Nazi book burnings of 1933, encapsulated the same sentiments with his usual pithy eloquence.

> Books cannot be killed by fire. People die, but books never die. No man and no force can put thought in a concentration camp forever. No man and no force can take from the world the books that embody man's eternal fight against tyranny. In this war, we know, books are weapons.

Encapsulated into a simple slogan, 'Books are weapons in the war of ideas', this became the motto of the American Council of Books in Wartime, a committee of publishers and policymakers eager to put the resources of the book industry behind the American war effort.[2]

This perception of the power of books was equally shared by Hitler, Lenin and Mussolini, though their concept of civilisation was somewhat different from those of the great democracies. They were also more determined to put their words into action. Gustav Abb, director of the University Library of Berlin and president of the Association of Research Librarians, recognised the leading role books would play in the Nazi project:

> Just as a book, the Führer's *Mein Kampf,* prefigured the radiant fundamental idea of our Movement, so in all the world's history there has been no radical change, no spiritual revolution that more strongly recognises the power of the book and of libraries than National Socialism, none that has taken libraries more thoroughly into its service.[3]

All of this had significant consequences for both the management of libraries and the development of the publishing industry. If books were the agents of civilisation, the inanimate missionaries of the cause, then publishers ran the munitions factories.

As with several aspects of our investigation of the home front in the following chapters, the impact of the First World War on the publishing industry served as a muted rehearsal for the total reorganisation required by the war economy in the second. The First World War did, however, pit against one another what were undoubtedly then the two greatest forces in the world of publishing, Britain and Germany. While France boasted a mature and sophisticated publishing industry, and that of the United States was on a rapid upward trajectory, Britain and Germany were in a class of their own (tsarist Russia lagged some way behind). In the nineteenth century, Britain had developed an unrivalled global network for the trade in books, based on the thirsty reading nations of the British Empire, while Germany had established a towering reputation for the publication of scientific and technical literature. German became one of the principal languages of scholarship, a reputation it would retain in classics and medieval history until deep into the twentieth century.

German propaganda was quick to call attention to this cultural superiority when the Germans were labelled as barbarians for their conduct in the first year of the First World War, the notorious assault on Belgium and the rough handling of occupied northern France. Aided by the subtle propaganda of the British intelligence unit in Wellington House, the Allies won the battle for the sympathy of neutrals, particularly and crucially the United States.[4] The sense of outrage this caused in cultured, sophisticated Germany was epitomised by a scathing poster, 'We Barbarians?', which set out the contrasting stages of cultural development between Germany and its opponents in a sequence of powerful graphics. German book production was three times that of Britain. Expenditure on school-age education was greater than that of France and Britain combined. The poster also celebrated the famously generous German social security system and German superiority in science, as recognised in the greatest number of Nobel Prizes awarded to the scientists of any nation since their establishment in 1901. This was propaganda, in this case to reassure the home front that German had not abandoned civilised values in the cause of victory. But the facts tended to bear this out – at least as far as publishing was concerned. In 1910, German firms had published 31,281 editions, against 10,804 in Britain. The comparative figure for the United States was 13,470, 146 editions per million of population, as against Germany's 481.[5]

The economic miracle that had followed German unification in 1871, Bismarck's 'blood and iron' regime, was widely recognised as a major factor in its advance to great power status. The roots of its cultural renaissance lay rather deeper. The German Enlightenment long preceded reunification and found its most profound political expression in the thwarted liberal revolution of 1848, put down by Prussian and Austrian military power. The division of Germany into a jumble of smaller jurisdictions was perceived as a major cause of its military weakness, but its legacy in cultural terms was more nuanced. While the publishing might of France and Britain was historically concentrated in London and Paris, in Germany independent states all had their own smaller centres of the print industry. The new German Empire of 1871 thus inherited a decentralised industry with significant nodes of production in Hamburg, Cologne, Frankfurt, Munich and Leipzig as well as Berlin. The same could be said of its intellectual culture, with universities throughout the Empire each with long-established reputations. The strong reputation of German schools can be traced back to the German Reformation, which led to the establishment of hundreds of boys' and girls' schools throughout the Lutheran states. By 1900, Germany had the highest levels of literacy among all of the major powers, and a thriving book trade. The brutality of German militarism, set against the cultural sensitivity of German literature, music and its highly developed academic tradition, was a conundrum that would puzzle foreign observers throughout the twentieth century.

When war was declared in 1914, a swift resolution of the conflict was generally expected. German strategy depended on a quick victory on the Western Front, and in Britain the cheerful talk was of peace by Christmas. The reality of trench warfare was all the more traumatic for being totally unanticipated. In both Britain and Germany the publishing industry accompanied the fighting nation through the oscillations of patriotic fervour, optimism, the horror of mass casualties, disillusion and, in the German case, defeat. Although Britain and Germany faced up to the war in very different ways (there was no British equivalent to the German military's role in domestic government), the experiences of these two mature publishing industries were in many respects very similar. Both experienced a rush of demand for news: newspapers would play a crucial role as the principal vectors of public information. The competition between newspapers was so intense that in 1915 German authorities imposed restrictions on the number of special issues they could publish.[6] Newspapers also bore the brunt of censorship, though in truth potential violations were more likely to be as the result of an excess of enthusiasm than criticism. At this stage the publishing industry in both countries accepted the need for war, though not without regret, not least because relations between the two countries' publishers were close. In Britain, *Publishers' Circular* acknowledged that the war had been 'forced on this country by the high-handed action of Germany'. Nevertheless, 'in view of the very friendly relations which have always existed between the British and German book trades ... we are sure that German book-sellers regret as much as we do this sudden termination of business relations'.[7]

The book trade faced profound disruption at the beginning of the war, as publishers adapted to the new circumstances. The first months of the conflict saw heavy demand for war-related content. Stanley Unwin had taken possession of his new firm the day war broke out, and watched its value plummet in the first weeks of the war. Fortunately, he had early success with Philip Price's *Diplomatic History of the War* and Austin Harrison's *The Kaiser's War*; William Heinemann offered Alexander Powell's *Fighting in Flanders* and *On Active Service* by Major G. P. A. Phillips. Unwin also undertook, unwisely, a translation of Heinrich von Treitschke's massive *History of Germany*, a work regarded in Britain as a cornerstone of German militarism.[8] Fascination with the mystery of Germany would provide much work for British publishers in both world wars.

This early exuberance was checked in both nations by paper shortages, which led to reductions in both the length of newspapers and the quality of book paper. In Britain, the price of paper almost doubled in the first two weeks of the conflict; this led to an inevitable rise in the cost of cheap editions, which relied on large print runs for their margins. Stanley Unwin, as a new publisher, had no paper ration, and had to buy what he could on the open market: at one point he reported paying a premium of up to 600 per cent for paper of significantly inferior quality. Heinemann, who had been urged to change his name at the beginning of the war, feared he had been singled out by xenophobic officials in the calculation of his ration: in consequence his output plummeted.[9] In Freiburg, a pleasant university town uncomfortably close to the French border, paper shortages at least freed students from the burdensome requirement to print 200 copies of their dissertations in order to graduate, but in truth, the university had already been hollowed out by the rush of students and junior faculty to join up. Professors with time on their hands exerted themselves to prove the justice of the German cause, whether defending the conduct of German armies, as for instance in the destruction of the University of Louvain, or applying their academic research to demonstrate that, in the case of medieval historian Georg von Below, 'militarism was a part of the divine order'.[10]

A dilemma common to both nations was how far society should accommodate the coarsening of manners, and relaxation of boundaries, that seemed to be an inevitable part of the war. In Freiburg, moral reformers noted a plague of 'trashy books', all the more troubling because of the popularity of this pulp literature among soldiers. It proved easier to deplore the principle of bad literature than to define its parameters: one German clergyman took the prudent path, warning against an 'indiscriminate mania for reading'.[11] These anxieties would have been recognisable in any gathering of librarians in Britain or the United States, where a firmly held belief in the vocational responsibility to shape readers' taste was a fundamental tenet of the profession. This became more difficult to enforce in wartime, when the prolongation of the conflict inevitably led to a turning away from war titles to escapist literature. This provided profits to the publishers of pulp fiction to the frustration of the high-minded, doubly so for the conscientious objector Stanley Unwin, who found booksellers would not stock the pacifist titles which found a natural home in his list.[12]

London and Freiburg were united by one further shared experience, which represented a new phenomenon of war: while they sent their troops to war, the conflict came to them in the form of aerial bombing. Almost 300 bombs were dropped on Freiburg, causing thirty-one deaths: trivial in the wider context of the war, but desperately unsettling to the civilian population. In England, press reactions ranged from indignation to insouciance, well captured by two cartoons of 1916. 'The Zeppelin Triumph' by Louis Raemaekers shows a distraught husband by a hospital bedside, whose daughter asks, 'But mother had done nothing wrong, had

she Daddy?' *Punch* chose instead to highlight the relative inef-
fectiveness of aerial warfare, with the Kaiser reproving Ferdinand
von Zeppelin, 'Why didn't you invent something useful, like the
tank?'[13]

The low incidence and sporadic nature of bombing is an indication of how far short the conflict of 1914–18 fell of the total war
experienced in the Second World War. The primitive aircraft of
the earlier conflict had more success dropping leaflets than bombs.
This was a major feature of both the German and Allied campaigns, and a nice source of revenue for favoured printers. General
Ludendorff, together with Hindenburg the animating genius of
German defence on the Western Front from 1916, ordered that
any Allied leaflets dropped on the trenches should be handed in,
and was pleased when this harvested some 300,000 items. This was
only a small fraction of what was dropped on the front and civilian areas. In the last year of the war, the British dropped leaflets on
Constantinople and the Italians spread propaganda over Vienna.[14]
In 1918, aircraft were again pressed into service when the British
National War Aims Committee dropped 250,000 pamphlets on
crowds gathered in Birmingham for a 'Win the War Day Rally'.[15]

As this suggests, propaganda was also a leading feature of the
home front, and here W. H. Smith, the newsagents and booksellers, were able to play their patriotic part. Smith's had made their
mark in the nineteenth century through the creation of a national
network of railway bookstalls: in 1914 they owned more than
1,500 stalls as well as 223 shops, in addition to controlling much
of the trade on the London Underground. Throughout the war
they worked closely with government bodies to ensure the smooth
distribution of propaganda, including rousing penny pamphlets
such as *The Commonwealth of Nations*, published from a speech
by the South African general Jan Smuts, and *Murder Most Foul*,
an account of the war crimes perpetrated by the 'Hideous Hun'
on the Western Front. In November 1918, the National War Aims
Committee thanked W. H. Smith for 'the firm's splendid effort in
distributing one-hundred million publications among the people
of Great Britain'.[16] This was the home front propaganda version of
the Schlieffen Plan, and in this case it worked.

*

The publishing houses of Britain emerged from the war relatively intact, though with personal wounds that would never be healed. J. M. Dent, Heinemann, Blackie and Longman all lost sons and cousins, and Edward Arnold a daughter nursing in France.[17] In the United States, direct involvement in the war was too brief to effect major changes in the industry. Though hardly unmindful of the moral aspects of the conflict, American business was also not oblivious to the potential to develop world markets while the European economic giants were locked in mortal conflict. In the spring of 1915, *Publishers Weekly* offered this thoughtful reflection:

> The happy faculty of laissez-faire which allows our country to loll comfortably unarmed in the face of a world war has also aided the general recovery of business by relegating the war to the somewhat objective and impersonal position of a spectacle. Meanwhile America goes about her customary tasks and diversions, and instead of rendering tribute to necessity through reduced tasks and diversion, as her English cousins are forced to do, bids fair to grow fat through the virtual stoppage of a large portion of the rest of the world's trade.[18]

The 1920s began with an economic boom that would transform the American economy, and its place in the world. This was a golden age of American literature, with the publication of Sinclair Lewis's *Main Street* and *Babbitt* and Edith Wharton's *Age of Innocence*. Thornton Wilder's *The Bridge of San Luis Rey* was the bestselling title of 1928. Scott Fitzgerald's debut novel *The Side of Paradise* was published in 1920 and *The Great Gatsby* in 1925; Ernest Hemingway published *A Farewell to Arms* in 1929 and Dorothy Parker was beginning to make her reputation. Americans were also reading Europeans: H.G. Wells, Winston Churchill, George Bernard Shaw and André Maurois with Erich Maria Remarque's *All Quiet on the Western Front* topping the bestselling lists in 1929.[19] Propelled by this literary energy, publishing flourished, with new firms entering the market (Harcourt Brace, publishers of *Main Street*, Viking, Simon & Schuster, Random

House) and expanding demand. Legal prohibition of alcoholic beverages (1920–33) was also good for business, increasing traffic in both bookstores and libraries. Radio and film, far from killing the reading habit, as doomsters imagined, provided new business through book and magazine tie-ins.[20]

This boom market came to a juddering halt with the crash of 1929, prompting a bout of introspection in the publishing industry. In 1930, the National Association of Book Publishers commissioned a report into the health of the industry, a meticulous survey undertaken by the banker O. H. Cheney. The conclusions of the Cheney Report were hard-hitting; no business likes to hear talk of 'blindness, planlessness, waste and inefficiency'. America's bookselling infrastructure fell far short of a national network. Most of the 4,053 bookstores were concentrated on the east and west coasts; in the hinterlands between, two-thirds of counties and half the towns and cities with populations between 5,000 and 100,000 had no place at all where books could be purchased. A quarter of the country's publishers were based in New York City.[21]

Publishers took the Cheney Report badly, but in the following years, a more efficient distribution network was devised. The Book of the Month Club, despatching books to readers direct, was the first of many such institutions offering readers both a regular reading choice and the assurance of quality guaranteed by a selection committee of eminent book people. Books also began to be marketed more like magazines, in department stores and chains of newsagents and general stores, some 70,000 in all. By 1941, and the American entry into the Second World War, the American publishing industry was ready for the assault on global markets that shaped its dominant position in the publishing world after 1945. These outstanding successes were a tribute to the sheer size of the American market, with over 100 million citizens over the age of fifteen, all potential customers. In 1933, American publishers turned out 110 million books; in 1943, this figure topped 250 million. This was an astonishing transformation and reflected growth in all portions of the market. By 1946, the Book of the Month Club was despatching 11.5 million books to its members every year: adoption as a main selection could make an author's career.[22]

*

The German book industry had weathered the Depression era remarkably well. In 1933, Germany was once again Europe's biggest producer of books, in terms of both volume and the number of individual titles: some 21,601 works produced by more than 3,000 separate publishing houses. Publishing made a considerable contribution to the German economy, with exports outweighing imports by a margin of three to one. Naturally, the book trade was an early target for Nazification, which encountered little outright opposition from within the industry. The excesses of Weimar culture, a movement in reality largely confined to Berlin, had already provoked strong reactions in the literature section of the Prussian Academy of Arts. The Nazi takeover of January 1933 provided the perfect opportunity for conservative elements in the German Association of Publishers and Booksellers (the Börsenverein) to seize the upper hand. In May 1933, the Börsenverein's executive issued a strongly worded denunciation of the authors whose books had featured in Nazi book burnings earlier in the year. The writings of Heinrich Mann, Erich Maria Remarque and others were 'to be regarded as damaging for Germany's reputation. The board expects the book trade to cease disseminating the works of these writers ... The literature of the bourgeois left in all its nuances' would be replaced by 'poetry in the old German sense'.[23]

This was of course disastrous for those firms publishing these authors, but the Börsenverein saw in the Nazi takeover the opportunity for a reorganisation of the book trade very much in its own interest. Already in April the association had presented to Germany's new masters a shopping list of its concerns, including the demand that all booksellers should be required to join the association, and that the selling of books in department stores and the '*Volk*-damaging expansion of the so-called modern commercial lending libraries' should be suppressed. As in Britain, the circulating libraries were seen as purveyors of cheap, low-calibre fiction.

What has been called the self-Nazification of the educated was a prominent feature of all the major professions, with doctors, lawyers and academics well to the fore. But nowhere was this eager compliance more evident than the book industries: the library profession, the press and publishing. Publishing firms in Jewish ownership were easy pickings, transferred into Aryan control at a fraction of their real value, the pitiful remains subject to swingeing export taxes if the original owners sought to leave Germany (as many did, some like George Weidenfeld, later building substantial new careers in Britain and the United States). A number of such firms, including Ullstein, the most successful publisher in the Weimar era, were absorbed by the Nazi Party's own publisher, Franz Eher. Propelled by the sales of what were essentially compulsory purchases of the works authored by leading members of the Nazi hierarchy, by 1932 Eher was already one of Germany's leading publishing houses. Acquisitions continued throughout the war, and with its output largely exempted from tax, by 1945 the Eher company was the largest commercial enterprise in the German Reich, with an annual turnover greater than the chemical conglomerate IG Farben. The German Labour Front also became a significant publisher, partly from the confiscation of the assets of the trade unions, many of which had developed their own substantial publishing arms.[24]

Germany was a bookish nation, and with such a tool at its disposal, the Nazi regime was able to make full use of the book trade to pursue its political and social agenda. As German troops advanced on all fronts, east and west, they were accompanied by their own book service, the *Frontbuchhandel*, bringing ideological reinforcement and recreational literature to the German occupying forces, from Norway to Ukraine.[25] These were glory years for German publishing, turning out 242 million books in 1940, rising to an astonishing 342 million copies in 1941. This boom market continued unabated until 1943, for, as Goebbels had observed in February 1942, 'Everything there is to sell continues to be sold out immediately.'[26] Where German firms alone could not meet this demand, the resources of printing houses and publishers in France and the Netherlands were pressed into service.

At first, much of the output was of war-related titles, though as the tide turned against German forces, the demand for more escapist light reading escalated. Already by October 1942, Goebbels was writing of the urgent need for 'light, captivating literature that does not demand a great emotional effort but unobtrusively leads the reader away from everyday cares'.[27] The German industry was also experiencing the first significant pressure on paper supplies. This nudged publishers towards seeking exclusive contracts publishing for the army, the Nazi Party or the Luftwaffe, since this brought with it a separate allocation of paper. So while German publishers turned out close to 100 million copies in editions for the troops, the civilian market atrophied. Many bookshops closed altogether, either because they had no books to sell, or because their staff had been called away to the front. The dreadful air raid on Leipzig, the heart of the book trade, in December 1943, obliterated 516 publishers, wholesalers and retail businesses, destroying an estimated 50 million books.[28] By September 1944, to maintain some sort of service for civilian readers, bookstores were required to turn over one quarter of their stock to establishing a lending service, a desperate measure for a regime that had closed commercial circulating libraries, only now to reopen them under a new guise. By 1945, Europe's proudest, most important and largest publishing industry had been reduced to rubble and ashes. Millions of copies of *Mein Kampf*, once prominently displayed in every household, were now employed for fuel in Germany's mutilated cities.[29]

For, the British publishing industry, the first years of the Second World War were undoubtedly difficult, despite the surge in demand for books of contemporary interest before and after the beginning of hostilities. The introduction of paper rationing, far more stringent than in the first war, meant that editions had to be smaller, titles carefully selected and compromises made in production quality. The paper quota was derived from the amount each firm consumed during the year 1938–9: at its most severe, the allocation was reduced to only 40 per cent of pre-war use. Established publishers fulminated as 'mushroom' ventures sprung up, mostly producing the 'pulp' fiction in demand as light entertainment. The iniquities of rationing were reinforced by the generous allocation the government retained for its own publishing, not just the numerous guidance pamphlets and posters necessitated

by new wartime regulations, but also a popular series of publications on the events of the war, from the Battle of Britain onwards.[30]
The major publishers also suffered greatly from the dangers posed
by submarine warfare to their overseas markets, the jewels in the
imperial publishing crown. A wary eye was turned on the American cousins, who were full of sympathy and goodwill for Britain
under siege in 1940, but also relishing the opportunity to move on
British markets in Canada, Australia and elsewhere. If all this were
not enough, conscription hollowed out publishing staff and, even
more critically, skilled workers in the bookbinding firms, creating
a critical bottleneck in the production process.[31]

The concentration of British publishing in London also
increased its vulnerability to air attacks, no longer the opportunistic Zeppelin raids, but a potentially obliterating assault of massed
bombers. On 29 December 1940, German bombers hit the publishing district of Paternoster Row, near St Paul's. The entire stock
of seventeen publishers went up in flames, along with the warehouse of the wholesalers Simpkin & Marshall. Six million books
were lost, including the entire back stock of many significant publishers. Elsewhere, Stanley Unwin lost 1.4 million books to a single
bomb. Reprinting of even popular titles was sometimes impossible.
By 1942, 580 of 970 titles in Everyman's Library, a staple of public
libraries, private collectors and the overseas market, were out of
print.[32]

Yet despite this early tribulation, British publishing not only
survived, but thrived. Simpkin & Marshall went bankrupt but
was brought back to life under the collective ownership of the
major publishers. None of the leading publishers was forced to
close during the war. This resilience needs some explanation. It
helped that British desperation to keep the economy afloat made
maintaining the book export market a major national priority, and
thus merited the full co-operation of the Royal Navy protecting
consignments of books despatched abroad. Compulsory war insurance (a further factor, along with binding costs, in the inflation of
book prices during the war) provided a measure of compensation
for books lost to bombing. A large proportion of the books lost
in Paternoster Row was slow-moving stock, sometimes more of a

burden than a critical asset. Monetising redundant stock turned a traumatic event into something of a lifeline.

Most of all, the restrictions imposed by paper rationing made certain that virtually everything published sold out. This removed from the equation what Unwin described as the most expensive item on the ledger: publisher's judgement. In normal times, excessive optimism could be the fast route to bankruptcy, as it had been since the dawn of print. Yet anticipating public taste required both experience and a large dose of luck. Now publishers no longer had to put their money on uncertain prospects, as everything was a winner: as in Germany, the book-buying public scoured the bookshops for comfort reading. Most of the established British publishers emerged from the war in better shape than they entered it.

This was especially so with one of the most recent, and to fellow publishers wholly unwelcome, additions to the publishing fraternity, Allen Lane's Penguin Books, offering new modern fiction and non-fiction titles in paper covers. Penguin did not invent the paperback. In one sense the paperback had been an aspect of the trade since the birth of printing in the 1450s, when all books were sold unbound. In these earlier eras, customers took their new books to the binder, where they could be bound in the cover of their choice, either individually or in collections of different titles. Pamphlets were often left unbound, a tradition maintained in the seventeenth century by the French series of cheap reprints, the Bibliothèque bleue. Even in the industrial age, when books first began to be marketed pre-bound, there was a role for soft-bound books, though generally at the bottom of the market, with the famed (and to librarians and Victorian moralists repellent) penny dreadfuls and two-penny bloods.

The major reprint series of the nineteenth century, and the much-admired Everyman's Library (established in 1906), kept to the respectability of hardback. In the United States the enterprise of Emanuel Haldeman-Julius only muddied the waters further, since his Little Blue Books, printed on poor-quality paper and with somewhat casual editorial oversight, were texts of a decidedly left-wing orientation, aimed at the American working man

Allen Lane, the ruthless innovator whose vision of affordable high-quality literature would completely transform the twentieth-century book market.

and woman. Detested by conventional American publishers, the Little Blue Books nevertheless sold some 300 million copies at five cents apiece, largely through direct sales to customers rather than by booksellers.[33] A more relevant model for Penguin was the German Albatross books. Albatross, established in 1932, offered European customers paperbound English-language reprints. The standard design and format, including a plain cover with the Albatross motif, was a striking innovation that would be adopted by Penguin, as was the colour coding of the cover according to genre.

Albatross was stunted both by its contractual limitation to the continental market and by the Nazi takeover. Its motivating force, Kurt Enoch, would later make a second career building Penguin in America.[34]

The consensus in 1935 was that Penguin would not last a year, since the concept of a paperback series of in-copyright, contemporary, quality literature was always extremely risky. The task of turning a profit on books priced at sixpence was daunting, particularly when the reprint rights had first to be bought from other publishers: had they kept to their initial determination to withhold co-operation from Lane they could have strangled Penguin at birth. Most held aloof until Jonathan Cape broke the deadlock by offering ten titles. He later told Lane that he had sold the rights only because he was sure Penguin would soon go bust 'and I thought I'd take 400 quid [pounds] off you before you did'.[35] Booksellers were initially equally sceptical, worried that browsing customers would damage the stock. But once the bargain store Woolworths had come on board as an alternative sales location, the design skill of the branding and the quality of the books on offer ensured that the gamble paid off. The reading public took to Penguins immediately. Penguin brought the pleasures of owning recently published books to a public that could not afford the seven shillings and sixpence that publishers demanded for new novels in hardback.

It was George Bernard Shaw, himself an iconoclastic outrider in the literary establishment, though now a rich one, who helped prod Allen Lane towards undertaking a crucial extension of Penguin's remit: a parallel range of non-fiction titles, badged as Pelicans. The first Pelicans were published in May 1937, and with the looming international crisis the most explosive new weaponry was wheeled out of the Penguin armoury in November: the Penguin Special. These were short, passionate disquisitions on the looming political crisis, often written by political protagonists or eyewitnesses from Central Europe. These powerful contemporary polemics could be published at extraordinary speed, sometimes within a month of the delivery of the typescript. They fed the need of a bewildered public for better information than that afforded by a befuddled government and newspapers hamstrung by Conservative proprietors, and they sold massively.

There were thirty-five Penguin Specials between November 1937 and the outbreak of war, and whereas Penguins and Pelicans generally sold around 40,000 copies, almost every Penguin Special sold a minimum of 100,000 copies. A sample of titles shows how focused they were on the international crisis, and preparing the public for the difficult times ahead: *Blackmail or War?*; *China Struggles for Unity*; *The Air Defence of Britain*; *Europe and the Czechs*; *Between Two Wars?*; *The New German Empire*. W. J. Rose's *Poland* was published two months before the German invasion. The grim realities of Britain's predicament were explored in *Our Food Problem*; more paranoid fears were stoked by *The Attack from Within*.[36]

In the two years before the war, Allen Lane published 150 Penguins and 50 Pelicans. Sales had already topped 17 million before the start of 1939. For many readers Penguins and paperbacks had become virtually synonymous, and this would only be reinforced by the astonishing production of another 600 editions during the war years. Competing British publishers learned their lesson. By 1940 they had banded together to create Guild Books, a monthly list of fiction titles to be republished in paperback contributed by ten of the major English fiction publishers. Penguin also found its echo across the Atlantic, with the establishment in 1939 of Pocket Books as a division of Simon & Schuster. The convenience of these pocket-sized editions seemed particularly appropriate to the stringencies of wartime, when the new standards in any case mandated crowded pages and inferior-quality paper. Troops could carry with them a few paperbacks, and discard them, without the serious investment in a hardcover book; they also fitted conveniently in the pocket of a combat jacket or trousers. Such considerations would in 1942 inspire one of the most successful publishing ventures of the war, the Armed Services Editions, 122 million copies of which would in due course be distributed free of charge to American forces scattered around the globe.[37] On the home front, too, paperbacks were read on the train, in the home, in cheerless digs on war service. London authorities kitted out their new shelter

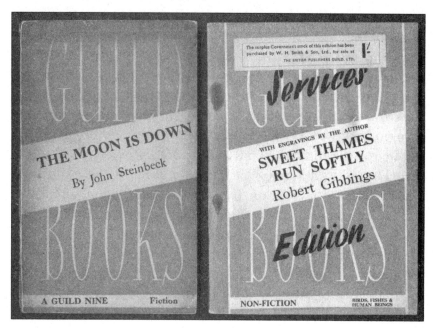

The established publishers were caught napping by the success of Penguin, and Guild Books was their attempt to take a slice of this buoyant new market. With titles like John Steinbeck's *The Moon is Down*, one of the bestsellers of the war, they could expect a decent market, but as the label on the other title here makes clear, not all their choices were successful.

libraries in Underground stations with inexpensive Penguins. Emergency bags packed against the need to evacuate in the case of bombing raids often contained a few paperbacks. This was a fundamental reorientation of the publishing market, begun in 1935, that took wings with the particular circumstances of wartime. Allen Lane rode his luck – the exceptional sales of the Penguin Specials in the pre-war years ensured him a generous paper ration – and his success changed the publishing world for ever.

Not everyone welcomed the jaunty new Penguins; in particular, this was a publishing development that left the public libraries watching from the side-lines. For the public libraries, the emergence of a new source of quality literature at a fraction of the price (fifteen Penguins for one new hardback novel) was a palpable hit at their place in the ecology of reading, and one in which they already faced competition from the commercial circulating libraries. Legitimate anxieties about the durability of paperbacks in a lending library held them back, but there was also something else to it. The Pelicans and Penguin Specials in particular had a decidedly leftward tilt, and library managers had no wish to purvey the sort of books that could also be bought in Woolworths. For the role of public libraries in wartime, this made for a bad start. It would be several decades into the post-war peace before libraries grudgingly accepted paperbacks onto their shelves. In the meantime, they would play a substantial role in the story of the book at war.

Wartime was challenging for publishers, and especially for authors, but also brought new opportunities. One branch of publishing that enjoyed extraordinary growth during wartime was the cookery book. In Britain, the outbreak of hostilities brought a cascade of titles offering simple recipes for harassed housewives. Many were short pamphlets issued by the Ministry of Food, available for four or six pence. These pragmatic little texts were usually unillustrated, but the publisher did commission for Frederick Grisewood's *The Kitchen Front* a charming dust-jacket illustration from Fougasse, whose Careless Talk Costs Lives posters made him the most visible artist of the war.[38] Commercial firms also cashed in on the anxieties of families coping with sharp reductions in the availability of crucial ingredients, mandating a move away from rich pre-war menus. Many purchasers were women shopping for themselves for the first time as domestic staff were called up for war work. One naval bride, who had never cooked before, was so terrified at the prospect that she pilfered a cookbook from her husband's ship's galley, only to be thwarted by the impossibility of measuring ingredients from recipes designed for the ship's full complement of 240 hungry sailors.[39]

Growing food, keeping chickens, making preserves and scouring the hedgerows all stimulated a range of titles: *Food Facts for the Kitchen Front* (with a foreword from the minister of food, Lord Woolton), *Cookery under Rations*, *The Penguin Book of Food Growing, Storing and Cooking*. The insistent repetition of 'the food front' or 'the kitchen front' drove home the message that the

Make Mars Last Longer. This sobering message in one of the first Penguin children's books (Puffins) made clear there was no escape from austerity in wartime Britain. The calorific tables make a strong case for chocolate bars, but since chocolate was rationed, gorging on Mars Bars was never an option.

prudent housewife was making a material contribution to the war effort, freeing up space on merchant ships for essential war materials. As the war wore on, Ambrose Heath's *Making the Most of It* (1942) probably expressed public sentiment more accurately. This was one of an extraordinary twenty-nine titles published by the food journalist Heath between 1939 and 1945, making him one of the war's most prolific authors.

In the United States, cookbooks beat the same drum, though with rather less conviction. 'Food will win the war' – or, more lyrically, 'the hand that cuts the ration coupon will win the war' – was less effective in a country still abundantly supplied.[40] Ruth Berolzheimer's *250 Tempting Desserts* was a text that would have been wholly redundant in 1940s Britain. Germany's crisis of supply also came much later in the war, but cookery did furnish one of the most extraordinary publishing stories of the war, the strange rebranding of Alice Urbach's bestselling *Cooking the Viennese Way*. Urbach ran a successful cookery school before the war and had a major success with her promotion of rich Austrian dishes and desserts, which went through three editions in its first three years, the third of 25,000 copies. Her life, like that of all Austrian Jews, took a sharp turn for the worse after Austria's absorption into the German Empire in 1938. Before she was permitted to emigrate, Alice was obliged to turn over ownership of her text to her publisher, who reprinted the book under the name of a non-Jewish male author. Apart from renaming 'Rothschild omelette' and 'beef Wellington', the main text was largely unaltered. Between December 1938 and 1941 a further 50,000 copies were printed. This Aryanisation of non-fiction was quite common in the German publishing industry, as with Paul Wessel's popular series of science primers, a major guide for legal ethics and *Knaur's Medical Encyclopedia*.[41] If publishers could cite necessity for this systematic plagiarism, it is less easy to forgive the continued exploitation of Urbach's text after the war, despite her frequent appeals to the publisher for the return of her intellectual property. It was only in 2020, when one of her grandchildren told this story in a book, that the rights of *So kocht man in Wien!* were released back to the family.

The cookbook boom was a reminder that while wars upended many lives, for others war was experienced as a series of uncomfortable adjustments to the mundane and everyday. For those on the home front, war was lived vicariously through friends and family in the armed forces or under the pathway of bombers. This variety of experience will be the subject of our next five chapters, from the home front to the front line, the book worlds of authors, troops and housewives, prisoners of war and the pedantic officials charged with regulating reading behaviour. All would play their part in the wartime life of books.

8

READING IN WARTIME

Forty years ago, the world was introduced to Nella Last, a forty-five-year-old housewife living in Barrow-in-Furness during the Second World War. Nella led a quiet life. She cooked, polished and shopped, chatted to neighbours and followed events, while caring for a household consisting of her husband, a man of few words who ran his own joinery business, and two grown-up sons. The older son would spend the war as an accountant in Northern Ireland, while his younger brother joined the army. The war also transformed Nella Last: we know this because from September 1939 she became a correspondent for Mass Observation (MO). This was a project established by the anthropologist Tom Harrisson, Charles Madge, a journalist, and the film-maker Humphrey Jennings to record everyday life in Britain's industrial cities. From the beginning of hostilities Mass Observation offered a wide cross-section of British society the opportunity to share their daily experience with a community of fellow authors and social scientists.[1] The MO archive, now at the University of Sussex in Brighton, offers a veritable treasure trove of information on civilian life in Britain during the Second World War. None responded more generously than Nella, who by war's end had despatched more than two million words to MO headquarters, a steady 1,000 words a day, usually written in the evening. Nella was a natural diarist, shrewd, sharp and with an acute sensitivity to the subtle gradations of social class in Barrow: she was never more withering than when observing other Barrow women taking on airs. All of this was poured out in the diary, for Nella was also unsparingly honest about her own not always creditable feelings.

What is most remarkable about Nella's Mass Observation

diaries is that in all this flow of words she said so little about reading: remarkable, because until the war broke out, Nella had been a voracious reader. A childhood injury had allowed her the space to read through the canon of English literature; Nella was a classic example of the working-class autodidact. But Nella's war left little time for books. Barrow had a major shipyard, and as a military base it was a natural target for Luftwaffe bombing. Nella volunteered for the Women's Voluntary Service, and served regular shifts cooking and cleaning in a WVS canteen. She opened a shop for the Red Cross: Nella was one of many women in whom the war revealed skills she had scarcely contemplated. She dug her garden for vegetables and kept chickens. She looked after the elderly members of her extended family. When Barrow was bombed, she sheltered under the dining-room table, then swept up the broken glass. No wonder she could manage little more than a glance at the newspaper before falling asleep.

This was the paradox of the home front in a nation at war. Many people read voraciously in wartime, as the Library Association, eager to be recognised as an essential wartime service, would tell anybody who would listen. There were many new readers among the troops, evacuees, land girls and industrial workers, all categories of adults prised away from the normal diversions of home life for service elsewhere. But fully 40 per cent of those polled by Mass Observation for its great survey of reading in wartime, undertaken in 1942, responded that they read less in wartime, often much less, or nothing at all. Books were an invaluable source of comfort in wartime, but they were a comfort that not everybody could enjoy.

In 1914–18, it was generally acknowledged that the British public libraries had had a bad war, particularly when contrasted with the cheery efflorescence of the public libraries in America. Latecomers to the party, the American libraries had thrown themselves into the patriotic cause, collecting books for the troops, selling Victory Bonds and offering the use of their facilities to the numerous voluntary organisations contributing to the war effort.[2] The twenty years before 1917 had seen an enormous amount of library building in the United States as Andrew Carnegie's programme of donations reached its zenith.[3] The war offered the

Nella Last. Caustic and chippy, but a shrewd observer of social nuance,
Nella became one of the great diarists of the war, thanks to Mass
Observation. If this seems to have been largely at the expense of reading
books, which she greatly valued, posterity is very much the beneficiary.

chance to embed the public library at the heart of the community,
and librarians seized it with open arms.

The public library movement in the UK had not reached
this state of development by 1914. Many communities, even substantial towns, had not yet adopted the Public Library Act, and
with campaigns to assist the war effort springing up all over the
country, libraries struggled to carve out a distinctive contribution. Budgets were cut and younger staff conscripted. The libraries
responded, sensibly enough, by stressing the merits of their technical and industrial collections, particularly those close to centres
of war industries in cities such as Sheffield, Leeds, Coventry, Wol-
verhampton and Birmingham. Sometimes this would lead, often

after the war, to the establishment of separate commercial and technical libraries.[4] Yet this activity, though worthy, scarcely resonated with the general public. Some libraries closed during the war or were requisitioned for war work, as was the Islington North branch library, converted to an annexe of London's Great Northern Central Hospital.[5]

The two decades between the world wars saw a transformation of the public library network in Britain. Spurred by the 1919 Public Library Act, which lifted the ceiling on local council spending by abolishing the restrictive 'penny rate' of the pioneering legislation of 1850, and passed responsibility to the county councils, a network of town and village libraries was established around the country. In 1939, many of those who had experienced the inertia of the management of libraries during the Great War were now leaders of the profession, so when war was declared, and the new Ministry of Information requested help in distributing its materials, the library movement was eager to be involved. Library staff, the Library Association pointed out, were well qualified to assist as Food Officers, with national registration schemes and organising Air Raid Precautions locally, and indeed many senior librarians would go on to play important roles in local administration. They also promised full support in the provision of library facilities for evacuated families, for troops based locally and for hospitals.[6]

This enthusiasm was genuine, though the library community also had more selfish reasons for demonstrating its importance to the war effort. It was especially keen to prevent its facilities being requisitioned by one of the myriad new war bureaucracies, and it was hopeful that library staff could be classified as essential workers and thus be exempted from conscription. They achieved more success in preserving their buildings: libraries were soon a hub of activity, providing information on new regulations, handing out pamphlets, displaying posters, providing meeting space. They failed, however, in their hopes that library staff could be protected from call-up, and over the course of the war, more than 2,000 members of the Library Association saw active service, many as volunteers. With that punctiliousness for which librarians are famed, those enlisted staff who failed to keep up their

Library Association subscriptions were removed from the roll of members.

The public libraries found themselves taking on extra duties, opening for extra hours and supplying books to many additional lending points, all with a greatly reduced staff. New, often female staff were taken on, but not enough to make good the deficiency. This was partly for the entirely laudable reason that the local authorities often made up the difference between library salaries and what their employees were earning in the forces and provided a guarantee that the job would be there for them at war's end; inevitably, this left less in the budget for recruiting replacement staff. In these difficult circumstances, libraries performed extremely well. The first major task, to meet the needs of mothers and children evacuated from London and other major industrial centres, was despatched with calm efficiency. New residents were issued with reader's cards, and collections, particularly of children's books, were augmented by voluntary transfers of stock from the urban libraries now denuded of readers.

Libraries that failed to recognise the urgency of the issue could expect no sympathy from their professional peers. When the librarian of Llandudno in North Wales revealed that he was insisting that evacuees show valid tickets from their home libraries before enrolling, the *Library Association Record* took the unusual step of publishing indignant responses castigating the unfortunate Mr Caul: 'With the exception of Llandudno, the whole country is at war.' On the whole, public libraries showed a commendable flexibility in adapting sacred procedures to accommodate the unusual fluidity of the population: not just troops and evacuees, but munitions workers, land girls and conscripted mine workers, all living away from home; to this would soon be added bombed-out families. In the course of the war, 62 million changes of address were registered, in a country with a population of 39 million.

Many library authorities opened new lending points, in village halls or even corner shops. A number of authorities introduced mobile libraries, servicing remote settlements or small wartime troop detachments. These facilities were all the more necessary as the reduction of public transport and removal of petrol rations for private cars along with longer hours of work made it difficult for many readers to get to the main branches to change their books. The most iconic symbols of library innovation were the libraries improvised by the London boroughs to serve those who had appropriated Underground stations as deep shelters during the London Blitz.[7] Collections of between a few hundred and 5,000 books were established in the shelters, often from newly bought stock and sometimes managed by a member of the library staff.

As symbols of the unquenchable spirit of London under fire, these Tube libraries were an important propaganda success, and did a power of good to the image of the library service. It was also an excellent opportunity to establish contact with potential readers who had previously seldom passed through the doors of the library. The war also brought new custom as men and women came looking for the myriad government documents that governed every aspect of life, food, clothing, trade, communication and recreation. The *Library Association Record* published a monthly list of new government publications, usually stretching to two pages. More palatably, libraries themselves issued lists of books of interest, such as gardening and cooking on wartime rations. Later in the war they would compile lists of titles on the issues of war, post-war reconstruction or unexpected allies such as Russia.

Many of those who came in search of information also took home a book to read. Not surprisingly, many libraries recorded a sharp increase in registered readers and in circulation. In 1941, Newcastle recorded 1.5 million issues, and Leeds an increase of 500,000. In 1943 Bristol, despite bomb damage, could report 2.8 million issues, and Manchester 6.1 million.[8] Optimistic reports of this sort flowed back to the Library Association, all reinforcing a sense of the library as the heart of the local community. But in the case of Leeds, this was reversing a similar reduction in the first year of the war, and the London boroughs also witnessed lower circulation as their populations sought sanctuary elsewhere. The question needs to be asked why, with conditions so favourable to reading, the use of public libraries did not increase more substantially.

When Mass Observation made its most systematic study of reading in wartime, in June 1942, the responses confirmed that

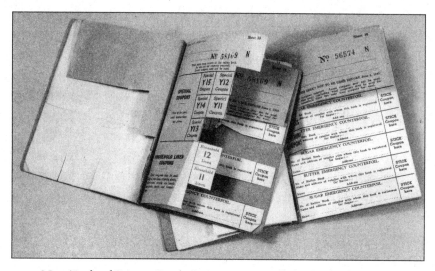

New Zealand Ration Book. Rationing was a fact of life even in the
Dominions, though they were not such an all-consuming preoccupation
in Australia and New Zealand or indeed the United States as in Britain.
Newspapers in the United States continued advertising new clothing lines,
furniture and food delicacies that would be unobtainable in Britain.

many readers were making heavy use of libraries.[9] But a full 40 per
cent of respondents reported that they were reading very little, if
anything. The experience of Nella Last could be replicated in millions of other cases. Much time that might previously have been
spent reading was now spent standing in queues: the complexities
of rationing absorbed the energies of both shoppers and the harried
butchers, bakers and grocers.[10] Many women were absorbed into
the workforce, or, like Nella, gave many hours to voluntary work.
Others were simply too stressed to take pleasure in books (reading
declined sharply during the Blitz).[11] Some could not get to the
library because they were working whenever the library was open.
The mobilisation of female labour, both in and outside the home,
had significant consequences for the public library, since women
made up such a large proportion of its regular clientele.

Even when readers made their way to the library, staff struggled
to provide them with the books they wanted to read. Public library
collections had been raided to create libraries for military camps
in their vicinity, and though donors met some of these needs, the

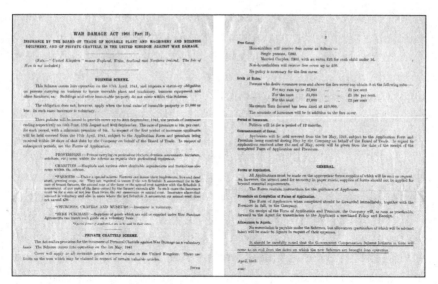

The blizzard of regulations that attended total war placed a
large burden on citizens, but some, like this explanation of war
insurance, were helpful, laying out the support offered to businesses
and city dwellers in the case of war damage. Public libraries
played a vital role in helping make such schemes known.

donated books were not always what soldiers regarded as recreational reading. Donations also had to be sorted, another task
to add to a busy librarian's day. In contrast to the first war, many
local authorities had increased library budgets to meet additional
demand, but even so, the war created a particularly adverse climate
for building library stock. The price of new books rose steeply, as
publishers absorbed new costs such as war stock insurance. Thus
libraries were buying fewer books, just as demand, particularly
for new fiction and books on the war, was rising. An even more
urgent problem was the conservation of stock. Books in regular
use were necessarily removed from circulation for repair or rebinding. Yet the cost of binding rose steeply as materials became scarce,
binderies suffered from bombing and lost workers to conscription.
Some skilled bookbinders left for better-paid work in munitions.
The result was that many binderies developed a backlog of work
of up to two years. Rather than take books out of service for this
length of time, many library copies were simply used to destruction. And readers did not like to take home soiled books, though,

paradoxically, they were often drawn to titles with many date stamps, as evidence that they were a good read.[12]

The shortage of staff also meant that public libraries could not seize the opportunity to get to know the potential new readers who came to the libraries primarily to consult government documents or pick up pamphlets. Normally this would have been the opportunity to provide them with an introduction to the book stock and guide their reading choice. To many librarians this was the heart of library work, yet impossible in the press of business. The result was that the opportunity was lost to make friends of the new working-class readers among the evacuees and war workers. To many of this sort of reader, the library represented a hostile environment, a place of disapproving glances, enforced silence and intimidating rules. It also did not stock the sort of magazines and recreational reading that they preferred. These readers often preferred the commercial libraries maintained by local newsagents or confectionery shops, generally known as tuppenny libraries, because books could be taken out for two pence, often with no joining fee. They stocked almost exclusively fiction, generally crime novels, adventure stories and romance, often books of few literary pretentions shunned by the public libraries. Here less confident readers could be assured of a welcome by proprietors who knew the sort of thing they liked and could provide a recommendation with a cheery smile and no judgement on their taste.[13] The public libraries did recognise that some of the pre-war idealism of 'improving' the reading taste of their patrons had to be abandoned, but old habits died hard. Library reports consistently celebrated high demand for non-fiction and technical literature even while, as Mass Observation reported in 1942, 75 per cent of readers still preferred light novels and thrillers.[14]

Many libraries suffered direct damage from the war, especially when the bombing moved on from London to industrial cities, ports and county towns. The heroic efforts to make good the damage and reopen a service in places like Plymouth, Portsmouth and Southampton showed the library service at its best but piled yet more pressure on budgets already stretched by high demand and increased costs. This made it even more difficult to provide readers with the recent titles they looked for in the library. Libraries were usually well stocked with the classics of English literature, also very much in demand during the war, thanks in part to the popular reprints of the Everyman's series, Nelsons and the Oxford University Press. But the waiting list for a new title by Dennis Wheatley or C. S. Forester might stretch for many months. The result was that public libraries not only lost working-class readers to the tuppenny libraries, but also a stratum of middle-class readers who in principle approved of public libraries, but relied on the subscription libraries at Boots or W. H. Smith for their recreational reading.

Reading through Mass Observation diaries, it is surprising how little those who read extensively relied on the public libraries. Arthur Hopkins, an Anglican minister in a working-class parish in Lincolnshire, had his own library of 2,000 books and a subscription to a commercial library. He alternated what he referred to as serious (that is theological) reading with old classics from his own library and contemporary reading, fiction and non-fiction, from his subscription library. He swapped recommendations and often loaned books to the friends he made on fire-watching duty.[15] Londoner Gladys Langford also obtained recent publications from a close friend who ran a small chain of four commercial libraries.[16] The bookkeeper Anthony Heap stuck it out in London for the whole war, where he spent much of his limited income on theatre tickets. He patronised Mudie's until it closed in 1937, and then joined Boots, having rejected *The Times* library on grounds of expense. In 1943 he upgraded to a class A subscription at Boots through frustration at never being able to get the titles he wanted: it was worth the £2 annual subscription as 'the satisfaction of being able to obtain any book I wanted as soon as published will justify the extravagance'.[17] Retired electricity board inspector Herbert Brush was also a Boots subscriber.[18]

Women made up the bulk of subscribers to Boots Book-Lovers Library, which had built its clientele around housewives who could rely on domestic help to provide leisure for reading. The subscription libraries could also rely on a newly empowered group of single young working women earning good wages in wartime jobs. Olivia

Cockett was twenty-six at the outbreak of the war. At the time she was employed as a clerical assistant at New Scotland Yard, though the offices soon moved to safer quarters at Putney. Olivia was intelligent and well educated, and read voraciously. She clearly had a considerable library of her own, augmented with regular trips to both the public library and library of W. H. Smith. She also received a monthly choice from the Readers Union book club.

One of the most interesting Mass Observation testimonies comes from Phyllis Walther, a graduate of London University who in 1939 returned to the family home in Dorset with her young son, leaving her husband to his war work in London (a common pattern). Phyllis's busy new life left little time for reading, but her response to the Mass Observation 'directive' of May 1942 (a regular call for a discursive response on a particular theme, on this occasion reading) opens a fascinating window onto the diverse reading environment of the middle-class family:

> The only books I read regularly are *Picture Post*, which I send to my sister in Australia for her birthday and Christmas presents, the *New Statesman*, which she gives me for my present, and *Reader's Digest*, which my father takes in. I used to belong to Boots Library but I found I took so long to read a book that I might as well buy it. I sometimes take out a book from there on my mother's subscription. My husband was a member of the Left Book Club before the war and I brought all those books down with me and read them slowly, and also a friend sent her books down with our furniture and I read them especially any new one in the Reader's Union, of which she was a member.

So many books, so little time. Now Phyllis barely snatches half an hour for herself, whereas 'when we had another maid and I did no housework I could read like this every day'.[19] Yet the range of sources from which Phyllis could obtain books, which also includes borrowing a book from her literary sister that she felt she 'ought to have read long ago', is not altogether untypical of Mass Observation diarists from better-off backgrounds. In the stratification of

Tom Harrisson, MO's director, Phyllis was a 'class A' reader. As a group, those who wrote for MO tended to the left, so the Left Book Club features often (disproportionately so considering its rapidly declining membership), along with the *Listener*, a high-brow magazine published by the BBC, and the *New Statesman*.

The book clubs, Boots, W. H. Smith and to a lesser extent *The Times*, are equally ubiquitous in the diaries, though strangely absent from Mass Observation's most extensive report on wartime reading of 1942. This may owe something to Tom Harrisson's own position as a well-known figure on the political left and so congenitally disposed to support the public library movement. While he was prepared to offer a serious analysis of the tuppenny libraries, as a place in which working-class readers felt comfortable choosing books, he seems to have had little time for the middle-class commercial libraries and their carefully gradated class hierarchy of subscriptions. Here the last word should go, as so often, to Nella Last, something of a favourite of Harrisson's and a nippy critic of social pretension. In February 1941, she was mystified why a vivacious and attractive woman of forty-seven should have committed suicide, since she had 'just about everything to make a woman happy'. This included a modern house, lots of housekeeping money (one of Nella's principal complaints against her own husband) and one of the loveliest fur coats in town. Furthermore, she 'was an "A" member at Boots Library – no free library books for her – and was in a magazine library at Boots as well'.[20]

Libraries also struggled because they could not take advantage of the major reading innovation of the era: the paperback. Librarians regarded Penguins with a sort of awed revulsion. In January 1939, the librarian of Nuneaton conceded rather tremulously in the pages of the *Library Association Record* that he had accessioned a few of the 'Penguin Special' tracts on contemporary affairs, but this prompted no response from the wider library community.[21] The London boroughs bought Penguins for the Tube shelter libraries, and other library authorities relied on them for the boxes of books they despatched to outlying military outposts, but this was because they had no great expectation that they would be returned. There was never any suggestion that paperbacks would be employed to build regular stock even when, from 1940, a consortium of publishers with long fiction lists established Guild Books to issue their own recent titles in paperback. These were precisely the sort of books for which public library readers were clamouring.

Librarians were of course correct that the new paperbacks would deteriorate very rapidly through frequent use. In November 1941, Denis Argent, a former journalist and now a private in a non-combatant unit in Bedford, visited a bookshop to buy *Labour Monthly* and *British Worker*, but recoiled from a Pelican of J. B. S. Haldane's *Science in Everyday Life*:

> Despite the good contents, this is just about the most villainously cheap Penguin that's yet been turned out – flimsy muddy paper, smudgy printing and bad binding. I decided it would be sixpence wasted as I can probably get a well-printed readable edition of the book from the library.[22]

Otherwise Argent was a voracious consumer of Penguins, often reading in meal breaks or while being driven back and forth from work assignments: for frequent readers, the economics were compelling. In 1941, *The Scarlet Impostor*, the latest Dennis Wheatley blockbuster, came out at 10s 6d. For that, the reader could buy twenty-one Penguins, and though sales were still brisk, the big four commercial libraries ordered 67 per cent fewer copies than was usual for a book by this author.[23] Ernest Hemingway's runaway bestseller *For Whom the Bell Tolls* was published that same year at 9s. This was a considerable purchase when compared to the 6d Penguin or Guild edition paperback, no more than the cost of a pack of twenty cigarettes. For a county library system to invest in twenty copies of Hemingway's blockbuster would not have been excessive, but this same £9 10s would have bought 380 Penguins, or 253 when the price was raised to 9d (with no discernible impact on sales).

For people on the move, like Denis Argent, from barracks to barracks, or on troopships to overseas postings, a paperback was attractive precisely because it could be read, shared with friends and then discarded. MO diarists clearly regarded buying a Penguin as a casual purchase, and one that could be made in Woolworths or a newsagent, without the need for a special visit to a bookshop. This was certainly the case with Kathleen Hey, one of the most interesting of the diarists: born in 1906, she lived with her mother and married sister and worked in the family grocery shop. Her reading tastes were highbrow, at variance with the preference for the wireless in her lower middle-class household. She had a library ticket but seems to have preferred to buy books, including a handful of 'sixpenny books' bought in a postcard shop while holidaying in Harrogate. These included *The Thought-Reading Machine* by André Maurois and *Russia* by Bernard Pares.[24]

For all these reasons, public libraries were unlikely to be the first port of call for readers seeking either recent fiction or the latest word on the progress of the war. They either stumped up the subscription from a commercial library, or, increasingly, bought the paperback. With paperbacks so cheap, a hardback novel, which they might not like and would possibly read only once, seemed a dangerous indulgence in wartime. Publishers took note, and prioritised proven bestsellers for their precious paper ration. Having failed to strangle Penguin at birth, publishers also made their peace with paperbacks, now thanks to the publishers' consortium Guild Books far more ubiquitous. Indeed, when MO diarists spoke of Penguins, they might have been using the most popular brand name to describe any paperback. Publishers had to take profit where they could, finding their way through the labyrinth of regulations, coping with bombed-out warehouses and binderies, consignments for export torpedoed, and paper shortages. Here, in the competition for limited paper stocks, they found one more formidable competitor: His Majesty's Government.

On 22 May 1943, Arthur Hopkins took the train from Boston to Lincoln, a rather convoluted journey in wartime conditions. To while away the time he had with him the Ministry of Information pamphlet *Combined Operations, 1940–1942*, describing the various sorties into enemy territory attempted in the first three years of the war, culminating in the disastrous Dieppe raid, for which it made the best case possible. Hopkins, an avid reader who followed the events of the war closely, was moved to mention this in his diary only because all other five passengers in his carriage were reading the same work.[25]

Combined Operations was the latest of a series of wildly successful accounts of British military endeavour on the war front; it was well written, lavishly illustrated and extremely affordable at one shilling. The series had begun with *The Battle of Britain*, a comparatively austere thirty-two-page pamphlet in light card, retailing at threepence. The text was supplied by the thriller writer Hilary St George Saunders, now writing anonymously for the Ministry of Information (MOI). Published in March 1941, it sold out its first printing of 50,000 copies in a day: 300,000 more copies were swiftly put to the press. An illustrated edition followed and then translations for distribution abroad. By 1942, *The Battle of Britain* had circled the globe with forty-three editions in twenty-three languages, not to mention numerous newspaper serialisations.[26] St George Saunders was able to fix in public consciousness a tale of plucky victory over Germany's ruthless fighting machine, a chink of light in a military landscape where until well into 1942 the tide resolutely refused to turn.

St George Saunders followed up his anonymous triumph with *Bomber Command*, four times the length of *Battle of Britain*, which sold 1.36 million copies. *Coastal Command*, *Front Line* and the *Battle for Egypt* were added to a growing list of titles. The popularity of the MOI's publications provided a steady income for booksellers, but left publishers with decidedly mixed feelings. It was one thing to be competing with industry colleagues who played by the same rules, quite another to be up against the government acting as a commercial publisher. This was especially the case while publishers were having to weigh the merits of each new project against the capacities of their measly paper ration, while the MOI enjoyed a quota six times the size of the entire book publishing industry. Maddeningly, it did not even keep to this bloated allocation, but overshot its nominal ceiling every year.

This must have been hard to bear, but the publishers would find that the steady stream of MOI bestsellers in no way exhausted demand for accounts of the military struggle and a running commentary on contemporary events. Each new phase of the war brought a wave of new titles. During the first winter of the war, the Russian assault on Finland gained a lot of attention. Readers anxious to learn more could seek out Ullmann's *Epic of the Finnish Nation*, Hampden Jackson's *History of Finland* and Herbert Ellison's *Finland Fights*.[27] Books on Germany, already popular before the war, continued to be published. Frederick Muller's *Freedom Calling* (about an anti-Nazi radio station), *Inside the Gestapo*, *Dachau the Nazi Hell* and Dr Rudolf Olden's *Is Germany a Hopeless Case?* set the tone in 1940. First-hand testimonies, such as Irmgard Litten's *A Mother Fights Hitler*, on her attempt to rescue her son from a concentration camp, and Madeleine Kemp's *I Married a German*, proved especially popular: Kemp's autobiographical memoir was into its fifth edition by 1939.

Hellmut von Rauschenplat's *How to Conquer Hitler* in retrospect looks too optimistic in 1940, as does the publication of *The Soldiers' English–German Conversation Book* in December 1939: for the first four years of the war, as it turned out, this would have been most useful for British servicemen in prisoner-of-war camps. Fiction writers chipped in: Bernard Newman's *Maginot Line Murder* (Gollancz) was advertised as the first crime novel of the war, closely followed by Wheatley's *Scarlet Impostor*, advertised as the 'first thriller dealing with the current war'. Albert Nesor's *Mad Dog of Europe*, a Hitler novel, was yours for 7s 6d. Publishers also employed the tried-and-tested weapon of humour and mockery, with Rolf Tell's *Sound and Fuehrer* and then the bestselling *Adolf in Blunderland*: helped by a dramatisation on the BBC, this went through three editions in eight days. One opportunistic author even published a biography of Lord Haw-Haw, the name given to William Joyce, broadcasting nightly from Germany. Foyles dedicated a literary lunch to Lord Haw-Haw. He was sent an invitation, but failed to show up.

This sort of sangfroid was perhaps forgivable in the phoney war, but vanished rapidly with Dunkirk, the fall of France and the Battle of Britain. For the next eighteen months, war books oscillated between the desire to explain the shocking speed with which France had collapsed in 1940 and celebrations of the courage and resilience of the RAF fighters. Notwithstanding the success of the MOI pamphlet, there was plenty of appetite for further eyewitness narratives. In September 1940, William Collins published books on all three of the services for 3*s* 6*d* each. In July 1941, William Buchan's *RAF at War* was available for 5*s*. Black published *RAF in Action* in December 1940, a book created with the co-operation of the Air Ministry. This assistance was important, because only with authorisation could a journalist or photographer access a military factory or an airfield, or hitch a ride for a bombing raid. Even at 7*s* 6*d*, *RAF in Action* sold out in two days. The publishers donated the royalties to the RAF Benevolent Fund, while Harrap's donated the profits from *Dive Bomber* to the Spitfire Fund, the most popular fundraising cause in 1940. Professional associations, voluntary groups and factory workers would club together to raise the £5,000 to build a Spitfire, the neat fighter that turned the Battle of Britain.

Each serviceman was obliged to write a letter to next of kin in case of their death on active service. In June 1940 *The Times* published such a letter (with the permission of the airman's mother), of a young airman in a bomber shot down protecting the evacuation from Dunkirk. *The Times* received so many requests for copies that a pamphlet version was published: it sold 500,000 copies by the end of the year. It was also made available as a poster for hanging in schools.[28] The outpouring of affection and gratitude for the RAF was heartfelt and unforced; at a time when the army was mostly lurking in camps around Britain, the RAF and Royal Navy took centre stage.[29]

When it came to France, commentators turned an unforgiving eye on the French governments of the 1930s, mapping the collapse of a nation in principle superbly well equipped to halt the German assault, as they had in 1914. As so often, foreign correspondents led the way, with an early analysis from Gordon Waterfield, correspondent for Reuters, with *What Happened to France*. The speed of the collapse caught some publishers napping. Dent were forced rather hurriedly to retitle Georges Duhamel's *Why France Fights*: in fairness to the author, the rather unfortunate new title choice, *The French Position*, was closer to the original French title. James

Marlow's *De Gaulle's France* rallied opinion to the leader in exile, while an English edition of the general's book on mechanised warfare burnished his reputation as a prophetic military thinker.[30]

Narratives of civilians caught in the carnage proved especially popular. Elie J. Bois offered *Truth on the Tragedy of France* and Alexander Werth provided *The Last Days of Paris*. The stiff upper lip was evident in Rupert Downing's *If I Laugh*, an account of his escape by bicycle with a Mrs Hawksley. Another escape story, *The Road to Bordeaux*, written by two Englishmen from the Paris theatre world who joined the French army as ambulance drivers in 1940, also struck a chord, and Nevil Shute had a huge success with a gripping sentimental novel on the same theme, *The Pied Piper*. Less sympathetic was Cecil F. Melville's *Guilty Frenchmen*, followed swiftly by Harold Cardozo's *France in Chains*, inspired by an opportunistic sortie by a journalist of the *Daily Mail* to the Franco-Spanish border. February 1941 brought André Simone's *J'Accuse*, on the collapse of France, 'The inner story of seven years' treachery in high places', swiftly followed by André Maurois with *Why France Fell*. This went through six large printings in three weeks. *France in Defeat*, a book by Percy Philip, the Paris correspondent of *The New York Times*, was more of the same.

The shock news of the German invasion of Russia brought a rush of publications. J. T. Murphy had the good fortune to have *Russia on the March* in proofs before the German invasion, but the future Labour cabinet member Jennie Lee was not far behind with *Our Ally – Russia*. Of course, the left, so confused by the Russian treaty with Germany in 1939, was exultant. Left-wing publisher Victor Gollancz had *Russia and Ourselves* written and produced in three weeks: it went through three editions before publication day. For the real enthusiasts, Lund Humphries offered an encyclopedic Russian–English dictionary, though it would set you back more than £2. For those wanting the whole story, Hutchinson's *Quarterly Record of the War* sold for 8s 6d. The first section, dealing with September–December 1939, was into its tenth edition by the end of 1940, and the third volume, dealing with the fall of France, its fifth edition.

This was a significant market, but no more so than the buoyant sales of current affairs publications in cheaper ranges. The war spawned a rash of new series: Cambridge University Press's Current Problems, Macmillan's War Pamphlets and the Oxford Pamphlets, which sold 2 million copies in their first two years. The home front war was an equally important source of business for the book trade. There were one million Air Raid Precautions officers, for whom the *ARW's Reference Book* was an indispensable guide. For the 1.5 million serving in the Home Guard, all wishing to do their bit for the war effort by burnishing their skills, Hutchinson's *Hints for the Home Guard* was a bargain at sixpence, and the whole *Home Guard Handbook* was available for a shilling. Sales of titles like these helped sustain booksellers when increased taxation and wartime austerity constrained the book buying of their regular customers. Here the testimony of bookshop owner Hubert Wilson, writing in the *Bookseller*, in October 1940, is thoughtful and insightful. Christmas 1939, he said, had been excellent. But then came the fall of France and regular sales tailed off, though happily footfall was sustained thanks to the astonishing variety of books and pamphlets for the civilian, budding soldier, nurse, ARP worker or 'pocket politician':

> There were books about ships, aeroplanes, and all weapons of war; pamphlets, memoranda and Acts of Parliament in constant flood from the Stationery Office, on every conceivable subject from garden produce to anti-gas drill; manuals of drill in threes; rifle drill; the use of the Bren gun; the duties of the Company Officer and a hundred other subjects.

All these together took up much of the display space, and most of the window. They brought in 'anything from a penny to 3*s* 6*d* but rarely more than a shilling . . . and they did bring a new public into the shop'. Wilson was also gracious enough to acknowledge that 'hundreds are now willing to enter that shop whenever they want a Penguin who had previously never dared to cross its threshold'.[31] Many in the book trade still hoped for a return to the good old days, with discerning customers spending larger sums on hardback books. But the experience of wartime and its new influx of

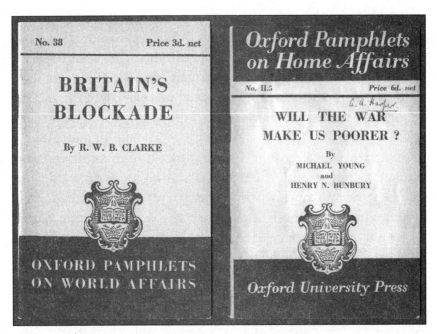

No. 38   Price 3d. net

BRITAIN'S BLOCKADE

By R. W. B. CLARKE

OXFORD PAMPHLETS ON WORLD AFFAIRS

Oxford Pamphlets on Home Affairs

No. H.5   Price 6d. net

WILL THE WAR MAKE US POORER?

By
MICHAEL YOUNG
and
HENRY N. BUNBURY

Oxford University Press

The neat, well-produced Oxford pamphlets found a large audience, though *Will the War Make us Poorer?* (1943) provided more optimistic reassurance than was strictly justified. The answer, of course, was yes.

one-shilling customers did much to prepare them for the paper-back revolution of the post-war years.

It is sometimes claimed that the latter stages of the war witnessed a decreasing interest in works on contemporary politics, though publishers' schedules show little sign of this. Rather, attention shifted increasingly to issues of post-war reconstruction. The Beveridge Report of November 1942, promising a total restructuring of social provision in Britain, was a bestseller in both its full and condensed versions. To judge by the Mass Observation diaries, it was widely discussed in British homes and the workplace (it is one of the few milestones of the war mentioned by virtually every Mass Observation diarist). One of the most striking features of the British war effort, particularly when we now know that the strategic outlook would be desperately challenging until at least 1943, is how early the thoughts of public officials, including the library community, turned to post-war planning. Books on architecture and social policy, and the visionary manifestos of the small cadre of politicians who shunned the wartime coalition, all found an eager audience. In retrospect this sublime confidence in eventual victory seems quite extraordinary, and certainly the diarists found space to reflect their frustration and anxiety at the conduct of the war. Nevertheless, apart from a brief wobble after the fall of France, few genuinely believed that Hitler would prevail.

Germans experienced quite a different kind of mass observation, though still generously funded and staffed by the government. The Gestapo was not the sort of body to which one could easily confide one's innermost thoughts on the progress of the war or gripes about neighbours, or express pleasure in reading books that might then turn out to be banned because of the subject material or the identity of the author. Diary keeping carried very real risks, and the extraordinary recklessness of a man like Friedrich Kellner, a civil servant and committed Social Democrat, was rare indeed. December 1942 was not a good time to be committing thoughts like these to writing, even in a carefully hidden private journal: 'Adolf Hitler is the most cunning criminal of all time. He is Satan and the Devil in one person. This Hitler has risen to be a glaring example of abomination for mankind.'[32] His diary's survival also owes something to the fact that Kellner was living in the small provincial town of Laubach. Even if others had risked keeping a diary, much personal material would be lost in the ruinous bombing between 1943 and 1945. In consequence of these two factors, reticence and war damage, we know much more about book production and consumption on the German home front through official sources than from personal reminiscence. The endless stream of memoranda passing back and forth between organisations with bafflingly overlapping jurisdictions, so characteristic of the Nazi state, tells us much about the book world, but ordinary obedient civilians come to the fore only when they step out of line.

As we have seen, the publishing industry, bookshops and public libraries all played a major role in Hitler's plans to create unity of purpose in the German nation in advance of the war, a role for which, in many ways, the library profession was well prepared. The public library network, vastly expanded in the years after the Nazi takeover in 1933, was already accustomed to an austerely pedagogic role in German society. Public libraries were seen essentially as institutions of adult education. A revealing report contributed to the *Library Association Record* in 1934, but describing the library world before the Nazi takeover, made little attempt to disguise this missionary purpose: 'The task of the public libraries is education through popular scientific literature, and educational entertainment, not merely entertainment, through fiction.' The concept of 'educational fiction' was interpreted very narrowly:

> We refuse all blood-and-thunder literature ... love novels, which depict a wrong and sentimental picture of life, writers like Courths-Mahler and her imitators ... mainly set in aristocratic circles, which have become the chief stock of the penny-cheap circulating-libraries in the poorer districts.

The works of Karl May, the purveyor of tales of the American West so much enjoyed by Adolf Hitler, were also excluded on the rather quixotic grounds that these stories were 'pure imagination', since May had never set foot in the United States.[33] The certainties of this iron-clad rectitude were carried over into the Nazi regime, as attested by Muriel Green, seconded from Halifax Library in Yorkshire for an exchange visit in 1936. Left to themselves, she was solemnly informed by her hosts, library users 'would always choose light literature of the same type and never improve their taste'.[34] In Berlin, patrons were only permitted to borrow five novels a month, in Frankfurt four. It is no wonder that readers fled in such numbers to the despised commercial libraries, or, indeed, that the Nazis also thought it important to impose regulation on this segment of the book market. As the war wore on, commercial libraries were closed altogether.

It was also common to charge new patrons for their reader's card, and a fee for each book taken out. This was not just an ordinary reader's card, but the *Leseheft*, a booklet in which readers recorded not only the books checked out, but also their preferred reading and titles they were keen to obtain. Since German public libraries religiously rejected browsing by patrons, all books being housed in a closed stack, these transactions all had to be negotiated through a librarian. Despite its pre-Nazi roots, this was a system perfectly calibrated for the needs of a totalitarian regime, and the Soviet Union adopted something similar. Robert Ashby, another English library visitor in 1937, was rather attracted to the *Leseheft* without recognising its manipulative potential.[35]

In the course of the war, Germany's increasingly desperate condition gradually eroded these unbending, pious verities. Public libraries had been obliged to turn over a considerable proportion of their stock to supply the 8 million books needed to create new libraries for troops and the Luftwaffe in 1939. This hollowed out their own collections, and as paper shortages bit deeper, new replacement stock was increasingly difficult to obtain. Although Hamburg proudly reported increased circulation for the first three years of the war, this came to a juddering halt with the famous firestorm bombing raid of 1943. All this had its impact on the unity of purpose so valued by the Nazi state. Librarians instructed to provide books for evacuees from bombed cities insisted the Reich authorities bore the cost. A steady stream of demands for more recreational material demonstrated the extent to which readers were abandoning the public library ideal: the requests passed on to the central authority responsible for supplying stock appealed for 'novels with cheerful content', 'novels for women' or 'adventurous travel'.[36]

By this point all library schools but Leipzig's had been closed and by war's end all male librarians except the congenitally infirm had been summoned to the front line. The effectiveness of Allied bombing led to an order in 1944 requiring public libraries to remove their stock to safekeeping, though there was an ever-diminishing range of safe places to which they could be sent. Through all of this, the Nazi library hierarchy remained in a state of denial. In his last annual message in 1944, Fritz Heiligenstaedt, director of the national agency for public librarianship, asserted that 'not only do circulation statistics climb steadily, but the readers have recourse to books that are more and more substantial and serious'. The copy of this circular in the Detmold archive has this last statement underlined, with a question mark and exclamation mark in the margin.[37]

In truth, the ideological mission of the public library movement had collapsed long before the Allied forces completed their destruction of the German cities, and their troops occupied the ruins. Hitler, living out his last days in the isolation of his Berlin bunker, would still have been astonished, as were the wary Allied troops, when the advancing columns of the Western armies were in some places welcomed by Germany's nation of readers dressed in their Sunday best, and offering flowers to their conquerors.[38] Allied soldiers exposed to the horrors of Buchenwald, Belsen and Dachau greeted this opportunistic pirouette with appropriate scepticism.

The drab uniformity of the German public library was a vivid contrast to the American book scene, embarked on a golden age of expansion. Even before Pearl Harbor, books sympathetic to the British cause, often written by American journalists who had experienced Nazi Germany and the fortitude of London during the Blitz at first hand, sold extremely well. They no doubt played their part in preparing public opinion for a full-hearted contribution to the European theatre of war, as well as America's leading role in the post-war settlement. We can track these publishing successes with some precision, because in contrast to the UK, American publishers had already since the beginning of the century had a well-respected and widely circulated bestseller list, compiled by the trade paper *Publishers Weekly* with the help of a representative sample of booksellers distributed around the country.[39] That said, these lists tell us only part of the story. Paperbacks, spreading very rapidly since the establishment of Pocket Books in 1939, were distributed mostly outside the established network of bookshops who helped compile the bestseller lists, through corner shops, newsagents and general stores. There would be no paperback bestseller lists until 1955. Even with this caveat, the bestseller lists tell us a great deal about American readers' engagement with the European war, and later the global conflict.

The difference between 1940 and 1941 was in this respect profound. The bestselling non-fiction titles for 1940 offered a fairly typical range of peacetime reading. Osa Johnson's *I Married an*

Adventurer, about her travels with her husband, topped the list, with Mortimer Adler's *How to Read a Book* in second place. The mixture of contemporary politics, reminiscences and evocative nature writing was typical of any peacetime year up to the end of the century. By 1941, the landscape was transformed. The three top sellers, led by William Shirer's *Berlin Diary*, and six of the top ten were all war books: this was impressive, considering that the United States would not enter the war until December. Douglas Miller's *You Can't Do Business with Hitler*, published on 1 January 1941, was a lesson well taken, though rather late in the day. The collected speeches of the English prime minister, *Blood, Sweat and Tears*, sold extremely well. It is noteworthy that in both of these years a British author topped the American fiction lists, Richard Llewellyn's *How Green Was My Valley* in 1940, and A. J. Cronin's *The Keys to the Kingdom* in 1941. Also selling well were Hemingway's *For Whom the Bell Tolls*, his novel of the Spanish Civil War published in October 1940, and Steinbeck's *The Grapes of Wrath* (1939). Both also sold well in Britain: the two markets were closely integrated.

In 1942, America's first full year of war, six of the top nonfiction books were war related, with Joseph E. Davies's *Mission to Moscow* beaten into second place by Marion Hargrove's more frivolous *See Here, Private Hargrove*, which offered the perspective of the civilian as temporary soldier. Originally a series of humorous newspaper columns, this light-hearted book sold 2.8 million copies.[40] Interestingly, four of these wartime bestsellers, including *Mission to Moscow*, were later turned into films. In the very different climate of the Cold War, the sympathetic portrait of Joseph Stalin in *Mission to Moscow* attracted the unwelcome attentions of the Committee for Un-American Activities.

The progress of American troops, in both the European and Pacific theatres, was closely followed: inevitably so, since so many American families had sons, brothers or sweethearts in the fighting forces. Journalist Richard Tregaskis's *Guadalcanal Diary*, a day-by-day account of the first decisive victory over Japanese troops on land, sold 1.5 million copies. Ernie Pyle, who had covered the Battle of Britain for a string of newspapers, generated two bestsellers from collections of columns filed while embedded with American troops in North Africa and France: *Here Is Your War* (1943) and *Brave Men* (1944). Seen from the perspective of the ordinary GI, these reports struck a chord with those anxiously watching and waiting at home. Pyle would be killed in one of the last engagements of the Pacific War in April 1945, the year *Brave Men* topped the non-fiction charts.

The perspectives of the traditional policymakers was represented in the bestseller lists by Wendell Willkie's *One World* and Walter Lippmann's *US Foreign Policy* and in 1945, looking ahead to his enormous influence on the post-war world, the biennial report of the US chief of staff, George Marshall, to the secretary of war. Wendell Willkie was Roosevelt's defeated Republican opponent from the 1940 election, and *One World* was the fruit of his travels around the world in the two years that followed as an informal emissary for America. A mixture of travelogue and passionate plea for a more just and integrated world, *One World*, issued simultaneously in hardback and paperback, sold 1.5 million copies in four months after publication in April 1943, a record for a non-fiction book. Willkie's early death, in October 1944, was a great loss to American politics.

These were serious times, and once engaged in the international crisis, American readers showed a commendable commitment to following it closely. For all that, and as in all other combatant countries, fiction remained the core of the book market, in terms of sales utterly dominant. The runaway bestseller of 1943–5 was Lloyd C. Douglas's *The Robe*, a blockbuster following the fictional journey of Marcellus, the centurion who supervised the crucifixion of Christ, leading to Marcellus's own Christian martyrdom. It topped the bestseller list in 1943, and in 1944 and 1945 was beaten only by two controversial novels, Lillian Smith's *Strange Fruit*, a tale of interracial marriage in 1920s Georgia, and Kathleen Winsor's *Forever Amber*, a genial historical romp set in seventeenth-century England. *Forever Amber* was banned in fourteen states in the United States and struggled to find a publisher in Britain. As so often, its notoriety only added to its appeal with readers. Perhaps the most distinctive feature of the American market was readers' insistence on access to the most recently published editions. A survey of the circulation of books from the public library of Montclair, New Jersey in May 1943 found that 65 per cent of the books issued had been published after January 1940; only 13 per cent had been printed before 1930. Whether they bought or borrowed books, Americans wanted what was new: indeed in one remarkable case in California in 1945 a woman obtained a divorce on the grounds that her husband would not allow her sufficient reading time to 'keep up with the current best sellers'.[41] The resilience of the publishing industry, albeit in far less challenging circumstances than those faced in Europe, ensured that this taste could be satisfied.

For all the interest in current affairs that can be tracked through the bestseller lists, pre-war patterns of book consumption in America ultimately underwent a far less radical readjustment than in other major combatant nations. During the years that the Americans were directly involved in the Second World War, only two novels dealing directly with the events of the war featured on the bestseller lists. These were John Steinbeck's *The Moon Is Down*, a sympathetic treatment of the confusion and moral dilemmas of life in occupied Europe, and John Hersey's *A Bell for Adano*, an account of the American occupation of a fictional Italian coastal town. As with the First World War, hard-hitting engagement with the horrors of war would be reserved for the decades that followed, with Norman Mailer's *The Naked and the Dead* and Irwin Shaw's *The Young Lions* leading the way in 1948.

For all the commitment of American troops and hardware, this was still a war taking place in faraway and scarcely known places: in this respect the home front in America would always be different from the experience of Britain, Germany or the occupied nations. It was not the case that Americans were entirely spared the wartime austerity ubiquitous in Europe. The rapid conversion of American industry to war production brought some shortages and a degree of rationing for civilians, for instance of tinned food. The publishing industry faced further controls on the use of paper. But America's forty-eight continental states were spared the bombing that transformed war on the home front: consequently, casualties were proportionally lower than any other combatant nation. Consumers still had money in their pockets, often, for war workers, rather more money than before. American newspapers still devoted lavish amounts of space to advertisements for stylish clothing and new furniture, both largely unavailable in Europe. This was a period of rapid growth for the American economy and some of this new energy rubbed off on the American book industry. If families waiting by the hearth for news turned to books for consolation, this was a laudable by-product of a society of plenty. It was not just through military muscle that the war years prepared the way for American post-war domination of Western politics and culture; the book industry also played its part.

9

BLACKLISTS

On 10 May 1933, the day that the Nazi regime staged book burnings across Germany, 100,000 people marched in protest through New York. It was a remarkably swift response and reflected a genuine and widely felt sense of outrage. American intellectuals and published authors, some of whose books had ended up on the pyre, hastened to condemn the evils of censorship. Eleanor Roosevelt, wife of the president, weighed in on the issue in her daily newspaper column.

The burning of books did more than any event to characterise the Nazi regime in the eyes of American opinion. It would be a recurring theme in President Roosevelt's speeches, contrasting the freedoms of American society with the assault on basic freedoms epitomised by libricide:

> If the fires of freedom and civil liberties burn low in other lands, they must be made brighter in our own. If in other lands the press and books and literature of all kinds are censored, we must redouble our efforts here to keep it free. If in other lands the eternal truths of the past are threatened by intolerance, we must provide a safe place here for their perpetuation.

Roosevelt returned to the theme again on what he had designated 'Victory Books Day', 17 April 1942, supporting the Victory Books Campaign:

> We all know that books burn – yet we have the greater knowledge that books cannot be killed by fire. People die, but books never die. No man and no force can abolish memory . . . No

man and no force can take from the world the books that embody man's eternal fight against tyranny of every kind. In this war, we know, books are weapons.[1]

The president was saying nothing that right-thinking individuals could not easily embrace. But the rhetorical power of this statement did require his fellow citizens to join him in a conscious effort to erase from their memory uncomfortably similar events in their own recent past. Less than twenty years before the pyres were lit in Germany, Americans themselves had been burning books, German books, with a righteous zeal. And in this, librarians had been happy to lead the way.

The declaration of war on Germany on 6 April 1917 had solved some difficult dilemmas for America's library community. The commitment to neutrality had been especially hard for the staff of public libraries, whose patrons wished to follow the European war, and were often strongly committed to the German or Allied cause. In 1915, the National German–American Alliance claimed 3 million members, many of whom were vociferous and demanding patrons of the public libraries. But in 1917, all hesitation was put aside. The die was cast, and Americans were expected to unite behind the common endeavour. The release of these pent-up tensions brought a surge of energy that focussed not just on the support of America's troops, but on the eradication of German influence on American life.[2]

When the European war had broken out in 1914, any discussion of the war by library staff was firmly discouraged. This advice was reversed when America entered the war. Library staff in Wisconsin, a state with a large German minority, were explicitly advised: 'The library, supported by public funds, is a part of the government which is at war with Germany and Austria and has necessarily taken sides . . . To be neutral is now to be disloyal.'[3] The legal framework was tightened to reinforce powers to restrict the circulation of any literature likely to damage the war effort. The postmaster general, who exercised considerable censorship powers through his control of what passed through the mail, promised to tolerate no campaign against conscription, enlistment, sale of liberty bonds or revenue collection. And indeed in 1917 the Post Office intervened to intercept all copies of Julius Koettgen's translation of *A German Deserter's War*. Clearly no one in the postmaster general's office had read this autobiographical memoir, which was profoundly hostile to the German cause. The Sedition Act, passed into law on 16 May 1918, prohibited any disloyalty, broadly conceived. There were more than 2,000 prosecutions under the act, resulting in 1,055 convictions.

Most damaging of all to the German-American community was a requirement, introduced in September 1917, that all foreign-language newspapers should provide the local postmaster with a sworn, correct translation of their text before publication. This was a major obstacle to continued publication. Leaving aside the issue of cost, the rhythms of newspaper publication, with its strict deadlines, made provisions of this sort particularly onerous. German papers could now be undermined by postmasters who found that they could not easily make time for such duties. At the beginning of the twentieth century, America supported an astonishing 800 German-language newspapers, a testament to an enormous wave of immigration from German lands that peaked in the 1880s, with almost 1.5 million new entrants in this one decade alone. Seven million Germans settled in America between 1820 and 1910. The First World War soured what had previously been a placid relationship. By the end of the war, half the German newspapers had closed.

The regulations put in place by the federal government were enthusiastically supported by both state and municipal authorities. Local authorities competed with one another to show the greatest zeal in the cause. In Sacramento, California, teachers were dismissed for not marching in the Liberty Loan parade. This sent a clear message to public librarians, and libraries adjusted their stock accordingly, assisted by *A Guide to Books for Patriotic Americans*, issued by *Publishers Weekly*. Patrons hurried to their local library to get news of the war, stimulating the first generation of instant histories that would become so popular in the Second World War. Seattle Public Library owned seventy-eight copies of Arthur Guy

Empey's *Over the Top* (1917); all had been checked out, and the library had a waiting list of almost 100 names.

At the same time as they stocked up with war books, librarians cleared their shelves of anything remotely pro-German. The atmosphere was now sufficiently toxic to induce librarians with German names to change them. The news that Benno Pfluger at the Cooper Union had lost his job on the pretext that he had not truly renounced his allegiance to the Kaiser when he became a naturalised citizen in 1912 had a suitably chilling effect.[4] Whatever scruples the library community had about the First Amendment, guaranteeing citizens the right to free speech, were now dissolved. Chicago Public Library banned all German books from the shelves, except those on non-military subjects published before 1914. Cleveland Public Library began 'retiring' objectionable books; Cincinnati Public Library sequestered all German-language books and cancelled subscriptions to German-language newspapers. The school board in Columbus, Ohio sold their German schoolbooks to a waste-paper company, topping them up with similar books from the public library. The music library in Hamilton, Ohio removed all works by German composers to the basement, which must have considerably restricted patron choice. Beethoven was now paying the price for the Kaiser's folly.

Librarians who stood out against the tide did so at peril of their jobs. E. H. Anderson, director of the New York Public Library, patiently explained that as a reference library, his institution was required to collect material on all sides for the use of scholars: 'If Satan should publish a pro-German book, we should certainly want it in our reference library.' This memorable if incautious flourish did not impress local opinion. On 13 April 1918, *The New York Times* carried a story headlined 'Pro-German books still circulated by Public Library'.

Through all of this the American Library Association stood mute; meanwhile, it willingly co-operated with the army's development of a list of books that it would not permit in army training camps. Inevitably this became a de facto deselection list for public libraries, and not all librarians were content simply to remove them to the basement. Many instances of book burning were the result of citizen activism: in Lewistown, Montana, all the German books from the local high school were publicly incinerated. Books were burned in popular demonstrations in Shawnee, Oklahoma as part of their Fourth of July celebrations, and in at least a dozen communities in Ohio. In March 1918, Hugh Tamisiea, director of the Missouri Valley Public Library, assured Herbert J. Metcalf, chairman of the Iowa branch of the Council of National Defense, that all pro-German material 'was burned last June'. Mary Wheelock of the Eldora Public Library reported, 'During the past summer and fall we had a number of pro-German books donated, but I burned them as they came.'[5]

It should be said that this level of public hysteria was not repeated when the United States joined the Second World War in 1941. Here public outrage was visited on the Japanese-American community, not on the book stock of the public libraries. In 1917, the democracies were in uncharted waters, and policy could always be distorted by an excess of enthusiasm. In the spring of 1918, libraries were requested, not unreasonably, to remove from their shelves all materials relating to explosives. But librarians were there before them: Jennie Doran of Denver Public Library had already recommended that the library turn over to the secret service the names and addresses of people who regularly consulted 'certain scientific or technical books'.[6] In the UK, it was the publishers who bore the brunt of the new restrictions, though most willingly gave themselves to the patriotic cause, not least because the demand for war books was as insatiable as in the United States. Friction was more a result of government bungling than malice. Among his many wartime publications Stanley Unwin published the *Polish Review*, a journal approved by the Foreign Office and largely financed by the British government; 250 copies were despatched to the Polish Information Service in New York. When these did not arrive, Unwin sent replacements, only for this consignment also to disappear en route. Unwin now sought an explanation, only to find, after much prevarication, that both shipments had been intercepted by the Post Office and handed to the War Office, which destroyed them. A Polish enemy of the editor had lobbied Field Marshal Sir Henry Wilson in Paris, and he had forbidden their distribution. The result was, in Unwin's caustic summary, that one government department had financed a periodical which a second department handed to a third to destroy.[7]

If the democracies could get so tangled in the complexities and moral contradictions of censorship, it was little wonder that the mid-century dictatorships should embrace it so wholeheartedly. The bonfires of 10 May 1933 were not, as some international apologists were inclined to argue, an example of student exuberance that got out of hand, but a carefully organised demonstration of Nazi power.[8] Their black and white division between authorised and proscribed literature represented their vision of Germany's future, and none of its traditional intellectual guardians would be permitted to stand in their way. Nor were they very much inclined to. Authors whose works had joined the conflagration hastened to find a refuge abroad, and if members of the library community mourned the assault on their collections, they grieved silently. Academics and librarians had in fact played a significant role in planning the burnings, which took place in ninety-three locations throughout Germany, including in most of its university towns.[9] Librarianship in Germany was a conservative profession, presided over by an ageing cohort of long-established placeholders, almost exclusively male. Its professional association made little attempt to resist or protest the Nazi reorganisation visited on all professional bodies. There were in any case more than a few active party members very happy to be installed in leadership roles, and many more joined the party soon after the Nazi takeover. Gustav Abb, a member of both the party and the SS, became director of both Berlin University Library and the Association of Research Librarians; in 1940 he was appointed head of the central administration of libraries in Poland.

For some former critics of the Nazis this involved a graceful pirouette, with little concern for dignity or self-respect. In the space of a few short months, the librarian Wolfgang Herrmann went from denigrating *Mein Kampf* (it contains 'no scientifically original or theoretically considered ideas') to helping prepare the book burning. Wilhelm Schuster, appointed in 1934 as director of

Nazi Book Burning 1933. Scenes such as this made a profound impact on opinion overseas, particularly in the United States. So much so that on the tenth anniversary the American Office of War Information could issue a poster using this picture captioned 'Ten Years Ago: THE NAZIS BURNED THESE BOOKS . . . but free Americans CAN STILL READ THEM.'

the Berlin municipal library and the school of librarianship, had in 1932 told a colleague that 'he would under no circumstances accept a book like Rosenberg's *Myth* for any library'.[10] This sudden enthusiasm did not necessarily make it easier to work out a coherent censorship regime. The Börsenverein (German Publishers and Booksellers' Association) was quick off the mark. In the issue of its trade journal for 13 May it published a declaration that the book trade should cease distributing works by a long list of authors. 'The literature of the bourgeois left in all its nuances' should be replaced by 'poetry in the old German sense'. This conservatism was quite attractive to many librarians, but it remained to be seen how far library patrons would embrace it. Wolfgang Herrmann, the caustic critic of *Mein Kampf,* worked his passage back to favour by compiling the first fiction blacklists. In July, a committee presented a compilation of works of 'belles lettres' that should be removed from the book market. Blacklists included not only Jewish authors but every figure of literary modernism. It meant, in effect, banning the entire Weimar canon.

This was a radical policy, and had it been rigorously enforced, it would have gutted many public library collections. Curiously, however, the various documents circulated among the library community failed to provide the clear guidance that would have helped librarians put these measures into effect. Herrmann's 'General Principles for the Compilation of Blacklists' of 1933 dealt in broad brushstrokes, more declamatory than a roadmap to action.[11] It offered a sweeping denunciation of 'Asphalt' literature – that is the experimental literature of Weimar – but should that apply to all imaginative writing of the period? And what of history, geography, biography and travel literature, all staples of the public library collections? Communist literature was of course proscribed, but then 'Not every Russian author is a cultural bolshevist. Dostoevsky and L. Tolstoy do not belong on the index.' The classics of English literature also generally escaped. Dickens remained a favourite under all forms of government, partly because his vivid sentimental narratives also offered an unsparing portrait of the deprivations of the Victorian underclass. The guidelines for public libraries and commercial libraries issued by the Kampfbund für deutsche Kultur (Militant League for German Culture) reiterated many of these points, while stopping short of precise recommendations: 'Specifically, it could not be the function of this list to enumerate the thousands of titles of trashy literature or other mediocre literature damaging to the spirit and the soul of the Volk.'

This denunciation of trash was a sentiment with which many British and American librarians would have agreed, but the German publishing industry was built on a mountain of cheap romantic novels and thrillers with a devoted following that encompassed readers from all social classes and political persuasions. As Joseph Goebbels recognised, in a society being shaped for war, an escapist literature of diversion and relaxation was an absolute necessity. So while the Nazis moved quickly to identify proscribed authors, it would have required more zeal and political skill than many librarians possessed to put into effect the thorough cleansing of collections, as Herrmann's elliptical instructions seemed to recognise: 'Technically, the cleansing should be done in stages. New acquisitions should be depended upon to fill the resulting gaps with German literature.'

It did not help that the banning of books became tangled in the usual chaos of competing authorities that characterised all aspects of the Nazi system of government. In December 1933, the Berlin publisher Wilhelm Jaspert wrote to the Propaganda Ministry to draw their attention to the fact that the more than 1,000 orders banning publications in the last year had been issued by no fewer than twenty-one different authorities. Even a year later, the head of the literature division in the ministry had to admit to Goebbels that the regulation of books was 'in a very sorry state'. There was still no 'unitary synopsis, and consequently no unified set of criteria and precepts' for the banning of books.[12] Even when it was decided that the Reich Chamber of Literature would have oversight, the Ministry of the Interior immediately reminded the police that these new arrangements did not nullify their own authority in this area. In 1934, the Bavarian Political Police issued a list of the publications they had seized or banned for distribution from commercial libraries, covering 6,834 titles by 2,293 authors. Circulating libraries were seen as key targets for the suppression of 'trash'. Between October 1936 and June 1937, Gestapo raids on around 5,000 bookstores and second-hand bookshops brought the number of confiscated items to around 300,000.[13]

All of this put publishers and booksellers on warning, but was far less helpful for librarians worried that their own collections contained inappropriate material. Publishers also had to comply with a complicated permissions procedure, which meant that eighteen months could elapse between a text being submitted for approval and its appearance. As the war progressed, the control of paper supplies imposed a further discipline on the publishing industry. Publishers also had to cope with their authors, not all of whom found it easy to adapt to the new political realities. The strain this imposed can be seen in the unravelling career of Hans Fallada.[14] The huge success of *Little Man, What Now?*

(1932), an almost unbearably sad picture of a small family struggling to make ends meet at the height of the Weimar economic
crisis, made Fallada into a public figure, and he reluctantly acqui-
esced with adjustments to the text necessary to keep the book
in print after 1933 (a thuggish stormtrooper became a football
rowdy). But Fallada did not join the party, which laid him open to
criticism in the Nazi press. In 1935 he was declared an 'undesirable
author', which banned his publisher from selling the translation
rights of his books abroad. This was a serious blow after the international success of *Little Man, What Now?*, which became a film
in America in 1934. *Wolf among Wolves* (1937), safely set in the
now-discredited Weimar period, won him a brief respite, and was
warmly praised by Goebbels. His reluctance to write the anti-
Semitic novel on which Goebbels insisted gradually soured their
relationship. Having missed the opportunity to escape abroad in
1938, Fallada sought anonymity in writing children's literature, but
his health deteriorated, particularly after his publisher and protector, Ernst Rowohlt, was dismissed from the Wehrmacht in 1943.
Fallada ended the war in a mental institution, an alcoholic and
drug addict, and it was here that he wrote *Alone in Berlin*, the book
which many regard as his masterpiece.

The sheer unpredictability of the system of regulation and
control was, as the Nazi hierarchy well recognised, the greatest
incentive to restraint and self-censorship. The censorship regime
was far kinder to authors long dead than to the living, as Fallada's tragic career would demonstrate, and with much of its talent
having taken refuge abroad, this was not a distinguished era for
German literature. But there was no doubt that in the six years
before the war, and for all its ambiguities and contradictions, the
regime had completely reshaped the German book world. Untan-
gling this mare's nest would pose significant problems to the Allied
powers in 1945.

In regulating the book industry, the Allied democracies could
muster nothing like the sense of purpose exhibited by the German
government. Indeed, it was important to the cause for which
they were fighting that democratic freedoms be retained, as far

as the exigencies of war allowed. In Britain, newspapers observed restraint in the publication of war news, and obeyed specific instructions (known as D-notices) to spike particular stories which were thought likely to have revealed information damaging to the enemy. Publishers too played their part and were generally not harassed. Having suffered in the first war through the vagaries of official regulation, Stanley Unwin, now a senior figure in the British publishing industry, made a point of praising the lack of government interference: 'There was no Gestapo lurking round any corner or behind any door. There was no official telling us what we might or might not print.'[15] Indeed, through their own choices, publishers, particularly those on the left, often pursued a greater ideological rigour than anything required by the authorities. In the pre-war period Victor Gollancz was fairly ruthless in excluding from the Left Book Club works that did not follow his own rather narrow definition of communist orthodoxy. George Orwell blotted his copybook by making the poor something less than heroic in his *Down and Out in Paris and London* (1933). It was published with a rare disclaimer from the publisher, disassociating itself from the author's views. Gollancz also rejected Orwell's memoir of the Spanish Civil War, *Homage to Catalonia* (1938), for publication under his label, because Orwell had signed up with the wrong communist faction in Spain.[16]

These were bad years for Orwell, a natural contrarian, who did not understand that the crisis of the times required simpler, clearer loyalties. Secker and Warburg printed 1,500 copies of *Homage to Catalonia* and there were still copies unsold when a new edition was issued in 1951. It must have been galling indeed to see Ernest Hemingway's own salute to the Spanish war, *For Whom the Bell Tolls*, selling half a million copies within months of its publication in 1940. Orwell's masterpiece, *Animal Farm*, was almost suppressed. Finished in February 1944, it was rejected by four publishers, including Gollancz. T. S. Eliot black-balled it at Faber and Faber, and Jonathan Cape abandoned it even after signing a contract, having been warned off by the Ministry of Information. With Soviet Russia still an ally, Orwell's portrait of the unscrupulous pigs was untimely. *Animal Farm* was not published until after the war, when Secker and Warburg once more came to the rescue. They were rewarded with 9 million sales by the end of the 1950s.[17]

A word in the ear from official sources, of the sort that had almost done for *Animal Farm*, also badly derailed the career of W. E. Johns, a decorated pilot from the First World War and now the best-selling author of the Biggles novels. Johns was also the editor of *Popular Flying*, a monthly journal that became so successful that in 1938 he was invited to add a weekly paper, *Flying*. Johns was an early critic of appeasement, and used his editorials to repeat these sentiments, climaxing in a trenchant denunciation of Chamberlain's betrayal of Czechoslovakia at Munich. Chamberlain did not take kindly to this sort of thing, and prevailed upon the proprietor, Lord Camrose, to dismiss Johns from the editorial chair of both titles.[18]

In Britain, at least two books were withdrawn from sale and pulped as a result of government intervention. The first of these was Arthur Bryant's *Unfinished Victory*, an untimely hymn of praise to the Nazi war machine, published in January 1940. It endorsed the Nazis' anti-Semitism, and the lyrical musing that the Third Reich might produce 'a newer and happier Germany in the future' was particularly unfortunate. A further twist was that the publisher, who apparently encouraged Bryant to persevere with the project, was the Conservative MP and future prime minister Harold Macmillan.[19] The book received a generally negative reception, and pressure grew for the author's arrest and possible internment under the Emergency Powers Act. The Oxford historian and wartime intelligence officer Hugh Trevor-Roper counselled against any drastic action. If the author was required to buy back the remaining stock, the problem would go away. Bryant clutched eagerly at this lifeline, retrieved the unsold copies, and settled down to enjoy the royalties of his soft-lens patriotic bestseller, *English Saga*. By the end of the year Bryant was dutifully referring to Hitler's rise to power as 'a terrible calamity'.[20]

Another title that fell foul of officialdom was the wartime bestseller *Diary of a Staff Officer*, published in February 1941. Widely read and admired (it went through six impressions in the space of three months), this day-by-day account of the doomed British

Expeditionary Force in France in May 1940 painted an unsparing picture of the chaos on the front line, and the disintegration of the French army. But it was not this that caused it to be withdrawn from circulation but the fear that an astute German reader might deduce from its text that the British had broken the German army's Enigma code. Reading the text today, this seems far-fetched. There is reference to a German wireless intercept on 20 May, and information of a German HQ conference on 26 May. But neither of these contain anything that would point to Enigma.[21] Officials might have been expected to take more offence to the less than complimentary references to the Allied leadership, particularly from a serving officer. Denis Argent, a soldier and an astute and voracious reader, thought it made clear 'the hopeless muddle and safety-first attitude that lost us that war'.[22]

Thus far, this elimination of the inconvenient or potentially indiscreet was a textbook study of how the British political establishment liked to work: behind the scenes, hush-hush. The problem was identified and taken care of. Newspaper proprietors might have known what was afoot (and in the case of the dismissal of W. E. Johns, were intimately involved), but they knew better than to publish a word in their newspapers. Those who found themselves on the receiving end of these interventions knew that public protest would only make their situation worse; they took their medicine and moved on. It was hardly a new phenomenon for authors to think ill of their publishers, or for journalists to be sacked. Arthur Bryant recognised his own folly and was no doubt grateful that nothing more came of it.

On the rare occasions when issues of censorship became a matter of public debate, the authorities moved swiftly to take control of the situation. The year 1940 witnessed some isolated incidents of agitation against the presence of leftist or pacifist periodicals in the public libraries. Sometimes this was the result of freelancing on the part of library staff. On 15 February 1940, Mass Observation diarist Tilly Rice confronted an employee at the county library, who admitted culling from a consignment of books intended for a local military camp anything likely to destroy their morale. 'Such as pacifist literature?' she enquired. 'Yes,' came the reply: 'there were two in the last lot that had to be put out.'[23] Oldham banned *Peace News*, the *Daily Worker* and *Tribune*; the *Daily Worker*, a paper sponsored by the Communist Party, was also removed from the shelves in Stepney, London. Yet these were isolated incidents. The *Library Association Record* reported with approval the trenchant response of the city librarian at Plymouth to similar agitation against communist literature. The newspapers and pamphlets would not be removed: freedom of speech was a valued privilege of democracy, and after all, *Mein Kampf* was approved reading for troops at the front.[24] This was indeed the case; there seems to have been a clear understanding that the more people who read *Mein Kampf* (or most likely, dipped in), the more committed they would be to the eradication of Hitlerism. *Mein Kampf* figured prominently on the Library Association list of recommended books for libraries in military camps and did steady business at the public libraries.

When, on 21 January 1941, the government closed down the *Daily Worker*, this had more to do with its relentless campaign for deep air raid shelters in London, a matter in which the authorities had proved to be seriously remiss. Five months later Hitler's armies invaded the Soviet Union, turning the strategic face of the war on its head. Libraries stocked up on books lauding the new ally, and readers devoured any book they could find on this surprising new friend. Dewsbury shopworker Kathleen Hey snapped up a Penguin volume of Russian short stories and Bernard Pares' *Russia* (1941), published as a Penguin Special.[25] In the years that followed, particularly while the tide of war continued to flow against British forces, there was genuine admiration for the fortitude and resilience of the Soviet troops. This was cunningly exploited by the press department of the Soviet Embassy in London, which distributed a regular digest called *Soviet War News*, a rather austere unillustrated news-sheet that was a fixture in British army libraries abroad, and widely circulated at home. In September 1942, the government permitted the *Daily Worker* to resume publication.

The most public cause célèbre was caused by the follies and misfortunes of a widely revered author, P. G. Wodehouse. This was

— SOVIET WAR NEWS —

PUBLISHED BY THE PRESS DEPARTMENT OF THE SOVIET EMBASSY IN LONDON

Phone : ABBEY 1470

Grams : SOVNEWS, LONDON

519-521, GRAND BUILDINGS

TRAFALGAR SQUARE, W.C.2

No. 100

November 4, 1941

ONE HUNDRED ISSUES OLD

A Message from I. M. Maisky,
Soviet Ambassador in Great Britain

This is the hundredth issue of "Soviet War News," which appears at the beginning of the twentieth week of the Soviet-German war.

I am very gratified by the reception which this daily bulletin has had in Great Britain. Its circulation has risen steadily, and we have received many letters of appreciation from all sections of the British people. The Press, also, has given us a generous measure of support.

There are trying days ahead for my people. But now more than ever we are certain of ultimate victory. If this bulletin, by creating a clearer understanding of the Soviet Union in this country, has helped in strengthening the ties between the two great anti-Fascist Powers in Europe, it will have fulfilled a valuable task.

OUR FINEST HOUR

"Pravda" writes :—

For a month fierce fighting has been in progress at the approaches to Moscow. The enemy has formed a battering ram of huge mechanised forces on the road to the capital and is gambling with large numbers. The German High Command thought that the blow which they were going to inflict at the beginning of October would be decisive. They miscalculated again.

During the first two weeks of their attack the German forces were able to force back our troops. This advance, however, was gained at a great price. New tanks and planes can be produced, especially when stolen European raw materials and machinery are utilised, but Hitler's man-power continues to decrease. Men cannot be produced in factories.

Ignoring his heavy losses, the enemy continues to thrust towards Moscow, throwing more soldiers into the flames of battle. He has staked all his cards on an effort to gain important successes before winter. We are entering a period of the most intense and heavy battles for Moscow. The enemy will try to penetrate our defences. In order to achieve this he is bringing up fresh forces.

To all our fighters in the Mozhaisk, Maloyaroslavets, Volokolamsk and Kalinin districts, to all our fighters defending the approaches to Moscow, we say that a tremendous historical task now faces us. Not one step back ! Each individual Muscovite, each Red Army man and commander defending positions on the roads to the capital must realise the full historical significance of a stubborn and active defence of the city.

The successful defence of Moscow will increase further the unrest on the German home front and hasten the demoralisation of the Nazi troops. By daring attacks, rapid annihilating counter-manœuvres and decisive counter-blows we must wear out and bleed the German Army to death, forcing it to strew new divisions of German dead in the approaches to Moscow.

By the courageous defence of Moscow we will point the way to victory to all our forces fighting on other fronts. Such is the great task in present and future battles.

These hours and the names of the heroes defending Moscow will be remembered with pride.

In the Arctic regions and Siberia, in the Soviet Far East and the Ural mountains, in the wild northern waste or the sunny republics of the Soviet south ; wherever, in the face of difficulties, new life, new factories, collective-farms and towns are springing up —Moscow is the guiding star. Moscow is not only our capital, not only our beloved and sacred town ; in Moscow every Soviet citizen feels that there is a small part of his heart and his aspirations. The name of Moscow is connected with the finest feelings of our Soviet people. That is why, in these days of great danger, in these days of fierce battles, Moscow and the Soviet people are one.

To-day, the life of every individual fighting in the approaches to Moscow or giving his knowledge and labour in the defence of the capital, belongs to our native land. We know that the battle will be hard, that it will demand sacrifices. The enemy is striking at our heart. Spare no efforts. Go into battle determined to win or to die.

In the future every Soviet citizen will be judged by the way he defended his native land at this time.

BATTLE FOR CRIMEA

The mid-day communiqué from the Soviet Information Bureau on November 3 states that during the night of November 2 Soviet troops fought the enemy on all fronts.

An earlier communiqué stated that during November 2 fighting was especially fierce in the Crimean sector.

On November 1, 28 German aeroplanes were destroyed for the loss of eight Soviet aircraft. On November 2, four German aircraft were destroyed near Moscow.

1

Soviet War News, published in London, was one of the great publishing successes of the war, and especially valued by Allied troops.

an issue that could not be resolved through the usual channels, because his idiocy was so egregious, and because the establishment was deeply divided in its response. Wodehouse was already a hugely published author when in 1934 he moved abroad to reduce his tax burden. Settled in Le Touquet in northern France, he was a generous host to members of the British Expeditionary Force in 1940 and was reassured by their optimistic predictions for the likely failure of any German assault. In consequence, he was slow to react when the German Panzers tore through Belgium. He and his wife were arrested at their home, and swiftly interned.[26]

Wodehouse had many fans in Germany, and in these difficult circumstances he found their flattering attentions very comforting. Always eager to please, he was easily persuaded to record some funny sketches to be broadcast to America. Wodehouse no doubt had the best of intentions, but the fact remained that by 1941 he was living in Berlin's most luxurious hotel, the Adlon, and broadcasting for the enemy. When this became known in Britain, the reaction was immediate. *The Times* and the *Telegraph* were bombarded with letters, some frankly contemptuous, others more supportive (as, for instance, from fellow author Dorothy L. Sayers).[27] More damaging to Wodehouse was a full-fronted assault from William Connor, Cassandra of the *Daily Mirror*, subsequently repeated on the radio in a BBC 'Postscript': 'I have come to tell the story of a rich man trying to make his last and greatest sale – that of his own country.' Wodehouse was compared unfavourably to British prisoners of war: 'Fifty thousand of our countrymen are enslaved in Germany. How many of them are in the Adlon Hotel tonight? . . . They suffer – but they do not sell out.' In the House of Commons, the foreign secretary, Anthony Eden, condemned Wodehouse for having 'lent his services to the Nazi war propaganda machine'.[28]

Public opinion was aroused, and councillors in Southport decided that all Wodehouse's books should be removed from the shelves of the public library and pulped. Colne, also in Lancashire, followed suit. But after protests, Colne decided the offending volumes should be placed in the reserve rather than destroyed. When the president of the Library Association argued that the 'lamentable utterance that he was flattered into making does not affect the quality of his writing at all', he seems to have spoken for the majority.[29] In the wise and measured judgement of the *Bookseller*, 'If he has forfeited the affection of his readers, let him pay the penalty, as he assuredly will, in loss of sales.'[30] When it came to it, readers did not want to deprive themselves of Jeeves and Blandings, while depriving Wodehouse of nothing at all. The author's own reckoning came at the end of the war, when he was arrested and detained in France. Although the British government declined to take further action, Wodehouse subsequently settled permanently in the United States.

This ragbag of semi-scandals and idiotic behaviour hardly amounts to rigorous censorship: indeed, many thought the government's control of book production in wartime should be more interventionist. Just as citizens sometimes appealed for more stringent rationing (cake, for instance), many voices pleaded for stricter controls on publishing. There was frustration that readers could not get the books they wanted, while shops were filled with 'trash'. Kathleen Tipper, a clerk in a shipping company and avid reader, was one who expressed these sentiments, complaining to a bookseller in the Strand that she had searched in vain for some works by John Galsworthy, best known for the *Forsyte Saga*, trying dozens of shops:

> I think, and she agreed, that it is disgraceful to allow printers to waste their paper allocation on the trashy books that are coming out in their thousands, whereas good books, classics and decent modern books, are nowhere to be had. She said they are offered this trash, much of it very expensive, or the alternative of having their shelves empty.[31]

In July 1942, the Library Association joined the fray. If the waste of food was unpatriotic and anti-social, then so too was the waste of paper: one man's liberty to read *The Corpse at the Brothel* should not interfere with another's to read *War and Peace*. This was a well-chosen example, because many popular classics including *War and Peace* (the quintessential wartime long read) were out of print for much of the war.[32]

The government's response was the Moberly Pool, a reserve of paper that could be released for individual projects that publishers could argue were 'essential'. Beneficiaries of this elastic and unspecific criterion ranged from additional copies of Shirer's *Berlin Diary* to legal textbooks, after Butterworth's publication on the government's behalf of thirty-eight acts resulting from wartime emergency powers had exhausted their paper quota. The Moberly Pool was always unpopular among publishers, even if they reluctantly made use of it. Publishers worried that the hunger for paper was shaping their lists in undesirable ways: that is, that they might abandon a project to which they were intellectually committed in favour of another book for which it was possible to argue the case for extra paper. This, of course, was exactly what did happen. In the course of their work the four-man panel considered 10,000 individual requests, all pleading their literary merit, high demand and the national significance of their works. The system succeeded, despite some persistent critics, thanks to the patent integrity of the panellists, exemplified by the refusal to grant a paper allocation to reprint Winston Churchill's much-admired biography of his ancestor the Duke of Marlborough, of which stocks were now exhausted. It is to his credit that the prime minister made no move to have this decision reversed: *Marlborough* remained out of print until 1947.[33]

What the Moberly committee could do nothing about was the voracious demand of government publishing, which routinely ate up more than its allotted allocation, and the so-called mushroom publishers, which sprang up outside the mainstream system and, scrounging paper where they could, were responsible for much of the 'trash' bemoaned by the established firms. By 1945, the Moberly committee was responsible for half of all the paper allowed for book publishing: by the time it was wound up in 1949, it had allocated 23.7 million tons of paper. With no sinister intent, it had become a major force shaping the output of books.

If we want to take the true temperature of wartime censorship in the UK, we should also give credit to what was permitted to be published. Throughout the war, critics of government policy were given a fairly free rein, most spectacularly with the publication of a fierce denunciation of pre-war appeasement policy, *Guilty Men*. Co-authored by three journalists, under the pseudonym Cato, it was written in four days, and hurried into print by Victor Gollancz in four weeks. Coming a month after Dunkirk, it was a controversial project. W. H. Smith and the wholesaler Simpkin & Marshall both refused to handle the book, but its notoriety ensured its success. It was sold on news-stands and street barrows and went through twelve editions in July 1940, selling 200,000 copies. By 1941 it was in its thirty-fourth impression. The authors, who included the future leader of the Labour Party, Michael Foot, chose anonymity not from any fear of reprisal, but because they all worked for Lord Beaverbrook, a strong supporter of appeasement, and writing the book breached their contract of employment.

The war years generated a steady stream of similarly sceptical works. In April 1942, the conscientious objector Denis Argent read both Alex Comfort's *No Such Liberty* (1941), a pacifist novel critical of Britain's heavy-handed policies towards evacuees (eviscerated in a review by George Orwell, unpredictable as always), and *Bless 'Em All: An Analysis of the British Army* (1942), by an anonymous Australian soldier who wrote scathingly of army routines and form-filling, the misuse of skilled soldiers, snobbishness and poor leadership.[34] Of course the marquee exhibit of British insouciance in the field of propaganda was permitting the publication and circulation of *Mein Kampf*. The heavily shortened version first published in English sold 53,738 copies and was placed third on the *Bookseller* bestseller list in November 1938. No unabridged version was available in the UK until 1939, when Hutchinson published James Murphy's translation. *The Times* remarked charitably that 'the translator has made an excellent job of 570 difficult pages.'[35] Despite a cover price of 8s 6d (which would have bought seventeen Penguins), sales were brisk, with 32,000 copies sold in the first few months and perhaps 150,000 overall. When war broke out in September, Hutchinson diverted the royalties to the Red Cross, responsible for the book service to British prisoners of war. In March 1940, Worcester Public Library reported to the *Library Association Record* that *Mein Kampf* was their best-borrowed nonfiction title. The library had so many readers on the waiting list that it increased the number of copies in circulation from four to twelve. In 1939, showing an admirable sense of balance, the Kent county library system reported circulating fifty-two copies of *Mein Kampf* and forty of Douglas Reed, *Insanity Fair* (1938), an account of the Nazi takeover in Austria and Allied appeasement of Hitler by *The Times*'s Central Europe correspondent.[36]

Those who made their way through the '570 difficult pages' deserve our congratulations, but there is no evidence that the exercise made any converts. The impact of *Mein Kampf* can be adequately gauged by a glance at the diary of physiotherapist Joan Strange, a committed Christian who deplored the war and was a member of the Peace Pledge Union. She was also heavily involved in organisations dedicated to helping refugees from Germany, and, probably influenced by their experiences, was patriotically committed to the Allied cause. In September 1939 a German friend, Sep Strasser, had sent Joan an English translation of *Mein Kampf*, confident that it would turn her into an ardent National Socialist. Her diary entry the following day is characteristically terse: 'Read a few pages of *Mein Kampf* in bed – much as I'd imagined. No possibility of Sep's prophecy coming true. Busy day at work.'[37]

In a world at war, every country recognised the need for some form of regulation of the flow of information, even those that were ostensibly neutral. The application of these regulations provide us with a few moments of low farce, none more absurd than the fate of W. E. Johns' *Worrals of the WAAF* (his new female heroine) in Ireland.[38] When war broke out in 1939, President Eamon de Valera had little choice but to declare Ireland's neutrality: memories were still raw from the independence conflicts, and anti-British sentiment was widespread. Behind the scenes, De Valera was more helpful, not least in permitting the Coastal Command squadron based on Loch Erne in County Fermanagh to overfly Irish airspace on Atlantic patrols, extending their range by a crucial 200 miles. But De Valera was well aware that many influential figures in his Fianna Fáil party harboured pro-German sympathies; his crafty strategy was to place these old colleagues in non-critical but important-sounding positions, which is how Frank Aiken came to be in charge of censorship. This was not a negligible role, since Ireland, respecting the Catholic origins of the state, issued regular lists of books forbidden to be imported into the country, because they were either 'in their general tendency indecent' or 'advocate the unnatural prevention of conception'. Most well-known British publishers at some point fell foul of these regulations, including Cape, Cassell, Collins and Constable, Heinemann, Methuen, Macmillan, Penguin and Putnam.[39]

Aiken fulfilled his responsibilities with commendable thoroughness, even to the extent of demanding to see proofs of the book review pages of the *Irish Times* before publication. Much to the fury of its pro-British editor, R. M. Smyllie, this resulted in more than a hundred reviews being hopelessly mutilated or banned altogether, including the review of *Worrals of the WAAF*. Smyllie bided his time before resubmitting the same review, but now under the title *Lotte of the Luftwaffe*. To no one's surprise the review was cleared for publication. Smyllie could now authenticate the pro-German sentiment of the censor's office and raised an enjoyable rumpus. The patriotic W. E. Johns would have enjoyed this farrago rather more than his own experiences of the subtle pressures exerted over authors in the purportedly free democracies.

PART IV

BOOKS FOR THE BOYS

10

TROOPS

When Allied troops hit the Normandy beaches on 6 June 1944, books were not far behind. Within a week, cartons of paperback books were among the myriad stores pouring into the bridgehead. In the days before D-Day, to calm nerves in the marshalling yards in southern England, one book from the popular Armed Services Editions of paperbacks had been issued to each of the American soldiers. Many passed the anxious hours steaming over to Omaha and Utah beaches reading, swapping books and reading more. The carnage on Omaha left a tragic number of dead; to survivors, one of the most macabre sights, as they pressed on from the beachhead, was the sight of gravely wounded soldiers propped up against the base of the cliffs, reading.[1]

One American officer engaged in the assault on France recorded his gratitude for this issue of books, though his fondness for Betty's Smith's blockbuster hit, *A Tree Grows in Brooklyn*, was not without peril:

> Our column got hit by a Boche battalion. We hit the ditches. Once I was tempted to read some more while they had us pinned down pretty tight. I was wounded slightly that day, too. The point is, I was thinking about that book even under pretty intense fire, it was that interesting. This is surprising because I never was in the West Point library except by order, but I liked that book.[2]

It is be doubted whether a detachment of GIs would have welcomed their commanding officer taking solace in a book while they looked to him to lead them out of a tight spot, but the wider point is clear: for a great number of soldiers, many not particularly bookish, books were a tangible reminder of a life away from the danger, monotony and the rigours of army life. Books were passed around the detachment, as soldiers eagerly awaited their turn for precious reading material. As one corporal bore witness, 'The books are read until they're so dirty you can't see the print. To heave one in the garbage can would be tantamount to striking your grandmother.'[3]

All the main protagonists in the Second World War made it a priority to supply their troops with reading matter; this, indeed, was one of the success stories of the war. From 1939 onwards, an effective co-operative effort between government agencies, publishers and public libraries ensured that books would follow the troops to Europe, to North Africa or island-hopping with the American forces in the Pacific. Public libraries ensured that travelling libraries would provide a regular service to isolated detachments manning anti-aircraft batteries or garrisons. The public pitched in by donating books from their private libraries to stock collections for the troops.

Of course, a Normandy ditch under fire was not ideal conditions for reading, though it makes for a good story. The reality of army life was often very different: long intervals of waiting, drilling, polishing kit and waiting for an engagement which often never occurred. Denis Argent, as a conscientious objector, was assigned to a non-combatant unit in Bedford, and the army struggled to find them worthwhile employment. With sometimes as little of two hours of army duties in a day, Denis read voraciously, mostly from the local public library.[4] This was an unusual case, but it was a fact of army life that each fighting army was accompanied by a mass of support units whose responsibilities for maintenance, transport, clerical duties, communications or supply meant that they were never destined to see action. Service abroad, far from home, left many hours for reading, for some soldiers for the first time in their adult lives.

The provision of reading material for troops in the First World War was less successful, but still something to which the army, and civilian bodies, devoted a great deal of energy. When the United States entered the war in April 1917, providing 'books for Sammies' heading first for the training camps and then to the Western Front was one of the most tangible ways in which citizens could show their support.[5] At first communities organised their own collections for local detachments, before the American Library Association, prompted by the government, took on the role of co-ordinating a national effort in August 1917. The August issue of *War Library Bulletin* alerted members to these new responsibilities:

> The ALA has been asked by the War Department to under-take the collection, distribution and circulation of reading matter in the thirty-two principal army camps ... Every library should give the widest publicity to this campaign of book collection, through the press, through slips put in books circulated, through the churches, the movies, and through other agencies co-operating in the same work.[6]

The response to the first book drive of September 1917 was disappointing, as the libraries worked out how best to engage with their local communities, but a second drive in March 1918 netted more than 3 million volumes, two-thirds of them fiction, not least because librarians were prepared to adopt more forthright tactics, notifying householders in advance that a collection cart would be coming their way. Through this coerced generosity, libraries could be established in more than 500 locations, including military hospitals. The largest proportion of books was sensibly assigned for the libraries established in the thirty-six major training camps around the United States. Almost all the new recruits would spend a period of three months training here, before shipping off to the front, and the libraries were sure to be well used. The Carnegie Foundation had allocated $320,000 for the erection of the library buildings, each providing space for 10,000 books and 200 readers. They were subsequently stocked with both the gifted books and others bought from funds provided by the army. The ALA's Library War Service became a high-profile organisation, chaired by the Librarian of Congress, Herbert Putnam, and in addition to the donations, it raised more than $5 million to spend on new stock. The ALA played a huge role in shaping the camp collections, not least by seconding experienced librarians to act as volunteers in the camp libraries. The names of those who offered themselves for this service read like a *Who's Who* of the leaders of the profession in these years. Their brief service in the camps helped craft reading facilities which by any estimation were of high standard.[7]

The war would end before more than a modest proportion of the books donated could be sent abroad, but the efforts of the ALA and citizen donors did result in the establishment of the American Library in Paris, founded in 1920 with some of the late-arriving donations, a beacon of American culture in a Europe battered by war. The enthusiastic commitment of the American public to the rebuilding of Louvain University library, destroyed in the German army's march through Belgium, was also a notable signal of America's new commitment as a bastion of civilised values in troubled times.

In Britain, the Library Association was able to exercise far less influence over the provision of books for troops than the ALA in the United States. Debilitated by budget cuts and the loss of staff to the armed forces, the public libraries concentrated their limited resources on making appropriate facilities available to the domestic war effort.[8] The mammoth task of supplying books to troops abroad was largely ceded to the voluntary sector. First into the breach were long-established organisations such as the Red Cross and the YMCA. The Red Cross dealt primarily with military hospitals, where its services were soon tragically much required. The YMCA established a string of mobile libraries and reading huts in Britain and near the front line in France. Nothing in the nineteenth-century experience of war had prepared charitable organisations for military operations of this scale and duration. The main burden of the supply of reading matter would be managed by the Camps' Library organisation and the Fighting Forces Book Council. The establishment of a director general of voluntary organisations allowed the War Office to provide some degree of co-ordination between the voluntary groups, and help with the logistics of supply, providing not only books and magazines, but

A YMCA Reading Room in Beauvais for troops from New Zealand, 1918.
Periods of recuperation away from the front offered the best opportunity
for reading and catching up with correspondence, though this carefully
posed picture may not reflect the troops' top priorities for leisure time.

also food and recreational facilities. The very effective field post
service was handled by the army itself.

In the course of the war, the Camps' Library administration
was able to distribute more than 16 million books and magazines
to soldiers and prisoners of war. Many were examples of middle-
brow Edwardian fiction, the sort of books that members of the
donor classes allowed themselves for relaxation at home. The
Camps' Library was also able to exploit contacts in the publishing industry to secure publishers' remainders from some firms. The
Camps' Library stock was distributed in 'trench boxes' of approximately 500 titles per unit.

Officers, and to a limited extent enlisted men, also received
books in parcels from home. The social divide between the officer
class and troops was evident not only in this aspect of trench
reading, but also in one of the most eccentric schemes of the
war, *The Times* broadsheets. This endeavour was the brain child

of Lionel Curtis, a well-networked member of the British foreign policy establishment, apparently inspired by a group of young officers on leave, 'reading aloud great passages of English literature from books on my shelves'.[9] By despatching carefully selected excerpts from the classics of English literature, it was hoped that this experience could to some extent be replicated on the front line, as a memory of a better and more civilised world. Geoffrey Dawson, editor of *The Times*, was enthusiastic, and Sir Walter Raleigh, Merton professor of English literature at Oxford University, was recruited to make the selections. Each series comprised thirty-six broadsheets, with excerpts from Shakespeare, Dickens and Jane Austen (not to forget Tolstoy's *War and Peace* and the *History of the Peloponnesian Wars* by Thucydides). The English poets were well represented. Sets of six extracts in a pictorial envelope were sold for one penny.

Launched in August 1915, with more than 1 million sales, the scheme terminated abruptly with broadsheet number 180 in December. One can easily see why. To those not brought up in this tradition of English letters, these disconnected gobbets of tightly packed text would have meant very little: they were essentially nostalgic memories of home and schoolroom for public-school boys, likely better provided with reading material in any case than the enlisted men with whom they shared the front line. Even so, their time was short, both in the general sense that they were kept ceaselessly active in the duties layered upon them by superior officers, and because many would soon be killed leading their men in one of the ill-conceived charges across no-man's-land. The average newly minted second lieutenant posted to the front would be killed within six weeks of arrival.[10]

When it came to the enlisted men, there was an obvious mismatch between the books despatched from the Camps' Library depots and the demographic intended to benefit from this generosity. Many of the books collected were donated from houses in the middle-class suburbs and towns of the shires. The British army was recruited overwhelmingly from the industrial cities.[11] At this date, books were not a major feature in working-class homes, where the most likely scenario would have been a small collection of books, consisting largely of reference works and a Bible, tucked out of sight upstairs.[12] Books for recreational reading, usually for the women of the family, came mostly from commercial libraries, to which they would be returned when finished. The worn-out copies of Victorian and Edwardian literature or volumes of sermons donated from more prosperous homes would not strike an immediate chord with the Tommies marching to war. The Red Cross, in fact, retained much of this material for military hospitals, rather than sending it to the front. So, if we ask ourselves the question, 'what did Tommy read?' then the answer, at least as far as front-line troops were concerned, was not very much at all. In first place, by a considerable margin, would have been letters from home, followed at some distance by newspapers. Of books there is very little sign.

This is hardly surprising; the trenches were unsympathetic environments for literary pursuits: routinely flooded with malodorous mud, the dugouts tunnelled out of the sides, rat-infested and dark. Who would have wanted to sit down with a book, even if guard duty, fatigues and other time-consuming duties left any opportunity? Periods of recuperation behind the lines offered a more congenial environment, but here too Tommies had other priorities: writing home, getting drunk and sexual encounters which, if they contracted venereal diseases, offered some chance of hospitalisation or a ticket home. It is scarcely a surprise that most of the hard evidence we have of British troops reading comes from hospital wards, which offered precisely the circumstances (enforced leisure, boredom) conducive to the reading habit.

This is not, it must be said, the consensus of those who have written on life in the trenches, which takes a more optimistic view, even to the extent of suggesting that the novels of John Buchan were so ubiquitous that discarded dustjackets of *The Thirty-Nine Steps* fluttered around no-man's-land. But there were many such myths of the trenches, such as the Angel of Mons, miraculously intervening to save the British troops at a decisive stage in the battle. Given how minutely the experience of the trenches has been examined, reading in the trenches may be one case where absence of evidence does indeed represent evidence of absence. We know far more about games of football, boxing matches and front-line theatricals than reading. As the junior officers charged with vetting letters home would have been painfully aware, the general standard of functional literacy among the troops was often extremely low: this would be one respect in which the transformation between 1914 and 1939 was most profound.[13]

The question we probably need to address is not so much what Tommy read, but what he liked to have read to him. The answer was trench newspapers, news-sheets edited and published by the troops for their own entertainment. *The Wipers Times* is the best-known example, but during the war, more than a hundred trench newspapers were published in the Allied and Dominion detachments, with many more in the French army.[14] Articles were 'bright, brief and topical', exactly the sort of thing that could easily be shared and spark a discussion in a platoon engaged in the endless digging, lugging sandbags, sharing out of rations, brewing tea and other chores that filled up every waking moment. Jokes, songs, gossip, digs at French allies, complaints about food, drills and pointless fatigues made up the rest of the copy. As the *RMR Growler* of the 14th Canadians promised, 'Our columns are open to every grouch in the Battalion, and a growl on any subject, whether the grievance be either real or fancied, will be joyfully received and have immediate insertion.'[15] Their popularity owed a great deal to disdain for the newspapers at home: their jingoism, their refusal to report bloody setbacks, their presentation of a stereotype soldier, courageous, undaunted, sardonic and endlessly cheerful. To the real-life soldiers, living in squalor, exhausted and intermittently terrified, this travesty was an insulting addition to their other burdens.

In the Second World War, both America and Britain seemed initially to think that the correct recipe was more of the same. In Britain, the public libraries were especially keen to make up for their underwhelming performance during the Great War. Aside from their role as information centres and prompt and successful action to ease the way of evacuees into local life, the public libraries, encouraged by the Library Association, engaged themselves swiftly in providing books for the troops. The first priority was equipping army camps and RAF stations in their vicinity. With the camps they were on familiar territory, and were soon equipped with a booklet, *Books for the Services*, published by the National Book Council in October 1939. While readily aware of the demand for light reading, some of the older librarians took a little time to adjust their expectations to the reading tastes of young men, a group not prominent among their most regular clients. And some old habits died hard: all public libraries insisted on a guarantor before issuing a card to temporary residents such as servicemen. Normally their unit officer would sign off the required chit.

These necessary formalities apart, there certainly was no lack of goodwill. Several libraries, like the one in Kirkcaldy, Fife, adjusted their working hours, and even opened the reading room on Sunday to accommodate men and women in uniform who could not easily get off base during the working week.[16] The public libraries also made it a priority to provide boxes of books for small outlying stations, which would be exchanged every few weeks for new stock. The Hertfordshire county library put together special collections made up of Penguins, Collins Classics and Nelson Classics: in the case of the Penguins they were almost certainly specially purchased for this purpose. Many libraries set up a mobile service to tour temporary billets: by 1941, the Liverpool library was running four vans to take books to several hundred sites where troops were stationed. These services were maintained throughout the war; in the case of the Kent county library service this involved regular supplies for almost 200 stations. When libraries could not meet demand from their own resources, they turned to the library community for help: in May 1940, Derbyshire county library service appealed for novels, especially Wild West and detective stories. Penguin books and magazines would also be much appreciated.[17]

It was swiftly evident that the needs of the troops could not be met simply by transferring books from the general library stock, particularly at a time when home demand was also rising. The result, inevitably, was the announcement of a Books for Troops campaign, urging the general public to look out suitable materials from their shelves and cupboards. As was always the case, this produced a great deal of unusable material, in the case of Derbyshire in 1942, generating 44 tons of paper for salvage. Conversely, when the government embarked on its major paper salvage drive in 1943, the Library Association made a crucial intervention to ensure that everything donated was not pulped before trained librarians had had the chance to examine the material for books that should be preserved. The dangers of too indiscriminate generosity in this regard had been dramatised by a discovery of a rare sixteenth-century Bible among the materials donated for salvage. The Library Association had been rather controversially frozen out of the managing committee of the Service Libraries and Book Fund, but in developing the protocols that should guide the examination of the materials donated for salvage they were allowed to take the lead. The result was that of the more than 80 million books donated to salvage an estimated 12 million volumes were saved and carefully sorted to rebuild libraries damaged by bombing or to be despatched to the Services Book Depot for distribution to the troops. Trade handbooks, financial directories, maps, street guides and industrial photos were retained on behalf of the Ministry of Economic Warfare; books in foreign languages were put aside for rebuilding libraries on the soon-to-be-liberated European continent. Genuinely antiquarian items, meanwhile, were offered to the main county library collection.[18]

When, in February 1945, the Library Association offered its own report card on the libraries' performance in the war, there was much of which they could be proud. In contrast to the first war, staff had shown a good deal of flexibility and imagination; they had also worked extremely hard, keeping the libraries open longer and serving an expanded clientele with far fewer staff. Between January 1941 and December 1942, 6 million books and 5 million magazines had been distributed to troops. As the war wore on, and thoughts turned to post-war reconstruction, the public libraries also pitched in to support the army's own education programme, publishing bibliographies of their holdings that might be relevant to the courses. It was a record of which they could be rightly proud.[19]

In the United States, the provision of books was recognised as an urgent problem, not least because the camp libraries of 1917–19 had deteriorated significantly in the intervening two decades.[20] In

1921, the new Army Library Service had inherited responsibility for 228 libraries, but the funds necessary for their upkeep had been progressively trimmed back during the years of peace. By 1941, they were essentially moribund. Little new stock had been added, and with the army's consent, many of the more attractive books had been transferred to local public libraries. Policymakers were also acutely aware, after the Japanese attack on Hawaii, that this would be a global war, with commensurate logistical problems for the delivery of the reading material appropriate for a citizen army.

The ALA's response was the Victory Books Campaign, placed under the direction of one of the most able and dynamic members of the library community, Althea Warren of the Los Angeles Public Library. Warren was determined that every effort would be made to alert Americans to the urgency of the task: 'It is going to take a full month of radio spots, pictures, stories, editorials and half a million printed posters to get the mass mankind of our country to give in quantity.'[21] Given the commitment to raise 10 million books in 1942, it would need all this and more. An initially sluggish response, as in the first war, was berated by the press, and in May 1942 the target had been met.

The problem was that, as before, a high proportion of the books were not fit for purpose. Many were battered or filthy; others were simply not the sort of material that troops wanted to read. The most trenchant critic of the Victory Books Committee was Isabel DuBois, head of the library section of the navy. DuBois oversaw 1,000 navy libraries and eight hospitals. Having opposed the Victory Books scheme in the first place, she saw no reason to change her mind. 'Are gift books worth it?' she asked. If the titles she had received were

> a sample of the books which have been sorted by librarians, it is the worst indictment of my profession I have ever seen. These were the same titles which I discarded in 1917 and 1918 and the 25 years in between has not made them any more valuable ... When I think of the tremendous waste in transportation and handling, it leaves me simply appalled.[22]

This hit home. Recruiters were acutely aware that 250,000 potential soldiers had been rejected from the service on grounds of illiteracy. A random selection of redundant polite fiction did not meet the needs of the new army or navy. In a global conflict, DuBois' last point about logistics was particularly pertinent. The miscellany of hardcover books and magazines donated provided useful material for camp libraries in the Unites States, even though only half the 10 million items donated were ultimately thought suitable for use. But for transportation abroad, these books were not well adapted. The authorities were alerted to this when the general in charge of a fleet embarking for the North African campaign left the books on the quayside pleading lack of space. And in the Pacific war, clearly destined to be a long-drawn-out campaign of island-hopping, such books were even more inappropriate. A new solution was needed. The Victory Book Campaign was terminated in 1943 and left-over books dumped on to the Japanese internment camps in the western states.

Fortunately, help was on hand, thanks to the quiet revolution in the publishing industry, with the coming of the paperback, championed by Penguin in England and Pocket Books in the United States. By 1941, when the major London publishers, acting together as a consortium, challenged Penguin's virtual monopoly, Penguin had made not only considerable profits, but also a signal contribution to the war effort. Penguin books were a popular addition to the travelling libraries supplied to outlying units, such as anti-aircraft batteries in Britain. In 1940, 200,000 Penguins were shipped out to the men of the British Expeditionary Force in France. Allen Lane, left in sole command of Penguin when his two younger brothers joined the navy, was always on the lookout for new ways of developing his market, and in 1943 launched his Forces Book Club. For an annual subscription of £3, ten titles a month, specially chosen for this bespoke service, would be mailed to individual officers or units abroad. The Forces Book Club was in fact one of Allen Lane's rare failures. Either the prescriptive nature of the monthly selection or the choice of books was not alluring enough to appeal to anyone but a limited officer class of habitual readers. He was warned as much by a unit commander who asked for 'a more liberal supply of fiction and adventure books, as we find that the majority of the books are of a heavy type, and seldom find any demand by the men of this unit'. Lane admitted defeat:

> You mentioned three categories stressed by you – 'warm' fiction, westerns and crime – and as we have never published any books in the first two categories, and not more than two titles a month out of a total of ten for the last category, I can readily understand how unsuitable as a whole our list must be.[23]

Penguin completed the contracted year, though printing only a fraction of the 75,000 copies per title originally envisaged, and then closed down the Forces Book Club.

The Penguin contract with the army for the Forces Book Club was a coup Allen Lane plotted with long-time crony Bill Williams, now comfortably installed at the Army Bureau of Current Affairs: it brought with it a precious allocation of paper from the government reserve. The news of this exclusive contract brought predictable indignation from other publishers, who attempted to challenge the Penguin monopoly with a service library scheme of their own. Williams thought Lane should not be overly concerned. 'If I know anything of the PA [Publishers Association] I think we may well be in for a protracted correspondence and at the end of it get nowhere.'[24] That, as far as histories of the triumphant march of Penguin books would have it, is pretty much the end of the story. But in fact, the publishers' consortium did launch their own paperback strand, Guild Books, with titles competitively priced at 6*d*, 9*d* and 1*s*. The participants in the new Publisher's Guild, which included Cape, Cassell, Murray, Faber and Heinemann, had considerable firepower; possessing as they did the copyright of a large proportion of contemporary fiction, they could supply the sort of materials craved by soldiers. In due course they issued their own Services Edition as a purely commercial venture.

Paperbacks made up an ever-increasing proportion of troops' libraries, indispensable in the camps of North Africa, on board troopships or in the small collections troops carried with them in their kitbags. When, from time to time, librarians serving in the forces wrote to the Library Association with their experiences of libraries in the field, paperbacks were a ubiquitous presence. One, charged with setting up a troopship library for 1,700 men, put out an appeal for donations from those on board that brought in forty Penguins to augment titles from the Everyman's Library and Nelson Classics. P. Hepworth, formerly of Sheffield Public Library, was stationed at a major service facility in the North African desert. This had three libraries, including an Information Room stocked with twenty copies of the *Egyptian Mail* (an English-language daily paper), miniature airmail issues of the *Manchester Guardian* and *The Times* and the ever-popular *Soviet War News*. Readers could also find Pelicans such as Sharp's *Town Planning*, Ifor Evans's *English Literature* and a Penguin Herodotus; these tended to vanish and would, in Hepworth's view, have been better off in the station's main lending library. The reading room next door had more Penguins of a purely recreational nature.[25]

With so much creative energy in the industry, soldiers were spoilt for choice. In 1945 Hutchinson gave away a million paperbacks as a free victory gift for the forces, which suggests they must have had a large stock on hand. My own copy of the Guild Books Services edition of Robert Gibbings's *Sweet Thames Run Softly* (1944) was repurposed after the war when the government sold off surplus stock. The stern injunction on the back cover, 'this book must not be resold', was now superseded by a label on the front indicating that the stock had been transferred to W. H. Smith and would be sold for one shilling.

By far the most famous and successful venture in providing books for the troops was the Armed Services Editions (ASE) published in the United States: this built effectively on the ongoing paperback revolution. When the Victory Books Campaign was suspended in 1943, the future of book provision for the troops lay in the hands of the Council on Books in Wartime, an industry body established in March 1942. It took some time to find its direction; initially it was, in the words of one observer, 'a committee in search of a project'.[26] Gradually opinion converged around the idea of a series of specially printed paperbacks, to be distributed free to troops in the field. Publishers would nominate possible titles, which would then be examined by members of the council. When they had made their choices, these would then be submitted to the army and navy, in the persons of Raymond Trautman and DuBois, for approval. The emphasis was on variety: a good portion of the list would be contemporary fiction, but with plenty of historical novels, mysteries, books of humour and Westerns: the evergreen Zane Grey led the way, with nine titles in the series. But there was also a rich layer of modern literary fiction, Hemingway, Dorothy Parker, Sinclair Lewis and John Steinbeck, who featured with eight titles. There was a smattering of poetry, from Longfellow and Shelley to Rupert Brooke and Robert Frost. The classics were well represented: Dickens with his three most accessible titles, *Oliver Twist*, *David Copperfield* and *The Pickwick Papers*, Thackeray, Conrad (five titles) and Voltaire's *Candide*. The grunt who drew Thoreau, Sterne or Tolstoy might well have gone looking for an exchange with Bram Stoker's *Dracula* or any one of the six books by Mark Twain reproduced in the series.

A strong feature of the list was the presence of English authors, Somerset Maugham (six titles), J. B. Priestley, A. J. Cronin, a best-seller on both sides of the Atlantic, and Richard Llewellyn's *How Green Was My Valley*. The all-time favourite, with no fewer than twelve titles, was C. S. Forester of Hornblower fame. Non-fiction was added to the series much more sparingly, with books about war, and especially the current war, making up only a tiny fraction of the 1,322 titles in the series. The non-fiction titles included Embree's *Japanese Nation*, issued during the occupation, and Dietz, *Atomic Energy in the Coming Era*. The war books included a selection from Homer's *Odyssey* and highlights from *Yank*, the soldier's magazine.

A special effort was made to push science, with *Science Goes to War*, *The Science Yearbook* of 1944 and 1945, and *Men of Science in America*. More consequential was the decision to include titles by Edgar Snow, the journalist responsible for the book that introduced Mao Zedong to the West, and Howard Fast, the post-war bête noire of the Committee of Un-American Activities. Soldiers seem especially to have enjoyed *The Postman Always Rings Twice*, a salacious and violent crime novel banned in Boston, but printed twice in the ASE series. *Forever Amber*, a semi-pornographic historical romp banned in fourteen US states and Australia, also seems to have found favour. It topped the US bestselling list in 1945 and went on to sell 3 million copies. Another striking choice for a segregated army was Shirley Graham's *There Was Once a Slave*, the story of Frederick Douglass.

Most innovative of all was the format, a paperback approximately 16 by 11 centimetres, bound along the short side. The text was set in two columns for ease of reading. Initially 50,000 copies would be published of thirty titles per month. The first 1.5 million copies were distributed in September 1943, and print runs rose steadily as their reputation spread among the troops. By the time the scheme was discontinued in September 1947, the council had distributed some 122 million copies of 1,322 titles to millions of serving men all around the globe. This was in itself a tribute to the US forces' mastery of military logistics. Bundles of books were flown into the Anzio bridgehead in Italy; others were delivered by parachute to garrisons on small Pacific islands. Charles Rawlings, a war correspondent for the *Saturday Evening Post*, witnessed a distribution on a Pacific station – an orderly queue filing past to take one book at a time: 'No time to shop and look for titles. Grab a book, Joe, and keep goin', you can swap around afterwards.' As for the soldier who grabbed *A Tree Grows in Brooklyn*, 'the guy that got that one howled with joy'. Rawlings was pleased to be included in the allocation when he travelled with the GIs on a troopship to Australia: 'We read out twenty-five blessed days on them.'[27]

A Tree Grows in Brooklyn was an established bestseller, and a real forces favourite. An overnight sensation, this sentimental tale of a young woman growing up in New York in the first decades of the century was one of the most successful titles of the war. The author, Betty Smith, received many letters from readers, including one from a young Marine, convalescing from malaria: 'I have read it twice and am halfway through it again . . . Every time I read it, I feel more deeply than I did before.'[28] The small landscape format turned out to be ideal for reading in a hospital bed. Many authors were delighted and honoured to be included in the series, and for

Scott Fitzgerald it led to a positive revaluation of his masterwork, *The Great Gatsby*. After a disappointing reception on its publication in 1925, its inclusion as an Armed Services Edition rescued it from comparative obscurity. Among the books that accompanied the troops onto the beaches of Normandy in 1944 were Lloyd C. Douglas, *The Robe*; the biography of Paul Revere by Esther Forbes; *The Adventures of Tom Sawyer*; and, inevitably, *A Tree Grows in Brooklyn*. Many of the books published as Armed Services Editions were titles that had been banned in Germany. It was one of the happy ironies of the book in wartime that they would arrive back in Germany in the knapsacks and fatigue pockets of the young soldiers of the liberating armies.

With this lyrical picture of the soldier-reader, we can celebrate one of the most imaginative and successful initiatives of the war. But the authorities were smart enough to know that it did not meet the needs of every GI: for all the popularity of the Armed Services Editions, by far the most popular reading was miniaturised versions of weekly magazines (*Time, Newsweek, Life*) and comic books. The Second World War coincided with the golden age of the comic. Superman made his debut in 1938, and Captain America took on Hitler on the cover of his first issue (March 1941) even before America entered the war. After Pearl Harbor, just about every comic-book hero, including Superman and Batman, took a break from their usual villainous opponents to concentrate on saboteurs, spies and evil Axis scientists.[29] The army brought comic books in bulk to distribute along with more than twenty sports, hobby and political magazines. For the American soldier, it was not all Scott Fitzgerald and Somerset Maugham.

The Second World War also brought an efflorescence of forces' newspapers, much more professionally produced than the trench newspapers of the First World War. The *Orkney Blast* was one of the first to be published, with weekly eight-page issues in an elegant broadsheet format. Much of the British army spent the years between 1941 and 1944 in camps in Britain, where access to newspapers was relatively straightforward. This was less true of the Scottish islands, and the 60,000 service personnel stationed around the fleet at anchor in Scapa Flow were unlikely to be

Indian NEWS REVIEW

VOL. 1   CAIRO, SATURDAY, SEPTEMBER 30th, 1944   No. 43

"GREEN DEVILS" FLEE

INDIANS IN EIGHTH ARMY'S DRIVE

GERMAN RETREAT IN ITALY

IN the mountains just west of the Adriatic sector, Kesselring pulled out his men so quickly that the Eighth Army lost contact with them.

For the first time the German "Green Devil" parachutists became disorganised and fell back in disorder.

The German retreat is now into an ever-widening plain. British and Indian troops in the mountains on the left flank of the sector are driving to debouch on the plain west of San Arcangelo, which is itself west of Rimini. They have crossed the river Rubicon.

In their 30 miles advance since the break through the Gothic Line a month ago, the Eighth Army has taken nearly 9,000 prisoners, and inflicted a total of 25,000 casualties.

On the Fifth Army front, although the vaunted Gothic Line defence zone has been smashed on a wide front, the Germans are now attempting to make up for the loss of prepared positions by reinforcing the critical central sector with seasoned troops.

NEW DEFENCE LINE

A desperate attempt is being made to set up a line along the forward slopes of the high ground north of the Gothic Line.

American troops repelled three fierce counter-attacks in the vicinity of Monte La Fine and Pratolungo, 20 miles south of Bologna. Two miles south of Castel del Rio, street fighting is reported in Moraduccio-on-Firenzuola.

The key features of the terrain on both sides of the road have been taken.

They occupied San Benedetto, 20 miles south-west of Forli, and captured Monte Scarabattole and Monte Carnevale, near Marradi.

Indian Prisoners in Epinal Released

A number of Indian troops imprisoned in the French town of Epinal have been released following the capture of the town by units of the 3rd Army, says "Reuter's" special correspondent with the United States forces in France.

ROYAL SUSSEX HONOURED

Brighton is to confer the Freedom of the Borough on the Royal Sussex Regiment on October 27.

ADVANCE IN ITALY

The town of Tavoleto was not taken without comparatively heavy fighting. The enemy held on well. Gurkhas and Camerons, supported by tanks and artillery, pushed him out. A Sherman in a side street of Tavoleto.

THE JEMADAR'S STORY . . .

Mount Citerna Fell in Night Attack

ON the top of a mountain I met Jemadar Fateh Mohamed, writes an Indian Army observer. He told me a story.

It was the story of the capture of Mount Citerna, a conical thickly-wooded feature forming a stronghold in the Gothic Line.

"My company attacked the hill under the cover of darkness," said the jemadar. "Two platoons were leading. The enemy, I suppose, heard our footfalls, but he held his fire until the leading troops were upon his wire defences only some 50 yards from five machine-gun posts. Hand grenades came rolling down the hill and burst amongst us. Two Sepoys were killed and others were wounded. The fire was accurate, and we had to think of a new plan.

"The Colonel Sahib had come up and upbraided us. If we could not capture that hill, we should never manage far bigger features that lay ahead. So we attacked again and made it."

"But how did you do it the second time?" I asked.

A grin appeared on the jemadar's tired face. "We are Indians, Sahib," he said. "We can move silently at night.

OUT THROUGH WIRE

"One platoon crept to the right and another to the left. A third put four bren guns on the ground to give covering fire. Our two-inch mortars ranged on the hill crest.

"Our platoon cut its way through the wire, although there was enemy fire and more grenades were rolled down on us. When our men charged to the top, fifteen Germans surrendered.

"One of our runners, Ghaus Mohamed, shot two Germans on his way back from Company Headquarters. Five more Germans were killed that night.

"We found the enemy had almost expended his stock of grenades on us, but he still had plenty of machine-gun bullets. He did not use them."

This was the jemadar's story. While he talked, his men were putting a captured enemy dugout into a state of defence.

Over a period of months, the Germans had hewn away a rock and made a cave from it. From it, deep connecting trenches led to weapon pits which covered all possible approaches to the mountain top.

JAPS BREAK CONTACT

Fifth Division Continues to Advance

THE 5th Indian Division has continuously crossed the Manipur River and has continued its advance down the Tiddim Road. A further 20 miles has been gained during the week.

The retreating Japanese put in one counter-attack but withdrew, abandoning their guns and leaving 160 dead.

Enemy rearguards shelled the river crossing points.

A S.E.A.C. communiqué issued on September 27th states: "the

V.C. CHARGED TO HIS DEATH

The Victoria Cross has been posthumously awarded to Captain (temporary Major) Frank Gerald Blaker, M.C., of the Highland Light Infantry, attached to the Ninth Gurkha Rifles, Indian Army, whose company attacked a vital position on the summit of an important hill overlooking Taungni, Burma, last July.

When the advance was stopped by close-range machine-gun fire, Captain Blaker advanced ahead of his men and, in spite of being severely wounded in the arm, located the machine-guns and single-handed charged the position.

Three rounds hit him in the body, but he continued to cheer his men on, while lying on the ground, so inspiring them that they captured the objective.

Japanese have broken contact with the Fifth Indian Division moving south on the Tiddim Road.

In the Arakan, active patrolling continues.

In North Burma, British patrols operating south of Hopin are probing in the Nazima area.

The German Gothic Line fixed defences were incomplete at the Adriatic end, as evidenced by this Tiger tank turret standing near an unfinished pit dug for it.

Indian troops fought gallantly but not without reservations about the imperial cause. Newspapers like *Indian News Review*, published out of Cairo, were a means of controlling the narrative when the news from home was often disquieting.

content with the one local paper, the *Orcadian*. The respected novelist Eric Linklater was brought in to oversee the first edition of the *Orkney Blast*, sportingly printed off on the *Orcadian*'s presses. From these modest beginnings the Empire forces developed a plethora of forces' newspapers and magazines: *Canada Press News* for Canadian troops in Britain, *Fauji Akhbar*, an English-language newspaper for Indian troops, *Springbok* for South African forces in the Middle East, and *AIF News* for Australians. The New Zealand and Canadian troops involved in the invasion of Italy both had their own papers, the *New Zealand Times* and *Maple Leaf*.

Airflow, a monthly magazine published for the RAF in Sri Lanka (then Ceylon), is a good example of what could be achieved for a settled garrison away from the front line. Its seventy-two-page small format was modelled on *Lilliput*, a popular magazine offering cheerful morale-raising stories along with cartoons, wry observations on human behaviour and some serious articles. *Airflow* followed its example, with photo plate sections, pages of advertisements for local services and artistic representations of the female anatomy (a *Lilliput* speciality). The RAF required four ground staff for every flier, who worked frantically to keep the aircraft functioning but did not face the terrors of combat. It is a reminder that in many parts of the world, boredom and homesickness were far more common dangers to military efficiency than enemy action.[30]

The Desert War in North Africa was by far the most active front for British forces in the middle years of the conflict, and not surprisingly made a major contribution to the development of forces newspapers. *Crusader* and *Eighth Army News* were the brain child of Warwick Charlton, formerly a journalist on the *Daily Sketch*. A tabloid man at heart, Charlton was determined that his papers would be the voice of the soldier, without intervention from High Command:

> This is a desert paper. It originates in the desert and is for the desert rats. Our chief interest is what you want and not what other people think you should have.[31]

This did not go unchallenged, but when General Montgomery gave Charlton his personal authority to publish what he wished, the matter was settled. But there was still no daily newspaper for the troops, until Churchill saw a copy of the American *Stars and Stripes* and tasked Harold Macmillan, then minister in Algiers, to see that there was a British equivalent. For this task, Macmillan recruited Hugh Cudlipp, later managing editor of the *Daily Mirror* and one of the most influential newspapermen of the 1950s and 1960s. The result, *Union Jack*, faithfully reflected the great issues most preoccupying troops, pay and leave, and, as the tide of the war turned, the prospect of demobilisation and post-war housing and employment. When the war moved to Italy and Montgomery was summoned home to help with the planning for D-Day, Charlton was removed and Cudlipp placed under stricter supervision. Frank Owen faced similar problems as the editor of *SEAC*, the service newspaper of the South East Asia Command, and survived only because of the protection of the theatre commander, Lord Mountbatten. But since the *Daily Mirror*, despised by Churchill and often critical of his government, was by far the most popular paper with the troops, *Union Jack* and *SEAC* would have lost credibility with their readers had they ignored their concerns.

With its apparently limitless resources, it is no surprise that the US Army should have produced two of the most successful and widely distributed service publications of the war, *Yank*, a weekly magazine, and *Stars and Stripes*, a daily paper produced and distributed in every foreign theatre of the war. *Yank*, a glossy made up of feature stories, correspondence and striking photography, honoured its commitment to be the voice of the ordinary GI by excluding officers from its staff. Except for a few officers in New York liaising with High Command, each issue was put together by a staff of privates, corporals and sergeants. Not all went smoothly. The cover of the first issue, celebrating a substantial increase in pay, had to be replaced, on the grounds that it made it seem like the American soldier was motivated largely by money. Two weeks later, the chair of the organising committee, Colonel Egbert White, was rebuked for an illustrated story on close combat training; throttling a sentry from behind was deemed 'unsporting and contrary

CRUSADER

BRITISH FORCES' WEEKLY   No. 101, Vol. 10   Two Lire   FOUNDED BY EIGHTH ARMY

Sunday, May 7, 1944

● The story of Pte V. KENNARD, of Wood Green, London

I WAS IN A CASSINO "LULL"

It meant 15,000 shells in nine days to the Infantry of the Line!

CASSINO HAS MISSED THE HEADLINES RECENTLY. THERE HAS BEEN A "LULL." BUT THE SHATTERED RUIN OF CASSINO IS STILL IN THE SAME PLACE AND THERE ARE SOLDIERS IN IT. LIFE IS NO LULL FOR THEM.

Private Kennard spent nine days in the town with his unit. Nine days of waiting. Nine days under continuous shellfire, nine nights of furtive prowling in No Man's Land. Such is the routine in Cassino to-day. On being relieved, Kennard gave the following vivid daily-day account.

FIRST DAY: My home is a hole in the ground a few feet square. It was dug and reinforced with stakes by the New Zealanders we relieved last night — a pit roofed with steel girders and an experiment of wooden beams. It houses a couple of pals and myself. Company is a boon in what promises to be a really hot spot. We arrived here last night, picking our way in the dark across the ruins of former houses, seeking cover as occasional mortar fell near, striking our ears for passing forms along the stunted buildings. I expected to be met by heavy mortaring and machine-gun fire, but all was comparatively quiet.

SECOND DAY: I slept little last night. I was waiting for something which failed to materialise. The artillery and

As told to CRUSADER staff reporter **SYD FOXCROFT**

gunfire shells appear to be falling thicker to-day. I learned this morning that over 5,000 shells fell in our area to-day. Many of the others have received direct hits, some as many as ten in a single day. There are casualties and stretcher-bearers are busy outside. Across the road an M.O. is serving both German and British wounded, and stretcher-bearers of both sides are exchanging cigarettes and attempting to conduct conversations.

I was talking with one of our stretcher-bearers. He wandered about the buildings with his Red Cross displayed, collecting the wounded and is undisturbed by Jerry.

To-day has been the worst day's shelling I've ever experienced and I'm thankful indeed when dusk falls and the shelling subsides somewhat. After an hour or two of comparative quiet the artillery recommences and among the casualties is Private A. Green, whose back wound is the first he has experienced since joining the battalion.

THIRD DAY: I still cannot accustom myself. I have been in action several times before but have never felt so helpless. Mortars and shells again. Several fall near to our dug-out, covering us with dust which clings to our already gritty faces.

Nearby a complete section is buried, and while shells drop round his Lieutenant Symmonds clears away beams and masonry and digs to extract all all comrade.

Occupants of a dug-out only ten yards away are less fortunate. Twelve of them, stretcher clerks and stretcher-bearers occupy the single dug-out. A direct hit by a heavy shell kills two and wounded five of them.

FOURTH DAY: I feel increasingly thirsty. The slightest movement acts me on my guard. I imagine danger at every corner, but in tight-hearted chatter we attempt to keep up our spirits. The periods of shelling are nightmares. We wait for bursts at intervals as the cramps abound to indicate the proximity of the bits.

Wandering around for a hot evening meal my attention was drawn to Castle Hill. Diaries of small arms fire pricked the darkness and the explosion of occasional small arms beacons again in much gaze on positions. The exchange of fire appeared much of us and such considerations made our position appear hopelessly precarious.

Supplies are coming through constantly. Jeeps transport the food, water and ammunition to within half a mile of our positions. We then manage respectively, covering the remaining stretch on foot under cover of darkness.

FIFTH DAY: The 5,000 shells which the enemy is estimated to be dropping in our area daily don't appear as terrible as each day we arrived. Men are, however, still killed and wounded and the stretcher-bearers and Jeep ambulance deliver two extremely busy. One driver, Driver Foskett, has been busy day and night taking back the wounded to forward dressing stations and hospitals.

Throughout my stay I have been awaiting the order to attack. I felt that we had to do so, and I prepared myself for little street-fighting.

SIXTH DAY: Enemy mortar and artillery shells rained on us in low. Our comrades are having a hell of a time, attempting to maintain line communications. Jumps are quickly so infrequent they are established installations in turn to shreds by shells. We have abandoned line communications to-day and depend now on wireless.

At times we count the shells as they fall round us — four at a time. Hardly a square yard of earth is undisturbed by shells or shrapnel. Stumps of buildings are reduced to the ground — only craters remain intact.

The seventh and eighth days passed uneventfully.

On the ninth day news of our intended relief filtered through and, frankly, we were glad. In nine days it was estimated that the enemy had rained fifteen thousand shells into the area we occupied, and we were ready for a rest.

We withdrew under cover of darkness. As the moon came up over surrounding hills we were able to discern the skeleton outlines of the buildings and the pot-holed roads. It made me wonder how we had been able to live nine days in such a hell on earth.

Pte. J. Hearn, of Boulder City, Western Australia, climbs on the shoulders of Corporal W. W. Williamson, of Maylands, Western Australia, to put down a Japanese flag from a tree near a Japanese H.Q. in New Guinea.

THEY PREFER THE FRONT

THEY could hold well-paid Home Front administrative jobs, relax at New York's entertainment centres, forget the war and earn the fares. But they preferred to stand by the side of Eighth Army men at Tobruk, Alamein and Mareth, and to follow the Army to Italy.

To-day, two companies of volunteers of the American Field Service work with the Eighth and Fifth Armies, conveying hundreds of wounded monthly from the battlefields to hospitals.

Founded during the opening stages of the First World War by a group of Americans living in Paris, the organisation was consolidated in the American Army when the United States entered the war.

STARTED IN FRANCE

Shellmen commenced work in France in 1939 doing continuous work during the harried evacuation of rebirths in southern France. Many of the volunteers were injured—others resolved to join a noble approach mostly one hundred men who a month after America entered the war, left the States to join War II's Western Desert Force.

They have been in Italy since the opening of the campaign, and are now well known to frontline troops, from Anzio to the Adriatic.

They come from all walks of life—actors, artists, writers, cab drivers, students, business men, engineers—youths of 18 and men of 65, all of whom volunteered for this frontline service. Many are disabled—two have wooden legs and many only one eye. All are considered medically unfit.

Equipping themselves, initially, in America, they live hard over here on pay which amounts alone to a monthly canteen allowance.

Four volunteers have been killed in Italy alone. They were members of the company which has accompanied the Eighth Army through the desert.

A Scout-car served as the "royal coach" when the King, Queen and Princess Elizabeth inspected Britain's invasion forces somewhere in the Home Counties.

Crusader was one of the most successful of the British troops' newspapers, thanks to editors determined to reflect the soldier's point of view and having, as the war progressed, an increasingly optimistic story to tell.

to American ideals'.[32] After a third offence, Colonel White was sent to cool his heels in Alaska before being released to set up a British edition of *Yank*.

Despite these early tribulations, *Yank* grew into a major venture, with twenty-one editions published in seventeen countries, a total of 2.25 million weekly copies.[33] Army planes carried the main-page formes to printing places abroad: editors could replace four pages of the master issue with copy of local relevance. All but combat troops paid five cents per copy. As a weekly, *Yank* relied on feature stories, and produced some of the best journalism of the war. Journalists, photographers and artists needed to be in the front line to do their job, and four would be killed in action.

Stars and Stripes built on the success of the troops' newspaper of the same title of 1917–18, which circulated up to half a million copies in the last year of the war to American soldiers on the Western Front. From 1942, *Stars and Stripes* produced a daily bulletin for troops in active service from the Mediterranean to the Pacific. The patient Colonel White took charge of the Mediterranean edition first issued in Algiers on 9 December 1941. This spawned a chain of editions published in Casablanca, Tunis, Palermo and Naples. A second chain emanating from London extended to Ireland, France and ultimately Germany. The Mediterranean edition was a paper of eight pages, with a longer Sunday edition of twenty-four to twenty-eight pages. Since it carried no advertising, there was a lot of space to fill.

Generating, printing and distributing such a mass of copy posed major logistical difficulties even for the American army. Plant, ink and paper had to be 'borrowed' from local businesses or the British ally. Local car owners were also persuaded to surrender their vehicles to the task of delivery. The Anzio beachhead was serviced by a daily boat from Naples. The provision of news, particularly home news, was a source of difficulty. Sports news was provided by the Army News Service. The forthcoming presidential election, however, blighted attempts to report domestic politics. It was only after the election was concluded and Roosevelt safely returned to office that *Stars and Stripes* was permitted to subscribe to the AP news service.

Stars and Stripes generally did a good job of reporting the soldier's point of view. In reporting from the front, they recognised that troops despised nothing more than sugar-coating reverses or understating casualties. Correspondence, often critical of regimental officers, was received and published, and no soldier was ever disciplined for opinions expressed in these letters. Some cases were investigated and egregious faults rectified. *Stars and Stripes* also received 300 poems a week, and those published were a popular feature. Even bad poetry made a point as it reflected so well the GI point of view. The poetry of 1939–45 is far less celebrated or studied than the war poets of 1914–18, so it is as well to be reminded that poetry still remained a valued expression of fears and emotions on the front line.

Not all forces publications were on this scale. Individual services and divisions had their own publications such as *Air Force Magazine*, the *Bureau of Naval Personnel Magazine*, *Cavalry Journal* and, for the Ordnance, *Army Motors*. American soldiers in Alaska and the Aleutians had their own newspaper, *Kodiak Bear*. Two Yank staffers on a long Pacific crossing even put out an illustrated ship's newspaper, *Salt Water Taffy*. The forces papers were perhaps most valued for their cartoon strips: Will Eisner's Joe Dope in *Army Motors* and David Breyer's GI Joe in *Yank*. The most successful of all was George Baker's Sad Sack, again in *Yank*, a well-intentioned yet hapless soldier whose good deeds were never rewarded. Even the *Orkney Blast* had Sylvia, a blatant clone of Norman Pett's Jane for the *Daily Mail*. Sylvia proved as unlucky as Jane in divesting her clothes, sometimes appearing naked except for a copy of the *Orkney Blast* covering her modesty: racy, for the good folk of Orkney.

In the first years of the war, as the German armies made their victorious way through Europe, their troops could make free with the libraries of the occupied nations. They could read German books in the special libraries created for them in Poland, where the Polish books were destroyed. Those who read English could pick over the 200,000 Penguins left behind by the retreating British Expeditionary Force in Belgium and France, and for those who read French, the libraries and bookshops of Paris were at their disposal. For those locations less well furnished with books, the High Command ensured that they did not go short.

For all the normal chaotic administrative overload of Nazi power, the provision of books for fighting men was both meticulous and generous. More than a thousand libraries were established on aerodromes for the pilots of Goering's Luftwaffe. In contrast to the Western powers, in Germany collecting for the troops focused first on publishers and booksellers: it was only when their compulsory donations had been distributed that the German state turned to contributions from private citizens. Even these had an air of menace. House-to-house collections, conducted by German youth organisations, allowed authorities to inspect the books to test the orthodoxy of donors, in case they had been unwise enough to add to their gifts any proscribed books.[34]

After the fourth public campaign in June 1943, which brought in 10.5 million books, Albert Rosenberg boasted to Hitler that the German people had 'given its soldiers the largest library in the world'. By the winter of 1943–4, Rosenberg's donation campaigns had yielded 43 million books. This is a remarkable figure, all the more so when we consider that the citizens who made up donor groups were by this point also suffering from war-related book shortages. It was far and away the largest and most successful of the book drives in any of the combatant nations.

The growing book scarcity on the home front may help explain why by 1942 the German High Command was complaining of the 'often shamefully poor content' of donated books. This also reflects a debate within the military and political leadership about what the troops should be reading. If we examine the monthly lists of recommended reading issued by the Wehrmacht between 1939 and 1942, we see a remarkably austere list of political propaganda, works glorifying war and practical military manuals. Fiction and poetry are largely absent. A survey of Wehrmacht soldiers on the other hand, at the end of 1941, demonstrated that these were far from the preferences of the troops themselves. They preferred detective stories, the Winnetou novels of Karl May and, perhaps more surprisingly, romantic fiction. Conceding the point, in February 1942,

Walter Tiessler, director of the Reich Ring for National Socialist Propaganda, asked that 95 per cent of the books sent to the front should be recreational reading.[35]

In a totalitarian state, this was an ideological dilemma that could only be resolved at the highest level. Goebbels, on many issues the most astute of the Nazi leaders, came down decisively on the side of the surveyed troops and Tiessler, though not without a dig at the distinguished colleague who had conducted the book drives with such efficiency. He regretted that there were still ideologues who believed a submariner, emerging from the engine room of his vessels, longed to read Rosenberg's *Myth of the Twentieth Century* (which was famously impenetrable).

> Of course that is pure nonsense. This man sees things differently and is in no mood to accept ideological lectures. He is living out our ideology and doesn't need to be instructed about it. He wants to relax, and we must give him the opportunity for relaxation through literature of the lighter sort.[36]

Mental recuperation and entertainment were now officially recognised as a matter of state importance. Goebbels found it 'psychologically quite understandable that in this, the fourth year of the war, interest in war books and political books has declined steeply'. This was equally true of the civilian population: 'The nation flees from the hardship and pressures of everyday life into mental spaces that have nothing to do with the war'.[37] But there were no longer the books, nor the paper reserves, to give those left at home the recreational literature they also craved. A large proportion of what could be printed was directed towards the troops.

This was partly because troop morale was a more pressing issue than the cowed and compliant home front, but it also represented a degree of self-interested cynicism on the part of publishers. The co-ordination of supply of books to the front, and their retailing to the troops, had been delegated to a new organisation established immediately on the outbreak of the war on 4 September 1939, the *Zentrale der Frontbuchhandlungen* (ZdF). Working through the German Labour Front, the ZdF ensured that German troops

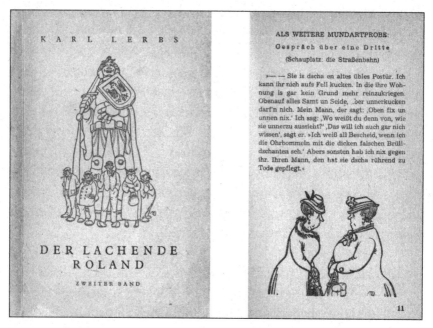

Books like these comic tales of life in Bremen were precisely what German troops needed to take their minds off the increasingly desperate military situation. The author, Karl Krebs, had accommodated himself easily enough to the Nazi regime and would commit suicide in 1946.

had easy access to books, wherever they were stationed. Ten large depots were established in major distribution nodes from Paris and Brussels to Oslo, Riga, Lviv and Rome. From there they could be distributed to more than 300 sales outlets on the frontline, established in field hospitals or the soldiers' billets. France alone had ninety-eight such sales outlets (confirming the reputation of France as a cosy posting). There were also a dozen bookmobiles, travelling sales vans, touring the front lines, and in Norway, also a desirable billet, several motorboats. Unlike the free distribution of the American Armed Services Editions, German soldiers had to pay for the books they bought from the network of sales outlets.[38]

Families were also encouraged to send books to their relatives, for which purpose lists of the recommended books could be obtained free of charge from bookstores. These lists comprised mainly books published by Nazi firms and were heavy on political and ideological literature, whereas the ZdF's own list offered 2,600

Although huge resources were invested in bringing books to the troops wherever German forces fought, there was no doubt that the softer postings, such as Norway, were best supplied, as here by this book boat, cruising the fjords to reach the more isolated units.

titles, drawn from a broader range of publishing houses, including works by authors outside the stable of party apparatchiks. This discrepancy probably reflects a recognition that while troops wanted to read fiction and entertainment literature, their families would not want to send anything through the army post that could put either themselves or their loved ones in danger.

As the war wore on, the supply of books to the troops became the most attractive and lucrative work available to the publishing industry. This was particularly the case when paper supplies ran short, and publishers with contracts with armed forces organisations could access paper supplies from the army's own generous reserves. The actual printing was often delegated to companies in the occupied countries, in France, the Netherlands, Norway or Belgium. In total, around 75 million copies of books were produced in this way between 1939 and 1943: between 1942 and 1943, the proportion of books published using the Wehrmacht paper allocation rose from 7 to 55 per cent of the total available paper stock. These included at least 35 million of the bespoke front-line editions, the German equivalent of the American Armed Services Editions, the production of which in Germany involved seventy-one separate publishing firms.[39] As the German economy was progressively degraded, the survival of German publishing depended ever more on contracts from the Nazi state, not only from the Wehrmacht, but separately from the High Command, Luftwaffe, the navy and the Waffen SS. The result was that as the war wound its way to an end, publishing would emerge in much better shape than many other sectors, albeit with a mountain of stock that in the new political circumstances was completely unsalable.

11

THE AUTHOR AT WAR

On 2 September 1914, Charles Masterman, author, journalist and serial loser of parliamentary elections, convened an extraordinary meeting at Wellington House, the home of the National Health Insurance Commission in London. Around the table sat the most distinguished and successful English writers of the age: Sir James M. Barrie, Arnold Bennett, A. C. Benson, Sir Arthur Conan Doyle, John Galsworthy of the *Forsyte Saga*, Thomas Hardy, Anthony Hope (author of *The Prisoner of Zenda*), H. G. Wells, the poet laureate Robert Bridges. This was the first assembly of what became in effect Britain's Ministry of Propaganda, later formalised as the Ministry of Information, with Masterman promoted to the cabinet to direct the effort. On 2 September, the twenty-five present, along with Rudyard Kipling, unavoidably detained elsewhere, committed themselves unambiguously to assisting the war effort with their writings, advocacy and influence: they also promised not to reveal the fact that they were writing under government direction.[1]

Over the course of the next four years, the Wellington House operation turned out a remarkable quantity of newspaper articles, pamphlets and contributions to journals. Many of the pamphlets were directed at then neutral America, an enterprise in which Britain was assured not only of the help of its own literary giants, but also the expatriate Americans Henry James and Edith Wharton. The American operation, supervised by Sir Gilbert Parker, was especially crafty. The jingoistic excesses of the English newspapers were largely avoided: the war was framed as a battle for the future of democracy. The sympathy for suffering Belgium, overwhelmed in the first months of the war by the German assault, was repeatedly called into play; *Germany's Violations of the Laws of War* was presented as a gift to numerous American public libraries, as was Parker's own *World in the Crucible* (1915). Parker built up a card index of 10,000 American influencers, who were bombarded with books and pamphlets, many of which they passed on to libraries.[2] America's admiration for French culture was also deftly exploited. Since the existence of the Wellington House operation remained largely secret, most of these publications were channelled through British commercial publishing houses, which willingly co-operated in the patriotic cause; other books were described as published by the Paris Chamber of Commerce.[3] The History Faculty of the University of Oxford contributed a magisterial series of essays on *Why We Are at War* (1914), and Lord Bryce, former ambassador to the United States and author of the highly respected *The American Commonwealth*, put his reputation behind the *Report of the Committee on Alleged German Outrages* (1915) which documented, with fabricated precision, many of the most outlandish rumours circulating in the popular press. Here the forensic skills of the historian were trumped by the duty of the patriot.

We are accustomed now to think of the literature of the First World War through the works of the war poets, the lost generation of Rupert Brooke and Wilfred Owen who left their indelible mark on our perception of the horrors of trench warfare. But the literature of disillusionment was largely confined to the decade of reckoning in the years following the war: the enduring masterpiece of this era, Erich Maria Remarque's *All Quiet on the Western Front*, was published only in 1928. Ernest Hemingway's reflection of his service in an ambulance unit in Italy, *A Farewell to Arms*, was issued the following year. More characteristic of the war itself were the rip-roaring yarns of 'Sapper', the alias of Herman Cyril McNeile and later author of the *Bulldog Drummond* novels, a serving officer who contributed a series of short stories on his war service in the *Daily Mail*.[4] These were subsequently published in two collections, *The Lieutenant and Others* and *Sergeant Michael Cassidy, RE*, both of which sold over 135,000 copies. Three more collections followed before the end of the war.

This trajectory, from serial publication in newspapers or journals to reissue as a book, was characteristic of many of the patriotic contributions offered by the Wellington House authors, and proved lucrative as well as influential: Arnold Bennett reckoned by 1916 to have made £2,000 from his war journalism (£205,000 in 2022 values). Sir Arthur Conan Doyle, too old for active service, nevertheless recalled Sherlock Holmes to the colours for one last adventure, in which he comprehensively outwitted German spy chief von Bork, in the process rolling up his entire English espionage network. 'His Last Bow' was published first in the *Strand* magazine and then in an anthology of short stories under the same title. John Buchan, veteran of the Boer War and accomplished surfer of the corridors of Whitehall, published *The Thirty-Nine Steps* (1915) first as a serial in *Blackwood's* magazine. When reissued as a book it sold 25,000 copies in the first three months, and went on, with its sequel *Greenmantle* (1916), to be one of the most enduringly successful works of fiction of the war.[5]

Unfit for front-line service, Buchan nevertheless made a critical contribution to the war effort, not only in his encapsulation of suave English individualism in the heroic guise of Richard Hannay, but also through his creation of an instant history of the war which eventually grew to twenty-four volumes and 1.2 million words. In this *Nelson History of the War* and two spin-off books on the Battle of the Somme, Buchan cleaved close to the vocabulary of newspaper reporting of heroic courage and undaunted commitment to the cause. Even the catastrophe of the first day of the Somme was bathed in the language of chivalric sacrifice: 'Not a man wavered or broke ranks; but minute by minute the ordered lines melted away under the deluge of high explosive, shrapnel, rifle and machine-gun fire.'[6] For this, and other signal services to maintaining morale, John Buchan was in 1917 appointed minister of information in Lloyd George's reconstructed government. The following year Arnold Bennett would be appointed director of British propaganda in France.

Even at this late stage in the war dissenting voices were hard to find. Buchan had no excuse for naivety, but most of the authors saw the front line only in carefully orchestrated VIP tours. Arnold Bennett turned his experience as a privileged observer into *Over There: War Scenes on the Western Front* (1915), published, in the

John Buchan (1875–1940)

custom of the times, first as a series of newspaper articles. Kipling
was a past master of this sort of lucrative recycling. This gave readers
at the public libraries two bites of the cherry, first in the newspaper
rooms, then in book form. For this was first and foremost a newspaper war: the iron grip of the Northcliffe and Rothermere papers
permitted no realistic description of the carnage and futility of the
trenches. Men came home on leave astonished at the cheerful calm
of the home front.

    The British propaganda campaign, to which its leading authors
contributed so enthusiastically, was in this respect wholly successful. America entered the war on the Allied side in 1917, and the
British public remained largely oblivious of the realities of life at
the front. Arguably, this was ultimately to the disadvantage of the
war effort, throwing a protective blanket over the follies of army
strategy, and thus ensuring that the slaughter of the trenches would
continue. The British authors who contributed to this outcome
were all in their way men of sensibility, and this is evident at least in
their fiction even before war's end. In the Richard Hannay novels,

Buchan allowed his fictional characters to be far more reflective of the doubts entertained by real soldiers, compared to their newspapers surrogates. In *Greenmantle* (1916), Richard Hannay, on the run in Germany, is given succour in a woodland cottage. 'That night I realised the crazy folly of war.' Blenkiron, his rich, corpulent and fearless accomplice, is even allowed to muse, 'We in America respect the fighting of the British soldiers, but we don't quite catch on to the devices of the British generals. We opine that there is more bellicosity than science among your highbrows. That is so?'[7]

The war ended with Buchan and Bennett duelling over the post-war future of the Ministry of Information. Buchan, the decorated officer, prevailed, and Bennett returned to his career as a novelist. It was in the years of peace, responding to their different wartime experiences, that writers reflected more systematically on the folly of war, and their own responsibility for its perpetuation. John Galsworthy's *The Burning Spear* (1919) is a complex satire of the Ministry of Information, which ends with its protagonist, a Don Quixote figure, failing in his attempt to immolate himself on a pyre of war propaganda books, pamphlets and newspapers. Arnold Bennett also published a fictional satire of his war work in *Lord Raingo* (1926), where the eponymous hero (based on Lord Beaverbrook) duels with the odious Andy Clyth (Lloyd George). The most substantial and enduring of these therapeutic efforts at cleansing and exculpation is Ford Madox Ford's *Parade's End* (1924–8). Ford, who had only recently adopted this anglicised name, had, as Ford Madox Hueffer, rather unexpectedly abandoned a life of bohemian dissipation and scandal to join up for what proved to be a miserable life as a junior officer. *Parade's End*, published in four discrete parts, reflected in full this disillusionment and seriousness.

None made the transition from a conception of the cleansing joy of war to disillusioned heartbreak more completely than the arch-Imperialist Rudyard Kipling, whose only son John had been posted missing in the first Battle of Loos in 1915. It was only after many months, and thanks to the efforts of fellow author Henry Rider Haggard, that it could be confirmed that John was dead (an agonising death of which Rider Haggard spared the grieving father the details). Kipling never really recovered from this blow, and in taking on the official history of John's Irish Guards was forced to confront the reality of war's squalor and sacrifice. The full fury of Kipling's tortured apotheosis was articulated in a piece entitled 'A Dead Statesman', a contemptuous dissection of Lloyd George, who knew General Haig had failed, but dared not remove him.

> I could not dig; I dare not rob
> Therefore I lied to please the mob.
> Now all my lies are proved untrue
> And I must face the men I slew.
> What tale shall serve me here among
> Mine angry and defrauded young.[8]

The literature of the Second World War was shaped by the shadow of the first, only twenty years past, and by the spirit of disillusionment that followed. The disenchantment of the 1920s, followed by the depression of the 1930s, saw a changing of the guard, as the giants of the Edwardian era shuffled off the scene, and new voices emerged. The new generation embraced both the bohemian spirit of Weimar Berlin and left-wing politics. Its testing ground was the Spanish Civil War, where several prominent men of letters joined the republican cause, including George Orwell and Ernest Hemingway. The hammer-blow of the fascist victory in Spain was compounded in 1939 by the alliance between Russia and Germany, humiliating the anti-fascist left. When leading lights of the movement, Christopher Isherwood and W. H. Auden, decided to flee Britain and sit out the coming war in the United States, it only accentuated the feeling of disorientation and defeat among their abandoned admirers.[9]

War, as Orwell pointed out, was in any case difficult for writers. In a time of existential threat to the nation, many felt literature an inconsequential activity, a sentiment brusquely articulated by the English author and journalist Storm Jameson: 'In September 1939 it seemed highly unlikely, as well as slightly indecent, to think of earning a living as a novelist.' Should writers offer their services to the war effort, or stay true to their vocation? For many, it was an impossible dilemma, one articulated by Phyllis Bentley: 'It appears that we are false to life if we don't write political propaganda, and false to art if we do.'[10] This was essentially the predicament of the left: those who embraced the war had few doubts. Hilary St George Saunders, who wrote several runaway bestsellers for the Ministry of Information, would argue trenchantly that:

> In time of war, writers [and publishers], like everyone else, have the duty of putting such skills and talents as they possess at the service of the country for an agreed wage, and no writer worthy of the name would seek to become a 'best-seller' by describing deeds in which he took no personal part.

He was true to his word: his skilful texts for *The Battle of Britain* and *Bomber Command* were published anonymously, and St George Saunders received no royalty for his handiwork.[11]

The answer of course, was that authors took a variety of positions, from the self-exile of Auden and Isherwood (mercilessly satirised in Evelyn Waugh's *Put Out More Flags* as Parsnip and Pimpernel) to the self-effacing patriotism of St George Saunders. Some hurried to do their bit, either by joining up to fight or offering their services to the myriad government agencies, not least the revived Ministry of Information. Many writers felt overcome by a profound lethargy. Naomi Mitchison, a well-connected leftist writer, spent the war running a farm and estate in Argyll, and wrote hardly at all.[12] Even for those whose creativity was undimmed, normal sources of income dried up, not least because of the closure of so many literary magazines as a result of paper rationing.

For those who could keep writing, the demand for new books was insatiable. Publishers struggled to meet the somewhat contradictory demands for escapist fiction and comment on contemporary events. In the realm of fiction, the desire for comfort and reassurance meant that many of the bestseller writers were authors who had built a following in the pre-war years. This was especially the case with children's literature, for which publishers were reluctant to allocate a share of their precious paper ration.

New children's books were thin on the ground, and the field was dominated by perennially popular authors such as Enid Blyton and Captain W. E. Johns of the Biggles novels.[13]

The best opportunities for new authorial talent lay as chroniclers of the war. The interest in following the news provided an opportunity for instant books that journalists, in particular, seized with relish. The war correspondent James Lansdale Hodson published with Victor Gollancz his chronicle of the Blitz, which would turn out to be the first of seven volumes of diaries.[14] In this market, American war correspondents initially enjoyed a considerable advantage since they could report from both London and Berlin. The standout bestseller in this category was William Shirer's account of his time as Berlin correspondent for the American radio network CBS, *Berlin Diary*. Published in July 1941, *Berlin Diary* sold 600,000 copies in its first year, and is widely credited with helping shape American public opinion in advance of America's entry into the war. It was apparently the first book that prompted Roosevelt to ask the author for their autograph.[15] The book was also hugely admired in Britain and became a staple of lists of books most borrowed from public libraries. Shirer freely acknowledged having disguised the identity of his German sources to protect them from retribution. He was less candid about alterations disguising his more favourable impression of Hitler during the first years of his posting.[16]

English readers were also voracious for first-hand accounts of the fighting from military personnel. The reminiscences of pilots caught up in the Battle of Britain were guaranteed a warm reception. After the puzzling inertia of the phoney war and the relief of Dunkirk, the airborne assault on Britain was the first occasion in which the majority of citizens would be directly engaged. The failure of Goering's initial plan to eliminate the RAF as a defensive force made heroes of the young pilots who had battled against the apparently invincible Luftwaffe and stalled plans for invasion. The Ministry of Information's eponymous pamphlet, *The Battle of Britain*, flew off the shelves, and accounts by those involved in the air battles were in high demand. The standout in this soon crowded field of battlefield journals was Richard Hillary's evocative memoir, *The Last Enemy*.[17] Hillary's period of active service was, not untypically, brief. His squadron went into action on 27 August 1940 and Hillary was shot down and ditched in the sea on 3 September, a crash in which he sustained horrible burns to his hands, body and face.

As far as combat flying was concerned, this was the end of Hillary's war, but his account of his love affair with the Spitfire, especially the lyrical description of the sheer joy of flying, his courage and the unsparing description of the many months of reconstructive surgery that followed his injuries, touched a nerve with a public eager for heroes. It helped that Hillary was confident, athletic and well connected; one of the most moving parts of the book is the matter-of-fact recording of the loss, one by one, of the band of Oxford contemporaries with whom he had signed up. When *The Last Enemy* was published in June 1942, Hillary found that a project meant to honour the comradeship of a noble brotherhood had made him a celebrity. Despite the consolation of a brief affair with the actress Merle Oberon, Hillary found this uncomfortable, and bullied weak officers into allowing him to return to the air. He died on a training flight, still patently unfit for active duties, on 8 January 1943.[18]

With what remained of London's literary left drowning its sorrows in the bars of Soho, the absence of new voices cleared the field for the old warhorses of pre-war fiction. Pre-war bestsellers, such as A. J. Cronin's *The Citadel* (1937) and Daphne du Maurier's *Rebecca* (1938), continued to sell briskly. In 1940, three American blockbusters were firmly established high on the UK bestseller list, led by Margaret Mitchell's *Gone with the Wind* (1936), its already enormous sales further boosted by the film version, which swept the Oscars in 1940. John Steinbeck's masterful portrait of poverty in dustbowl America during the Great Depression, *The Grapes of Wrath* (1939), was hardly comfort food for a nation at war, but it proved extremely popular in Britain. Steinbeck would score a second success with *The Moon Is Down* (1942), a timely exploration of occupied Europe set in a lightly fictionalised Norway. The book was criticised at the time for presenting the occupying power in too sympathetic a light, but its empathetic reconstruction of the dilemmas and compromise of occupation struck a chord throughout Europe, where it was widely circulated in clandestine translations. It was also read and admired in the Soviet Union, as well as selling well in the UK. The third of the American bestsellers of 1940 was Ernest Hemingway's novel of the Spanish Civil War, *For Whom the Bell Tolls*. This was a huge transatlantic success, which finally gave him the bestseller status that he craved and cemented his reputation as one the premier authors of the twentieth century. In 1944, Hemingway, armed with a press pass, would accompany the American troops on the Normandy landings.

The taste for American literature was a noticeable trend in wartime Britain, but established British authors also contributed to bestselling contemporary fiction. The aeronautical engineer Nevil Shute combined top-secret work on naval weapon design with a steady output of war-related fiction. After two books in 1940 with popular RAF themes, Shute touched a nerve with *The Pied Piper* (1942), a taut and touching story of an English pensioner marooned in France by the German invasion, leading a growing band of children across France to the Brittany coast, and ultimate safety in England. Dennis Wheatley was another established author who combined secret war work (in his case in a special unit devising schemes of military deception) with a steady stream of new novels. Wheatley's robust and stylish thrillers made him a favourite with male readers; his debonair spy, Gregory Sallust, was thought to be an inspiration to Ian Fleming, later creator of James Bond, also an intelligence officer during the war. One of the most original talents in this largely male domain was Peter Cheyney, who adopted the idiom of the hard-boiled American detective for a series of wildly popular novels featuring the FBI agent and later private eye, Lenny Caution. Like Wheatley, Cheyney was a man of the right, having joined the New Party, Oswald Mosley's first excursion into fascism, something his millions of readers did not hold against him. In the preface to his 1945 novel, *I'll Say She Does*, Cheyney gleefully told the story of a captured English clergyman, walking round the compound of his prisoner-of-war camp, with his nose in his book of devotions, artfully concealing Cheyney's *Your Deal, My Lovely* (1941) tucked inside. By the end of the war,

Pulp Fiction. The English crime writer Peter Cheyney (1896–1951)
revelled in his success as a purveyor of tough-minded detective
fiction, and cultivated a lifestyle to match those of his heroes.

Cheyney's books were selling more than 1.5 million copies annually
to a worldwide audience.[19]

Female authors found the war hard. The disappearance of the
literary journals and many women's magazines cut off a number of
avenues for placing their work, while the disappearance of domestic
servants to war work meant that time previously spent on writing

was now occupied with cooking, queuing for food and running the household.[20] In February 1942, Eunice Frost at Penguin received this harrowing appeal from Kathleen Hale, author of *Orlando's Evening Out* (1941), the first illustrated work of fiction published in Penguin's strand for children, Puffin:

> I am wondering if you will be sending me a statement of royalties soon . . . I will tell you why I am worrying about all this – domestic servants can command a much higher wage than hitherto, and I am in danger of losing mine if I don't give her a rise very soon. I can't do this unless I get my royalties, for my husband's salary is, like everyone else's, halved by the increased income tax and he can't help me. I want to be able to say to my maid that on a certain date I will raise her wages. If I lose her then there'll be no more Orlandos, for I cannot possibly do without her.[21]

A cheque was despatched and four more Orlandos appeared between 1942 and 1946.

Those who persevered often saw their novels explicitly as a form of war service, their comfort to young men (the 'boys') who could have been their own children, grandchildren or younger brothers. Florence Barclay, wife of a clergyman and bestselling author of romances, spent much of the first war visiting wounded soldiers in hospital. She was touched by how many found some relief from their desperate injuries in reading her books.[22] In 1944, Alica Crang wrote to Allen Lane at Penguin to ask that the royalties from her *Preserves for All Occasions* be sent to the British Red Cross Prisoner of War Fund.[23] None of these female authors was held in higher esteem than Betty Smith, whose *A Tree Grows in Brooklyn* was, as we have seen, a firm favourite with young men far from home in the Pacific islands or France. Many wrote to Smith, who always replied, often enclosing a signed photograph; she estimated that she received 1,500 letters a year. Her grief at their sacrifice was poured out in an impassioned article when news came of the slaughter at Omaha beach:

Who died? I'll tell you who died . . . They all died. And I
don't know how any one of us here at home can sleep peacefully tonight unless we are sure in our hearts that we have
done our part all the way along the line.[24]

The most extraordinary of these authorial stories must be the
accidental celebrity of the journalist Jan Struther. In 1937, the
editor of the London *Times*, admiring her work for *Punch*, persuaded Struther to write a series of columns on the day-to-day life
of a fictional ordinary woman, Mrs Miniver. Gathered together in
book form in 1939, and later expanded with the wartime experiences of Mrs Miniver, the book touched a chord, particularly in
the United States. The books sold 300,000 copies, and when Struther moved to New York in 1940, she lectured on British society
for the Ministry of Information, earning an appreciative tribute
from Winston Churchill. Roosevelt told the author that the book
had helped hasten American entry into the war. The film won six
Academy Awards, and the grudging admiration of Joseph Goebbels, a shrewd and subtle judge of the art of persuasion:

> [Mrs Miniver] shows the destiny of a family during the
> current war, and its refined powerful propagandistic ten-
> dency has up to now only been dreamed of. There is not a
> single angry word spoken against Germany; nevertheless the
> anti-German tendency is perfectly accomplished.[25]

The writer's war was never uncomplicated: certainly the scale
and horror of the Second World War was not matched by a rush of
great literature. There were some exceptions, Hemingway among
them, and if the war was certainly not generally a great period for
English letters, it did play its part in easing the genesis of one of
the great novels of the twentieth century, *Brideshead Revisited*.
Evelyn Waugh was almost the antithesis of Richard Hillary: a
successful and admired author, but no natural soldier: pudgy and
unfit, middle-aged and overweight, undisciplined, self-indulgent
and insubordinate. With the outbreak of war, Waugh was in no
doubt he should play his part, and badgered friends, including Ian

Fleming, to help him to a position. Rather incongruously posted to the Royal Marines, he proved to be a terrible officer: he exhibited no perceptible military skills except undoubted courage. He was prone to quarrelling with fellow officers, obsequious to the more aristocratic, and utterly obnoxious to the men under his command. He made a point of falling out with his commanding officers to the extent that virtually no one would tolerate him under their command.

By 1943, Waugh was prepared to acknowledge his utter failure as a soldier, though unable to make the connection between his own ill-discipline and the refusal of his commanding officers to entrust him with responsibility. He recalled his own prediction that the chief use of war would be 'to cure artists of the illusion that they were men of action. It has worked its cure with me ... I don't want to be of service to anyone or anything. I simply want to do my work as an artist.'[26]

In January 1944, the beaten and defeated author-soldier wrote to his commanding officer requesting three months' leave without pay: to write a new novel. The letter combined an explanation of his total unfitness for modern warfare (lack of technical training, lack of physical agility) with a short disquisition on novel writing, most crucially that 'once an idea becomes fully formed in the author's mind, it cannot be left unexploited without deterioration'. Thus began a dance with authority that lasted for half a year. This was a crucial stage of the war, and every capable man was required: but that did not, in a military sense, include Waugh. The army authorities were torn between a disinclination to reward Waugh for his obstreperous attitude and a certainty that he was incapable of fulfilling any serious responsibilities, and only likely to cause further chaos and bad feeling.[27]

Recalled after one month of his three months' leave, he immediately offended the general to whom he was to be an ADC; a second general, no doubt forewarned, swiftly granted him six further weeks of writing leave. Redeployed to the SAS on his return, a further six weeks' leave was granted. When this was rescinded, his new commander granted him all the time he needed to finish the book, which he did on 8 June. The result was not the bitter-sweet semi-autographical war trilogy that cemented his literary reputation, *Sword of Honour*, published between 1952 and 1961, but *Brideshead Revisited*, Waugh's lyrical salute to a pre-war world of country houses, Oxford and Catholicism that continues to hold its place in the affections of readers in the English-speaking world.[28] In Clement Attlee's austerity Britain, it was a runaway success as it was in a United States not yet introduced to *Downton Abbey*. It swiftly sold half a million copies. True to form, Waugh grumbled that most of the royalties were swallowed up in punitive taxation; but he should have blessed the unusual pragmatism of the British officer corps, for which, on this one occasion, the successful pursuit of the war, unimpeded by Lieutenant Waugh, trumped strict adherence to protocol.

In Germany, the Nazis had both simplified and complicated the production of wartime literature with their rapid reorganisation of the publishing industry on coming to power in 1933.[29] The professional associations of publishers, librarians and authors were all swiftly brought under the wing of the new regime: any writers tainted by association with socialism, communism or the values of Weimar were summarily expelled; so too were Jewish writers. The literary section of the Prussian Academy of Arts was reorganised as early as 13 March 1933: Thomas and Heinrich Mann were among the first victims.[30] Public libraries and bookshops were required to remove from the shelves their holdings of disapproved authors, and publishers to destroy any remaining stock. The direction of travel was unambiguous, and many of Germany's most distinguished authors fled abroad.

The Nazi leadership seemed in no way discouraged by the loss in literary talent implied by these measures, since they already had in mind who would fill the gap: themselves. Hitler found his voice as an author during his brief imprisonment after the failure of the Beer Hall Putsch in 1923. When published in 1925, reviews of *Mein Kampf* were universally hostile, the *Frankfurter Zeitung* describing it as 'an act of political suicide'. The first volume sold a meagre 1,500 copies, and even devoted members of the Nazi inner circle found it hard going. Hitler was lucky that its publisher was a patron and supporter; otherwise the complex second volume (which contains much of the reflection on racial issues) would scarcely have merited publication. As it was, now ignored by the critics, it mustered barely 700 sales.[31] Business would pick up as the Nazis inched closer to power and by 1933, *Mein Kampf* had sold its first million. By 1945, 9 million copies were in circulation in Germany.

Joseph Goebbels also desired to be taken seriously as an author. His complex and passionate novel, *Michael* (1929), secured a respectable following, and was borrowed from public libraries much more frequently than most of the turgid literature written by supporters of the regime. His astute and acerbic diary was also clearly intended for publication: an edited version of the volumes dealing with the Nazi takeover was published in 1934.[32] The most unlikely bestseller was the vast, rambling treatise of the movement's chief ideologue, Alfred Rosenberg, *The Myth of the Twentieth Century* (1930). The other leaders of the movement mocked Rosenberg's impenetrable prose, and Hitler disliked the book, which he considered unreadable. He was also irritated when it threatened to cause a diplomatic breach with the Catholic hierarchy, since its open scorn for religion, singling out the Catholic Church for special opprobrium, led to calls for it to be placed on the papal Index. Nevertheless, forced purchase by public and even school libraries ensured its success, and *The Myth* would accumulate sales of more than 2 million copies, second only to *Mein Kampf* in the pantheon of Nazi bestsellers.

None of this would be of much interest to German soldiers and citizens seeking relief from the relentless demands of total war, particularly when the tide turned against Germany from 1942. Left to themselves, the tastes of most German readers were not so very different from those of their adversaries: detective stories, thrillers and romance (the German translation of *Gone with the Wind* sold 300,000 copies).[33] The all-time favourite among troops and on the home front was the prolific and long dead Karl May, the author of a conveyor belt of adventure stories, including his famous Winnetou novels, set in the American West. Party officials and librarians who denounced the reading of 'trash' and 'trivial literature' probably had May in their sights, and his books were banned from

Vienna municipal libraries in 1941. But May was protected from any further censorship by the knowledge that Hitler was a devoted fan. Towards the end of the war, when generals risked criticism of his strategic judgement, Hitler would recommend May's books to them. According to Albert Speer:

> Hitler was wont to say that he had always been deeply impressed by the tactical finesse and circumspection that May conferred upon his character Winnetou ... And he would add that during his reading hours at night, when faced by seemingly hopeless situations, he would still reach for those stories, that they gave him courage like works of philosophy for others or the Bible for elderly people.[34]

As for the myriad titles published by regime-friendly historians and political writers, German public librarians would later claim that the bulk of these works were seldom borrowed. But these affable revelations were generally offered after the war's end in a context where their own wartime conduct was under uncomfortable scrutiny.

The circumstances of life in the occupied countries also presented an impossible environment for free expression in literature: here, the reckoning would come only with post-war reflections on collaboration and war guilt and the celebration of resistance movements often largely invisible during the war. A partial exception to this silencing of literary life can be seen in France, where the emergence of a quasi-independent regime in Vichy cultivating the virtues of a traditionalist, agrarian society offered opportunities to authors who, like Marshal Pétain, scorned the discredited leftist politics that had led to humiliating defeat in 1940. Writers on the right made no secret of their admiration for the occupying forces, and they would pay a heavy price for their open advocacy of German values in the *épuration* after the liberation, while the more nimble politicians, François Mitterrand among them, were able to walk away from their earlier record of collaboration.[35]

Journalists were particularly vulnerable in this backlash,

because their views were set out in print, permitting no obfusca-
tion. De Gaulle commuted most of the death sentences passed by
the vengeful tribunals, but not that on Robert Brasillach, despite
a petition on his behalf from fifty-seven fellow writers, including Paul Válery, Colette, Jean Cocteau, Jean Anouilh and Albert
Camus. During the war Brasillach had been editor of the fascist
newspaper *Je suis partout*, and one of the most ardent supporters of the German regime, advocating the execution of left-wing
politicians and captured members of the resistance. But what
sealed Brasillach's fate was that de Gaulle had read his books, and
recognised his outstanding abilities: in later life he would recommend his work to his grandson. In 1945, Brasillach's distinction
as a writer only compounded his crime: as de Gaulle observed in
his only comment on the case, 'In literature as in everything talent
confers responsibility.'[36]

In truth, most French writers were neither committed resisters
nor ardent propagandists for Vichy. The confusion of the French
literary establishment under German occupation is well captured
by the oscillations of the grand old man of French letters, André
Gide. He excoriated his compatriots as the nation capitulated:

> How can one fail to approve Churchill? Not subscribe most
> heartily to General de Gaulle's declaration? Is it not enough
> for France to be conquered? Must she also be dishonoured?
> This breaking of her word, this denunciation of the pact
> binding her to England, is indeed the cruellest of defeats,
> and this triumph of Germany the most complete, by getting
> France, as she hands herself over, to debase herself.[37]

And with that, he settled down to brush up on his German. He
expected most Frenchmen would grumble their way through the
war, measured by 'less sugar in one's coffee, and less coffee in one's
cup'. He admired Pétain, favoured co-operation with Germany,
and practised it in the later stages of the war when he befriended
German officers in North Africa.

For those who could not disguise their contempt for the occupying power, the most immediate outlet would be the initially

highly secret, but ultimately ubiquitous resistance newspapers. Thousands contributed to the writing, printing and distribution of these newspapers during the course of the war, though at a heavy cost. In the Netherlands alone, 770 were executed for their role in clandestine printing and 2,000 in Belgium.

British publishers did face many challenges and frustrations during the war, but if they were inclined to complain, they had only to look across the Channel to occupied Europe and count their blessings. In the occupied nations, the Germans took control of the printing presses immediately. Some sympathetic newspapers were allowed to continue, but most were shut down. Continuing these newspapers underground was virtually impossible: their plant was too public and too prominent. Resisters had no legal access to paper, a printing press or indeed the very distinctive printer's ink. Here the communist underground had something of an advantage, having providentially stockpiled paper in the first stages of the war, but even so most of the early papers were printed on duplicators, one using a child's toy printing set.

Distribution was also a major issue. At first little more than a hastily produced single sheet, the newspapers were distributed exclusively within a small circle of fellow resisters: often this trust was misplaced. So although we can count more than 5,000 titles at some point published in Poland, France, the Low Countries and Scandinavia, most were fragmentary and very short-lived.[38] It should also be said that the greatest efflorescence came in the last year of the war, when the tide had turned, and many literary figures and publishers who had initially co-operated with the occupying force were anxious to burnish their resistance credentials.

With all these qualifications, the resistance press played an important role in keeping the cause alive and restoring the self-respect of peoples crushed by the speed with which they had been overpowered. The first issue of *Vrij Nederland* (*Free Netherlands*) appeared on 31 August 1940, the birthday of the exiled Queen Wilhelmina, and was sustained throughout the war, by which time 180 of its staff had been executed. In France, *Libre France* and *Pantagruel* began production in October 1940. The French communist newspaper *L'Humanité* was actually banned by the

SABOTØREN

ORGAN FOR SABOTØRENES LANDSFORBUND

NR. 1   JANUAR   1945

VI SKAL FRI VÅRT LAND OG FOLK!

Øksnevad overdrev ikke da han i BBC sa at siden svartedauen har ikke landet vært rammet av en verre ulykke enn tyskernes barbariske tvangsevakuering av befolkningen i Troms og Finnmark.

Redslene har ikke lammet den norske motstandsviljen. Tvert om. Det var den norske heimefrontens vilje Terje Wold ga uttrykk for i at alt er bedre enn på denne måten å la seg drive som slaktekveg av mordbrennerne.

Forsvarssjefen, kronprins Olav har gitt oss direktiver når tyskerne påny setter i gang den brente jords taktikk:

1. Adlyd ikke tyskernes evakueringsordre. Stikk dere unna og saml dere i grupper. Velg en leder og redd det som er mulig.
2. Angrip tyske patruljer som blir satt til å ødelegge norsk eiendom og anlegg.
3. Sett alt inn på å slukke branner.
4. Er det ingen lovlige myndigheter til stede sa sørg for å opprettholde ro og orden. Hjelp dem som trenger det mest.

Ordren forutsetter at vi i tide forbereder oss. At vi i størst mulig utstrekning har våpen og utstyr parat når vi trenger det. At vi fysisk er i form.

Forsvarssjefen understreket at tiden ennå ikke var inne for regulær reising av heimestyrkene. Men desto større krav stilles det til oss norske sabotører.

De norske militærenhetene vil snart sammen med vår russiske allierte og trolig med militær hjelp fra England og USA feie tyskerne ut av landet vårt. Vi sabotører forbereder grunnen gjennom aksjonene våre, og når hovedkampene setter inn skal tyskerne få føle at det vi hittil har utrettet vil blekne i forhold til det vi makter.

ALTA BATALJON

SPØKER FOR DIETEL'S ETTERLATTE

The Saboteur, January 1945. This was a vehicle of the Norwegian Communist party, and far more professionally produced than many of the Scandinavian resistance papers, which were mostly duplicated typescripts.

French government for approving the Nazi–Soviet Pact, so was already a clandestine newspaper when the Germans invaded. It maintained circulation through 383 issues printing up to 200,000 copies, and was distributed publicly for the first time on 21 August 1944, during the liberation of Paris. In Denmark, *Land og Folk* (*Country and People*) was published in twenty-five local editions, with eventually up to 130,000 total copies.[39] The resistance press had an easier time of it in Scandinavia, where the large distances between settlements and the relatively light-touch occupation made systematic repression more difficult.

While these more prominent titles played an impressive role, a newspaper was an importance certificate of importance for any small resistance group: many groups indeed were known by the name of their newspaper, as with Franc-Tireur, the Lyon-based movement established in November 1940. Newspapers could also play a role, as the war wound on, in drawing together the disparate resistance organisations into a common cause. In France, the resistance newspapers played a crucial part in establishing de Gaulle as a leader: from September 1943, the socialist newspaper *Libération* printed under the title: 'Un seul chef: De Gaulle'. The newspapers were also important because they were sufficiently low key to be acceptable to a wide cross-section of the population. In the first period of the occupation, popular opinion was overwhelmingly opposed to acts of sabotage or the assassination of German soldiers, since this always provoked severe reprisals. For the first two years under German rule, newspapers were the resistance.

The Dutch case is in this respect particularly revealing. The German invasion came as a shock: unlike Belgium, the Dutch had no experience of occupation from 1914 to 1918. Had they been left in peace, the Dutch would no doubt have remained neutral, and continued, as they had in the First World War, to place their heavy industry at the disposal of the German war machine. When Hitler came to power in 1933, the Netherlands was the first country to sign a trade agreement with the Third Reich. In the first stages of the occupation, many Dutch households cleansed their book collections to remove anything that might raise suspicion, and public libraries interpreted the instruction to remove anything potentially offensive to the Germans very broadly.[40] Yet from 1940, clandestine literature flourished in the Netherlands to an extent not matched elsewhere in Europe.

Between the two wars, printing was one of the largest industries in the Netherlands, with more than 2,000 firms, many of them very small, operating in the graphic arts industries. Yet the number of people involved in active resistance was relatively small, no more than 25,000, though drawn from the full range of Dutch society. Some resisters were instinctively conservative: many of those in the resistance movement would oppose Indonesian independence in the post-war period.[41] The Protestant newspaper *Trouw* (*Loyalty*, still published today) was founded when a group of the staff abandoned *Vrij Nederland* over its overly secular editorial stance. On the other side of the political spectrum, *Het Parool* (*The Password*) emerged out of the labour movement, another sign of the pre-war social fragmentation of Dutch culture. Ultimately, though, the increasingly virulent hatred of the occupying power was the great unifier.

In addition to newspapers, the clandestine press in several nations also turned out poems, broadsheets and even books. This was important, not least because newspapers were generally distributed for free, so the sale of books and poems could recoup some expenses. A poem protesting the execution of early protesters in the Netherlands, Jan Campert's *De Achttien Dooden* (1943, *The Eighteen Dead*), proved so popular that the profits allowed the printer to set up one of the most famous clandestine publishing houses of the war, De Bezige Bij (The Busy Bee, still active today). The taste for poetry spawned two important anthologies, titled *Geuzenliedboek*, drawing on the memory of the 'Beggar Songs' of the first war of liberation, from Spain in the sixteenth-century Dutch Revolt. The Busy Bee's nearest French equivalent, Éditions de Minuit, was founded in 1941 by the writer and illustrator Jean Bruller. By the end of the war it had published many important authors, including Louis Aragon, François Mauriac and André Gide. Bruller himself, writing under the pseudonym Vercors, made a contribution to the series now recognised as a literary classic, *Le Silence de la mer* (1942, *The Silence of the Sea*), the story of how an elderly man and his niece made their own protest against occupation by refusing to speak to the German officer billeted in their home. Distribution of *Le Silence de la mer* was also assisted by RAF air drops. Sadly the Dutch attempt to pay tribute to British help, *Wat de RAF voor bezet Nederland beteekende* (*What the RAF Did for the Occupied Netherlands*), was rather undermined when almost the entire stock of fifty copies was lost in an RAF bombing raid. The first attempt to publish a Dutch edition of *Le Silence de la mer* also ended in tragedy when the printers were discovered and executed. The standout literary success of the clandestine printing industry was not a text originating in the occupied countries, but John Steinbeck's *The Moon Is Down*, published in clandestine editions in French, Norwegian, Danish, Dutch and Italian.

What did all this publishing, and, it must be said, the bravery of those who risked death to bring out and distribute this literature, achieve? The Germans had four goals in their occupation of the Netherlands: to exploit the Dutch economy, prevent support for the Allies, deport the Jewish population of the country and persuade the Dutch that as a 'brother nation' they were natural friends. They failed only in their efforts to Nazify Dutch society. The Dutch economy was entirely at their disposal, and the Allied attempt to build an intelligence network in Holland was so totally compromised as to render it useless. Certainly the 'spirit of resistance' on which many post-war Dutch authors have prided themselves did not prevent the transportation of 73 per cent of the Netherlands' Jewish population to Nazi death camps, the largest percentage in Western Europe. This offers a rather sobering perspective on the key question, the potency of literature when a society's central values are unexpectedly overturned. Resistance literature has as much to do with restoring a measure of self-esteem as damaging the enemy. This ambiguity continued into the post-war period, when a reluctance to confront the cost of passivity and complicity during the war almost prevented the publication of what is now recognised as one of the war's great works, Anne Frank's *Diary*.

The experience of wartime reading in the occupied countries varied from extreme brutality to an eerie semblance of normality. While the literary culture of Poland and the conquered lands to the east was systematically destroyed, continued access to books and libraries was part of the occupying powers' attempt, ultimately unsuccessful, to conciliate the population of lands with close ties to Germany, such as Denmark and the Netherlands. The Jewish populations of these countries were of course excluded from this favourable treatment, yet out of their torment emerged one of the most extraordinary books of the war, *The Diary of a Young Girl* by Anne Frank. Anne was just thirteen when in 1942 she disappeared with her family into a prepared refuge in her merchant father's warehouse. For two years, Anne's diary offered a candid chronicle of life in these cramped quarters, with all the fear, bickering and, in Anne's case, adolescent angst. Books were a lifeline for Anne and her family, and one of the most remarkable aspects of their secret confinement was the delivery every week by one of their brave and loyal helpers of books from the Amsterdam city library. Anne recorded the thrill of their arrival in her diary entry of 11 July 1943:

> Miep [Gies, Otto's loyal secretary] has so much to carry she looks like a pack mule ... She's also the one who brings five library books with her every Saturday. We long for Saturdays because that means books. We're like a lot of children with a present. Ordinary people don't know how much books can mean to someone who's cooped up. Our only diversions are reading, studying and listening to the wireless.[42]

When their refuge was discovered, Miep Gies managed to hide the manuscript of Anne's diary, and after the war she returned it to Otto Frank, Anne's father, the only member of the family to survive the war. Anne died in March 1945 in Bergen-Belsen concentration camp. Otto was determined it should be published, but those he approached turned it down, including De Bezige Bij and Querido, a publishing house that had made its name with the works of exiled German authors and whose founder had, like

Anne, died in a German concentration camp. Only through a public intervention by the respected Dutch historian Jan Romein could a publisher, Contact, be found.[43] *The Diary of a Young Girl* was published in 1947, and became one of the first great literary monuments of the Holocaust. It has now been translated into seventy languages and sold more than 30 million copies.

12

THE GREAT ESCAPE

In the publishing world, nothing beats a captive market. This is why the market in schoolbooks is so cut-throat. Specialist firms invest huge sums on crafting texts and lobbying for adoption; success can result in millions of sales, spread over many years. The dictators of the twentieth century created a second type of captive market by limiting reader choice and making certain texts virtually obligatory purchases. Hitler's *Mein Kampf* was the most shameless wartime beneficiary, but his example was eagerly followed, from Mao's Little Red Book to East German leader Erich Honecker's speeches, many copies of which ended up in landfill in 1989. The third, most poignant of these captive markets was created in prisoner-of-war camps, where many thousands of young men faced what might be many years of separation from home, family and useful occupation. Books offered one of the few opportunities to enlarge their imaginative world beyond the square mile of earth and wire to which they were confined. Though many indulged in fantasies of escape, and some even made it outside the wire, for most prisoners books offered the best opportunity for some sort of emotional freedom. Books ranked among the necessities of life: this voracious reading was the true great escape.

The POW population included among its number some of the most committed readers of the war. Second Lieutenant Francis Stewart read 350 books during five years of captivity, as we know from his meticulously recorded log.[1] The life of captivity also encouraged a rather different sort of reading from the broader mass of the reader population. Outside the camps the circumstances of wartime life, not least the paper shortage and longer working days, encouraged the production and reading of shorter books – a brief tract on the current war or novels where the plot was resolved in less than 200 pages. POWs, in contrast, had time for the long read: in many cases, the longer the better. In POW libraries great works of literature found a devoted following they certainly could not have hoped for at home. Flight Lieutenant Robert Kee, later a distinguished journalist and broadcaster, was shot down on a mine-laying mission off the coast of Holland, and spent three years in Stalag Luft VIII, made famous for its celebrated escapes. During three years he read systematically through the canon of English literature:

> We could not have lived without books. They were the only sure support, the one true comfort. When food was short, clothing scarce, blocks overcrowded and underheated, and news bad, there were always books. In reading one had a pleasure of which, like sleep, one could never be deprived. I remember the books which I read in that time with a great love.
>
> I think chiefly of Hardy, *Adam Bede*, *Tristram Shandy*, *The Newcomers*, *Henry Esmond*, *The Old Wives' Tale*, *Sentimental Education* and many others, but every sort of reading was happiness. As supply was limited, and controlled by censorship, reading was conventional, but one soon discovered that it would be possible to spend a life-time reading books which were not obscure and still not exhaust everything that was worthwhile.

When there were no novels available, Kee read plays, 'the whole of Shakespeare, Shaw's *Androcles and the Lion*, and Thornton Wilder's *Our Town*'.[2] Camp life also encouraged reflective reading: poetry was both read and written. In 1943, Basil Blackwell at Oxford would publish one collection of such works, the poems of Sergeant R. P. L. Mogg, shot down over Germany.[3] Many readers arrived with relatively simple reading tastes and gradually moved on to more demanding texts, as Stewart, the veteran of 350 titles, recognised:

Early on in this diary I claimed that though in many ways we may have deteriorated in prison, in some ways we have definitely progressed. Reading & the instruction & thought resulting from it is probably the most obvious example of this & certainly the most universal. No prisoner, I suppose, can deny that he has read more & over a wider field in prison than he would have done at home, even if there hadn't been a war on.[4]

Some would come to recognise their years in the camp libraries as formative for their later lives. For others, books were just one way of dealing with the discomfort and endless, unremitting tedium of camp life. Books also provided some form of insulation from the lack of privacy, since prisoners were usually housed in shared rooms with up to nine other men. Some of the bolder prisoners claimed to have welcomed a spell in solitary confinement as respite, so long as they could take a book with them: 'One could settle peacefully to reading or writing and I managed the greater part of *The Forsyte Saga*. Five days in the cooler was pure holiday, ten a shade too long.'[5]

Not all camps were equally well provided for. The provision of books was far better in the second war than in the first, and better in officer camps than in camps for other ranks. While officers could not be obliged to work, non-commissioned prisoners were often assigned to work details. Some relished the opportunity to get out of the camp: 'work from 6 a.m. to 7 p.m., then wash, eat, bath and bed ... Surrounded with lovely country, with rabbits, squirrel, etc.', in the words of one cheerful Tommy in 1944.[6] Though efforts were made to supply work detachments with travelling libraries, this was a life that left little time for reading. There was also considerable variation depending on the theatre of conflict and the host power. In the First World War none of the participants were psychologically prepared for a long war, nor for the large number of prisoners that would have to be cared for: 8 million in all, including 5 million on the Eastern Front.[7] In Britain, where the build-up of POWs was very slow, there was far more concern in the first stages of the war with how to deal with resident aliens from the combatant nations than with battlefield prisoners.

*

In the First World War, public hysteria over the 'enemy within' led the British Parliament to legislate for speedy incarceration of German nationals in hastily prepared internment camps, the largest of which (as it would be in the Second World War also) was situated on the Isle of Man. This camp also had the largest library, with 18,000 volumes for German inmates.[8] In the first year of war, there was in any case a significant imbalance between the number of Allied prisoners in German hands, already half a million by early 1915, and the trickle of German prisoners arriving in Britain.[9] As the number of prisoners in the UK grew, so too did the number of camps, from twenty at the beginning of the war to 500 in 1918. Many of these were extemporised, in derelict factories or converted country houses. The provision of recreation facilities was also fairly arbitrary. The Hague Conventions of 1899 and 1907 which governed the treatment of POWs in the First World War offered little guidance beyond the requirement that prisoners should be fed and housed appropriately. More broadly, the Conventions required POWs to receive equivalent treatment to the men in their armies; given the conditions prevalent on the Western Front, this would not have been very reassuring.

In practice, the case for providing some sort of recreational facilities was strong, if only to prevent the explosion of pent-up frustration that could lead to violence; it was left up to the prisoner's own government or charities to provide the reading material. How much of this would be passed on to the prisoners would vary considerably from country to country. In 1918, a German officer was complaining to the Württemberg War Ministry about the lack of facilities in French camps: 'Mental activity together with physical engagement is the only salvation and means of bearing the long years of internment . . . the German soldier needs this mental work.'[10] The fact that the soldiers were requesting copies of Clausewitz to brush up on military tactics may have explained the French authorities' reluctance in this particular case.

Even after they had been donated, books had to overcome a number of hurdles before they would reach their intended destination. Books and newspapers were subject to double censorship:

first they were checked to ensure that they contained nothing that might give away information about the economic and military situation at home or contained useful technical and scientific information. Then on arrival they would be examined by the recipient administration to remove anything expressing propaganda or sentiments hostile to the host power. Application of these principles could be lax or stringent depending on the zeal or indolence of the responsible local officers. Mostly it was fairly arbitrary: the prisoners were not in the position to complain, and mostly would have had no knowledge of the books they were due to receive. The lack of competent linguists also hindered the efforts of censorship. The bureaucratic process meant that despite the best efforts of neutral bodies like the Danish Red Cross, it could be many months before books reached their intended destination, and prisoners would never know what had been confiscated en route. Even so, many prisoners welcomed the arrival of a consignment of reading material with almost as much enthusiasm as food parcels.[11]

Newspapers were a more difficult problem, though still eagerly devoured, even if the news contained in them was many months out of date. Most belligerent authorities forbade the circulation of newspapers from the prisoners' home country or other enemy nations. Sometimes, but not always, newspapers from neutral nations were permitted. The most easily available newspapers were the specially produced propaganda vehicles in the prisoners' own language circulated by their captors. English-speaking prisoners in Germany were provided with the *Continental Times*, and at least at the beginning of the war there were regular issues of the *Bulletin pour les prisonniers français en Allemagne*. There is little to suggest these newspapers had much success in their ostensible purpose of influencing minds. The French *Zeitung für die deutschen Kriegsgefangenen* (*News for German POWs*) was widely ridiculed for its frequent linguistic errors. Officers wishing to brush up on their languages could at least read the local newspapers, which circulated fairly freely in the German camps, and were certainly more current. Some of the more interesting nuggets could be abstracted into the ubiquitous camp newspapers. One captured German officer incarcerated at Barcelonnette in the French Alps indulged himself with a subscription to the London *Times*.

Prisoners from different nationalities were not necessarily housed separately. Münster, in Westphalia, relatively close to the front line, had three camps, the biggest of which had a library of 7,000 books, with titles in English, French, Russian, Polish and Flemish. There were even some books in Esperanto, the then fashionable attempt to fabricate a universal language. In February 1915, the German government began to sort prisoners into separate camps for different nationalities, an arrangement that became standard practice by the Second World War. This involved experimentation with 'privileged' camps for ethnic groups who might be induced to turn against their own governments. Prisoners from Belgium's Flemish population, of which the Germans had high hopes, were brought to Göttingen, where the more intellectual among them were even given access to books from the renowned Göttingen University. The camp itself had a library of 6,300 books. Sir Roger Casement, a diplomat in the British Foreign Office who nursed a passionate attachment to Irish nationalism, was allowed to tour the British camps to recruit soldiers for an Irish brigade, but with little success. It was a venture that would cost him his life; Casement was arrested when a German submarine attempted to land him back in Ireland in 1916, tried for treason and executed.

A variety of organisations laboured to provide British prisoners in Germany with reading materials. The Camps Library project, not altogether liberated from the didactic zeal of public librarians, aimed to supply books of a 'solid character': 'historical and scientific works, poetry, essays . . . pocket dictionaries and grammars' and pocket Shakespeares.[12] These were self-evidently more suitable for the officer class than enlisted men. The Prisoners of War Book Scheme, meanwhile, endeavoured to supply books of an educative nature, particularly technical titles, for those attempting to use their time productively to enhance their professional qualifications.

> Can those of us at home . . . imagine what it must be to have
> days and months of time in enforced inactivity and never a

line to read? Can we picture to ourselves the state of the energetic young man, working hard to rise in his calling, leaving
the books and classes, on which depended all his hopes, in
order to join the colours, and now condemned to eat his
heart out, in some far-distant camp, surrounded only by the
enemies of his country?[13]

Hopefully this purple prose opened the purses of donors, but in
truth most prisoners did not endure 'enforced inactivity': more
than 90 per cent of those imprisoned by the Germans were put to
work on farms or industrial sites. Many of those on work parties
had no access to books at all. Most of the accounts of reading in
imprisonment came from officers, and it is from them that we
hear of books retained by censors and books passed on with their
covers ripped off, on the rather feeble pretext that items sent to
French prisoners had maps concealed in the bindings. A scheme
to improve the flow of books by ordering from a firm in Leipzig
went nowhere when it was argued that British authors would be
done out of their royalties.[14] With books in such short supply,
British prisoners, officers and men, mostly read whatever came to
hand: the authors on their wish lists, the established favourites of
detective and adventure literature, G. A. Henty, Conan Doyle and
Baroness Orczy, along with Ethel Dell, a wildly popular author of
romances set in the British Empire, remained unobtainable.

There was an air of improvisation about some First World War
internment facilities that would not be replicated in the second
war. British civilians trapped in Germany in 1914 were despatched
to the racecourse at Ruhleben near Berlin. Here they had space,
reasonable food and a row of shops ('Bond Street') including the
camp's official bookshop ('the Mecca of booklovers') and a printing works. This was responsible for the camp's elegant magazine,
a generous forty-eight to seventy-two pages printed on excellent
paper, with cartoons and illustrations. Issue number six, in June
1917, was published in an edition of 7,000 copies, 4,000 of which
were mailed by inmates to friends and family at home. A separately
printed prospectus of study opportunities for autumn term 1916
offered instruction in twenty-five subjects, including ten languages

along with the biological and physical sciences: the prospectus has a picture of the biology laboratory. For the less committed scholar there were literary lectures on Galsworthy and 'the new poetry'. Strolling the racetrack, you never knew whom you might meet. Issue two of April 1916 carried an appeal for a 'Who's Who in Ruhleben'.[15]

The period between the two wars brought important changes to the regulations governing the treatment of combatants in wartime. The barebones Hague Convention was expanded in a series of protocols agreed in Geneva in 1929. These made clear that prisoners were entitled to receive relief parcels and, crucially, the holding power was mandated to 'encourage intellectual diversions organised by prisoners'. From these stipulations followed an extraordinary effort in the Second World War to provide Allied POWs with food and books, the two forms of nourishment most badly needed by those behind the barbed wire. In Britain, the provision of books was placed in the hands of the Red Cross, in co-operation with another important humanitarian organisation, the Order of St John.[16] The books were largely donated by the public enhanced by purchases made possible by fundraising. During the course of the war these organisations despatched some 240,000 books directly to camps, while the YMCA sent a million books for the use of American prisoners on behalf of the American Red Cross. The British and Foreign Bible Society sent Bibles, including 5,000 copies of the Greek New Testament for those intending to study for the ministry.[17] Many of the Bibles, particularly in East Asia, were inevitably repurposed as cigarette papers, though one feisty padre, Noel Duckworth, insisted the men read the pages first.[18]

Relatives were also permitted to send newly purchased books directly to their loved ones, inspiring yet another of the schemes of the Penguin press, allowing POWs, in return for an annual subscription of £3, to receive ten titles a month from a specially created POW series. This selection included some remarkably provocative titles, including A. J. Evans's popular tales of First World War derring-do, *The Escaping Club*, first published in 1921. It is hard to see why this would have been let into the camps, but in a postscript

The Prisoner of War

THE OFFICIAL JOURNAL OF THE PRISONERS OF WAR DEPARTMENT OF THE
RED CROSS AND ST. JOHN WAR ORGANISATION, ST. JAMES'S PALACE, LONDON, S.W.1

Vol. 3 No. 31   Free to Next of Kin   NOVEMBER, 1944

The Editor Writes —

IT has always been evident that as the Allied ring tightened round Germany the situation of our prisoners there would, for various reasons, become more difficult. Prison camps near the frontiers would tend to be moved into the interior—and this must mean leaving well-organised permanent camps and probably moving into improvised and overcrowded quarters. Moreover, under the increasing weight of our bombing attacks the transport position inside Germany was bound to become more and more disorganised. Both these processes have already started, though not as yet on a large scale. The latest figures as to stocks in camps bring us up to September 15th and indicate that until then, at any rate, Geneva were still managing to get our parcels through. Clearly, the seriousness of the situation will depend on whether the Germans fight all the way back to Berlin or whether organised resistance ceases fairly quickly.

Four Ships at Lisbon

There is good reason for hoping that the Lisbon-Marseilles-Geneva route will very soon be re-opened, though on a limited scale, owing to the reduced capacity of the Marseilles-Geneva railway. In anticipation of this four of our ships, fully loaded, are waiting at Lisbon. In addition, there is an accumulation in our warehouses that it will take some time to work off, so that it may be some time, too, before

despatches from this country can be resumed.

Christmas Parcels

The suspension of shipping made it impossible to despatch the Christmas parcels, which were ready at the end of July, so that I am afraid that the chance of their arriving in time is not great. Efforts are now being made to give them priority, but I wonder if it is realised that one week's food parcels for 160,000 prisoners weighs about 800 tons. The prisoners will, of course, be disappointed, but will appreciate the reasons, of which they have been informed. In contrast with this I am glad to be able to record that we have managed, in spite of recent difficulties, to get through to Geneva a not inconsiderable quantity of urgent supplies, mostly medical.

Planning Their Return

With victory approaching hopes are centred on the speedy liberation of

A rugger team at Stalag XXB.

prisoners of war and their quick return home. The problem is, of course, one for the military authorities and not for the Red Cross, although the Red Cross will have a hand in it, and I understand that plans are being worked out in great detail with the object of bringing them home with the least possible delay. But obviously 160,000 prisoners scattered in innumerable camps and labour detachments cannot be assembled and brought home in a few days.

Back from Switzerland

The 1,000-odd officers and men who arrived back from Switzerland so unexpectedly, recently, were in exceptionally high spirits and good health. During their two days in a pleasant dispersal camp just outside London they were entertained by continuous films and E.N.S.A. shows. After that, they all went on six weeks' leave.

Service at Belfast

Nearly 1,200 next of kin of prisoners of war recently attended the special service of intercession at St. Anne's Cathedral, Belfast, arranged by the Ulster Gift Fund. The Governor and the Prime Minister of Northern Ireland were present, and the service was conducted by the Dean, the Very Reverend W. S. Kerr, B.D., the Rev. R. J. F. Mayston, M.B.E., Deputy Assistant Chaplain-General for Northern Ireland, being the preacher. The collection on behalf of the Red Cross was taken by six officers from the three Services, the Naval officer being an ex-prisoner of war. Realistic plans for the building up of our national and home life were urged by Mr. Mayston

Prisoner of War offered relatives a generally upbeat view of life in the camps, with features on sporting fixtures and camp entertainment. It also offered clear guidance on what families could and could not send their incarcerated family members, including what books were most in demand.

of a letter to Allen Lane at Penguin, Evans confirmed that it had a wide readership: '*The Escaping Club* was translated into German and Italian and was compulsory reading for guards in the POW camps.' It was also eagerly studied in the libraries on RAF bases.[19]

The Prisoner of War, a periodical distributed to families of

POWs free of charge by the Red Cross, often contained lists of books wanted in the camps, and recommended that families send paperbacks because they were much more economical to post. Penguins were ubiquitous in the camps, though the company suffered a temporary setback when a Penguin book including an advertisement for a Penguin pen (presumably intended for the domestic market) fell into the hands of a guard, who was not surprisingly outraged as it showed a cartoon Adolf Hitler impaled on a soldier's bayonet.[20] All Penguins in the camps were banned. When the authorities relented after the Normandy landings, a backlog of 25,000 Penguins was released to the camps.

When the books arrived at the camps, the German authorities, often older servicemen no longer fit for front-line duties, proved accommodating. They would far rather that their charges be reading, playing football or gardening than tunnelling (though often they did all of these things). Space was made available for a library and reading room, and a librarian appointed from among the prisoners to take charge of the collection. In Oflag VII-B at Eichstätt in Bavaria, the library was curated by Elliott Viney, who had marched off to war with a detachment recruited from his family printing firm, only to be captured in the retreat to Dunkirk. Viney ran the camp newspaper as well as the library and seems to have especially enjoyed his duels with the German censor. Buchan's *Thirty-Nine Steps* and *Greenmantle* were banned, but the omnibus *Adventures of Richard Hannay* made it through. Although works by the unfortunate American novelist Winston Churchill were all confiscated, the authentic prime minister's *My Early Life* slipped through the net because it was published under the name Winston Spencer Churchill. According to Viney, the only banned book they never succeeded in obtaining was the English translation of *Mein Kampf*. Viney also, employing his skills as a printer, made sure that the escape stories survived the frequent hut inspections by having them 'carefully rebound with the first and last pages of some other more innocuous title'.[21]

Oflag VII-B was one of the bigger camps, and Viney built its library from 500 books in 1940 to an astonishing 50,000 titles in 1945.[22] This was exceptional, but the library at Stalag Luft III

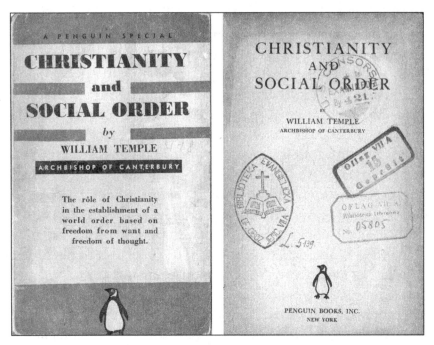

The censor doing his job. Archbishop Temple was a trenchant supporter
of the war and the benign title was no defence against a careful reading.
The numerous stamps allow us to trace the arduous journey to a Polish
officer camp in Bavaria. At the last moment, the censor stepped in to
ban the book, which is probably why it survives: almost all the books
in camp libraries were left behind when the camps were liberated.

had 8,500 volumes, not including the 20,000 books in prisoners'
private libraries, which generally circulated just as generously.[23]
These resources had been carefully curated because many of the
books were intended to support the courses in professional development being pursued by camp inmates. Most of the camps put
on courses of lectures of various degrees of seriousness, and in the
bigger camps these achieved an astonishing range. In Stalag Luft
III at Sagen, 1,500 prisoners attended 200 classes a week from 1942.
The following year, 100 students sat their City & Guilds exams in
the camp cinema, with tables and chairs obligingly provided by the
guards. This drive to allow POWs to obtain formal qualifications
was one of the most inspired initiatives of the war, mostly under
the aegis of the University of London, with its extensive experience of external examinations. During the course of the war, the

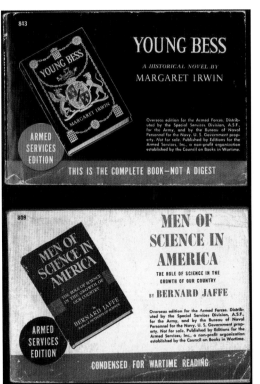

17. The overwhelming publishing success of the Second World War, the American Services Editions delivered 122 million copies of 1,322 titles to servicemen stationed throughout the world, a logistical feat as impressive as the publishing venture itself. Fiction predominated, with a smattering of non-fiction titles.

18. The Staff of the *Orkney Blast*, the first of the British troops papers in the Second World War. Sixty thousand service men and women were stationed on Orkney, largely to service and protect the British fleet at anchor in Scapa Flow, and any sort of diversion was gratefully embraced.

19. *Time* Magazine. An example of the miniature editions of popular magazines specially produced for American troops overseas. The military authorities were well aware that not all the troops wanted to read the novels in the American Service Editions, and sports magazines also featured prominently in the reading matter distributed.

20. The soldier as reader. The citizen army put into the field by the United States in 1917 was conspicuously better educated than the conscripted troops of most combatant nations. With three million books donated by the public, the military created a network of over 500 libraries, including in military hospitals.

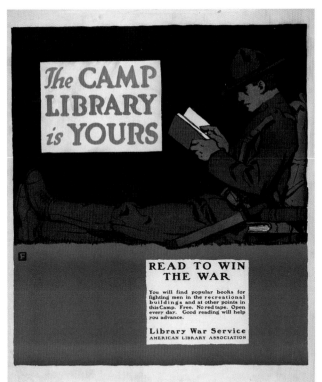

21. The American Library Association was campaigning for donations right up to and beyond the cessation of hostilities. A large tranche of the late-arriving books was used to establish the American Library in Paris, founded in 1920, a beacon of American culture in a Europe battered by war.

22. It took a great deal of credulity to believe this presentation of neatly stacked books being eagerly consumed by German troops in well-laundered uniforms in the front line. Trench life was antipathetic to serious reading, and the rats, mud and constant discomfort would have made short work of books and clean uniforms.

KNOWLEDGE WINS

PUBLIC LIBRARY
BOOKS
ARE
FREE

AMERICAN LIBRARY ASSOCIATION

23. 'Knowledge wins: public library books are free' (1918). For soldier and civilian alike, book learning created a pathway to gainful employment and prosperity. The public library ideal was very much alive, though librarians well knew that the vast majority of their patrons came to a library for light entertainment and relaxing reading.

24. Edward Murrow and William L. Shirer. Their radio broadcasts provided American listeners with some of the most vivid reporting from Germany and London, and Shirer the material for his bestselling *Berlin Diary*.

25. Adolf Hitler, bestselling author, discerning book collector and devotee of the corny adventure novels of Karl May (1842–1912). This was awkward, as most German librarians were dedicated to eradicating such literature from their shelves.

PELICAN
BOOKS

READING
FOR PROFIT

MONTGOMERY
BELGION

26. *Reading for Profit* (1945) published the lectures on English literature given by Montgomery Belgion to his fellow officers while imprisoned in Germany. Belgion warned his auditors that they would be demanding, but both he and the lectures were extremely popular. Fastidious to the last, his preface thanks 'the courtesy of the German military authorities in enabling me to typewrite a portion of my MS. and in allowing me to send the whole of it home'.

27. The fortress monastery at Monte Cassino was originally conceived as a refuge for books from other libraries, and only as the front came nearer was the abbot persuaded to send the treasures to safety in the Vatican. This is one of the irreplaceable ancient manuscripts that survived as a result.

The evidence of love

DAN JACOBSON

READERS NEWS

July 1961 · 23rd Year · Volume 24 · No. 2 · (Whole Number 286)

The Difficulty of being South African

A Note about Next Month's Choice at 5s 9d

THE EVIDENCE OF LOVE

by Dan Jacobson

'IN THE minds of both of them was the thought of Kenneth and Isabel being carried to their respective prisons to be stripped, shaved, shouted at, bathed in lysol.

'"Be comforted, sah," Cornelius Makeer cried out.

'Violence makes a strange ending for a love story, even if the setting is South African. But because Dan Jacobson has the ability to create sensitive, intelligent people and make them act sensitively and intelligently despite the background of guilt and shock, *The Evidence of Love* is neither propaganda nor sensationalism. It is, instead, a considerable artistic achievement, all the more impressive because it was written calmly out of the same tensions as created the South African explosion.

'It is the story of a love affair between a Cape Coloured boy and a white girl. Kenneth Makeer is bright, dissatisfied and ambitious, with a desperately respectable father and a complexion white enough to 'pass' outside his own group; Isabel Last is wealthy, anxious to please, confused, lonely and 'liberal'. Both live in Lyndhurst—the setting of most of Jacobson's work—and both, throughout the larger part of the book, scarcely know of each other's existence. Both are lost and casting around for their identities, and both are taken up by a rich, eccentric spinster called Miss Bentwisch who, to atone for a shadow of bastardy

28. This searing tale of interracial love in South Africa and its tragic consequences was published in London in 1960, where its South African author Dan Jacobson had moved to pursue his career as a writer. It would be another twenty-five years before the prohibition of interracial marriages was relaxed, one of the first steps to towards the dismantling of Apartheid and its censorship regime.

29. The smug sneering of the German officer to the captured British Tommy, 'For you the war is over,' now has an ironic ring, since *Commando* books certainly helped perpetuate tropes of the brave and ingenious British soldiers and their villainous but easily outwitted foes. They were a ubiquitous presence in boys' schools and playgrounds in the 1960s and 1970s, collected, swapped or bartered.

30. This book of quotations from Chairman Mao, universally known as the Little Red Book, was the publishing phenomenon of the twentieth century, with more than a billion copies published between 1964 and 1971. Generously distributed abroad and ubiquitous in China, the Little Red Book played a critical and often oppressive role in China's Cultural Revolution.

31. The poet Anna Akhmatova (1889–1966) lived through five decades of the Soviet experiment, initially lionised but then suffering greatly from official disapproval. Her son and partners experienced long spells in the Gulag, but Anna somehow survived to enjoy renewed esteem in the last years of her life.

university set 1,305 examination papers, though some of the questions on the history papers were lucky to get through the censors: 'War is the national industry of Prussia'; 'For the past fifty years Italy has been regarded as a first-class power only by courtesy.'[24] (The German censors might well have agreed with the second of these.) Examinations were held in eighty-eight camps.[25]

Other professional bodies, including the Institute of Civil Engineering and the Chartered Insurance Institute, also provided a syllabus. The Library Association ensured that their members in captivity could continue to work towards their qualifications. One of the most eye-catching initiatives was the course in English literature designed by J. R. R. Tolkien and C. S. Lewis: this was the first external examination authorised by the University of Oxford.[26] It dovetailed nicely with the courses in English literature offered in several camps by the urbane Montgomery Belgion. Belgion was nearly fifty when captured in Greece in 1941 and a natural authority figure; his lectures were such a success that they were published as a paperback at the end of the war. His acknowledgements ended with a typically thoughtful recognition of the role of his guards in facilitating this project: 'Finally, let me acknowledge the courtesy of the German military authorities in enabling me to typewrite a portion of my MS. and in allowing me to send the whole of it home.'[27] The Pelican paperback was printed by the firm of his fellow POW, Elliott Viney.

Professional qualifications inevitably required textbooks and resources well beyond the capacities of a camp library. These were provided by the Educational Books Section of the Red Cross, which after an air raid in London in 1940 moved to the recently completed New Bodleian building in Oxford. Here, under the scrupulous management of Ethel Herdman, the staff of the section fulfilled a stream of orders sent either by individual POWs or the course director. Delivery was accelerated by the establishment of a warehouse of 50,000 books in Geneva covering the seventy-six most popular subjects.[28] But all requests were considered, including from the bus conductor interested in 'light psychology' which he thought might prepare him for promotion to inspector, or the rabbit tracker intent on becoming a gamekeeper. The request from

Write and tell them

with a Penguin Pen

THE PENGUIN PEN

is a precision made Fountain Pen fitted with an Iridium Tipped 14-Carat Solid Gold Nib (Fine, Medium or Broad).

The Ebony Streamline Holder, highly polished and unbreakable, embodies the latest design in safety screw caps which automatically shuts off the flow of ink when in the pocket.

Self-Filling, Large Ink Capacity, improved ladder feed ensures an equable and controlled ink flow.

BRITISH MADE THROUGHOUT

INCLUDING THE COST OF **5/6** POSTAGE AND PACKING

The Penguin fountain pen advertised with a grinning soldier impaling a cartoon Adolf Hitler. It was tactless to send books with this advertisement to POW camps: when recognised, it led to a ban on the distribution of Penguins.

Stalag Luft VI for gold leaf with which to decorate its prospectus was probably enjoyed as teasing humour.[29] By the end of the war, 263,000 books, helpfully furnished by Blackwell's bookshop conveniently next door on Broad Street, had been despatched.

There is little doubt that German prisoners of war in the UK were far less well supplied with reading material than was the case in the Allied camps in Germany. There were a number of reasons why this should be the case. Rather like in the first war, German prisoners were rather thin on the ground while the tide of war was flowing so heavily in their favour. The few that did fall into British hands, pilots downed over Britain or prisoners taken off submarines, were swiftly shipped off to Canada or Australia, where the prospects of their making a successful escape back to Germany were negligible.[30] It was only in 1944 that German POWs began arriving in Britain in any number, by which time their relatives at home and the German authorities were too preoccupied with the struggle for survival to organise a book drive for prisoners. Birger Forell, a Swedish pastor invited by Bishop Bell of Chichester to be the prisoners' advocate in Britain, suggested that the libraries left behind by the Wehrmacht in France could be distributed to the camps. This recommendation was followed, but exclusively to the benefit of POW camps in France and Belgium. For the English camps, Forell was reduced to recruiting two young women, ironically German Jewish refugees, to comb second-hand bookshops for suitable German texts.[31]

This paucity of reading material did, however, inspire one of the most interesting publishing initiatives of the war, a series of texts issued in German translation specifically for German POWs.[32] This was undertaken under the aegis of the United States government by a collaboration between the exiled German publisher Gottfried Bermann Fischer and the American branch of Penguin Books. From 1942, almost half a million Axis prisoners were transported to the US, including 380,000 Germans. The new series was conceived in part as a form of re-education in civil values for the more convinced Nazis, though not without a certain nervousness: concerns were expressed that it might provoke retaliatory indoctrination efforts on captured American soldiers. The titles chosen were mainly taken from the excellent range of German literary works for which Bermann Fischer held copyrights, including authors such as Thomas Mann and Erich Maria Remarque, who were both banned in Germany. The series was completed by translations of a handful of American titles, including Ernest Hemingway's *For Whom the Bell Tolls* and *The Rover* by Joseph Conrad. Wendell Willkie's *One World* set out an alluring vision of the possibilities for post-war Europe. The series, known as the *Bücherreihe Neue Welt* (New World Book Series), was printed in a standard paperback format and copies were sold in the camps below cost at 25 cents each. Two hundred and forty thousand copies were distributed, and reports from the camps suggest that they were widely read.

In Britain, the quality of library provision in the POW camps for German prisoners gradually began to improve, though mostly after the end of hostilities. In principle the Geneva Convention required prisoners to be repatriated as soon as feasible after peace had been signed. The British government, however, took advantage of the fact that the German unconditional surrender did not constitute a peace treaty to retain many of the prisoners in the UK to plug the labour shortage with so many British troops still on active service abroad. There was also a genuine fear that the return of thousands of unrepentant Nazis would be potentially disruptive as the Allied occupying forces struggled with the dilemmas of creating a denazified civil society. The problem was particularly acute with prisoners decanted back to Britain from Canada and the United States, since these soldiers and pilots captured in the first years of the war had no experience of the disintegration of Germany in the last stages of the war, and were often defiantly committed to the Nazi cause. Efforts to identify the more amenable were often impeded by the rigorous discipline imposed within the camps by the prisoners themselves.

The year 1945 was undoubtedly the bleakest time for German POWs in Britain, as news of the horrors of the concentration camps turned British opinion decisively against them. The sorting process made slow progress, but those privileged few identified

A basic reading facility in a British POW camp for German prisoners.
By the time German prisoners had arrived in any numbers, the position
on the home front was too parlous to be able to send many books from
Germany. Some camps had to rely on relief organisations sending volunteers
to scour second-hand bookshops for German language material.

for the 'white' camps of co-operative prisoners could enjoy the comparative luxury of a camp like Shap Wells in Cumbria, where newcomers found sheets on their beds and a decent library of 2,000 books (the camp's main building is now an elegant hotel). This was a small camp where 250 officers were served by eighty orderlies and kitchen staff. Cultural events figured prominently, including a series of university-style lectures provided by the erudite Professor Joachim Ritter of Kiel University. Ritter also contributed a study of T. S. Eliot for the camp magazine. More traditionally minded officers could enjoy lectures on foxhunting and shooting from the camp commandant.

One of the best organised of the camps was at Featherstone Park, near Haltwhistle, close to Hadrian's Wall. Like many POW camps it had originally been built to house American troops in the build-up to D-Day. Thereafter it was repurposed, first to hold

Italian prisoners, then as a camp for German officers, attended
by 580 orderlies.[33] The compound was divided into three parts,
to separate co-operative prisoners from the irredeemable (the SS
and submariners were automatically placed in this category) and
those yet to be classified. In the post-war years it became a huge
centre of adult education, with materials provided by the YMCA
and Red Cross. It gradually built a library of 5,500 books. Officers
could also buy books for their private collections; soon there was
an on-camp bookshop and a bindery. Among the visiting lecturers
were Pastor Martin Niemöller (who as a former First World War
submariner and early supporter of Hitler was seen as a turncoat
and was roundly booed) and a demobbed Hugh Trevor-Roper,
whose disquisition on 'The End of an Ideology' went down so well
that his listeners subsequently ordered 400 copies of his recently
published *The Last Days of Hitler*.[34]

Llanmartin near Newport had the best of the libraries, though
a more recalcitrant POW community. Watten in Caithness was
another camp reserved for hard-core prisoners, hence the remote
location. Gradually it accumulated a library of 1,000 texts, though
the cold drab climate ensured it was never a happy camp.[35] The
librarian at Grizedale was Major Hans Gerd von Rundstedt, a
trained archivist and reluctant soldier. He shared his quarters with
his father, Field Marshal von Rundstedt, which made Grizedale an
obligatory stop for the military historian Basil Liddell-Hart, who
shuttled round the camps interviewing the captured generals and
collecting material for his next book.[36] The purpose of re-education
was further pursued at Hilton Hall, where German officers could
be seconded for short residential courses. These pampered prisoners were provided with a large selection of German newspapers,
and an excellent library where *Mein Kampf* was shelved next to
one of the works of Winston Churchill.

By February 1947, German prisoners were spread between 1,400
separate units, and not all of them could be provided with libraries
of this quality. As was the case with Allied POWs, the best facilities were reserved for the officers. Even so, the other ranks in both
German and British camps were well looked after when compared

to the fate of significant portions of the POW population, many of whom were deprived of virtually any of the amenities prescribed for them under the Geneva Convention. The multitude of prisoners scooped up by the German advance into the Soviet Union were kept under bestial conditions. Rations calculated at a starvation level ensured that most of them would die before liberation. The Japanese also gave little regard to the welfare of the Allied prisoners under their care. Although the civilian internment camp at Singapore had a well-stocked library, the Japanese army had little respect for soldiers who surrendered. Many were worked to death on the infamous Burma Railway, while others died of malnutrition or tropical diseases against which their weakened bodies had no defence.[37] In camps like this any sort of reading matter was rare, though even on the Thailand–Burma Railway Stephen Alexander found a copy of *Gone with the Wind*, and in the hospital hut (a place for sustained reading for POWs in all theatres), *The Forsyte Saga* and *War and Peace*. Some camps had so few books that texts were divided into small segments so that ten or twelve men had something to read, a privilege that in the more liberally supplied German camps was reserved for *Lady Chatterley's Lover*.[38]

Alan Steele, a Penguin author who was captured by the Japanese in Java, spent almost three years in POW camps in Japan. There he reported:

> We had a fairly good supply of books but had little opportunity for reading as (a) our huts usually had no windows, and we weren't allowed to take a book outside, and (b) we were working all day. There were two big deliveries of American Red Cross books, one in November '43 and the second about the same time last year [1944]. The first lot they divided into lots of fifty books and sent them round to the twenty-three camps in our Fukuoka, Kyushu, area. They look on books as 'books' – so the result was that you might, and did, receive fifty Jewish prayer books, instead of fiction etc. After many protests I was allowed by the Japs to go to the warehouse in Fukuoka, and sort them myself for the various camps.[39]

Steele and his fellow prisoners were rescued by the Americans shortly after the Japanese surrender. The end of the war was far more chaotic for the POWs in Germany. With the Russians closing in, the prisoners were marched west. While rumours of a possible evacuation had been circulating since the beginning of 1945, the prisoners often had only a couple of hours' notice of departure. It was a mad scramble to gather warm clothes and treasured possessions. While most men kept their journals, with the careful record of friends moving in and out, hard-fought games of football or cricket and books read, the books themselves were usually sacrificed to the need to carry as much food as possible. Robert Kee managed to rescue *Tristam Shandy* and a paperback collection of poetry.[40] The carefully curated libraries were simply abandoned. Collectively, Allied POWs must have left behind something like 3 or 4 million books in the German camps, many by this time read almost to destruction. Yet they had served their turn. It is fair to say that nowhere in the war had libraries been more valued: indispensable helpmates through endless years of waiting.

PART V

THE BOMBER WILL ALWAYS GET THROUGH

13

SANCTUARY

Although civilian casualties were relatively rare away from the battle front, the sheer unexpectedness of death falling from the sky, on busy cities, killing civilians indiscriminately, was something for which the civilian populations of the combatant nations of the First World War were totally unprepared. Thomas Livingstone, a clerk living with his wife and son in a Glasgow tenement, was an avid consumer of war news and a devoted diarist. While recording his visits to Glasgow's excellent public libraries and newspaper offices, it is striking how often he refers to bombing raids and the casualties caused by Zeppelin raids and later aeroplanes. In April 1916, the prudent Thomas even insured the contents of his small flat against air raids.[1] By the middle of the war, as we see from Tommy's diary, such events would be relatively common: one horrifying incident in London claimed seventy-one lives; all told, attacks from the air were responsible for more than 2,000 fatalities in Britain between 1915 and 1918.[2] Allied raids on Stuttgart, Mainz, Freiburg and Frankfurt caused around 2,600 deaths, a tragedy, even if such casualty levels certainly could not be compared to the carnage on the battlefields (an average of 6,000 fatalities a day), or even what the population of France and Belgium suffered from artillery bombardment.[3]

This unwelcome new intrusion of the horrors of war into far-distant cities foretold the far greater terrors of the 1940s. In the two decades between the wars, aircraft design improved very rapidly, and much more rapidly than the defensive technology created to mitigate the threat. It became an axiom of war planning that 'the bomber will always get through'. Many, not least in the air forces of the combatant powers, believed that airpower would be the decisive force in winning the war. Bombers, it was anticipated, would pinpoint military targets, airfields and dockyards, and lay waste to essential industries, destroying the ability of enemies to continue the fight and eroding civilian morale. In practice, this was not an exact science; in built-up areas, public buildings and civilian housing would be equally at risk, as they had been when the Zeppelins floated into view. This posed a special challenge to cultural institutions, such as art galleries, full of irreplaceable treasures, and libraries packed with highly inflammable paper products.

All this was well known when war broke out in 1939, not least through the recent experience of the Spanish Civil War, which many journalists, authors and military personnel had experienced at first hand. Yet for all that, the protagonists in the Second World War took very different views, both on the questions of which of the nation's treasures would be removed to safety, or even whether they should be evacuated at all. While the masterpieces of Renaissance art sat out the war in comfortable safety in deep salt mines, books were very often left to take their chances: frequently with catastrophic results.

In this section of the book we turn away from the contribution that books made to winning wars, to auditing the cost. Books, as we have seen, played an essential role in maintaining civilian and troop morale. Books helped train officers, inform military strategies and prepare the population for the sacrifice of battle. Libraries were essential resources for scientists, intelligence organisations and cartographers. But there was a price to be paid for this contribution to the war effort. In the course of the two world wars, books in their millions would be wilfully destroyed, pillaged, pilfered and removed from their libraries. Others would be simply the collateral damage of total war. Librarians were aware that the books in their charge were both precious and vulnerable. This chapter examines the steps taken to mitigate the danger.

Italy's military contribution to the two world wars was far from glorious, but in terms of the protection and conservation of its book stock, it set the standard for others to follow. There was good reason for this, for Italy had a great deal at stake in the new era of industrialised warfare. Thanks to the country's Renaissance heritage, and its role in the development of typography, Italian libraries had by far most widely dispersed collections of medieval manuscripts and early printed books, many of them still in the hands of church institutions. At the beginning of the war many of these books were transported to safe havens in remote locations, such as the monastic mountaintop fortress of Monte Cassino. The monastery mostly took in boarders from other ecclesiastical communities, but the libraries in major cities like Bologna and Milan, likely to be early targets for bombing, also sought safe havens in the surrounding countryside.

In deciding what to secrete in these caves, mines and isolated castles, Italian librarians could rely on an admirably clear series of protocols.[4] Between 1935 and 1936, the General Directorate of Libraries established a tripartite order of priority that would influence conservation strategies all over Europe. In the first category came manuscripts, incunabula and early printed materials of special cultural significance. These were to be evacuated from institutions in cities as a matter of course. A second class of valuable books, including sixteenth-century imprints, was to be moved to protected rooms within the library building. More recent imprints, assumed to be less valuable and more easily replaced, should remain on the shelves. Civil servants and librarians were aware of the importance of books to maintaining civilian morale.

This triage and preparation took time, particularly when libraries lost staff to military call-up with the opening of hostilities. It was not until June 1940 that the evacuation of high-category items took place, around 200,000 volumes from the major state libraries (because of the late creation of Italy from a patchwork of smaller states, Italy had seven institutions classed as national libraries). Meanwhile, responsibility for the safeguarding of ecclesiastical libraries and archives, of which there were more than a thousand in Italy, fell to the Vatican, which provided both the possibility of sanctuary within the protected space of the Vatican State, and advice on good practice for the more far-flung institutions. The bombing of Genoa, Turin and Milan in the autumn of 1942 prompted a second round of evacuations, now encompassing books from the second conservation category. Library catalogues were also moved to places of safety, so that in the event of catastrophe the collection could at least be reconstructed from new purchases.

When in September 1943 Italy abandoned the alliance with Germany, and nominally joined the Allied cause, German troops moved swiftly to occupy the territory of its former ally. The next two years would prove the most difficult of the war for Italian libraries. As the Allied armies fought their way painfully up the rugged terrain of the peninsula, and bombing of Italian cities intensified, it was hard to observe the respect for Italy's cultural treasures originally envisaged. In December 1943, the supreme commander of the Allied forces, General Eisenhower, had reaffirmed his commitment to the preservation of cultural monuments, but with reservations. Italy, he reminded his subordinates, 'was a country rich in monuments which by their creation helped and now in their old age illustrate the growth of the civilization which is ours'. But, he continued, 'If we have to choose between destroying a famous building and sacrificing our own men, then our men's lives count infinitely more and the buildings must go.'[5] This qualification sealed the fate of Monte Cassino.

By the end of 1943, the mountain range on which Monte Cassino perched was an integral part of General Kesselring's Gustav Line, the network of fortified positions that barred Allied access to Rome and the plains of northern Italy. As the American and Empire troops fought their way towards the monastery complex, the local German commander persuaded the abbot to send the community's treasures, and those they were guarding for others, to safety in the Vatican, where they would join the books and manuscripts of a host of Roman institutions. The abbot reluctantly agreed, and 70,000 volumes were transported out. In the next months of brutal fighting Monte Cassino was reduced to rubble. The salvation of its books became a double propaganda triumph: for the Germans, who had obligingly provided the trucks to convey the books to safety (they were careful to make a film record of this philanthropy), and for the Vatican, which even before the end of 1945 hosted a public exhibition of the treasures to

Monte Cassino after four months of bombardment. No
books could have survived this level of devastation.

which it had given sanctuary. The published catalogue even had an
English-language edition; the presence of a copy in the St Andrews
University Library suggests this may have been widely distributed
to foreign institutions as a gift.[6] At a time when the papacy was
facing severe criticism for failing to protest more energetically the
extirpation of European Jewry, this gave it an opportunity to show
a more positive face, as the custodian of Italian civilisation.

An official survey commissioned after the end of the war concluded that Italy had lost around 2 million books, a remarkably
small figure given the intensity and duration of the fighting on
Italian soil. More tellingly, this included only 376 incunabula and
2,315 sixteenth-century books. Many of the more painful losses
were sustained during the German retreat, such as the 200,000
books lost from the libraries of Naples, as the Wehrmacht commander took all too literally Hitler's instruction to reduce the city
to 'mud and ashes'. No sort of careful conservation protocols, as
the Poles and Russians would also discover, could protect books
from the anger of a vengeful and desperate retreating army.

The measures taken by Italian libraries should in principle
have been mirrored by other combatant nations. For different
reasons this was seldom the case. In France, the national network

of university and municipal libraries was in some decay. Weighed down by the extent of their inheritance from the confiscations of the French Revolution, the municipal libraries had not yet emerged from the long slumber of the nineteenth century. As a result of the closure of church libraries during the Revolution, town and city libraries held spectacular collections of early printed books. These were generally of little interest to the growing population of an industrialised society, and budgets were not provided for the required renewal of stock. The university libraries of the French provinces were in scarcely better condition. In the interwar period, the universities of Paris attracted 50 per cent of the total number of French students and awarded three-quarters of the degrees.[7]

France emerged from the Great War victorious but economically ruined. For libraries the period between the wars was, by general consent, a period of decay and disillusionment. In every aspect of provision – reading space, new books and scientific periodicals – France lagged behind its neighbours. Yet its libraries, thanks to the events of the Revolution, still had enormously valuable stocks of rare books that had to be protected. The unlucky history of France's war meant that conservation measures proved wholly insufficient against the rapidity of the German advance and the pillage of the occupation.

On 28 September 1938, a circular letter had been despatched to the directors of the 183 municipal libraries, ordering them to prepare an evacuation programme closely modelled on that of Italy. In Paris, the energetic director of the Bibliothèque Nationale, Julien Cain, ensured that the library's greatest treasures were secreted outside the city. This required the filling and transportation of 2,000 cases, taken first to the château of Ussé in the Loire valley. Later, and only when the German invasion was well underway, the château of Castelnau in the South of France was also employed.[8]

For the municipal libraries, as always, the devil was in the detail, and the requirement that each of the most precious manuscripts and printed books should be individually wrapped stalled progress. The civic authorities responsible for the libraries were also likely to give equal priority to the conservation of their archives, reducing the amount of space and packing cases available for books. The only library that attempted a more comprehensive evacuation was that of the city and university of Strasbourg, still traumatised by the German bombardment of 1870, and the subsequent absorption of Strasbourg into the German Reich. In 1870 the German artillery had set the whole of the old city alight, leading to the destruction of all three of Strasbourg's main libraries. The German authorities had subsequently rebuilt the university library as a German collection, so the return of Alsace-Lorraine to France as part of the Peace of Versailles was deeply resented in Germany. Strasbourg's French authorities knew they could expect nothing good of a new German occupation, and in 1939 the library's books were evacuated to Clermont-Ferrand.[9]

Elsewhere in France, the logistical difficulties of even a more limited evacuation proved insuperable. The task was far from fully accomplished when the German army poured over the French border. The massed flight of the population of northern France clogged the roadways, fatally impeding the movement of troops to the front and making it impossible to entrust further library treasures to the road, particularly when German bombing made the railway network inoperative. Paris was declared an open city to preserve it from the bombing that had already laid waste to the libraries of Caen and Tours. Once France's leaders had sued for peace in June 1940, the libraries of northern France (and later of Vichy too) were effectively at the disposal of the occupying power, with consequences we will discuss in the next chapters.

In these early years of the war, the protection of books in German libraries cannot have seemed an urgent priority. The tide of war flowed heavily in Germany's favour, and many of its more energetic librarians were soon seconded to take part in the reorganisation and plunder of libraries in the occupied countries. Even when the risk of war damage became more urgent, as for instance after the incineration of the ancient Hanseatic town of Lübeck in March 1942, it was not easy for librarians to take appropriate measures to preserve their books. Reichsmarschall Goering's pledge that not a bomb should fall on Berlin was revealed as empty words, yet too eager an embrace of evacuation measures could easily be conceived of as defeatism. Even after a devastating attack on the state library in Karlsruhe in 1942, a news blackout was maintained. As Georg Leyh, long-time editor of the *Zentralblatt für Bibliothekswesen*, the professional journal of the library community, was obliged to warn the distraught Karlsruhe library director, 'Nothing is supposed to be published in the *Zentralblatt* about the bombing damage in libraries.'[10] Leyh was a widely respected elder of the library community who remained in post despite never joining the Nazi Party, yet even he had to respect the limits imposed on their freedom of action by the stifling grip of the regime.

Even so, news like this spread through the library jungle telegraph, and librarians began making their own discreet arrangements for the preservation of their treasures. Hamburg library had begun moving its most precious items, which included part of a priceless collection of early Reformation pamphlets, as early as September 1939. Small numbers of books were lodged in the vaults of the bank and town hall in the suburb of Harburg, others in the crypt of Hamburg's St Michael's Church. Even this deviated from the most recent official advice, that 'irreplaceable works of culture' should be moved to fire-proof bomb shelters.[11] More substantial evacuations took place later in the war, though mostly after the disastrous firestorm raid had carried off many of the treasures of the collection. Some of the selection decisions made by German libraries seem extraordinary today. The Hessische Landesbibliothek in Darmstadt had one of the finest collections of music in the world, including autograph manuscripts of Beethoven, Handel, Mozart and Vivaldi. Nevertheless, their librarians decided to send to secure storage a representative year's issues of cookery, gardening and fashion journals. The scores mostly burned when the library was destroyed in bombing by 1944.[12]

In responding to the increased destructiveness of Allied raids from 1944, libraries could take advantage of new guidelines which directed that whole collections should be considered for evacuation to areas less vulnerable to bombing. Because the aerial threat in 1943 came largely from the west, books were sent east. Hamburg had got 5,000 manuscripts and 3,500 more Reformation pamphlets away to Schloss Lauenstein, south of Dresden, a few weeks before the library's destruction. In April 1944 more books followed to the castles of Hermsdorf and Weissig. The unanticipated consequence was that at war's end many of these books would be located in the new Soviet zone, so were unlikely to be returned. It was only when transportation across Germany became too hazardous that Hamburg's stock was sent 200 kilometres south to the potash colliery near Helmstedt, from where they could be retrieved.

In 1944, Tübingen University's books were evacuated to a salt mine near Heilbronn, relatively nearby, from where they could be recovered. The books of the Berlin *Staatsbibliothek* (State Library) faced a more tragic fate. Several million books were dispersed to some twenty-nine places of safety, but mostly to the south and east. Once the new boundaries of Central Europe had been fixed, twelve of these were in the Soviet zone and eleven in what became Poland. One was in Czechoslovakia, and only three in the American zone, with two in the small French zone. Very few of these books would ever return: the fate of the rest will be surveyed in our chapter on restitution.[13]

The particular circumstances of the British library world also militated against a comprehensive plan of evacuation of library treasures. Although many of the larger municipal libraries had accumulated collections of great distinction, the principal libraries of early printed books were concentrated in three locations, Oxford, Cambridge and London. The capital was an obvious target for bombing, and the air raid sirens sounded within an hour of the declaration of war (a false alarm). Over the following weeks, the government undertook a large-scale evacuation of small children from the capital, though many of them drifted back to London when the expected German bombing onslaught failed to materialise during the war's first winter. Many key departments of the war administration were also moved to smaller towns around the home counties.

For the libraries of the capital, there was a limit to the extent to which they could remove their collections, given their likely importance to the war effort. By far the biggest collection, essentially the national library, was that of the British Museum, with its 5 million books. The curators of this collection did undertake to remove the most irreplaceable items to the National Library of Wales in Aberystwyth.[14] This was accomplished with admirable efficiency, and by 5 September 1939, 197 boxes, containing 10,000 volumes, had been despatched to Wales; these included 584 volumes of maps and 132 volumes of early newspapers. But this only touched the surface of the museum's collection of early printed books and accounted for only one-fifth of 1 per cent of the whole collection. A disastrous bomb attack that destroyed close to 200,000 books in 1941 prompted the despatch to safety of a further 50,000 books from the fifteenth- and sixteenth-century collections. The printed catalogues of the library's early Dutch and Italian holdings have a sombre appendix of the books destroyed in this raid. These include Bibles, liturgies and a rare text by the visionary Florentine preacher Girolamo Savonarola.[15]

Given the importance of this, the world's premier collection of early printed books, this insouciance might seem to come quite close to criminal neglect. Perhaps the key to understanding this very modest level of evacuation lies in the hybrid nature of the host institution, the British Museum. The library was important to Britain's scholarly community, but the glories of the British Museum encompassed many millions of artefacts that were quite literally priceless, and irreplaceable. The trustees of the museum had begun removing some of its most significance pieces in response to the Zeppelin attacks in 1918, and the artefacts were once again the first priority for storage space and packing cases in 1939. The evacuation of these antiquities and anthropological marvels was successful, so much so that the historian of the evacuation can state with some pride and only a glancing parenthesis that 'despite major damage to the building, no significant items (apart from books) were lost'.[16] In much the same way, the paintings of the National Gallery, removed to dry salt mines in North Wales, were also accorded much higher priority than mere books.

As for Oxford and Cambridge, it never seems to have been thought likely that these two ancient seats of learning would be serious targets for bombing. Many reasons have been suggested why this should have been the case, for instance an informal gentlemen's agreement that if Heidelberg and Tübingen were not visited by bombers, Oxford and Cambridge would also be off limits. A popular theory has Hitler personally instructing that Oxford would be spared, as he had it in mind for his capital in a conquered Britain. Hitler was a great admirer of architectural beauty, so this has a certain plausibility; the brutalist modern building of the University of London Senate House was, in contrast, designated to serve as the British headquarters of the Gestapo.

Even so, Oxford was pushing its luck. As undergraduates flocked to the services, many colleges were requisitioned for war work, including billeting members of several branches of British intelligence. Oxford was also an industrial city, with Morris's giant car factory at Cowley. During the war it switched production to observer planes and effecting repairs to crashed and damaged aircraft. The Bodleian Library hosted a range of important war departments, including the Admiralty's Photographic Library and the Royal Observer Corps. The Blood Transfusion Service also occupied space in the New Bodleian Building, where its as yet unfilled stacks provided a safe place for the plasma bank accumulated in advance of D-Day. It is hard not to think that in objective terms Oxford, and even the Bodleian itself, were legitimate war targets. In the event, Oxford relied less on Hitler's whimsical charity than on the resilience of the New Bodleian and its many floors of underground stacks. The library's priceless collection of early printed books was swiftly transferred from the old library to this deep storage, where the treasures of fifteen of the Oxford colleges would join them along with books from the Victoria and Albert Museum, the Science Museum and the libraries of both the House of Lords and the House of Commons. All told, eighty-seven separate institutions relied on the New Bodleian to protect their most precious books.[17]

Had the books been moved further afield, the potential damage that might have occurred during or after evacuation was a not insignificant consideration, as it was for all major collections contemplating evacuation. At least one truckload of treasures is reputed to have gone missing from the Bibliothèque Nationale during the chaotic flight of May and June 1940. The library of Livorno in Italy lost thirty-two crates of books when its refuge, the chartreuse of Calci, was flooded by a tributary of the Arno in 1945.[18] Libraries were also aware that the alternative accommodation available might not have the appropriate climactic conditions for book preservation. The east Yorkshire port of Hull was always likely to be a target for bombing, and the university college took immediate action to move its books out of the city. This involved calling upon a range of institutions and local clergy for help; one rectory provided sanctuary for 5,000 books. In the end, small collections of rare books and manuscripts were distributed around five rectories and 32,000 items from the general collection were spread around eight other institutions.[19] Clergy houses were not in the 1940s well-heated or climate-controlled environments for rare books, and at least one item, the manuscript catalogue of Holy Trinity Parish Library, came back in a seriously damaged condition. Although Agnes Cuming of the Hull library tried to keep an eye on the outhoused books, it was seldom possible to deploy library staff to look after stock sent for remote storage. This was why the British Museum was so grateful for the help of the National Library in Aberystwyth. In other circumstances, as we will see in the next chapter, displaced collections were very vulnerable to neglect, pillage or souvenir hunting.

If the library communities of Europe enjoyed only indifferent success in the battle to protect their stock, there was at least one protagonist determined not to be caught napping: the United States of America. The movement of library treasures out of the safe haven of American libraries might appear quixotic given the invulnerability of the American continent to air attack, but that is not how it seemed in 1941. The Japanese attack on Pearl Harbor was a bolt from the blue to the American public, many of whom had not been following the European war very closely. Had the Battle of Midway not been such a decisive victory for the American fleet in June 1942, the spectre of Japanese aircraft carriers cruising off the California coast might have become a reality. In the event, Japanese troops did land on American soil when they occupied the islands of Attu and Kiska in the Alaskan Aleutian Islands and it cost the US 5,000 casualties to expel them. In September 1942, an aircraft launched from a submarine flew two short missions over Oregon, dropping bombs. Casualties were minimal, and censorship ensured that this daring feat never became widely known. Six civilians were killed in Oregon by bomb balloons launched by the Japanese to drift over the American mainland, but these were mainland America's only casualties from bombing.[20]

Preparations for the evacuation of American collections were well in hand before the declaration of war, thanks to a committee established on presidential instructions, staffed largely by the directors of major East Coast institutions. This resulted in the compilation of a bulletin on *The Protection of Cultural Resources against the Hazards of War*.[21] Planning in the Library of Congress involved the physical examination of more than 600,000 books to identify priorities for evacuation. After Pearl Harbor, space was found in the storage facilities of a number of university libraries for the most precious materials, 4,000 crates in all. Meanwhile the original copies of the Declaration of Independence and United States Constitution were despatched to the Bullion Depository at Fort Knox in Kentucky. The New York Public Library evacuated rare holdings to the vaults of New York banks. The Houston Public Library moved its holdings of local newspapers to the bomb-resistant San Jacinto Monument.

While the West Coast was plausibly in the line of fire, these precautions in the East Coast libraries seem rather superfluous, as must have been the 2,705 extremely boring hours of fire watching logged by staff of the National Archives in the first year of the war. Although it was at one point rumoured that the Italian military planned to drop torpedoes in New York harbour, attacks on the scale likely to cause major damage in the cities was never plausible. What we can say is that this sort of vigilance on the part of leading cultural institutions probably helped adjust citizens to a wartime frame of mind, and also, after the intelligence failure of Pearl Harbor, helped reassure them that the country's leaders recognised the seriousness of the challenges that lay ahead.

*

There were many circumstances militating against the effective protection of books against bombing in the Second World War: among them the sheer number to be conserved, and the lack of staff to identify the rarest and most precious items, not all of which would have been early printed books. The bizarre decisions made by the library in Darmstadt are an indication of this confusion. There was also a general sense in cultural institutions that priority should be given to the irreplaceable – antiquities and paintings – rather than books, which were produced in large editions. Such thinking, alas, did lead to the loss of old and precious books that were often the only known surviving copies of a particular printed work. These we can trace, like the early editions of Low German publications from the sixteenth century in the possession of the libraries in Königsberg and other German cities on the Baltic coast, only from catalogues compiled before the war.[22] Even if libraries did take the chance to move books from city centre locations vulnerable to bombing, they were still far from safe when their hiding places were overrun by invading armies, or 'liberated' at the end of the war. Plunder and the appropriation of the spoils of war would compound the destruction of the bombing; because it had not been anticipated, it was in many respects more painful.

14

PLUNDER

By 1942, German military conquests had exceeded even the wildest dreams of the Nazis' nationalistic academic geographers and cartographers. It was time to make hay with the riches of the sub-jugated nations. The Nazi regime plumbed new depths of cruelty and horror, most evidently, of course, in the obliteration of Jewish and Polish culture. But in their rapacious appropriation of the treasures of the conquered nations, they were following a strong historical precedent. Throughout the history of warfare, the troops and generals of victorious armies regarded the possessions of the lands they had invaded as fair game: most armies lived off the land, taking food, livestock and crops as they went. Their generals were more discerning, appropriating the contents of palaces and castles to decorate their own residences back home. In this, at least, the Nazi robber barons were in good company. And despite attempts in the twentieth century to regulate the conduct of invading forces, and their conduct towards civilians, the Allied troops occupying Germany also removed a great deal of valuable property.[1]

The Nazi High Command was unusual, not in its eager embrace of the perquisites of military triumph, but for the system-atic manner in which it pursued them, marshalling personnel and scarce ordnance to haul trainloads of treasures back to Germany. Even here Germany could point to historical precedent, not least in the figure of Napoleon Bonaparte, the greatest battlefield general of the nineteenth century and the first since Charlemagne to aspire to a truly European empire. In reorganising the govern-ment of Europe to French advantage, Napoleon also took the opportunity to restock France's galleries and palaces with the best of European art.

As was customary, Napoleon and his revolutionary predecessors clothed such rapacity in the language of the common good. The choice of masterpieces to be purloined was placed in the hands of a Commission for Research on Objects of Science and Art, a shameless attempt to reconfigure the appropriations in the fashionable language of the Enlightenment. The commission was staffed by a compliant assembly of French connoisseurs and scholars, botanists, scientists and mathematicians as well as sculptors and art experts. But the plans were executed by soldiers, with inevitable damage to the artworks cut from their frames and hauled back to France. The extent of the plunder was often stipulated in the treaties of peace enforced on Napoleon's victims: the Vatican, for instance, gave up 100 paintings. Among the most striking of the French trophies was Paolo Veronese's enormous *Wedding Feast of Cana*, ripped from its moorings in the abbey of San Giorgio Maggiore in Venice. It remains in Paris alongside the *Mona Lisa* in the Salle des États in the Louvre.[2] It is sometimes possible to trace the tides of war in the fate of individual artworks: Michelangelo's *Madonna of Bruges*, for example, his most distinguished piece outside Italy, was removed to Paris in 1794, and having been returned to Bruges was then taken by the retreating Germans in 1944.

The programme of military acquisition was inaugurated long before Napoleon seized power, and indeed books also featured prominently in the cultural agenda of the French Revolution. Already in 1792, the keeper of printed books at the Bibliothèque Nationale was setting out his requirements:

> Citizen minister. Allow me to bring myself to your recollection, and to ask you to have the kindness to inform General Custine, who is marching on Mainz, that there is in the metropolitan chapter library a copy of the earliest dated printed book, of which I add the title. It is the famous Psalter of Mainz, from 1457, in folio. May it be convenient for him to procure it or to have it presented to him.[3]

The revolutionary commissioners were nothing if not systematic. Often they worked from printed catalogues of old books published by the proud owners. Between October 1794 and January 1795, Gaspard Michel made a wide sweep of institutions in the Low Countries and northern Germany, taking in Brussels, Liège, Aachen, Cologne and Koblenz. The descent into Italy in 1796 brought cases of incunabula from Bologna and Milan. These depredations were not entirely confined to volumes from the first age of print: modern scientific books, useful to the advance of knowledge in the new republic, were also a high priority. One zealous commissioner, Anton Keil, working in the book rich German city of Trier, confiscated old books which he then sold to raise money for the purchase of recent editions. In the words of the minister of the interior, Pierre Bénézech:

> The project aimed to form in the Bibliothèque Nationale a collection as complete as possible of books in all fields and in all languages, and to collect as many different editions of these same books as possible, taking advantage of a unique situation which no other government has yet faced.[4]

This 'unique situation' was the opportunity to commit theft on a scale unprecedented since the glory days of the Roman Empire: here M. Bénézech proved himself a master of the euphemistic phrase worthy of the twentieth-century dictators who followed so enthusiastically in his footsteps.

Napoleon's agents in the plunder of books included the novelist Stendhal, who was given responsibilities that the young man was very happy to fulfil. Among Stendhal's trophies was an early Bamberg edition of Boner's *Fables*, wrested from the ducal library in Wolfenbüttel. To add insult to injury, this volume was rebound and the imperial eagle stamped on the cover as a mark of its new ownership. This became a point of sensitivity when, as a result of the peace treaties of 1814 and 1815 following Napoleon's defeat, the stolen bibliographical treasures were ordered to be returned to their owners. The librarians of the Bibliothèque Nationale, who had expended so much effort in their acquisition, co-operated with the utmost reluctance, complaining that they had expended more on rebinding than the value of the books. This elicited no sympathy from those who had experienced the arrogance of the conqueror over the past fifteen years.

In the twentieth century Napoleon was still revered as the most brilliant battlefield general in history, and his deportment as ruler of a subjugated Europe created a dismal precedent. But for a comparison with the wholesale plunder of the type undertaken by the Germans in the 1940s we have to look further back in time to the contesting armies of the Thirty Years' War (1618–48). After the conquest of the Calvinist Rhineland Palatinate by Duke Maximilian of Bavaria, the contents of the university library of Heidelberg, one of the oldest universities in Europe, were offered as a gift to the pope. Its entire collection of manuscripts and early printed books was carefully packed into cases, and a heavily armed caravan of mules made its way across the Alps to its new home in the Vatican library (where much of it remains).[5]

This was a disaster to the new network of Protestant universities established across Europe in the wake of the Reformation, but for a few short years in the 1620s and 1630s, the Protestants found their own conquering general, and the battle of the books was resumed. In his descent on Europe, King Gustavus Adolphus of Sweden had as his primary goal to establish a corridor of security in the Baltic region; it was only the unexpected victories of Swedish forces over the Austrian Habsburgs that allowed him to posture briefly as the arbiter of Europe. In the first phase of Swedish conquest the Catholic libraries established along the northern European coast were a primary target. The Jesuit libraries of Riga, Braniewo and Frombork were seized and ransacked. The books were inventoried and packed for transport back to Sweden. Here they were carefully sorted, and the best items shared between the royal collection and the library of the University of Uppsala. In the final years of the Thirty Years' War, spoils from Bohemia and Moravia would be added as well; in all of these instances the Swedes worked on the principle that if they seized the contents of foreign libraries in their entirety, they could sort and redistribute the books in safety at home. In Uppsala the Catholic books were stored on a separate floor of the library, accessible only with a special key: it was necessary to know your enemy to combat their pernicious doctrines, but only those of iron-clad faith should have access to them.[6] As we will see, very similar motives prompted the looting by the Nazi state.

Books and knowledge would be at the heart of the Nazi agenda, but until now this aspect of plunder has received only a fraction of the attention lavished on the paintings and other artefacts removed to Germany. Hitler, it should be said, had little reason to plunder for personal gain. The massive royalties from the compulsory purchase of *Mein Kampf* and, more quixotically, royalties for the use of his image on German postage stamps, made him a wealthy man. His interest in plundered art was focussed on the masterpieces of early German painting, which he appropriated for the planned Führermuseum in Linz, his Austrian hometown, scheduled to open in 1950. Goebbels, Ribbentrop and Albert Speer built substantial collections, and Reichsmarschall Hermann Goering, with the lack of measure that he brought to all aspects of his life, collected on a massive scale.[7] The entire Nazi inner circle, including Hitler for his museum in Linz, availed itself of coteries of experts who fanned out across Europe to seek out suitable pieces. Goering was a great admirer of the art of the seventeenth-century Dutch Golden Age, which featured heavily in the 2,000 pieces collected for his bloated country estate at Carinhall outside Berlin.

The Nazi collectors built a network of collaborationist dealers in Paris and Switzerland. The art world is, at the best of times, a business of glistening smiles and steel-tipped teeth, and the war brought out the worst in many previously respected traders. A host of experts proved happy to facilitate the trade in plundered and confiscated goods. Paris, the centre of the European art world, established a roaring wartime trade. Swiss art dealers profited vastly from dealings with the Nazi leadership during the war, then refused (on the instructions of their professional body) to co-operate with Allied attempts to recover looted art in 1945. They maintained this uncooperative stance after the war, while piously excluding from Switzerland some of the most notorious Nazi dealers in plundered art, thus securing more of the market for themselves. The records of the Swiss Art Trade Association, which might throw light on these devious manoeuvres, have mysteriously disappeared for the years 1945–80.[8]

Paintings, rather than books, were the main focus of this collecting, though the two were inextricably linked, not least because the major art dealers had themselves assembled distinguished reference libraries: these, too, were targets for the most serious collectors. Goering was able to obtain the famous art reference library of Allen Loebl, director of the Garin gallery in Paris. This rather complicated transaction was brokered by Bruno Lohse, Goering's art buyer in Paris. Goering refused to pay cash for the library, as he had no wish to be indebted to a Jew: instead the collection was exchanged for a picture by Utrillo, itself plundered. A second major art library was assembled at the Führerbau in Munich, a holding station for the looted art destined for the museum in Linz.

In this way, the Nazi leaders built substantial private libraries, partly because they indulged themselves with every marker of status, but also because some of them were genuinely bookish. In his private life Hitler was far more austere than the bandit circle to whose excesses he turned a blind eye, and his library was of moderate size and carefully assembled. The library at Berchtesgaden numbered around 2,000 volumes, concentrated on subjects in which he had a genuine interest, such as history and architecture. There are also specially bound copies of gifted books, though some, like the windy theorising of Bishop Alois Hudal, demonstrating the compatibility of Catholic teaching with National Socialism, show little sign that he read beyond the first sixteen pages.[9]

This collecting fever continued to the very last months of the war, even as the Allied troops fought their way across Germany and the Nazi hierarchy sought, mostly in vain, to identify a place where their collections could be concealed and safe from bombs. By the end of the war the Nazi leaders and German institutional collections had had their pick of millions of books scooped up as part of the confiscations from emigrated Jews, or those despatched to their deaths in concentration camps. A large proportion of these books, for which no immediate use could be found, was abandoned or pulped for salvage. This process of destruction identifies one significant difference between books and the appropriated artworks, by their very nature unique items and therefore individually more valuable. The confiscated books included many quotidian items of little resale value, functionally indistinguishable from other copies in the same edition.

This partly explains, along with their lack of glamour, why plundered books have received only a fraction of the scholarly attention devoted to the lost artworks, and there has been comparatively little effort to restore the surviving copies to their former owners. There has never been a database of lost books compared to the systematic notification of artworks still missing from the Second World War, which continue to surface in surprising quantities on the market, or more embarrassingly in the basements of renowned institutional collections. Indeed, books would probably have remained little more than a footnote in the story of cultural loot, had it not been for a scheme of Nazi library building on a scale and ambition that put even the Swedish plunder of the Thirty Years' War in the shade. Here one must credit the maniacal megalomania of the Nazis' chief ideologue, Alfred Rosenberg.

For Hitler and his inner circle, the Thousand-Year Reich was not a casual piece of rhetorical bombast, but something that required careful planning. Even after the subjugation of east and west, defeated and humiliated enemies would not be entirely eradicated. It was therefore necessary to keep these phantoms alive, at least through their texts, so that Judaism, socialism, the Bolshevik menace and other challenges to National Socialism could be thoroughly researched and crushed in the event of any resurgence. This was the basis of one of the greatest plans of library building ever conceived in wartime: Rosenberg's grand scheme for ten scholarly institutions, spread around Germany, each with a library of up to 1 million books.

Rosenberg was something of an outsider among the Nazi old guard, a Baltic German and an intellectual, all too aware that Hitler's cronies (and secretly Hitler himself) regarded his magnum opus, *The Myth of the Twentieth Century*, as incomprehensible gobbledygook. It was only with difficulty that in 1934 he secured official confirmation as the movement's chief ideologue. With the start of the war, and the riches of the conquered territories at his disposal, Rosenberg was appointed to head his own cultural taskforce, the Einsatzstab Reichsleiter Rosenberg (ERR). By the end of the war Rosenberg had built up an enormous bureaucracy, responsible for purloining millions of books from libraries all over the continent, in addition to archives and works of art. Once the Nazi hierarchy's collecting mania had been sated, priceless works of art piled up rather aimlessly. After the war, the US Army reckoned to have tracked down 10.7 million artefacts in some 1,500 repositories and hiding places.[10] The destruction of libraries, on the other hand, was never without purpose – either to appropriate books to the needs of the new regime or eradicate the culture of subject nations.

After its defeat in 1939, Poland was the first to be subjected to the new cultural agenda of the Nazis. This task was placed in the hands of a special unit, Sonderkommando Paulsen, led by a former professor of archaeology, Peter Paulsen, now in the SS. Paulsen divided his efforts between the eradication of Jewish institutions, and the confiscation of Polish libraries: all that was to remain in Poland was a core of scholarly libraries for the use of the local German population and the occupying forces. This saved at least a portion of the library of Kraków University, one of the most distinguished collections in Europe.[11] Elsewhere, libraries suffered near total destruction; this extended even to school libraries. The church of St Michael in Poznań became a central depot, where books regarded as serviceable, particularly scientific texts and periodicals, were set aside to be taken to Germany; the rest were pulped. This nihilism continued until the end of the war, with the destruction of 300,000 books in the Warsaw Public Library as the last German forces abandoned the city. All told, Poland is reckoned to have lost 90 per cent of the content of its school and public libraries and 80 per cent of private collections and specialist libraries, and 50 per cent of its scientific collections, some 15 million books in all.[12]

With the foundation of the ERR in 1940, the plunder of libraries became more purposeful and deliberate. In the event, only one of Rosenberg's ten institutes, the Frankfurt Institute for Research on the Jewish Question, would ever be realised. Hitler ordered

Rosenberg to concentrate on this, and the new National Socialist university to be built on the shores of the Chiemsee in Bavaria. The building was suspended to the end of the war, but Hitler was keen that Rosenberg should persevere, 'particularly so that the research and creation of a library can go on'. According to the newly appointed director of the planned new university, a former librarian of the Rothschild collection in Frankfurt, 'the goal is to create the first great scientific National Socialist library'.[13]

To stock these two libraries, and a project of his own, the *Ostbücherei* (Library of the East), Rosenberg turned first to the newly conquered lands in the west. The ERR squads made more than 29,000 raids in the Netherlands, harvesting 700,000 books from house clearances, mostly of Jewish residences. Some of these books were passed on to schools in the Netherlands. A major target was the two most distinguished historical libraries of Judaism, Ets Haim and the Bibliotheca Rosenthaliana, both in Amsterdam. Both were impounded and carried off for the Frankfurt Institute, despite brave efforts on the part of the Dutch librarian Herman de la Fontaine Verwey to save the most distinguished books of the Rosenthaliana.

The ERR had established its western headquarters in France, where it would ultimately confiscate 723 libraries with a combined total of 1.7 million books. These included the Ukrainian and Polish libraries of Paris (the Bibliothèque Polonaise generated 136,000 books) as well as the library of the Alliance Israélite Universelle and the Bibliothèque Russe Tourguenev.[14] The assault on Russia in 1941 brought new opportunities. The ERR searched at least 2,265 institutions in the east, 375 archives, 957 libraries, 531 research and educational institutions and 402 museums. This was an extraordinary endeavour that required not only a huge logistical effort, but also the advice of a shoal of librarians and archivists seconded from German institutions. When these planned confiscations are added to the damage sustained during the German assault and later retreat, the USSR is reckoned to have lost more than 100 million books.[15] Vilnius, now the capital of Lithuania, was a particular target as the capital of Eastern European Jewry. Its two major libraries, YIVO (the Yiddish Scientific Institute) and

The plunder in the East was so indiscriminate that there was no
possibility of putting all the books appropriated to any useful
purpose, never mind cataloguing then. This stockpile in Riga,
Latvia, was probably ultimately destined for destruction.

the Strashun Library, were almost completely destroyed: 40,000
books were sent back to Germany, and the rest were pulped.

By 1943 the finest Jewish library in Europe, around 500,000
volumes, had been assembled in the warehouses of the Frankfurt
Institute on the Jewish Question. But by now the tide of war was
turning against Germany, and little progress could be made in creating a working library. Most of the books remained in their crates,
and only 25,000 of the new acquisitions were ever catalogued.
Many of the eastern acquisitions were set aside for Rosenberg's
other major project, the *Ostbücherei*. This new library in Berlin
was intended for all books relevant to the study of Bolshevism
and Eastern Europe: in the year after the invasion of Russia this
absorbed half a million books, 300,000 from Smolensk and
200,000 from Riga.

The only real restraint on this manic collecting came, as
ever, from competition from other Nazi institutions. Himmler's
Reichssicherheitshauptamt (Reich Security Main Office, RSHA)
built a huge library in Berlin in the former Freemasons' Lodge on
Eisenacherstrasse. Some 3 million books flowed into Berlin during
the war, and half a million remained in the Eisenacherstrasse

depot at the end of the war. Himmler also appropriated the third major Jewish collection in Amsterdam, the private library of Isaac Leo Seeligmann.[16] The Gestapo had assembled its own library in Munich, 200,000 volumes at the point that the Gestapo head-quarters moved to Berlin. The efforts of Gestapo units sorting through confiscated property swelled this to more than 600,000 books. Occasionally, competition for the best libraries led to unseemly squabbles. The archive of the International Institute of Social History in Amsterdam, with its treasure trove of mater-ials on trade unions and socialist parties, became the object of a four-way tussle between the ERR, RSHA, the German labour movement and the local Nazi leader Arthur Seyss-Inquart. The ERR prevailed because they had established physical possession, not only of the Amsterdam headquarters of the Institute, but of the Paris office as well.[17]

With so many books flowing through Germany, there were plenty left over for established institutional and public libraries. Germany's librarians played an important though inglorious role in the plunder of European libraries. Just as they had easily accom-modated themselves to Nazi rule in 1933, so they now hastened to offer their expertise in the identification of desirable books, and the administration of major libraries in the conquered territories. The new German library in Kraków was placed under the direc-tion of Gustav Abb, formerly director of the Berlin University Library.[18] Following the dismissal of the Jewish director of the Bibliothèque Nationale in Paris, his successor worked under the scrutiny of a trio of German administrators. In return for their co-operation, German librarians were able to take their share of the booty. The Königsberg Library, strategically located at the east-ernmost extent of German territory, benefited from an influx of 50,000 volumes from the confiscated library of the Catholic sem-inary at Płock, including 400 incunabula and 100 manuscripts. All of these would be lost as Königsberg burned in the climactic Russian assault of 1945. The director of the Königsberg Library had by this point been drafted into service digging trenches. As he remarked to a library colleague, with admirable understatement, 'Research is out of the question.'[19]

The principal libraries in Berlin, the State Library and the public library, played a major role, both in offering their expertise in the examination of books, and as a central clearing house for the torrent of books pouring into the capital, from east and west, and from the confiscation of Jewish collections in Germany. The Berlin *Staatsbibliothek* distributed books to more than thirty German universities: by the end of the war most institutional collections shared complicity by benefiting from the plunder of Jewish libraries.[20] Many of the Jewish books went with their other possessions to the city pawnbroker, where libraries could apply for books to make good their losses from bombing. In 1943, when the Berlin Public Library applied for 40,000 books to compensate for war damage, it was made clear that the sums paid would be applied to the 'solution of the Jewish Question'. The librarians would have been perfectly clear what this entailed; nevertheless, the purchase went ahead.[21]

This tawdry trade can be set alongside another sort of insidious plunder that flourished unchecked in the German library world after the Nazi takeover in 1933. The trade in rare books and manuscripts was an intimate business: rare-book librarians knew the dealers well, and relationships of trust had been built up over the course of many years. Many of the antiquarian booksellers were Jews, who from 1933 onwards were increasingly keen to liquidate their stock and make their way abroad. Librarians were able to obtain valuable books and manuscripts for only a fraction of their real value, but because money changed hands, items purchased through these lopsided contracts were not regarded as plunder.

One particularly squalid transaction came to light only as the result of a devastating fire caused by an electrical fault at the famous Anna Amelia Library in Weimar in 2004. Discovering what had perished (50,000 books) required a review of the library archives, with disturbing results. It turned out that 35,000 books had been added to the library between 1933 and 1945, many of dubious provenance. One particularly stunning acquisition, transferred to the library from the Goethe and Schiller Archive, was a collection of 2,000 almanacs from the sixteenth to eighteenth century, including a number in which Goethe had personal involvement. These formed part of the collection of an erudite businessman, Arthur Goldschmidt, forced to sell after the confiscation of his family firm. Goldschmidt valued the collection at 50,000 Reichsmarks, but the director of the Goethe Archive, Hans Wahl, knowing his predicament, would offer only one Reichsmark per book. Goldschmidt, he wrote, should be delighted they were going to such an appropriate home. In 2006 the Anna Amelia Library made a shamefaced settlement of 100,000 euros with Goldschmidt's heirs, though this is an almost unique case. Most German libraries have not made the identification of plundered goods in their libraries a priority for staff time.

In 1990 Joe Meador, formerly of the US Army's 87th Armoured Field Infantry, would make the news for all the wrong reasons.[22] In 1945, Lieutenant Meador had been part of a unit charged with securing the famed treasure of Quedlinburg Cathedral in the Harz mountains. Quedlinburg had obtained a certain notoriety through the patronage of Heinrich Himmler in his search for the roots of an Ottonian German Empire, and the cathedral treasure survived the war intact, secreted in a nearby mineshaft. Meador managed to appropriate a substantial portion of these valuables, including the Samuhel Gospel, a richly jewelled ninth-century manuscript, and then to mail his treasures home. Meador, an art major at North Texas State University, had a discerning eye, and after his return to Texas, he made no attempt to sell his hoard: it came to light only after his death when his brother and sister tried to find a buyer for the Samuhel Gospel. News of the reappearance of this extraordinary treasure soon spread among manuscript specialists, though no respectable institutional collection would buy from the Meadors. In the event, a German cultural foundation paid what was in effect a ransom of $3 million to secure its return to Germany.

This was a better outcome than for many of the GI magpies, though one that led to protracted legal action when the Meadors were charged by the US attorney with trading in stolen property. The Meador case made headlines because of the exceptional nature of the stolen artefacts, but less spectacular pilfering was routine: few Allied soldiers went home without some sort of souvenir from

Germany. Though the Allied High Command in principle depre-
cated such behaviour, all ranks, including senior officers, gathered
their mementoes. At the Potsdam Conference in 1945, Field
Marshal Sir Alan Brooke, Marshal of the Air Force Sir Charles
Portal and Admiral of the Fleet Lord Cunningham found time to
examine the books in the royal library in the Cecilienhof Palace,
and a few antiquarian volumes reportedly found their way into
their luggage.[23] Eisenhower issued reproving orders, but the true
position of the American generals in the field is better exemplified by the laconic report from Charles Gerhardt's 29th Infantry
in April 1945: 'We're advancing as fast as the looting will permit.'[24]
There is, of course, no suggestion of moral equivalence between
these acts and the systematic rape of European culture by the Nazi
regime. For the Soviet army, revenge for the despoliation of their
own homeland was pitiless and thorough.[25] In the Western armies,
each enlisted man made their own decisions based on opportunity
and the dictates of their own conscience.

There was an etiquette of plunder on the Allied side, even if it
was honoured to varying degrees in different theatres of the war.
Service personnel with real criminal intent profited more from
illicit dealings in Allied stores and medical supplies than from what
they could extract from the already ravaged German economy.[26]
The principle of 'living off the land' justified the appropriation
of any amount of food, wine or spirits discovered. Many service
personnel lived in high style in requisitioned country houses,
from which the residents were peremptorily expelled: some were
given the chance to remain and act as domestic servants to their
new tenants. Souvenirs were tolerated everywhere. Every English
Tommy wanted a German handgun and camera, a Luger and a
Leica. Soviet troops were obsessed with watches, and often wore
four or five.

The units charged with securing caches of Nazi loot, or the safe
places in which valuables were stored, faced temptations of a different order. The baggage of the newly incarcerated Reichsmarschall
Goering yielded a number of gold watches. Processing officer Paul
Kubala handed them out to his subordinates, thus securing their
complicity for his more ambitious schemes.[27] A certain amount

of art went missing, though it was mostly disposed of among the network of corrupt dealers rather than secreted in baggage sent home (a fair quantity ultimately made its way into institutional collections via the trade). For the opportunistic souvenir hunter, this was one respect in which books were preferable to paintings, being portable and more easily concealed.

Joe Meador was not the only American GI to have filched rare books. Lieutenant Bud Berman chose two early manuscripts, one of which contained two pages of the *Hildebrandslied*, the oldest extant poetical writing in the German language. This extraordinarily precious fragment had survived the looting of the Fulda monastery in 1632 during the Thirty Years' War, and the Allied bombing, only to fall victim to a casual piece of souvenir hunting. Berman sold the manuscripts on his first furlough in New York for $7,000. From New York the more valuable of the two manuscripts found its way to the collection of a Californian oil heiress, before making its way back to Kassel, after protracted legal proceedings, in 1972. Sergeant Walter E. Clark was similarly required to disgorge the Golden Book of Saarbrücken, which he had made off with under the eyes of the horrified local staff, though again not without a protracted tussle with the US customs service.[28]

While America's community of book experts was not greatly concerned to see ordinary soldiers deprived of their purloined treasures, different standards were found to apply when a major institution was offered the opportunity to secure an outstanding item like the Mainz Psalter of 1457. This had come into the hands of William A. Jackson, curator of the Houghton Library at Harvard, and he was very much minded to retain it, notwithstanding that its true owner, the Dresden State Library, was not really in doubt.[29] Jackson proposed that its fate should be resolved by a jury of three, made up of himself and representatives of the Library of Congress and New York's Morgan Library. Given that the Library of Congress had happily absorbed half a million books from Germany after the war without payment (an episode discussed in our chapter on cleansing), Jackson felt assured of a sympathetic hearing.

The Mainz Psalter, one of the seminal works of early typography, and four times as rare as the Gutenberg Bible, was a difficult book to give back. It was the first dated printed book with an identified printer, as well as one of the earliest attempts at printing with musical type and in two colours. The Dresden Landesbibliothek had sent it for safekeeping in Bohemia, from where it was liberated by a Soviet soldier en route to Moscow with the rest of the Dresden treasures. When it made its way from Prague to New York, Jackson was all too willing to offer it protection in the spectacular Houghton collection. Alas, the State Department took a different view, and by 1950 it was on its way back to Dresden.

More typical of the GI experience was Churchill Brazelton, who looted to order for his mother. She received a miscellany of valuables, including a fur rug, a Gobelin tapestry and some illustrated Spanish books and knick-knacks: 'You asked for two small figures for the little shelves so I found two in a wrecked house and confiscated them.'[30] Brazelton was a liaison officer attached to the US press corps, and the journalists insisted on a comfortable berth at night, preferably in an elegant 'chateau'. Brazelton did his best to oblige:

> The last one was very nice but had been wrecked by the hordes of Americans who had stayed there from time to time. However this is Germany and the way these men hate the Germans no one gives a darn what happens to anything they own. After the horrors and destruction they have thrown to the rest of the world they deserve and will get no sympathy. Nothing we can ever do will repay them for all they have done.[31]

This was a common view, articulated with equal force by an officer who had taken no action when troops under his command laid waste to a requisitioned house that its German owner, Dr Bernhard Limburger, had filled with priceless porcelain and other treasures:

> To me, who is fairly acquainted with Mr Limburger, he is just another suave, shrinking, pious, non-party, pro-American who caused some 10,000,000 American men and women to waste four or five years of their lives at war, some of whom

were buried in one of his fields today, and he complained to me that we were using up his fields.[32]

In this lack of concern, Captain Francis E. Ewing spoke for the vast majority of the citizen soldiers who had freed Europe, at the cost of many of their friends' lives. The continuation of such attitudes would greatly complicate relationships as Germany made its gradual transition from despised enemy to ally and bulwark of democracy in Western Europe.

15

PULP AND ASHES

In 1939, Poland was the first country to experience the reality of total war. In May 1940 it was the turn of Rotterdam in the Netherlands, and later that year and the next, London, Liverpool, Plymouth and Coventry. From 1941, Russian civilians found themselves in the path of the Wehrmacht's murderous advance, before the turning of the tide brought three years of terror for Germany's urban populations. This was a new chapter in the history of warfare. Civilian populations had always suffered when their homes were invested by marauding armies. But never before in the history of conflict could so many far distant from the battlefield be brought directly into danger, their houses obliterated by bombs falling far from their intended targets, buried or incinerated with all their possessions, widowed, orphaned or maimed by a whimsical twist of fate. Many suffered in a spirit of mute resignation, but others conveyed their thoughts in letters and diaries. It is to these that we turn to learn how ordinary people experienced the war, and how it changed them.

After a year of war, months of inactivity and the relief of Dunkirk, Britain's civilian population faced a new test of their courage and resilience. The diarists of Mass Observation collectively present a vivid picture of life under the bombs, and the response of their fellow citizens. We will come to the impact of the bombing on libraries shortly: the diaries give us a notion of how individuals reacted to the war on their doorstep or crashing through their roof. Many had prepared for nights in the shelter or the prospect of sudden evacuation, with a few books in their emergency bag by the stairs. But all the evidence suggests that reading fell off sharply during the Blitz: some gave up reading altogether in the most intense phases of the bombing. They were too traumatised, too busy or simply exhausted by the strain of waiting, interrupted sleep and uncomfortable nights in the shelter. Though direct testimony is much less widely available from Germany, it seems likely the assault on German cities, over a far longer period, would have produced a similar effect. On 25 April 1945, Hans-Friedrich Blunck, tucked away relatively safely in the northern duchy of Holstein, sat down to read, but with little success. 'In these times extremely detailed descriptions are unreadable, and it is also unbearable to think of the wonderful Vienna described [in Stifter's *Nachsommer*, a classic novel of the nineteenth century].' Blunck, an author himself, had been president of the Reich Chamber of Literature between 1933 and 1935, but as the Reich dissolved, even he could not lose himself in books.[1]

By 1944, in any case, the supply of books for civilians in Germany had largely dried up, as publishers, for commercial reasons explained in an earlier chapter, prioritised books for the troops.[2] Libraries, too, were barely functioning as staff were summoned away to the front, and even the libraries that could open their doors were difficult to reach because of the disruption to public transport networks. The year 1944 was also when the dire state of the war economy required German women to give up some of their unusual privileges as the idealised wives and mothers of the Reich. Hundreds of thousands were called up to work in war industries; equally significantly, some 400,000 female foreign workers providing domestic labour in German homes were reassigned to factory work. This sharply curtailed the opportunities for reading, as under the barrage of bombs and advancing armies, normal life collapsed around them. Food, cooking and finding somewhere safe and dry to sleep were the overwhelming priorities in Germany in the last years of the war.

In the British Mass Observation diaries of 1940 and 1941, there was one other consistent theme: a sense that the women of England had now faced the same dangers as their menfolk in the front line and had not been found wanting. Olivia Cockett, a twenty-seven-year-old clerical assistant at New Scotland Yard, experienced the Blitz near the family home in Eltham, south London. 'The Blitz on London has been on since late August,' she noted on 6 October, 'and we are all still alive – the "all" I know, at any rate – though 10,000 Londoners are dead ... Have seen literally hundreds of houses down, probably thousands uninhabitable. Feel sick but not sick to death. It is not so terrible in the present as it was in the future.'[3]

That seems to have been a common sentiment. Phyllis Warner, another Londoner, described a similar personal journey. 'I'm glad to say that I'm not as frightened as I was. Last week I couldn't sleep at all ... but this week I feel much stronger.' During the first week, Phyllis noted quite a bit of stop the war sentiment, but that had quietened.[4] An anonymous twenty-eight-year-old from Maida Vale recognised a fundamental change in herself as a result of the September bombing:

> I feel much more certainty and self-confidence, and much less shyness and inferiority complex as a result of the discovery that I am not the coward I thought, and have more good in me in the way of 'taking it' than I would have believed ... I have a greatly increased feeling of personal responsibility all round – as head of the house, as a citizen, and simply as an individual human being.[5]

Many women might miss aspects of their pre-war lives, such as the help around the house, and the opportunities this created to sit down with a book. But equally, these were lives to which they would not return. Tested in the fire of wartime work, and having displayed courage under fire, they had become quite different people with new and various responsibilities: work, queuing for food, work for voluntary organisations and creating a kitchen garden. Any sort of leisure-time activity was bound to be at a premium.

Most of the attention thus far directed towards the destruction of libraries in the Second World War has concentrated, understandably enough, on bomb damage to the major public collections. These were institutions that stood at the centre of the community, often in imposing purpose-built buildings. Their loss was deeply felt, a demonstration of vulnerability and a tangible

Keep Calm and Carry On. An iconic (and undoubtedly posed) photograph of phlegmatic browsers examining the books at Holland House, London, largely destroyed in an air raid of September 1940, its valuable library miraculously preserved. A famous gathering place of the Whig political aristocracy in the eighteenth and nineteenth centuries, Holland House was never rebuilt after the war, though its preserved remains can now be seen in Holland Park, Kensington.

blow to morale. They were collections built and curated over centuries, often containing unique materials devoted to the history of the city or locality. In this sense, they were also a repository of the community's collective memory.

In Germany, the largest city libraries were sometimes based on princely collections dating back to the seventeenth and eighteenth centuries: the same could be said of university libraries, which in many parts of Europe often performed a wider public function for the local population. And up until the moment the bombs fell, libraries all over Europe had been a hive of activity: the source of information, advice and the myriad forms required in wartime; a place for meetings, signing up for voluntary organisations, donating to war savings, as well as borrowing books. Now they were gone, and the community grieved for far more than their weekly visit to take back their loans.

All protagonists in the war, with the exception of the United States, suffered grievous blows. In the five days of fighting before the surrender of the Netherlands, the distinguished library at Middelburg was engulfed in flames, with the loss of 150,000 books. Miraculously, the Rotterdam libraries escaped the destruction of the entire city centre. In Belgium, the University of Louvain was destroyed, as it had been in the First World War, and once again the German forces denied responsibility. On neither occasion did the German protestations of innocence, although dutifully supported by German academics, find much resonance in the international community. In 1940, the targeting of the library may have been fuelled partly by resentment of the contribution Germany had been obliged to make to replenish the stock of the destroyed library after the First World War. Each of the 300,000 books donated was supplied with a bookplate memorialising this German humiliation. This probably sealed Louvain's fate in 1940.[6]

France suffered twice, first in 1940 with the German invasion, which accounted for the libraries of Tours and Caen, and again in 1944 when Allied forces bombed railheads to inhibit German troop movements. The fabulous collection of Chartres had been removed to safety in 1940, was returned to the library in 1941 and was then destroyed in 1944.[7] The libraries of Ukraine and Belarus were almost obliterated, first in the German advance in 1941 before the battered retreating troops fought their way back to Germany with devastating results.

The Blitz destroyed libraries in several London boroughs, and University College London lost 100,000 books to a single attack. Liverpool, Plymouth and Coventry, inevitably, suffered grievous losses: in the case of Coventry, this involved the destruction of an important collection of scientific and technical literature of considerable value to the local war industries. This illustrates the difficulty of protecting public libraries. Because their collections were so important to the war effort, it was impossible to send them to safety and still perform their essential role in providing books and other resources to the civilian population.

Given the intensity of the bombing, it is remarkable how many city-centre libraries escaped largely unscathed. But overall, the major institutional collections, publishers and wholesalers in the different European nations must have lost something in the region of 50 million books to bombing (with the most destructive single bombing raid being the attack on Paternoster Row in December 1940, home to most of Britain's publishing industry; a similar calamity was suffered in Leipzig in 1943). But even a long trek down the Via Dolorosa of beautiful collections and imposing buildings reduced to dust and ashes only scratches the surface of the damage inflicted on the book stock of Europe during this war. In addition to the destruction of public libraries, we must consider the damage to private collections inflicted by the bombing and artillery, and the deliberate destruction, with flamethrowers, dynamite or vandalism by individual soldiers, perpetrated by the German occupying forces. Many libraries died simply because they fell into the path of attacking or retreating armies. This contributed many more millions to the losses, as did the abandonment of books by their owners, fighting men leaving behind books as they abandoned a theatre of war, or civilians engaged in one of the tragic treks away from the fighting or expelled by their homelands' new owners at the end of the war. And then we must not forget one of the most curious of all aspects of the destruction of books: the voluntary surrender of books and magazines by their patriotic owners for salvage and recycling. Overall, the scale of the damage to the continent's book stock is probably ten times that accounted for by the bombing of libraries, and this before we consider the millions of other pages of printed matter, issued in support of the war effort, and just as quickly discarded.

Between D-Day and the German surrender in May 1945, the American armies fired 23 million artillery shells in the European theatre of war, many of them directed against German towns and villages that had disregarded orders to surrender (usually because the German troops stationed there refused to permit it). Often it is impossible to disentangle the damage done by bombing and artillery fire, or, at closer range, shells fired by tanks. The small

Wesel in 1945. Although this could be any one of many German
towns, Wesel was unlucky in its importance guarding a strategic
crossing of the Rhine. By this point of the war, the Allied armies
were happy to leave the clearing of obstacles to their artillery
and air power. No one wanted to be the last casualty.

historical town of Wesel, uncomfortably situated on one of the
major Rhine crossings, was bombed on 16–17 and 19 February
1945, after which the Germans destroyed the bridge, the last Rhine
crossing in German hands. On 23 March, Wesel was subjected to
an artillery bombardment of astonishing ferocity, involving 3,000
guns, reinforced by RAF bombing. By the times the smoke cleared,
97 per cent of the town's buildings were destroyed. Of Wesel's
pre-war population of 25,000, only 1,900 remained at war's end.
The rest had either fled or died in the bombardment.

The example of Wesel could be duplicated a thousand times
over from the suffering towns and villages of Europe, from France
to Lithuania. It is reckoned that in addition to 60,000 civilian casualties, the German bombing of Britain destroyed 2 million private
dwellings. The Allied assault on Germany accounted for some 3.6
million German homes. The number of books lost in this destruction is hard to calculate. Many working-class British householders

who took part in the Mass Observation survey of 1942 professed to have few if any books at home. They preferred to borrow reading matter, or stuck to magazines or newspapers. But many would still have had a cookery book, a Bible, a dictionary or encyclopedia, even if they were not displayed in public rooms. Some working-class households accumulated considerable numbers of books, often kept in upstairs bedrooms. The pamphlets issued by the government to guide wartime conduct were ubiquitous in every household and, as we have seen, the books published by the Stationery Office celebrating British feats of arms were bought in huge numbers. So if we estimate a modest average of fifteen books per household for the destroyed properties in Britain, and twenty for the famously bookish Germans, for whom some patriotic purchases, like *Mein Kampf*, were in any case compulsory, this gives us a total of 102 million books destroyed in British and German homes in the course of the war. With figures like this, the estimate of 100 million books lost from the libraries of the Soviet Union, fought over for four agonising years, does not look exaggerated, though it has been disputed by German scholars.

Even if we regard the destruction of books in private hands as collateral damage, the purposeful destruction of the collections of countries under occupation went far beyond those books lost in the first attacks, plundered to replenish the libraries of Germany or for the new projects of Rosenberg's fevered imagination. Libraries were particularly at risk when the German armies were in retreat, when anger, frustration and fear reinforced the military logic of scorched-earth tactics. The municipal library of Dieppe, France, was destroyed in August 1944 by retreating troops, as was the library of the French National Assembly in Paris – a disdainful gesture comparable to the destruction by British troops of the Library of Congress in Washington during the War of 1812.[8] Before abandoning Greece, the Germans looted or burned much of the stock of the National Library in Athens, reckoned at 400,000 volumes. The National Library of Naples was incinerated because German troops claim to have been fired on by snipers as they abandoned the city. The burning of the collection of the Warsaw Public Library in the last days before the German evacuation, by troops sent into the stacks with flamethrowers, completed the destruction of Polish library culture.

Belarus suffered during the German advance in 1941, and again during their retreat in 1944. It has been calculated that 83 per cent of the country's collections were plundered, stolen or destroyed. Most of what survived was retrieved from Germany, Czechoslovakia or Poland after the war. In Smolensk, the Germans burned down all the libraries and twenty-two schools before they abandoned the city, with the loss of 646,000 books. It is significant that much of this detailed information comes from the proceedings of the trials in Nuremberg in 1946, a clear indication that crimes against humanity encompassed these cultural crimes, as well as the egregious acts of barbarism and mass murder committed by the SS and the Wehrmacht.

In all of this destruction we can note three other particularly egregious cases: Poland, Bohemia and the Jewish libraries. All had their own particular purpose. In the case of Bohemia, books were destroyed to eradicate Czech culture, and reclaim these lands wholly for Germany. Libraries were searched for the works of Czech writers, which were removed along with Czech books dealing with geography and history, or patriotic biographies. The Germans dug deep into history to identify the texts to be removed: the fifteenth-century reformer Jan Hus here stood shoulder to shoulder with the author of historical novels Alois Jirásek and the poet Victor Dyk. A decree of 1942 ordered university libraries to hand over all early Czech printed works. All told, Czech libraries lost something in the region of 2 million books, about a quarter of their total stock. In the year after the war, as the old borders were restored, the Czechs would take a savage revenge for their treatment during the occupation on their now defenceless German minority.

When the Polish armies laid down their weapons on 27 September 1939, after a gallant and costly struggle, the libraries of their homeland remained relatively intact. Five and a half years later, when the last German soldiers withdrew from Warsaw, the entire book stock of the nation had been laid waste. This reflected the German plan for Poland as a whole: that its civilisation should be utterly obliterated. Schools would close: Polish children would be offered four years of elementary education, to fit them for useful work. This was to be a peasant society, with a limited industrial proletariat. Intellectuals and other civic leaders were rounded up and many taken to the camps or shot. Poland was to be deprived of leadership, and also the accoutrements of civility, such as books.

Poland was a sophisticated, multilingual society, used to accommodating many ethnic groups and religious faiths within its borders. Its libraries, which included the medieval university library of Kraków, had many books published in German. These were seized and divided between the Germanised university library of Poznań and a new library to serve the military administration in Kraków.[9] Other books were passed to the German universities at Breslau, Königsberg and Berlin. But most of the Polish items in these collections were simply pulped. For the contents of school libraries and smaller institutional collections a central sorting depot was established at St Michael's Church in Poznań, where more than 2 million volumes were processed; what remained in the church was destroyed in an air raid in May 1944. Publishing firms, meanwhile, were obliged to turn over their presses to the services of the occupying forces. Publishing in Polish was limited to German–Polish dictionaries and the posters and instructions of the governor, Hans Frank, and local military commanders. Bookshops were closed; most would have shut anyway for lack of saleable stock.

Poland also provided the German conquerors with the first opportunity to trial their radical solutions to the 'Jewish problem'. Here, the eradication of Jewish worship and cultural practices was made into a form of public theatre not seen since the book burnings of 1933. All the synagogues were closed, and their libraries and sacred texts consigned to the flames. Special *Brennkommandos* (arson squads) were assigned to burn down the synagogues and their books. In Lublin, the Nazis celebrated the incineration of the books of the Talmudic Library: 'For us it was a matter of special pride to destroy the Talmudic Academy.'[10] The local Jewish population was assembled to witness their treasures burn, much as the Spanish conquistadores of the sixteenth century had forced the indigenous peoples of Mexico to watch the destruction of their books. In Lublin, a German military band drowned out the cries of the heartbroken watchers.

The conquest of Poland came before the establishment of Rosenberg's ERR (see above, Chapter 14), at which point Nazi policy shifted abruptly from destruction to the preservation of the literary remains of Jewish culture. The attentions of the ERR, and its competitors in library building, concentrated first on the rich pickings in France and the Netherlands, before turning back to the east. The equally impressive collection of Jewish texts amassed by Himmler's security service for their library in Berlin was destroyed by bombing in November 1943. The library of the ERR survived largely intact, to become the major focus of efforts of cultural restitution after the war.

As the tide of war turned against Germany, efforts to exterminate Jewish culture became more intense. Next in the line of fire was the Lithuanian city of Vilnius, the 'Jerusalem of the North'. The fate of Jewish books in Vilnius has attracted a great deal of attention in recent years, not least due to the heroism of the Jewish workers designated to sort the books of the Yiddish Scientific Institute, YIVO, a collection swollen by material looted from other Jewish institutions. Working under the supervision of the Frankfurt Hebraist Dr Johannes Pohl, the oldest and most valuable books were set aside for removal to Germany; the rest were sent for pulping.[11] The sorters' brave efforts to rescue what could be saved, at the risk of their lives, provide one of the most uplifting stories of the war.[12] How much their books mattered to the Jewish community can also be discerned by a deeply moving, though ostensibly dry, report from the librarian of the Vilnius ghetto's public lending library.[13] A collection of some 45,000 volumes, the library enjoyed brisk business despite the removal of its card catalogue by the German occupying authority. Yiddish and Hebrew books made up a surprisingly small proportion of the stock (30 per cent) and an even smaller proportion of the loans. As successive German round-ups winnowed the population, borrowing from the library became more feverish, up to 400 books a day. Readers favoured light fiction and mysteries over instructional texts: the sort of escapist literature that could still be enjoyed in conditions where each resident was limited to 700 square centimetres (7 square feet) of living space. The remains of the YIVO collection and the ghetto library were both lost when the ghetto was liquidated in September 1943. The books left undestroyed were sent for pulping when the Red Army occupied Vilnius: an ominous indication of the likely fate of Lithuanian culture in the forty-five years of Soviet occupation during the Cold War.

Not all the destruction of books was so dramatic: some books simply outlived their usefulness. This was the case with the POW libraries: the emptying of the camps meant leaving behind both the carefully curated libraries and the shelves of books collected by individual prisoners – all told, something in the region of 4 million volumes. This was not the only example of books abandoned because they had outlived their purpose. The service of the German *Frontbuchhandel* (Front-Line Book Service) was especially appreciated by troops garrisoning the occupied countries regarded as more comfortable berths, France, the Low Countries, Denmark and Norway. Once the Allied troops had landed in Normandy and the South of France, there was little time for reading, and many books were abandoned with other kit in retreat after retreat. Of the 100 million books distributed to German troops, few would have accompanied them home, or even to the prisoner-of-war camps where several million German soldiers would be incarcerated, in the case of those captured on the Eastern Front, for up to ten years. The 122 million books published in the American Armed Services Editions were hugely popular, but collectively owned; most were read over and over again until they disintegrated. Many were abandoned in foxholes in the Pacific islands or the Ardennes; most did not survive the war, by which time their work was done.

Then there were the books abandoned out of malign necessity: the libraries of Jews deported from Germany, France and the Netherlands, the libraries of the ghettos when they were emptied out into the concentration camps. German defeat brought a whole new wave of forced evacuations, of the German populations of East Prussia, Pomerania and Silesia, desperately trying to stay ahead of the Russian armies. Walter Kempowski, in his last great novel, *Alles Umsonst* (2006; *All for Nothing*), presents this evacuation through the eyes of an East Prussian noble family, determinedly ignoring the war until the time comes to join the crowd of refugees on the roads, with a cartload of valuables progressively abandoned.[14] The German navy performed its last significant service by transporting 2 million refugees along the Baltic to safety in the west. The end of the war brought another painful mass of refugees, as the Czechs turned on the German oppressors and repossessed the Sudetenland. An estimated 2.1 million ethnic Germans were deported to either the American or Soviet zone; none had the opportunity to liquidate their property or carry much with them. With a further 7 million evacuated or expelled from the German lands ceded to Poland, the total number of ethnic Germans forced to emigrate to Germany easily exceeded 12 million.[15] Books were seldom priorities for rescue.

We know that the new Polish masters of the formerly German provinces of Silesia and Pomerania appropriated more than 6.5 million books from the institutional collections and major private libraries in the German-speaking areas, though many were subsequently sent for pulping.[16] A more common fate was that the books were destroyed as the advancing troops looted and laid waste these neat German properties. A family expelled from their property in Danzig returned to find a typical scene of disorder:

> What we saw was unholy chaos and great destruction. We couldn't get the kitchen door open at all. There lay the books, torn from their bindings, paper and ripped fragments all over the place. The dining room was exactly the same.[17]

It would be possible to be more sympathetic if these same households had not watched in mute indifference as this sort of treatment had been meted out to neighbours from other ethnic groups in the years of German supremacy. This was payback: a point hammered home in one property, where amid the smashed furniture and other desecration, the returning owner found a carefully penned note left by a Soviet officer by the wrecked piano. 'Do not conclude, from the destruction here, that the Soviet people had an evil nature and no culture – everything that is happening here is for revenge.'[18]

The losses from this sort of wilful destruction are literally uncountable, but collectively they must have amounted to many further millions of books. Then we have to consider the disappearance of hundreds of millions of the sort of wartime texts that were never intended to survive, the posters, pamphlets and leaflets pumped out by all the combatants as part of the war effort. Does this come into the category of 'books'? Certainly, this was not the sort of material that most people would regard as part of their library, but these pamphlets, posters and flyers do constitute some of the best-read literature of the war. For a butcher or grocer failing to adhere to the ever-changing rationing protocols, neglect of these powerful little bulletins could mean their business being closed down, or a prison sentence. Posters pricked the conscience and inspired loyalty and obedience, ever more difficult to maintain as the war wore on. Millions of leaflets were dropped by air: sometimes these leaflets or flyers gave the occupants a twelve-hour warning of an impending raid. Picking them up and reading them might save your life.

Sometimes a leaflet was just one way of cheering yourself up when nothing else was happening. A very good example comes from the stagnant front outside Monte Cassino in the first half of 1944. Thanks to the terrain and the skill of German troops in building strongpoints in the mountains, the Gustav Line, a formidable chain of defences on the road to Rome, proved as hard a nut to crack as the German commander, General Kesselring, had intended. The Allied forces took heavy casualties inching their way forward, capturing mountaintops, crossing deep fast-flowing rivers and overwhelming machine-gun emplacements. The Germans defended their positions with extraordinary tenacity, condemned to days and weeks lying inert under constant bombardment, plagued by thirst, damp and lice. This became a war of attrition in which the morale of the contesting forces would play a large role in deciding the outcome: the nearest thing to First World War trench warfare experienced in this conflict.

The appeal to the vulnerabilities of troops whose nerves were already shredded by the constant shelling and machine-gun fire must have seemed worth a try: certainly it seems to have brought out the creativity on both sides. The Germans had fun inviting the British troops to imagine what handsome GIs were doing with their wives at home and asked the New Zealanders why they were being sacrificed for their imperial warlords.[19] Linguists in the German forces created flyers in a range of languages for the multi-national Allied troops, though frequent changes of detachments in the front line meant that they were often misdirected. The men of the Beds and Herts Battalion must have been rather challenged by the leaflets in Arabic intended for the Goumiers – Moroccan irregulars in the Free French contingent, much feared by the Germans for their effectiveness in broken terrain. The Allied leaflets hammered away at a single rather obvious theme, which had the great advantage that it was patently true: why were the Germans continuing to die for a lost cause? They also published their own multilingual flyers to prey on the insecurities of the international detachments in the German front line, though with a lack of success that surprised even the Germans.

The leaflets were printed on a mobile press that travelled with the American army on a giant tank carrier: it could turn out 8,000 leaflets an hour. These were then delivered by artillery fire, stuffed into a canister after the smoke-producing shell had been removed. About 750 copies could be delivered in a single shot. For a soldier immobilised in a shallow dugout with little cover throughout daylight hours, it might offer some minimal distraction. The Allies even produced a German-language weekly newspaper, *Frontpost*. One German soldier taken prisoner asked his interrogator for a copy of the latest issue, 'as if this was a regular service to which he had subscribed'. The pamphlet war became so intense that the forces began exchanging leaflets about leaflets, as in this German example, shot into the Allied lines:

> Those of you who are lucky enough to get out of this inferno
> of Cassino will always remember the German parachutists,
> the most ferocious of them all. Yet just imagine, some greasy,

slick-haired guy sitting safely way back of you tries to soften us with leaflets, asking us to wave a white handkerchief. Let this guy come to the front and find out that the paper with his trash on it is just good enough to wipe the arse with. On second thoughts, let him continue sending his leaflets – toilet paper is becoming rare at Cassino, and, tough as they are, even German parachutists don't like using grass.[20]

This captures one other aspect of this brutal and tragic episode, the strong element of mutual respect between the contesting forces. The intervals between assaults were marked by well-observed truce periods so that both sides could retrieve their wounded. The Allied leafleteers persisted, and sometimes managed to hit the mark. After the 1944 attempt to assassinate Hitler, volunteer German POWs were sent back through the lines to post flyers claiming the army was in general insurrection. And in the last days of the war, several hundred Czechs defected from the German army carrying leaflets specially written for them, calling upon them to join the patriotic cause of an independent Czechoslovakia.[21]

Hardly any of the many millions of flyers and leaflets dropped, fired or hand-delivered during the war would have been preserved. As the German troops indicated, they came in quite handy for wrappings and ablutions, though on the home front, being caught with an Allied leaflet in a German city might have been regarded as treachery. This probably limited the extent to which German civilians could make use of them, even during the paper famine of the last months of the war.

To conclude this tour of destruction, wilful or casual, we should consider the extraordinary story of wartime salvage drives. These focused most urgently on pots, pans, iron and aluminium, and gradually embraced paper products. This was not through any ecological anxiety, but a product of the shortage of wartime paper supplies. Poster campaigns stressed how many cartridges or essential industrial products could be fashioned from waste paper, and how many merchant ships could be released for other vital supplies if they were not carrying Canadian wood pulp. Municipal collectors scooped up used newspapers and magazines (in British households, magazines were often confusingly referred to as 'books'). Recycling paper was compulsory: from 1941 it became illegal to kindle a fire with newspaper, and from 1942 those refusing to sort their waste faced a possible two years in prison.[22] Towns and cities used the spur of competitive local targets to encourage generosity: Glasgow pledged a million books. Small towns and villages aimed to collect a mile of books (around 10,000 volumes). The process of inspection and sorting also gave a sobering lesson to librarians, confronted with the low quality of reading matter found in so many British homes.[23] Hopefully this helped nudge them to a more inclusive view of their own service, and the final abandonment of the settled prejudices against thrillers, romance and murder mysteries that had so limited the appeal of public libraries to large swathes of the reading population. In all, the great British book drives of 1943–4 raised 87 million books, with something over 60 million going to pulp. This striking number was more than equalled in Germany, where block leaders and enthusiastic teenagers from the Hitler Youth and the League of German Girls going from house to house could ensure that generosity to the patriotic cause would be enhanced by the fear of being seen not to contribute.

Pulp and ashes: all told, it seems more than likely that the events of the war – bombing, artillery fire, house-to-house fighting, evacuations, salvage and targeted destruction – accounted for something close to 500 million books being lost, destroyed or abandoned. At least another 200 million leaflets, pamphlets and posters were scattered around the battlefields, or recycled back into salvage. This was an astonishing assault on the collective reading culture of Europe, as well as Asia, where destruction in China, Malaya, Indonesia and Japan was if anything more critical, in places where mass literacy was only just emerging. Japanese bombing destroyed many libraries in China, including both main university libraries in Shanghai. Beijing's National University Library lost 200,000 books. Four-fifths of China's public libraries were looted or destroyed, with the loss of 10 million books.[24]

Allied bombing of Japan in the last years of the war accounted for half of the country's total book stock.[25]

These were grievous blows, but in Europe recuperation was relatively swift. Certainly there were, particularly in the destruction of the larger and more specialised collections, losses that could never be replaced; this was especially true of the historic Jewish collections of Eastern Europe, and of the historical heritage of the Poles and other subject peoples in the east. Yet by far the largest proportion of the reading matter lost was relatively easily replenished, or, in the case of leaflets, never intended to be preserved. To set against the loss of 500 million books in Europe, we have the astonishing statistic that in Germany publishers turned out 584 million books in the two years 1940 and 1941 alone.[26] In Britain, publishers recovered from the elimination of their entire collective back stock in December 1940, to embark on five years of remarkably creative publishing. For some, when they had banked their war insurance compensation for these losses, the freedom from this huge mountain of slow-moving stock, the physical legacy of so many over-optimistic decisions, might have been something of a relief.

In the post-war period, as paper restrictions were gradually unwound, the publishing industry embarked on a new golden age, with global markets, the growth of the paperback business, and millions of people in all parts of Europe hungry for familiar reading pleasures as they painfully recreated shattered homes and broken families. But before that, there was one more trauma to be undergone: the question of how many more books must be sacrificed to win the peace. In the five years after the war, millions more books would be consigned to destruction to eradicate the ideologies that had contributed to the extraordinary resilience of the Nazi regime. Others would be appropriated in compensation for the plunder and destruction of the war. This was an uneasy time for occupying forces who had gone into the war celebrating books as beacons of freedom, but ended as their destroyers.

PART VI

1945–89: WAR AS PEACE

16

CLEANSING

The years after the end of the Second World War were bound to be messy: the moral clarity of the war soon disintegrated under the pressure of circumstances. The occupying forces in Germany, faced by millions of displaced persons, helped the French and Dutch on their way home, while forcibly, on Stalin's instructions, repatriating former Soviet citizens to the east, where many faced imprisonment or death.[1] When the Allies sat in judgement on the Nazi elite at Nuremberg, evidence of Allied atrocities was specifically excluded. The Soviets, perpetrators of the Katyn massacre, in which they murdered nearly 22,000 Polish officers and prisoners of war, supplied two of the judges. Vessels taking Jewish survivors to Palestine, at least until the creation of the state of Israel in 1948, were turned back by the British navy. British investigators hunted down and executed any soldiers who had taken part in the killing of British POWs, while senior Nazis survived to build careers in the universities, judiciary and business community of the new Federal Republic of Germany.[2]

Faced with starving and traumatised populations, solutions to the manifold problems of the tortured continent were bound to be rough and ready; opinion back home generally accepted that the occupation forces were doing their best with an impossible job. But there were flashpoints, not least when it seemed that the American authorities, embarked on a purification of the German library system, were prepared to destroy millions of Nazi books. In 1933, 180,000 had marched on the streets of American cities to protest the Nazi book burnings. President Roosevelt had led the national condemnation: America would stand firm for the book as a critical marker of civilisation. Now, in the wake of the liberation, millions more books would be sacrificed to the cause of liberty.

The protests and public hand-wringing provoked by this paradox no doubt provided a welcome diversion to Germany's hard-pressed academics and librarians, who in 1945 risked being enveloped in the general opprobrium felt by the occupying forces since the discovery of the concentration camps. Pleas for the preservation of German culture rang hollow, particularly a culture so thoroughly Nazified, often with the enthusiastic assistance of these self-same academics and librarians.[3] When Allied troops overran German towns, the first instinct was to close all schools, libraries and bookshops. Only when the town was fully secured were these institutions allowed to reopen, though by this stage of the war bookshops had little stock, and many of the schoolteachers, if they and their charges had not been summoned to the front, would lose their posts as a result of denazification. But in the second half of 1945, and the brutal winter that followed, libraries were not the Allies' first priority. One British officer cheerfully admitted that they looked to library shelves as a source of firewood and building materials. 'Public libraries? We took their wooden shelves. What was important in 1945 was milk for babies, wood for buildings and coal for heat.'[4] The integrity of libraries' book stock came very low on the occupying forces' priorities.

This indeed remained the case, but with the passage of time this also allowed librarians freedom, once the roof had been repaired, to set the terms of the curation of their collections rather more than might have been consistent with a total repudiation of Nazi-era books. In principle, the removal of such books was an absolute necessity for the creation of a new society committed to democratic values. In practice, it required close supervision by experts who knew the canons of German literature intimately, and these were in short supply in the post-war occupying forces. Whatever their professed policies, the local representatives of the Allied military authorities were reliant on the expertise and good faith of the local librarians in order to carry them out.

*

Certainly, had the British military government been seriously interested in a fundamental cleansing of German libraries, they would not have entrusted a supervisory role to the poet Stephen Spender. Despatched to undertake a survey of post-war German institutions largely on the strength of his command of German, Spender proved a rather indolent inquisitor, more urgently concerned with the deficiencies of the car provided for his tour of the libraries of the Ruhr than with the contents of their collections. He was easily charmed by the learned librarians and academics with whom he took tea, and was willing to take at face value their presentation of their impeccable anti-Nazi credentials. Then it would be on to the next, for more tea and excuses, graciously received even when the previous host had warned that this particular individual was a fervent Nazi.[5]

Professor Kroll of Cologne opined reassuringly that he did not think that the influence of Nazi literature was very great: at least that was his impression from an investigation of readers' cards. It was astonishing, he told Spender, how few readers had interested themselves in Nazi books: Nazi literature was just too dull and humourless. Then it was on to Düsseldorf, and a warm reception from Dr Reuter, librarian of the combined town and state library. Despite its significant losses to bombing, his library still had many Nazi books, but since no one but librarians had access to the closed stacks, he felt they could safely be left where they were. Since Spender proved a sympathetic listener, Reuter also treated him to a discourse on the difficulty of disentangling the Nazi from non-Nazi influences in learned periodicals, which during the last ten years had presented a strange mixture of articles of real learning and valueless propaganda. Spender's narrative of these conversations provides a first-hand account of many such exercises of exculpation. The German universities came very well out of this process, partly because British, American and French academics had no wish to think ill of colleagues with whom they had enjoyed close and amicable relations before the war – but also, more pragmatically, because academics, like lawyers, businessmen and the clergy, were essential to any hope of rebuilding civil society. The full extent of academic complicity with Nazi rule was left carefully unexplored.[6]

Dr Peters, librarian of the Düsseldorf *Volksbücherei* (Public Library) and a party member (though only, he claimed, because this was a prerequisite for retaining his job), led Spender down a different avenue of this moral maze. While he had already put aside books in the categories identified as potentially poisonous, it would take three to four months of his staff's time to read this mass of material. Thus, the effect of British policy would be to make lots of Germans read hundreds of Nazi books which no one had opened during the Hitler regime (librarians seemed particularly insistent on this last point). Spender did not dispute this self-serving syllogism, partly because he had already come to very similar conclusions himself. 'Anyone who wanted to obtain Nazi books in Germany could easily do so, so to withdraw Nazi books seemed a piece of window dressing which would give us the reputation for treating literature in the same way as the Nazis themselves had done.' With this gloomy prognosis, he was easy meat for the charming female librarian of Aachen:

> Please, don't trouble, Mr Spender. We understand exactly what you want, and there is no difficulty whatever about carrying out your instructions. You see, throughout the Nazi regime, we kept all the books by Jewish and socialist writers in a special cellar, under lock and key, as having only historical and scientific interest. All we have to do now is to take out these books and put them on our open shelves, while at the same time we lock up all the Nazi books, because now they only have historical and scientific interest.[7]

Even so, books were culled, most urgently school textbooks and public library collections for the young. The Allied troops had been appalled by the youth of the soldiers who had been sent against them, and that they had frequently been forced to kill or themselves be killed. This was even more the case because these child soldiers were often the most fervently committed to defending the Reich to the last days of fighting. In February 1945, Lieutenant Van Ooteghem of the Flemish SS regiment was given a platoon of forty young volunteers, 'all youngsters of fifteen to seventeen years – most had been working in the Junkers aircraft factories – and they were convinced they would win the war'.[8] Many of these teenage recruits were targeted as potential members of the Werewolf movement intended to continue a guerrilla campaign after Germany's defeat.

The total management of the life of German's young, from the age of ten onwards, had had its effect, not least on the school curriculum. These militant adolescents were the products of Nazi education, and if Germany were to be saved, a whole generation of school textbooks would have to be swept away.[9] History books were an obvious example, but so too were geography texts and atlases. The French, in their zone of occupation, made a point of removing from all bookshops and libraries, including school libraries, any book that contained a map that deviated from the boundaries established at Versailles. The cartographical task of reconciling Germans to the new restricted boundaries of the 1945 settlement was one that would be entrusted to a new generation of school atlases.[10] Science books could normally be rescued, particularly if prefatory material lauding Nazi science had been cut out. But mathematics texts were more problematic, since many of the working examples were often drawn from the military field:

> If it takes 50,000 members of the Wehrmacht three days to conquer Holland [area of the country stated], how many days will it take 80,000 men to conquer England [area of the country stated]?[11]

Removing such texts was necessary and important work, but by the time of Spender's mission it had become increasingly clear that the four occupying powers were taking very different approaches to the problems of cleansing German book stock. Speaking for the Soviets, Marshal Zhukov favoured a much more stringent policy, including an investigation of private collections. The Russians would compile a 526-page catalogue listing books banned from the Soviet zone. While the French concurred, the British and Americans were against such wholesale purges. The Americans circulated a brief twenty-eight-page 'illustrative' list of the sort of

DR. CURT WUNDERLICH

Schamlos erinnern britische Marken
an einträgliche Sklavenmärkte und
den Raub strategischer Schlüsselpunkte.

DAS EMPIRE

BRITISCHER RAUB UND VERRAT

AMTLICH BELEGT DURCH POSTWERTZEICHEN

ERNST STANECK VERLAG BERLIN

Hitler had promised so to dominate the lives of German youth that 'they
would never be free again'. Even stamp collecting did not escape Nazification.
In this 1941 survey of British Empire stamps, the crimes and treacheries
of British empire-building are paired for their young readers with the
stamps of each of the colonial possessions of which Hitler was so jealous.

works that librarians might wish to exclude from their collections, such as cheap war novels and texts on racial superiority and colonial expansion. The British, meanwhile, worried that it would be difficult to define what was 'genuinely German' but at the same time 'neither militaristic nor Nazi'.[12]

The notorious Allied Order Number 4 of May 1946 that set off a storm in the American press was intended to resolve this question while restoring a common front between the four occupying powers. It prohibited works that promoted fascism, militarism, racism and anti-democratic ideas. All such books should be removed from library shelves and (here lay the problem) 'placed at the disposal of the Military Zone Commanders for destruction'. The press contingent at the American headquarters soon zoomed in on this last provision. Responding to questions, a low-level official ventured unwisely that 'billions' of books might be seized, and was not able to identify any clear difference between this order and the Nazi book burnings.[13]

The reaction in the United States was instantaneous. 'Allies to wipe out all pro-Nazi books' was the headline in *The New York Times*, to be followed the next day by a scathing editorial:

> It not only imitates but exceeds one of the earliest orders issued by Hitler after his accession to power – the burning of democratic pacifistic and 'Jewish books' ... if Germany is to be cured of Nazism it will be not by driving it underground, but by proving its fallacies to the Germans.[14]

Librarians and scholars joined their voices to the chorus of disapproval, leading to a formal admonition from the American Library Association:

> With full endorsement of the obvious motive to stamp out Nazism, we are confident that the method will be condemned in America and all over the world as short-sighted, unsound, and contrary to democratic principles. If the report is true, we urge that the order be revoked.[15]

The American library community was especially sensitive, because the reaction to the Nazi book burnings in 1933 in the United States had been so visceral and intense. In 1943, more than 200 libraries had held special events to mark the tenth anniversary of the burnings, celebrating the contribution of literature to the cause of freedom. Faced with this unwelcome scrutiny, putting Order 4 into practice proved an unwelcome extra burden for the occupying forces, though it was made clear to all concerned that pulping not petrol would be the preferred agency of destruction. There were to be no embarrassing pictures for the vultures of the press.

The Americans eventually squared this circle by appropriating a considerable proportion of these now forbidden books for their own purposes. Some 2 million were sent back to the Library of Congress, to be distributed to research libraries around the United States. American libraries had paid a heavy price for the isolation of the inter-war years. The military and political leadership in 1941 had been made acutely aware that they were lacking the materials to create a political, industrial or psychological profile of their new enemies, Germany and Japan: hence the rather embarrassing public appeals for maps and relevant foreign literature.[16] A plan was devised for systematic collection of texts from all over the world, with each of America's major libraries being given specific responsibility for a particular geographical domain. By 1945, it was clear to the American foreign policy establishment that withdrawing from their new global role was not a plausible option. Specialist teams were despatched to scour Japan, Italy and Germany for books and especially archival materials of value.

The appropriation of Nazi literature, textbooks, technical literature and history writing formed part of this wider effort, though to its victims it no doubt seemed little more than plunder. The bulk of the Library of Congress appropriation was new stock from what remained in publishers' warehouses: American agents removed 150 copies of every book or pamphlet they desired for American libraries, and the rest were sent for pulping. But libraries and bookshops were also targets. The Interdepartmental Committee for the Acquisition of Foreign Publications was established as a sub-branch of the Research & Analysis unit of the OSS, forerunner

of the CIA. It was active during the war scouring up print materials for the war effort, and its officers, some former librarians,
entered Germany with the advancing troops. They found many
of the major cities utterly desolate: three-quarters of the centre of
Cologne had been destroyed. They nevertheless scooped up 'a tremendous mass of material'. The IDC reached Cologne before the
civilian affairs officers had arrived to begin reconstruction, and,
as they frankly acknowledged, 'it is during this period that the lid
is literally off and almost anything goes'. They helped themselves
to anything they fancied from bookshops and libraries, 'and the
richest haul came from the university itself'.[17]

Viewed in retrospect, this rapacious collecting had uncomfortable resonances of Rosenberg's ERR, and the leader of this raiding
party, Leonard Hankin, felt obliged to defend himself. In forward-
ing this material, he reported rather shiftily, 'our function is merely
that of shipping agents', and in any case, the poor condition of the
university library put the survival of the books at risk (it was a
rescue mission, then). Hankin was a cheerful pirate at heart. By the
time the team reached Bonn, the military government was in place
'so the period of the snatch is off'. Rather than plundering the university library, Hankin sought the co-operation of the librarian,
who promised help in gathering the books they sought. A bookshop promised a useful trove of periodicals and maps, though here
too, with many curious German civilians looking on, Hankin was
obliged to quash 'the inclination to just seize the stuff and stalk
off'.[18]

The book collectors were part of a much larger formation,
known as T Force, gathered as the Allied forces prepared to break
out from the Normandy beaches. This comprised some 1,800
individuals charged with identifying key enemy personnel and
documents. Paris itself yielded real treasures from documents left
behind by the German administration. These included 'maps,
correspondence, inventories, personnel files, secret military and
non-military orders, yearbooks, business directories, films, current
periodicals in German, French, Japanese, and Russian, and so
on'.[19] And this was only a foretaste of what would be available in
Germany.

Even after dividing the spoils among government agencies and military departments, as well as other research libraries, there were still half a million books for the Library of Congress. Today the library's website refers rather coyly to the 'Co-operative Acquisitions Project', without delving too deeply into details of provenance.[20] These Nazi-era collections include 1,200 books from the personal library of Adolf Hitler, housed in discreet storage away from the main library building. Fifty years after their acquisition, only half had been catalogued. Brown University has another eighty of Hitler's books, from the much smaller collection in the Führerbunker where he spent his last weeks. They were appropriated by one of the first American soldiers to visit the bunker, Colonel Albert Aronson, and donated to Brown by one of his nephews in 1986.[21] Compared to the Library of Congress, the British Library in London has a relatively modest collection of confiscated Nazi books, around 11,000. Half of these came from the Hanover Kriegsschule (War College), and some from the libraries of other Nazi institutions. Some were removed in the course of winding up Nazi institutions elsewhere in Europe. Books from Aarhus in Denmark, Königsaal (Zbraslav) near Prague and Lisbon testify to the broad reach of the Nazis' control of the European book world during their brief pre-eminence.[22]

The Soviets, as usual, painted with a rather broader brush, and without any of the moral qualms that troubled at least some of the Allied book hunters. Stalin's armies, in any case, had a far larger suite of new satellite territories on which to impose their will, stretching far beyond the battered, broken cities of the east zone of Germany, swiftly denuded of their remaining industrial plant and artistic treasures by well-manned and extremely efficient Russian trophy brigades.[23] In Poland, Czechoslovakia and other satellites, Stalin recognised the forms of self-government, but these countries' authorities too were encouraged to undertake their own cleansing of the national book stock. This cleansing would extend not only to the literature of the Nazi period, but also to the literary remains of the brief inter-war experience of democracy.

The Soviet regime took strong action partly because they

believed in the civilising power of books. From the very beginning of the Bolshevik Revolution, books and literacy played a critical role in Lenin's plans for the awakening of the proletariat. The result was an astonishingly rapid extension of literacy, and of the Russian public library network: even as the economy stuttered, this was one of the great achievements of the first decades of the Soviet state. It required an equally rapid expansion of the capacities of the publishing industry. The other side of the coin was close control both of reading and the activity of indigenous authors. Writing was a perilous job, particularly in the paranoid years on both sides of the Great Patriotic War, when authors were as likely as any other professionals to fall foul of the unpredictable shifts in ideological messaging which could condemn the unwary to a slow death in the Gulag.

The difficulties of navigating the pitfalls of Stalin's Russia can be exemplified by the long and distinguished career of the poet Anna Akhmatova.[24] Anna was a survivor, but at great personal cost. Born in 1889, and already well published by the time of the Russian Revolution, she decided not to abandon Russia, unlike so many other intellectuals, which made her initially a favourite of the Soviet regime. This ended abruptly with the trial and execution of her former husband, Nikolai Gumilev, in 1921. Anna's admirers melted away as her works were effectively banned, while her son and new partner were frequently imprisoned. An authorised edition of her works in 1939 was swiftly withdrawn and pulped. Her war work seemed to offer a way back to favour, until a visit to her flat by the Latvian/British intellectual Isaiah Berlin resulted in her expulsion from the Union of Soviet Writers. Stalin's death in 1953 allowed a partial rehabilitation, leading to nomination for the Nobel Prize for literature in 1965 and 1966, the year of her death.

It was obvious that the Soviets would apply these same standards of ideological purity to the buffer states, consigned to them by Stalin's successful arm-wrestling with an ailing Roosevelt and a pragmatic and resigned Churchill. Among the trophy states were two sophisticated reading nations, Poland and Czechoslovakia, though both had been battered by the experience of Nazi rule, and Poland had to absorb a substantial portion of former German territory. Hungary, as a Nazi ally and satellite, could also expect some rough handling. In the case of Poland, which had endured the almost complete annihilation of its public library network, as well as the closure of its schools, it might have been thought that the job of ideological cleansing had already been achieved. But the Soviet inheritance included the Germanic public library created in Kraków, and the large number of German library books, especially from the *Staatsbibliothek* in Berlin, secreted in caves in Silesia, now designated as part of Polish territory. These books would not be returned to Germany – the choice was whether to appropriate them as part of Russia's reparations for the destruction of its own libraries, or allow them to remain in Poland. Initially, without formal communist control over Poland, the Russians were inclined to be generous. Kraków was the beneficiary of many of these treasures, particularly many pieces of rare early music printing, and musical scores in manuscript.[25]

This was a good beginning on which to build a co-operative relationship. The Polish authorities were all too willing to make hay with the former German territories in Silesia and Pomerania, removing such cultural properties as remained undestroyed. The property left behind by Germans fleeing west could also be claimed by the state. The two main libraries of Breslau, the badly mauled university library and the municipal library, largely undamaged, were both incorporated into the new university library of what was now a Polish city, Wrocław. In all, more than 6 million books were retrieved from the former German territories, a quarter of which were destined to restock the libraries of Kraków's Jagiellonian University.[26] The new Polish state also achieved marvels in rebuilding the public library network. From the battered remains of 426 libraries left by the retreating Germans, with a total of 1 million books, by the end of 1949, these had grown to a collection of 6.5 million books, in a public library network that had expanded ninefold.[27]

Even so, it was soon apparent that Polish education and cultural priorities would in the long term have to be subordinated to socialist principles. Most of the books retrieved from Silesia would have been in the German language. While some were scientific and technical books of real utility, most did not meet the stringent specifications laid down by the Ministry of Education for retention as part of the Polish national collection. Large quantities of German-language materials were examined at the sorting centres set up in the main cities (often in the buildings of the universities) and sent for pulping. That Poland wished to turn its back on the German heritage of the newly Polish lands was understandable; that the university libraries and their staff were charged with consigning books to pulping was yet one more sorry episode in these dismal times.

Meanwhile, the Main Office for Control of the Press, Publications and Public Performances had already issued an initial list of banned books in October 1945, the first of seven such lists published between 1945 and 1947. Any works of a nationalist, fascist, anti-communist or anti-Soviet character were banned. The noose tightened further with the communist victory in the elections of 1947, initiating a period of cultural austerity all too familiar from the early history of public libraries in the west. In 1949, Jadwiga Filipkowska-Szemplińska urged fellow members of the Polish Librarians Conference not to loan out 'sensational and mystery books or sentimental romances', something that could have been said by any English or American librarian of the 1890s.[28] This, though, was the language of the new socialist library culture: popular literature, Filipkowska-Szemplińska believed, was 'full of bourgeois ideals, snobbery and the cult of lazy good-for-nothings'.[29] Librarians who could not accommodate the new puritanism in its socialist clothing were gradually eased out of their positions.

Czechoslovakia experienced a similar transition, from initial post-war optimism to increasingly rigid controls. Pre-war Czechoslovakia was remarkable for the strength of its public library network, much of which survived the years of Nazi rule relatively intact. While the Soviet Union could by 1967 offer forty-seven books per hundred inhabitants in its revitalised public library network (the comparative figure for 1914 was six per hundred), Czechoslovakia had reached sixty-five per hundred inhabitants already by 1937. Yet the cleansing of public libraries after 1948, the date of the communist takeover, would result in the removal of 27.5

million books from the shelves of the public libraries, a devastating impoverishment of reading culture. The nationalisation of the publishing industry also resulted in the destruction of 85 per cent of publishers' stock.[30]

The irony of this is that an unusually high proportion of Czech authors had supported the communists, and the opportunity to fill this yawning gap on the shelves of bookshops and libraries was one they eagerly grasped. Although the number of editions published fell sharply after 1948, print runs increased fourfold: if your works met with ideological approval, it had never been easier to pen a bestseller. The love affair with authority proved fleeting. Chafing at the restrictions on their creativity, Czech authors became first ardent supporters of the Prague Spring in 1968, then, in the new repression of the 1970s, exponents of the famous underground samizdat literature.

The process of adjustment to Soviet control in Poland and Czechoslovakia swiftly throttled any brief optimism for the restoration of the cultural freedoms of the pre-war years. In the shattered remnants of the Russian occupied zone of Germany, there were no illusions. In the four-power division of 1945, the Russians had inherited what was generally regarded as the historic heart of Prussian militarism and Nazi power. No one imagined they would proceed gently.[31] The denazification of libraries was far more thorough in the east than in the western zones, and far more indiscriminate.

Already in 1946, 1.2 million books wended their way east to libraries and repositories in the Soviet Union. This was only the first instalment of an ongoing process: all told, it is estimated that between 5.5 and 11 million books were removed from the German Democratic Republic (GDR – East Germany) during the Soviet occupation.[32] Some never made it to the shelves of libraries, but instead piled up unread in makeshift Russian warehouses, sometimes in the damp and unheated premised of former Orthodox churches, now unused. A reorganisation of local government in the GDR in the 1950s, removing some of the smaller units, resulted in some public libraries closing altogether, and considerable losses as inappropriate titles were weeded out. In due course, when the

Soviet appetite for vengeance had been sated, the GDR would build a formidable network of public libraries, with more books per head than its affluent West German neighbour.[33] Then came 1989, and a further revolution, which doomed most of these books to destruction, as inhabitants of the GDR rejected the closed and ideologically constrained market imposed on them for the last forty-five years. Soon the stock of the public libraries was on its way to the pulping mills, the last major act of cleansing of Europe's turbulent century. It was an unedifying end to a tragic story, played out in Europe's most bookish nation, a publishing giant since the beginning of the twentieth century, and one of the major fonts of literary genius. The twentieth century had not been kind to German literary culture.

17

RESTITUTION

Richard Kobrak should have had an unremarkable life. A decorated veteran of the First World War, Kobrak trained as a lawyer and settled for a comfortable existence working for Berlin's city authorities. He married, brought up a family and collected books, to which he attached a neat, unadorned bookplate. The family identified as Christian, and their Jewish background was well submerged, but after Hitler's accession to power neither this, nor Richard's war record, proved adequate to save them. A patriotic German, Kobrak was reluctant to be forced out of his home, but in 1936 he was dismissed from his job, and after the *Kristallnacht* riots of 1938, he finally recognised that his family was in danger. Barely months before the war his three children were sent away to safety, but there was no money left for the parents to plan their own escape. In 1943, Richard and Charlotte were deported to Theresienstadt and from there to Auschwitz, where they were murdered.

Seventy years later, a book with Kobrak's bookplate came to light in the Berlin Central Library. This is the city's main public library, build on the site of the *Stadtbibliothek* (city library) destroyed in the Second World War. According to Sebastian Finsterwalder, one of a small team charged with identifying plundered books in the library, it first came into the library around 1950, as part of a collection assembled by a man named Dombrowski. The book in itself is unremarkable, the work of a conservative politician of the inter-war period, Georg von Hertling, entitled *Recht, Staat und Gesellschaft* (*Law, State and Society*). This is not a valuable book, and in monetary terms one could certainly not justify the resources required to sift through the entire collection of the Berlin Central Library and trace the heirs of the original owners.

In this case, remarkably, after posting the book on the library's database of plundered books, Finsterwalder was contacted by someone who knew one of Kobrak's grandchildren, now living in England, to whom it was in due course returned. The grandchild, now in her fifties, does not read German, but to recover the book was nevertheless a hugely emotional experience: her only tangible connection with the German grandparents she never knew.[1]

One book, a poignant remembrance of the terrible violence done to millions of people, driven from their homes and deprived of their livelihoods and lives. It seems unarguably correct that such property should be returned, at whatever cost in labour and money. Restitution is an important part of the healing process that follows any conflict: a return of property to those from whom it has been unlawfully seized, or their descendants, and a symbolic act of atonement by those who have benefited from the original acts of appropriation, extortion or criminality. In practice, establishing the parameters of what should be returned, and to whom, is incredibly complicated, particularly in the immediate aftermath of war, when many of the victors have also suffered terrible losses, and emotions are running high. Decisions are made that in retrospect seem arbitrary and unfair. For many libraries and millions of Europe's stranded books, the war would continue for years, and with none of the glamour that has attracted public interest in the hunt for stolen art. Only the richest and most distinguished collections of books became in the immediate post-war period the subject of debate and controversy; it was left to small teams of dedicated librarians and military officials to see that as much as possible of the residue found its way home, if there was still a home for it to go to.

By the end of the war in 1945, the book stock of Europe was hopelessly jumbled. Millions of books had been appropriated and taken to Germany. The collections of German libraries had been belatedly moved to places of safety in castles or mines, many now outside the newly drawn borders of the post-war German states, to which they were unlikely to return. Many further millions of books had been abandoned in the bombings and migrations of this era; books from institutional collections were scattered between the

Allied and Soviet zones of occupation, a further complication that
would not be easily resolved. To rebuild libraries shattered in the
bombing, books were gathered up from abandoned houses with
little concern for questions of ownership; meanwhile, the troops
of the occupying powers helped themselves to anything that took
their fancy, which sometimes included books. We have seen in the
previous chapters examples of both casual souvenir hunting and
the more purposeful gathering of Nazi-era publications to stock
the shelves of American research collections, under the guise of
the cleansing of German libraries.[2] The American example was
followed by the Soviet Union on an industrial scale in the lands
under its control. This brought a new complexity to issues of restitution when these books had originally been plundered from other
western or eastern libraries by Germany.

The problem of restitution, then, went hand in hand with the
task of rebuilding Europe's shattered libraries. Issues of ownership
were sometimes subordinated to public utility. It proved far easier
to return whole plundered collections which had been kept in one
place than the jumbled remnants of many house clearances. Sometimes it is difficult to distinguish restitution from retribution, or
even reparations, when millions of books were seized in compensation for what had been destroyed; this is particularly the case in
the complex history of restitution in Eastern Europe and Russia.
Finally, we are left with the issue of what was to be done with
books when it was impossible to make restitution to families that
had been altogether obliterated in the Holocaust: an impossible
quandary, where even the best intentions brought bitter conflict
and unsatisfactory resolutions.

Germany's voracious plunder of Europe's libraries continued up to
the last months of the war. In Berlin, a handful of staff still worked
away in the ruins of the *Staatsbibliothek*, cataloguing books while
the building crumbled about them. The books from Rosenberg's
Institute for the Research of the Jewish Question in Frankfurt were
shifted to Hungen, 50 kilometres to the north, in 1943, where they
were housed in makeshift depositories around the town; new consignments diverted to Hungen continued to arrive almost until the

moment the Americans occupied the town in April 1945. Many of the new acquisitions had never left their crates.

Some of the books from libraries in Amsterdam or Paris were swiftly identified, but these easy wins proved to be only the beginning of a mammoth task of extraordinary complexity. By the end of the war none of the major libraries created by the Nazi regime from the plunder of the conquered territories were in their original location. The ERR's *Ostbücherei*, a library intended for Berlin, had been removed to Ratibor in Silesia in 1942; the books in the ERR's sorting centre not yet allocated to any library also made their way from Berlin to Ratibor. With additional consignments continuing to arrive from the east, the collections scattered around Ratibor amounted to some 2 million books when the Germans fled the fast-advancing Russians in January 1945. The huge library being assembled by Himmler's security service in Berlin also moved to evade the bombing, partly to Theresienstadt, and from there to castles in the Sudetenland and partly to Ratibor.[3] The library being assembled for the new Nazi university, the Hohe Schule, was also evacuated from Berlin in 1942, largely to Tanzenberg in Austria. The books intended for the library of the massive cultural institute planned for Hitler's home town in Linz were moved to Villa Castiglione and neighbouring castles in 1943.[4]

This enormous logistical operation involved some 10 million volumes frantically criss-crossing Germany in search of a safe refuge as the infrastructure of the state fell to pieces. The books at Ratibor were abandoned largely because there was no available rolling stock to take them to the identified places of safety in Bavaria. Of the five major collections, only the Frankfurt Jewish Institute came close to offering a functioning library service, and then with only a fraction of the books received; as the libraries surrendered staff to the desperate struggle on the front line, even cataloguing the new acquisitions became an impossible task. The futility of this whole venture aptly captures the sheer wastefulness of the totalitarian state.

While some crates headed east and some headed west, each of these libraries represented a jumble of books from all over Europe. The books from the west (France, Belgium and the Netherlands) came largely from private libraries and the libraries of specialist institutions: public library collections were left comparatively undisturbed, with the exception of some distinguished Jewish collections deposited in the library of the University of Amsterdam. In the east the reverse was the case, as the private libraries had very often already been integrated into state institutions; since the Nazis were keen to lay their hands on a comprehensive library (and archive) for the study of Bolshevism the contents of public libraries were very relevant to their mission. Some books from the east were designated for the Jewish Institute in Frankfurt, and books from France and Amsterdam libraries, such as the Ukrainian, Polish and Turgenev libraries in Paris, were sent to Berlin for the *Ostbücherei*, and thence to Ratibor. Books from an individual library might be spread between several depositories and libraries in Germany.

To complicate matters further, who had care of these collections depended on which of the occupying powers had possession on the ground when the fighting ceased. The books of the Frankfurt Institute at Hungen were in the American zone, and those from the Hohe Schule at Tanzenberg in the British zone in Austria. It was the Soviets who captured the lion's share, since their sphere of influence encompassed not only Ratibor (now Racibórz in Poland), but also Czechoslovakia, where the books of the Berlin library of the security service had been secreted. It was taken as read that the books of the German public libraries, which already contained many plundered books, sheltered in castles or mines now in territories allocated in the post-war settlement to Poland or Czechoslovakia would never be returned.

In the American zone, those charged with restitution of books found that doing the right thing was far from simple. The Hungen depositories fell into American hands in April 1945, about the same time that a further 100,000 looted German books were discovered in cellars beneath the rubble of the Jewish Institute in Frankfurt. These had to be moved swiftly, so the Americans requisitioned as temporary storage the library gifted to the city of Frankfurt by the local branch of the Rothschild family. Perhaps unwisely, the officer charged with managing the growing hoard placed an advertisement

US Army Chaplain Samuel Blinder examining looted Torahs in the cellar of the Frankfurt Institute. Of course, in most cases there was no synagogue or Jewish community to which they could be returned. Solving this quandary led to some of the most passionate disputes of the post-war restitution effort.

in the army newspaper, *Stars and Stripes*, calling for information on displaced books, only to be inundated with calls identifying caches of books in churches and castles, including one collection of half a million books on Freemasonry.[5] It soon became necessary to find a new sorting centre: a warehouse in Offenbach, opposite Frankfurt on the other side of the Main, was requisitioned, where the various collections could be brought together and sifted.

By the time this had been achieved it was February 1946, and scarcely a book had yet been returned to its owners. While many of the crates were clearly labelled as property looted from Jewish institutions, much of the stock had been hopelessly mixed in the hasty move to Hungen. The Offenbach operation was also very short of trained librarians, since the MFAA, the Monuments, Fine Arts and Archives Program, established in 1943 to protect cultural property in liberated countries (popularly known as the Monument Men), was mainly concerned with high-value art, and the Library of Congress mission was entirely focused on obtaining materials for American research collections. It took two graduates of the University of Chicago, Seymour Pomrenze and Isaac Bencowitz, to devise a system capable of processing books in this quantity and at speed.[6] Books recognisable as belonging to institutions, such as the Rosenthaliana in Amsterdam and the Domus Spinozana in The Hague, were placed in 'national rooms', where Dutch and French restitution officers could claim them. Bencowitz also trained the local German workers to recognise bookplates, library stamps and markings in Hebrew that would identify the libraries to which they should be returned. This resulted in the identification of 4,000 library marks and the *ex libris* of 500 private owners. Books continued to flow in, including 700,000 books from the Berlin *Staatsbibliothek*, found in a Frankfurt railway siding, and the remains of 425,000 books from the library of the Reich Main Security Office, left behind in Berlin (Offenbach was by now receiving books from all over the American sector). By the end of 1948, 3.5 million books had passed through the depot, and all but 367,000 had found a home. In the circumstances, it was a remarkable achievement.[7]

The work undertaken in Offenbach was particularly sensitive because of the large number of books looted from Jewish institutions to build Rosenberg's Frankfurt Institute. The British, dealing with the half a million books collected for the library of the proposed new Nazi university now located in their zone of occupation in Austria, had it comparatively easy. These were efficiently sorted into national sections to be returned to their countries of origin; this included 2,517 crates returned to France, including books from the libraries of the pre-war prime minister Léon Blum, members of the Rothschild family and many other private Jewish libraries. Approximately 55,000 books in 659 crates were despatched to Moscow in May 1946, with a further consignment of 397 crates sent to Leningrad a year later. This latter batch comprised books purloined by the Germans from the imperial palaces around Leningrad during the epic three-year siege.[8] This gesture of solidarity was not one the Soviets would reciprocate; their refusal to return books from Western libraries that had found their way into the

This book stamp identifies the original owner of the volume as the Volhynia Theological Seminary in northern Ukraine. Despite the extraordinary work accomplished in Offenbach, the plundered books were so jumbled that it was often impossible to match books to either private or institutional collections. In many cases, the library to which they might have been returned no longer existed.

collections of the Soviet Union would continue to cloud diplomatic relations into the twenty-first century.

Of course, there was every reason why the Soviet Union should take a different approach towards questions of restitution. For all the hardships of occupied Europe, and the sacrifice of the Allied troops before Germany was defeated, Russia had suffered incomparably more: in the damage to property, human casualties and the destruction of its cities and cultural institutions. In Belarus, the State Library of Minsk reckoned to have lost 83 per cent of its books. The damage to the libraries of Ukraine in the German advance, occupation and retreat was in a very real sense incalculable (not least because the Soviets were reluctant to acknowledge that they had contributed by blowing up public buildings on their retreat, and the bombardment before Kiev was retaken).[9] Although the Baltic republics had initially welcomed liberation from Russian rule, their libraries had also suffered grievously during the German occupation. If the Soviet Union had lost a hundred million books, as was plausibly deposed in evidence to the Nuremberg trials of the principal Nazi leaders, then no sort of reparation, however arbitrary, could ever fully compensate.

The complex of repositories in and around Ratibor was the first to experience the Soviet approach to restitution. Within a few weeks a train of fifty-four freight cars, holding more than a million books, was on its way to Minsk. Some of the books were indeed part of the huge appropriations from the libraries of Belarus. But these were mixed with books from libraries from a range of Soviet institutions and libraries in France, Belgium and the Netherlands: approximately half of the million books emanated from these Western sources. No distinction was made in handling the material destined to remain in Minsk, after a portion had been siphoned off for Moscow and Leningrad. The Russian libraries laid claim to almost all the archival material swept up in Germany. This was the case even for documents of importance to Ukraine, Belarus or the Baltic nations: obtaining their return was an issue that preoccupied librarians in these nations for many years. They were less concerned with questions of cultural ownership of books from France and the Netherlands that they were now examining for accession in their own collections.

Before any of the books from Western libraries could be absorbed into the collections of Minsk or Moscow, they had of course to be examined for suitability. The provisional report of the Soviet censorship department in Minsk was simultaneously reassuring but cautious, hedging its bets in the style required of Russian officialdom:

> The library administration has made a provisional examination, so in my inspection I did not find any literature with anti-Soviet propaganda, although to be sure the entire holding will require further 'cleansing' since it is littered with scattered bourgeois apologetic philosophical and sociological publications.[10]

How such 'scattered bourgeois apologetic' publications would practically be identified in a collection of half a million books was left appropriately vague. That was the way to stay alive in Stalin's Russia. The library reported that it had retained 60 per cent of the Western books in the consignment. If this was true, then some

200,000 books that would have been gratefully received in Paris or Amsterdam were consigned for pulping.

This one trainload was the first of many, but it highlighted many of the issues raised by the shipment east of vast quantities of books from German libraries and the repositories dotted around Poland and Czechoslovakia to which they had been consigned. It must be remembered that in the immediate post-war period, the libraries of the war-ravaged parts of the Soviet Union were hardly equipped to undertaken serious re-cataloguing work: particularly after the immediate post-war purge of any librarians who had co-operated with the German occupying forces. Once a building had been made water-tight, for a period any books to fill the emptied shelves were gratefully received. This involved accepting many books in French and Dutch which were hardly likely to be central to their core mission. This was even more the case with the millions of books gathered in Germany by the Soviet trophy brigades.[11]

In Stalin's plan for making good the damage wreaked by German aggression, the stockpiles of Nazi plunder represented only the low-hanging fruit. When Russian troops first advanced into German territory, Stalin's infamous order of February 1945 established no limits to the pillage to be extracted from a society which, to the eyes of the advancing troops, still seemed to be astonishingly rich after five years of warfare. In the parts of Germany occupied by the Soviets, industrial plants were dismantled wholesale and shipped back to Russia: sometimes this was done so crudely that the machinery was rendered unserviceable in the process. The German destruction of Russian cultural treasures would also bring reprisals. The trophy brigades are reckoned to have swept up some 900,000 works of art. Books, too, formed part of the programme. Staff from the Lenin Library in Moscow had made their way to Berlin by June of 1945, looking for books with which to build library collections at home. The first priority was technical books published in Germany during the war, though medical books were also targeted. To facilitate the search, Soviet officials transported to Berlin the entire stock of twenty-five libraries, including major public libraries in the eastern zone, for sorting and appropriation: this represented a total of some 1.3 million books. Only when all the interested parties had examined the stock were the remnants returned to the libraries. All told, it is reckoned that something in the region of 10 million volumes were removed from the libraries of the Soviet-occupied eastern zone of Germany and the depositories elsewhere, to replenish the libraries of the Soviet Union. Half of these were destined for Moscow and Leningrad, home to the most prestigious Soviet libraries.[12]

This left the libraries of what became communist East Germany (the GDR), already battered by bombing, utterly denuded. For the task of rebuilding the libraries in Berlin, the Central Library established a series of collection points around the city, where the books found in the ruins of bombed and now unoccupied homes could be deposited. Books from Nazi ministries, or private libraries including those of leading members of the regime, such as Goebbels and Albert Speer, were also appropriated (the Soviets encouraged similar confiscations to rebuild the shattered libraries of Poland). These 'rescued' books joined the collections of books the libraries had received from the city pawnbroker, the product of the house clearances following the round-up of Jewish families in Germany and occupied Europe.[13] This ensured that unnumbered quantities of books from Jewish households remained in German libraries long after the liquidation of the library of Rosenberg's Frankfurt Institute. Little would be done to attempt to identify these items until the last years of the twentieth century.

The 7–10 million books removed were a savage blow to the German library community (as they were intended to be), but, the technical books apart, they did little to restore the damaged libraries of the Soviet Union. Many of the plundered books were in German, whereas the Soviets' most urgent need was for educational texts and literature in Russian and the languages of the other nations of the Union. The desire to appropriate trophies of value also led to many books from the first centuries of print being added to the freight trains. Many of these disappeared into the vaults of the major libraries in Leningrad and Moscow, where hundreds of thousands remained uncatalogued, and unavailable to readers, for the next forty years. It was impossible for librarians in Germany even to establish which books the Russians had taken, and which had been destroyed in the war. For many years the cata-logue entry for many of the sixteenth-century books in the Berlin *Staatsbibliothek* was a plaintive 'Kriegsverlust möglich': 'possibly lost in the war'.

The fall of the Berlin Wall in 1989 and the subsequent political turbulence in the Soviet Union paved the way for a possible reset in the relationship between the library communities. The cata-logue entries in the Berlin State Library were gradually changed to reflect the present location of books from their library in Russia or Poland. The issue of repatriation remained, however, deeply div-isive. One of the first fruits of glasnost was the revelation that 2.5 million books from Germany allocated to the Soviet Academy of Sciences had in fact been stockpiled in a church in Uzkoye outside Moscow and there left to rot. They were still there in 1990, now reduced to an indistinguishable mass of pulp.[14] This created a sen-sation in the library world, raising hopes that the new climate of openness might encourage conversations about the return of books to Western libraries. Quiet work on the provenance index of the National Library of Belarus has revealed many works from French private libraries, and a Dutch researcher identified a number of books from Dutch collections. It was thought that at one point Minsk had some 20,000 books in Dutch, though some seem to have been moved to Moscow in the 1970s. A portion of these, 608 books in 663 volumes, was returned from the Moscow State Library for Foreign Literature to Amsterdam in 1994.[15] The Minsk library also offered further clues to the fate of the 100,000 books from the famed Turgenev library in Paris, confiscated by the Nazis for the *Ostbücherei*, and then later transferred to Russia. These were prized because Lenin had studied there, though the library also aroused suspicion as a hotbed of émigré literature. In 2002, the Russian State Library acknowledged that 10,000 books from the library were in Moscow; many of the rest had been destroyed in 1951.[16]

The repatriation of books to Amsterdam raised hopes that would never be realised. In Russia, conservative and nationalist forces were already mobilising against the return of books: one representative in the Duma described such transactions as 'spitting on the graves of the 27 million Soviet citizens killed in the war'.[17]

In 1998 the Russian Constitutional Court forced President Yeltsin to sign a law forbidding further restitutions. We are still far from knowing the full extent, or location, of books from Western libraries that remain in the countries of the former Soviet Union.[18]

The tragedy of the plunder, dispersal and destruction of Jewish cultural property during the war was also compounded by unseemly squabbles over the destination of the unclaimed books. Even in 1945, the Offenbach centre received numerous delegations from representatives of the Jewish community, and scholars anxious to work on texts in the warehouse. The burden of dealing with these unwelcome visitors fell on the liaison officer, Koppel Pinson, who felt understandable frustration that the small, hard-pressed team were doing 'all the hard work and all the dirty work, while our great leaders of Jewry send telegrams from their offices or come on inspection tours of three to five days'. Pinson wanted the world to know 'that what we are dealing with is not a library in any sense of the term, but a large deposit of loot'.[19] The stock of unclaimed property might have been depleted, but its symbolic capital was enormous, and the number of powerful interests clamouring for attention called for a resolution that could only be made by the highest authorities.

Pinson's outburst may have expressed the frustration of an overworked officer, but it also laid bare real divisions within the international Jewish community over where the future lay. Six million Jews had been murdered, 90 per cent of the pre-war population in some parts of Europe. Was it even possible to conceive of a future for the Jewish people in post-war Europe? Many thought not, and to restore property to its original homelands would, in the words of Jerome Michael, chair of the Commission for European Jewish Reconstruction, return to them a quantity of books that would far exceed the religious and cultural needs of these 'ghost communities'. In this particular exceptional instance, it was necessary, in the view of the Librarian of Congress Luther Evans, to make decisions, 'less from the point of view of specific property rights than from the point of view of the cultural value of material to the Jewish people'.[20] So no books for the scattered remains of the

Polish and Soviet Jewish communities, and none for any German institutions like the University of Frankfurt. But where was now the spiritual home of Jewry – the United States or Palestine?

The leading role of American intellectuals in this debate, and the presence of the American occupying forces on the ground, seemed to tip the scales in favour of the United States, but Palestine too had its advocates. A growing if contested Jewish population had settled in Israel in the early twentieth century and created significant cultural institutions which would be a plausible home for unclaimed Jewish property.[21] But Palestine was still part of the British mandate until 1948, and it would be May 1949 before recognition of the state of Israel by the United Nations placed its claims on a secure legal footing. The proposal for a new Jewish library in Copenhagen, briefly championed by UNESCO, kept alive the guttering flame of a European centre of scholarship and memory, though this plan was never supported by any Jewish representative body.

We can see this debate played out in the correspondence and memoranda of a remarkable woman, Lucy Dawidowicz (née Schildkret). Dawidowicz was a scholar and archivist with strong pre-war connections to the Yiddish Scientific Institute (YIVO) in Vilnius. She returned to Europe in 1946 to serve the body charged with supporting the 250,000 people in camps for Jewish displaced persons in Germany. She arrived in Offenbach to select the last portion of 25,000 books promised by the American authorities for the camp libraries. Sifting through the remaining stock, she repeatedly came across the library stamp of YIVO, and of the second major Jewish library in Vilnius, the Strashun. Dawidowicz was convinced that these two collections should be sent to New York, where YIVO now had its headquarters, and in this she would prevail. But Dawidowicz also had strong views on the future of the Offenbach centre, which she believed should be wound up; this would mean abandoning the effort to identify individual owners who were probably dead, or institutions which had largely been destroyed.[22]

Dawidowicz made no effort to disguise her disdain for several of her colleagues, exposing serious maladministration in the delivery of earlier consignments of books to the displaced persons' camps, whose arrival could not be verified. Dawidowicz suspected Pinson, who had been in charge at this point, of building his own private library from the Offenbach stock. Five other cases of materials from Offenbach, including 1,100 manuscripts, ended up in Jerusalem, a theft that two American officers at Offenbach would later admit to having assisted. The case for Jerusalem was also powerfully made by the faculty of the Hebrew University of Jerusalem, established in 1918 and formally opened in 1925. At war's end the university's representatives toured Europe to search for looted books and gather support for Jerusalem as their home. The bibliographic resources of the city had been considerably enriched by the arrival in 1935 of the magnificent library of the German retail magnate Salman Schocken. This was intended as a research resource for scholars working in the National Library, which traced its origins back to 1892. Most of all, Jerusalem could make a case of simple moral clarity. In the words of the president of the Hebrew University, Judah Magnes, 'We are to be the chief country for the absorption of the living human beings who have escaped from Nazi persecution . . . By the same token we should be the trustee of these spiritual goods which destroyed German Jewry left behind.'[23]

The advocates of the United States were not convinced. Koppel Pinson weighed in with a warning that 'claims from Palestine, a state from which none of this collection originates, and which unfortunately is not recognised as a legal side to this property restitution, are not likely to be accepted'. General Clay, representing the American occupying authorities, was inclined to agree: 'We deal only with governments, [and] are not free [to] effect unilateral changes.'[24] There was also the fear of carnage and destruction should Israel be worsted in the inevitable conflict with dispossessed Palestinians; moreover, the rackety history of Jerusalem's negligent custodianship of its treasures in the nineteenth century did not inspire confidence. European scholars had been able to raid the libraries of Jerusalem at will, selling thousands of irreplaceable manuscripts to the British Museum library, the Imperial Library in St Petersburg and the Prussian State Library in Berlin.[25] In the event, the post-war spoils were shared in equal portions between the United States and Israel, with each taking about 40 per cent of the residue of dispossessed books. Ultimately half a million Jewish books looted by the Nazis would make their way to the National Library in Jerusalem.

Here they were joined by the 'abandoned property' of Palestinians who had fled their homes in 1948 and then again after the Six-Day War in 1967. To the librarians of the National Library, some of whom had also worked on the salvage of Jewish books from Europe, this was more an act of preservation than appropriation: 'The best part of the libraries of the Arab writers and scholars are now in a safe place.' These books have never been offered to the heirs of the dispossessed owners, but at least they have avoided the fate of the library of the Palestinian poet and teacher Isaaf Nashashibi, forced to leave his books behind when he fled to Cairo during the war of 1948. 'For months after Nashashibi's death and wholesale pillaging of the house that Spyro Houris built, certain neighbourhood grocers could be seen using pages of Nashashibi's most valuable books to wrap cones of sugar and salt.'[26]

Restitution is messy; in the turmoil of troubled times, there is often no clear path to a morally unimpeachable solution. Today, several libraries in Berlin and Potsdam have begun the examination of their own collections for plundered books, an expensive and painstaking mitigation that the Jewish American scholar Lucy Dawidowicz had denounced as pointless in 1946. Should all cultural property plundered or dishonestly obtained be returned, or remain in current locations where it will be professionally curated and easily available to scholars? All researchers who use the major historical collections of Europe benefit from a disorderly mountain of donations and purchases of books obtained by their original owners through a million small acts of deceit, coercive acquisition or confiscation. Only the most egregious cases are widely publicised, but in truth, the collections of few galleries, museums or libraries would survive detailed scrutiny without embarrassment and moral hazard.

The truth is that any post-war settlement includes arbitrary elements. There are winners and losers, some who go unpunished and some who do not receive their due. That, it turns out, is as true for the book assets of libraries, communities and individual owners as for other forms of human capital. The particular problem of the Second World War was that while amnesty can often work reasonably well as a method of resolution in the peace-making process, this was simply not possible in 1945 given the appalling scale of the crimes against humanity. This too applied to the deliberate misappropriation of books conducted on a truly industrial scale and with an almost manic resolve by the agencies of the Nazi state. The restitution of Richard Kobrak's book makes for a heart-warming story, but it is the only volume of his library that can now be traced. We should not too easily deprecate the efforts of those who struggled to ensure that cultural heritage eventually found sanctuary far from the scenes of the gruesome crimes perpetrated in mid-twentieth-century Europe.

18

HEARTS AND MINDS

Looking back on the dawn of the Cold War era, what most surprises is the speed with which the elation of victory dissolved into a gloomy consciousness of a new age of conflict. Perhaps the lesson of recent history was that hopes of a genuine laying down of arms were never likely to be realised. We tend to forget that after the armistice in 1918, British soldiers were shipped straight out to reinforce the Russian forces fighting the Bolsheviks in the Russian Civil War. Only on the Western Front were the guns and artillery silenced: in Finland, Poland, the new Baltic republics, Ukraine and the Balkans, the defence of the newly established borders provoked vicious fighting. Between 1918 and 1921, the reborn Polish state fought six wars against almost all of its neighbours.[1] In 1945, once again it would be Russia, pushing relentlessly forward in Central Europe, that preoccupied the Allied powers: not least the (to them) alarming level of support for communism in the countries liberated from fascism, most notably France and Italy.

The necessity that those responsible for the horrors of Nazi rule should be held to account was soon moderated by an understanding that if Soviet power was to be contained, Germany would have to be rebuilt as the eastern cornerstone of the Western alliance. If the munitions king Alfried Krupp had taken his father's place at the first Nuremberg trial, the 750,000 victims of his brutal forced labour regime would have seen him hanged. As it was, by 1951 he was free, restored to his vast industrial empire, and recasting himself as an European idealist. The grain merchant Alfred Toepfer effected an equally adroit resurrection by establishing a foundation for European dialogue with a cascade of cultural prizes and scholarships.[2]

The uncomfortable truth was that a new Germany could only be fashioned with the help of the lawyers, doctors, industrialists and professors who had often served the Hitler regime with enthusiasm, or no visible sign of conscientious objection. The same went for the bishops and pastors who had blessed the war effort. Notwithstanding the fact that churches would haemorrhage members in the second half of the twentieth century, in the immediate postwar period they would play a major role in the rebuilding of civil society, as the only civic institutions operating throughout liberated or defeated Western Europe. Centre-right Christian democratic parties would dominate the reconstructed political systems of all the six countries that in 1951 would form the hub of the later European Union. In 1945, a stable political future must have seemed an impossible dream. The spectre of starvation haunted much of the continent, as did the destruction of much of its housing stock and the disruption of basic infrastructure. This was a challenging context for inhabitants and the occupying powers alike, and with it came a yearning for restoration of a normal life freed from ideological controls and unconstrained by shortages.

The American publishing industry had prepared for this moment, and the opportunity to penetrate new markets around the globe. As we have seen, the Allied occupying forces had made the denazification of library stock a major priority, and this and the destruction caused by bombing left a huge gap to be filled. The German publishers that had served the Nazi war machine so enthusiastically could hardly be trusted to fill it. Then there were the newly liberated countries emerging from five years of Nazi occupation, eager for new reading material. But if American publishers had their eyes on new markets (and the British publishers had every intention of defending theirs), so, too, had the CIA. One would not normally see the West's most active intelligence service as a major player in the civilian publishing market, but in the strange times of the early Cold War, it made a sort of sense. Even before the dust had settled in Germany, it became clear to the Western powers that the greatest danger came not from the revival of militarist ideologies in Germany, but from the continuing allure of Soviet Russia.

*

Despite the tumultuous welcome given to Charles de Gaulle on the liberation of Paris in June 1944, his imperious assumption that he would preside over the re-establishment of French nationhood did not go unchallenged. The result of the first post-war elections in October 1945 was ominous: the communists polled strongly, and in partnership with the socialists could have commanded an absolute majority. Although de Gaulle was unanimously re-elected to lead a coalition government, his determination to deny the communists key ministerial portfolios frayed the fragile consensus. In January 1946, he resigned; he would not return from his self-imposed rural exile for twelve years.

Meanwhile, the settling of wartime scores continued, particularly viciously among the intellectuals. In October 1945, the French National Committee of Writers, established during the occupation, issued a list of 156 poets, publishers and writers who should be blacklisted for collaboration. Those at risk scrambled to publicise their covert service to resistance, real or imagined. Several of those most egregiously linked to the German cause were sentenced to long terms of imprisonment, or even, in the case of Robert Brasillach, executed. The communists, now free of de Gaulle, could justly claim they had earned their place in government by their unquestionable sacrifice in the war, though always somewhat inflated in the telling of their irrepressible leader, Maurice Thorez. In the neat encapsulation of one wry observer, of the 29,000 resistance fighters who had perished, 75,000 had been communists.[3] Liberated Italy, too, required a firm steer from the CIA, and the liberal distribution of dollars, to secure victory in the 1948 election for the Christian democrats.

With Roosevelt having ceded half a continent to Stalin, it seemed fleetingly in these years that, through these nations' own choice, the communist empire might stretch as far as the English Channel. This prompted the Marshall Plan, a huge effort to alleviate the real prospect of starvation in Western Europe, and to assist the process of reconstruction. But winning hearts and minds also demanded a more proactive cultural policy, to convince the population of Europe that the values of the democracies were to be preferred over those of their erstwhile ally, Soviet Russia.

In principle, this was a moment for which both the library communities and publishing industries were well prepared. The devastation of European libraries was clear for all to see. Already in 1941, the Rockefeller Foundation had reached out to the American Library Association (ALA) for co-operation in stockpiling runs of scientific and medical periodicals from the war years that would help rebuild library collections after the war. Over the next decade, the ALA would distribute 6,037 journal titles in 9,320 sets among thirty-three countries, from France to China.[4] The countries ceded to the Soviet sphere of influence, especially Poland and Czechoslovakia, profited greatly from this programme before the shutters came down. The point was rammed home by Ksawery Pruszyński, a member of the Polish delegation to the United Nations, who had been asked by friends to remind America that 'Poland needs not only bread and clothing, not only medical supplies and tools and bulldozers but food to satisfy her spiritual hunger: books, books, books!'[5] Scholarly books were also collected for shipment from the American Book Center for War Devastation. By June 1948, 4 million books, mostly in the fields of medicine, science and engineering, had been shipped to forty-five recipient nations.

Assistance for the universities was easy enough to justify, but winning the peace also required restoration of the shattered retail book markets. The American Office of Wartime Information had been carefully stockpiling books in London, but it was clear the English-language editions of American authors would not on their own prove sufficient. What followed was a new publishing initiative, the Overseas Editions, to bring translations of books that would best represent American values to the European market. The emphasis was on non-fiction: eventually some forty-one titles were chosen to be published in editions of 50,000 copies each.[6]

Proponents of the scheme had envisaged cheap paperback editions on the lines of the highly successful Armed Services Editions, but from the outset this new scheme was beset with problems. Securing the rights took time, as did the translations, though here European refugee writers proved a useful resource. In due course the series would include twenty-two books in French, twenty-three in German and five in Italian. A more pressing problem was money. Not surprisingly, some members of Congress were far less keen to provide cheap books for Europeans than free books for GIs. Faced with these obstacles, the committee established a parallel venture, Transatlantic Editions, published in smaller print runs in French and Dutch in London. Many books made it into both series: Carl van Doren's biography of Benjamin Franklin; *US Foreign Policy and US War Aims*, a combination of two books by Walter Lippmann; Stephen Benét's *America*; Ambassador Joseph Grew's *Mission to Tokyo*; along with two books on the Tennessee Valley Authority, the marquee project of Roosevelt's New Deal. The overall tone was serious and high-minded, yet although it was July 1945 before the first Overseas Editions went on sale in France, they sold out immediately. In all, seventy-two editions of forty-one titles were published in French, Italian, English and German, a total of 3.6 million copies.

As so often, the Allies got most propaganda value from books they did not have to pay for, like George Orwell's *Animal Farm* and *1984*. In Japan in 1948, forty-six companies bid for the translation rights for *Animal Farm* (which also demonstrates how well Japanese publishing had weathered the war years).[7] Especially important at the time in the Cold War struggles, though far less well known now, was Victor Kravchenko's *I Chose Freedom*, first published in 1946 and subsequently translated into twenty-two languages. Kravchenko's eyewitness account of Soviet Russia provided the first widely read evidence of the violence of forced farm collectivisation and the Ukraine famine (Holodomor). The publication of a French edition was delayed until 1947, since none of the major houses would take it for fear of communist reprisals: it still sold 400,000 copies. It provoked a barrage of criticism from the Stalinist left, including the claim that the book had been written by American intelligence agents. Kravchenko sued for libel in what became, as he intended, a trial of Stalinism and the Soviet Union. The verdict in his favour, after three months of excruciating testimony, did much to discredit Soviet communism in France, though leading intellectuals such as Jean-Paul Sartre and Simone de Beauvoir proved immovable.

By 1950, the battle lines were drawn. With the Marshall Plan

At the end of the Second World War, the Soviet Union went from admired ally to detested foe in the space of less than five years. These publications testify to the infatuation with all things Russian in wartime Britain. The songs, one scored by Dmitri Shostakovich, might have made a welcome change from 'Roll Out the Barrel' and 'We'll Meet Again'.

beginning to alleviate living conditions, and the Western show of resolve in the Berlin airlift, communism lost much of its allure. In Eastern Europe, Russian power had been consolidated by the extinction of democracy in Poland and Czechoslovakia; in 1950, the Korean War opened up a new front in the ideological conflict that would dominate European politics for the next forty years. Both sides settled in for the long haul. The cultural struggle also entered a new phase, symbolised by two duelling conferences: a gathering of Marxist intellectuals in the rather incongruous luxury of New York's Waldorf Astoria hotel in 1949, and the launch in Berlin of the Congress for Cultural Freedom in 1950.

The Waldorf Astoria turned into something of a fiasco, a demonstration of the extent to which the literary left was now divided, in Europe as in the US, between those who continued to honour Russia for its part in the Allied victory over fascism, and those who could not forgive Stalin for the Gulag and his pact with Hitler.

The consequences were vividly on display at the Waldorf, where Lillian Hellman, Dashiell Hammett and Arthur Miller attended the conference, while based in a suite upstairs, Mary McCarthy, the poet Robert Lowell and his wife Elizabeth Hardwick, Arthur Schlesinger and the editors of the *Partisan Review* turned out a torrent of press releases and leaflets and heckled the proceedings below. The uncomfortable demeanour of the conference's star participant, the composer Dmitri Shostakovich, largely mute until told to speak by his KGB minder, was not the best advertisement for the Soviet system. The only moment of light relief came when a young Norman Mailer denounced both the US and the USSR and was roundly booed by both sides.

The Berlin conference also attracted a star cast of literary lions, led by Arthur Koestler, Tennessee Williams, Nicolas Nabokov, André Malraux and, fresh from the Waldorf, Arthur Schlesinger. This meeting was also not without excitement, not least the discomfort of the British delegation, which included the philosopher A. J. Ayer and the historian Hugh Trevor-Roper, at the meeting's militant tone. This contretemps did not prevent Arthur Koestler ending the congress with a rousing declaration of literary war: 'Friends! Freedom has seized the offensive.'[8] While the Waldorf Astoria was not to be repeated, the Congress for Cultural Freedom would be a constant presence for the next two decades selling Western values on the European continent: and it was generously funded by the CIA.

When CIA involvement in the Congress for Cultural Freedom was revealed in 1967, most of those involved in its management affected pained astonishment. But in truth, anyone with the least curiosity, or experience with publishing, would have known that sales of its publications would only have covered a fraction of its costs: the salaries of the headquarters staff in Paris, the sponsored conferences, generous fees paid to contributors to its journals and lavish travel budget. Of the publications, by far the most successful was *Encounter*, a well-crafted, serious journal of current politics, culture and thought that appeared monthly. It soon established a solid position in the intellectual framework of British cultural life. Much of this success was owed to its odd-couple editors, the

driven and irascible Irving Kristol, succeeded in 1958 by Melvin
Lasky and the British literary grandee Stephen Spender.[9]

Last seen motoring around post-war Germany interviewing
librarians, the tolerant and easy-going Spender rose easily through
the ranks of the literary left to establish himself as a much-respected
cultural commentator, even as his own productivity as a poet dried
up. In the end his own story is much less compelling than the fact
that he pops up in everyone else's, at almost every critical moment
in the literary Cold War. He also achieved the unusual distinction
of being simultaneously under scrutiny by MI5 and the FBI while
being groomed by the CIA and the British Foreign Office (which
paid his *Encounter* salary).[10]

Encounter was the best known of a radiating circle of cultural
magazines managed by the congress. The first to be launched was
Preuves, a vehicle for hard-pressed anti-communist intellectuals in
France and an open challenge to *Les Temps modernes*, established
by Sartre, de Beauvoir and Maurice Merleau-Ponty. *Preuves* was followed by *Encounter* (1953), the Spanish *Cuadernos* (1953) and the
Italian *Tempo Presente* (1956). For Germany, there was *Der Monat*,
first published during the Berlin airlift of 1948 and sustained until
1971. Beyond Europe, the congress sponsored *Quest* (1955) in India,
Quadrant (1956) in Australia and *Transitions* (1961) in Uganda.
All of these magazines offered a welcome source of income to literary intellectuals across a wide political spectrum. In the case of
Encounter, its left-leaning contributors offered the best cover for its
CIA backing: when the Labour Party returned to power in Britain
in 1964, a full third of Harold Wilson's cabinet had written for
Encounter. The embarrassment of these high-minded statesmen at
the revelation of CIA involvement was commensurately great, and
stimulated a great deal of sour commentary from those not drawn
into *Encounter*'s warm but compromising embrace. When seventeen leading Anglo-American intellectuals published in *Partisan
Review* an editorial denouncing CIA journals, presumably they
were unaware that *Partisan Review* had itself received funds from
CIA front organisations.[11]

Despite the size of its investment in journals, the CIA did not
ignore the book market: *The New York Times* alleged in 1977 that

it had contributed to funding more than a thousand books. These projects certainly included translations of T. S. Eliot's *The Waste Land* and *Four Quartets*, anthologies of Russian literature, Pasternak's *Doctor Zhivago* and, appropriately enough, Machiavelli's *The Prince*. A major part of this budget was expended on trying to infiltrate Western literature into the Soviet Union and its satellites in Eastern Europe. These initiatives included the quixotic Bible Balloon project of 1954, which involved floating 10,000 balloons carrying Bibles across the Iron Curtain. But this was the opposite of a precision weapon; even the most committed Cold Warrior could see that there was little point in littering the Czech countryside, and the programme was swiftly abandoned. Attention shifted from ideological propaganda to more diverse works of economics, sociology and the social sciences. These were valued by universities, where the precious permits to import Western books were generally reserved for the hard sciences. In 1970, the Czech authorities warned their scholarly libraries that such works were even more dangerous than works of propaganda in effecting the gradual infiltration of bourgeois ideology. When they could not contact librarians directly, the programme, channelled through Radio Free Europe, did its best to ambush visitors from the Eastern bloc, such as visiting sports teams and trade delegations. Fishermen landing their catch in Western ports could also sometimes be persuaded to take books and pamphlets back with them. All told, the Free Europe programme published over half a million copies of books, periodicals and pamphlets. Whether they received much return on this investment is more doubtful.[12]

The best works of propaganda are not intended as propaganda. This nostrum held as true in the Cold War as in any period of 'hot' conflict. The Cold War intelligence war was an unambiguous triumph for the Soviet Union, which was offered a steady stream of nuclear intelligence from well-placed scientists. The discovery of the Cambridge spy ring also sowed dangerous distrust between British and American intelligence. But if the intelligence war was inglorious, there is no doubt that the literary spy war was a clear victory for the West. Both the works of Graham Greene and John Le Carré's *The Spy Who Came in from the Cold* were required

A runaway bestseller from its first publication in 1963, *The Spy Who Came in from the Cold* went through thirteen impressions in its first eight months. Its appeal to readers behind the Iron Curtain was not welcome to the Western intelligence services, who were worried that such an unromantic and realistic view of intelligence work gave too much away.

reading in the KGB, and, for the same reason, the two authors were both despised by the CIA. But the character that caused Soviets the most irritation was James Bond, the creation of the former British intelligence officer Ian Fleming. We first met Fleming as assistant to Admiral Godfrey, the head of naval intelligence in the Second World War, a post that Fleming occupied with great success, but which did not fulfil his yearning for action.[13] The life he missed as a desk-bound officer during the war he lived vicariously through his tough, insouciant and glamorous agent, 007, and this provoked a quite astonishing response from the communist powers.

Casino Royale, published in 1953, was well reviewed, but sold modestly. Fleming diligently turned out a Bond book a year until his death in 1964, but it was only with the release of the first film, *Dr No*, in 1962, that Bond became a global phenomenon. The

Russians had somehow got wind of the film: the first review came three months before its premiere, in *Izvestia*, the leading Soviet newspaper. Entitled 'Love and Horrors', it pulled no punches: 'Obviously American propagandists must be in a bad way if they need to have recourse to the help of an English free-booter – a retired spy who has turned mediocre writer.' Fleming was delighted. A plot was hatched to use the Russian review on the dust jacket of the forthcoming Bond, *On Her Majesty's Secret Service*, adorned by an economical appreciation by the author: '(Ouch. I. F.)'.[14] A hundred or so copies of the dust jacket were supplied for the proof edition. But then wiser counsels intervened. This was the height of the Cold War, the year of the Cuban Missile Crisis. To goad Soviet officialdom was probably a risk not worth taking. It was left to the managing director of Fleming's publisher Cape, Michael Howard, to pass on the bad news to the disappointed author.

This was only the first salvo in what became a concerted effort to denigrate Bond behind the Iron Curtain. *Pravda* opined in September 1965, one year after Fleming's death, that Bond could not be allowed to die because he taught those sent to kill in Vietnam, the Congo, the Dominican Republic and many other places. East Germany's *Neues Deutschland* saw the Bond films and books as vehicles for all the obvious and ridiculous rubbish of reactionary doctrine.[15] In 1967, the Bulgarian author Andrei Gulyashki was persuaded to serve up a Bond pastiche, *Avakoum Zakhov versus 007*, in which Bond was thwarted by the local hero (in the English edition, the first o was removed as 007 was covered by the Fleming estate trademark). In the 1970s, half of the East German population sat down to watch on TV *The Invisible Gunsight*, with Alexander, a handsome but proletarian Stasi agent despatching Western enemies: no martinis for Alexander, just beer down the pub with his postman friend. And between 1976 and 1989 Polish TV served up *07 Come In*, featuring Civilian Militia Lieutenant Sławomir Borewicz.

It was probably Maya Turovskaya, a well-respected Russian author and critic, who came closest to getting under James Bond's skin, with her thoughtful analysis of the Bond phenomenon in the Russian literary journal *Novy Mir* (*New World*) in 1966.

Turovskaya presented Bond as comfort food for a country in decline not prepared to face its own problems: 'The Bond myth demonstrates the public's rejection of the problems of the "Angry Young Men".'[16] There is truth in this; when Fleming began his Bond series, Britain was at a low ebb. The year before he began writing *Casino Royale*, Fleming had been at a dinner party where food was delayed because one guest was absent. The hostess was finally persuaded not to wait when another guest, the art historian Anthony Blunt, suggested the absentee would probably not be joining them. In fact, he knew this to be the case, because the errant guest, Guy Burgess, had defected to Russia that day, and his friend Blunt had spent the afternoon making sure Burgess had left no compromising material in his flat. This was the social crowd in which Fleming circulated; he was touched very personally by the treason of the Cambridge spies. James Bond was not just a money-spinning frivolity, it was also presenting the other side of the coin, the true patriots, like Fleming, who had defeated fascism. James Bond was a defence of Fleming's fragile, embattled caste.

In the West, the Cold War was experienced as a series of frightening episodes: the Berlin airlift, the Korean War, McCarthyism, the Cuban Missile Crisis, Vietnam. In between, life could go on as normal. For many in the Soviet bloc, it would have been more like forty-four long winters, a life defined by poor housing, travel restrictions, consumer shortages and surveillance. We see this vividly expressed in the memoirs of those who fled, often leaving behind families to which they remained very attached, but with whom they were allowed little contact. The German-American author Nina Willner's mother Hanna was one such tragic case. Hanna fled the Soviet zone of Germany in 1948, leaving behind her parents and grandparents and eight siblings. They would be reunited only after the collapse of the Berlin Wall, but her defection cast a constant shadow over their family life and careers.[17]

Hanna's father was a schoolteacher in the small village of Schwaneberg, south of Magdeburg, an intellectual and well-respected member of the community. Initially, he welcomed the substitution of Soviet for Nazi rule, and diligently studied

Marxism. Three of the children would become schoolteachers; another benefited from the famous East German elite athlete programme. Their father owned a large and sophisticated library, which offered his children a window on the outside world, the Louvre in Paris, the Prado in Madrid. When his enthusiasm for the regime paled (he objected to handing out pamphlets denouncing the educated), like many in these countries his library became his retreat: until one day government officials arrived and carried off armfuls of books, a shrewdly painful punishment, and a warning. When he finally went too far, criticising the regime to his neighbours, he was dismissed from his job and exiled to a smaller home in a village 80 kilometres away. Only a quarter of his library could go with him; the rest was distributed to his children, now well established in their own careers.

We see these personal tragedies echoed in the stories of many who fled East Germany before the building of the wall, those who left Hungary after the uprising of 1956, and Czechoslovakia after the Prague Spring in 1968. But most, willingly or not, remained. This invites another perspective, what one historian has called a form of 'participatory dictatorship'.[18] In this reading, citizens reconciled themselves to their rulers; they knew when and how to protest, and the regime listened. They welcomed the absence of unemployment, greater opportunities for higher education, the enhanced role of women in the workplace, the elite sports programmes, the easy accommodation of divorce and termination of unwanted pregnancies. After 1989, a few looked back with nostalgia on what they had lost; in the case of Nina Willner's schoolmaster uncles, all three were dismissed from their jobs after reunification, even the one who had refused to join the Communist Party.

In all of these societies, a vibrant cultural programme was integral to the socialist vision of society, and ensured that books would be plentiful, and cater to most consumer tastes. The richness of this book culture is revealed in the biography of Paul Lendvai, nineteen years old when he joined the staff of the leading communist paper of Hungary, *Szabad Nép* (*The Free People*), before a precipitous fall from grace with the purging of former social democrats from the Communist Party. A search of his flat and that of his parents would result in the removal of 129 foreign-language books, 120 foreign-language periodicals, 110 notebooks and numerous books and periodicals from his parents' home.[19]

In East Germany, the government rebuilt the public library network and required factories to provide libraries for their workers. In 1981, their leader Erich Honecker proudly contrasted his own 'country of readers' with the 'bestseller consumers' of West Germany. It seems rather quaint that in the 1970s the East German government was concerned at surveys that revealed that only 35 per cent of its citizens read 'serious literature', a figure that today would seem unimaginably high. An international study of reading literacy, carried out after the fall of the Berlin Wall, found that reading comprehension of East German eighth graders was significantly higher than that of their West German contemporaries. Among adults, a large number attended writers' circles and poetry clubs, many organised round the workplace. Even the Stasi, the feared security police, had their own poetry circle.[20]

To square these two visions of the trapped Soviet satellites, we must acknowledge that a great deal changed between 1945 and 1989, when Mikhail Gorbachev finally liberated the captive nations to go their own way. By 1989, elderly cadres ruled over crippled economies, and the patience of many citizens had worn thin. East Germans practised what has been called 'defection by television', where even the commercials on the West German programmes reminded them of the everyday poverty of their consumer choices. But the great transformation of 1989 was not a revolt led by academics or the professional elites; in Poland it was a workers' movement, while the East German demonstrations were led by the Protestant churches. Hungary had for some time practised its own form of soft communism, so was ready to make the leap. Only Czechoslovakia broke the mould with the playwright Václav Havel, as it had done in the Prague Spring of 1968.

It all looked very different in 1945, when a high proportion of those who survived the war were ready to welcome their Soviet liberators. Poland was a wreck coming to terms with a westward shift of its borders, Germany a pariah nation. Those who had led Hungary and Romania to disaster in the war were too compromised to offer any hope for right-of-centre parties. With the former regimes so discredited, many were prepared to embrace a new beginning of leftist politics, and for those who were not, Soviet tanks could be persuasive. The remains of the library accumulated by Paul Lendvai's parents were destroyed by tank shells in the Budapest uprising of 1956; by a grim irony the only survivors were the works of Marx and Lenin, which the parents had put in the laundry closet because they dared not throw them away, but inadvertently created a place of safety where they escaped the conflagration. Yet in the first decade after the war, Hungarians had embraced the new order with at least an intelligent interest: *Stalin's Short Course History of the Communist Party* was published in Hungarian in a giant edition of 560,000 copies.[21]

During the war, Stalin had won many admirers, even in the West, where he was twice crowned 'Man of the Year' by *Time* magazine, in 1939 and 1942. But for Soviet academics and intellectuals there was little peace dividend: they would be the principal victims of the increasing mental inflexibility of that most bookish of revolutionaries. The ageing leader was still fighting the last war. In 1948, he devoted endless care to the publication of a justification of the 1939 pact with Nazi Germany, prepared on his behalf by a team of historians. Two million copies were printed to be distributed by embassies abroad, with translations into English and other languages.[22]

Nonetheless, the new satellite regimes initially dealt with their intellectuals with some care. They recognised an opportunity and ideological need to open up universities to those from a proletarian background; this was a genuine revolution. On the other hand, to rebuild these shattered societies, they needed the help and expertise of lawyers, doctors, scientists and academics, many of whom had served the old regimes with little sign of discomfort, at least until new generations could be trained up. Life in the rebuilt universities reflected these tensions.

Authoritarian regimes had a range of tools at their disposal to impose control over universities. The first was to apply political criteria for entry as students or appointment of faculty, accompanied almost inevitably by a purge of the existing student and staff body. In most parts of the Soviet bloc this led to privileged access for the children of the working class, accompanied in both East Germany and Czechoslovakia by restricting entry for children of families identified as bourgeois: this is one reason why, before the building of the Berlin Wall, so many members of the professional classes moved to the West.[23]

The purging of the faculty and restriction of the pre-war independence of university governance was not always a matter of regret. In Hungary it was recognised that the institutional autonomy of the inter-war years had protected many mediocre scholars. In Czechoslovakia, the overwhelming majority of intellectuals had welcomed the Soviet liberators, and many joined the Communist Party. This did not prevent them supporting the Prague Spring; the 1956 revolution in Hungary also demonstrated that the mass enrolment of working-class students had not produced loyalty. In Poland, what remained of the established professoriate did rather better: the role of Polish intellectuals in wartime resistance gave those who had survived a prestige that their colleagues elsewhere in Eastern Europe lacked. But here, as elsewhere, the research culture was reshaped in line with the priorities of the new regimes. Adopting the Soviet model of separating hard science into separate academies, Polish universities were stripped of their medical faculties and veterinary science, along with theology; the teaching of philosophy was also largely abandoned.

Academics left behind in the stripped-down universities complained of heavy teaching loads, and resented the time occupied by administration and political meetings. Most serious of all was the separation from the wider academic community, the inability to travel to international conferences, or even, during the most paranoid years, to exchange articles and papers with colleagues in the West. Nevertheless, compared to their fellow citizens, university faculty enjoyed a privileged life. In 1952, the top income of a professor in East Germany could be ten times that of an average worker. This upper stratum consisted almost exclusively of research scientists, and the premium wages they enjoyed came down sharply with the building of the wall, inhibiting escape to the West.[24]

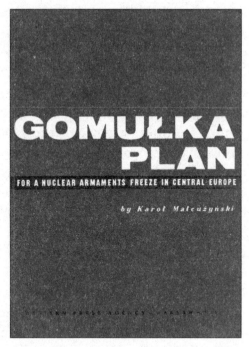

The Gomułka Plan (1964). Nothing irritated the Western powers
more than the Soviet appropriation of the vocabulary of peace.
In this instance, there was little chance that the Polish leader's
proposal for a nuclear-free zone in central Europe would be
adopted, given the huge Soviet supremacy in troops and tanks.

Writers and artists who toed the party line were equally
coddled. Bertolt Brecht was rewarded for his decision to keep
faith with the East by reduced income tax, a generous pension and
access to the special shops that were reserved for leading members
of the regime. The relationship with the government was complex
and subtle. Writers were allowed a little creative anger, so long as
that did not stray into open criticism. In return, paper would be
found for larger editions of their new books, the party would help
organise promotional tours and they might even be permitted to
publish their works in the West. Books were an important part of
the planned economy, and an extensive bureaucracy helped shep-
herd new projects from the first synopsis to publication and sale in
the state-run bookshops.

*

After the fall of the Berlin Wall, and the collapse of this whole system, the East German book censors looked back nostalgically on the world they had lost. They had little doubt that they were a force for good; their carefully planned diet of crime, romance, war stories, Westerns and science fiction had books for most readers, in a publishing programme for 1989 that would place 11.5 million copies of 625 authorised titles onto the market. They saw themselves less as censors than as advocates of literature, leading books through the labyrinthine structure of successive levels of approval before they could be sent to the printers. Very rarely were titles submitted to them rejected: writers knew what would and would not be accepted, and where they crossed a line, their editor in one of East Germany's seventy-eight publishing houses would soften the rough edges.[25]

This may seem like a very sanitised view of life as a censor (or more properly, an employee of the Head Administration for Publishing and the Book Trade), but it was a characteristic of the age that those who patrolled the boundaries of propriety, whether in Romania or the United States, believed they were doing good. In the United States, freedom of expression was guaranteed under the Constitution (as it was also in East Germany), but it did not prevent books coming under fire during years of McCarthyism, Hollywood blacklists and red scares. Library staff were required to sign a loyalty oath as were, in Texas, the writers of schoolbooks. Even in 1955, as McCarthy's influence waned, young readers of the school text *Exploring American History* (1955), co-authored by a Yale academic, were reminded: 'The FBI urges Americans to report directly to its offices any suspicions they may have about communist activity on the part of their fellow Americans.'[26]

Howard Fast, an author who had spent the Second World War working with the United States Office of War Information, was a particular bête noire: public officials in their loyalty hearings could be asked 'Do you read Howard Fast?' Sentenced to prison for refusing to name contacts in the Communist Party, he spent his three-month sentence sketching out what became his masterpiece, *Spartacus*, an account of the famous slave uprising in the Roman Empire. Since no American publisher would touch it, Fast was forced to self-publish, with some success. He had no such problems in the Soviet Union, where 2.5 million copies of his books were bought, translated into twelve languages.[27] Most toxic of all was the purge of American libraries overseas maintained by the State Department. Among the 30,000 works removed were the Sam Spade novels of Dashiell Hammett, who also lost his radio series on NBC. However popular they were, the State Department could not be seen promoting a communist writer, and the TV networks were happy to follow the patriotic line.

Even humble comic books could not escape the new puritanism. In 1952, comics were removed from the on-board bookshops of the US Pacific Fleet, on the grounds that they were too violent and graphic for marines and sailors. By 1955, a raft of US states had passed legislation against comic books, including, most damagingly, New York. With a ban on the use of 'crime', 'terror', 'horror' or 'sex' in the titles of comic books, some eighty titles were rendered illegal. A ban on sales to anyone under eighteen was another body blow; some publishers abandoned all their comic-book titles, and some closed down altogether.[28]

There were many justifications offered for censorship: political, religious, ethnic or judgements of taste. Between 1937 and 1961, students at the School of Librarianship at the University of Montreal in the French-Canadian province of Quebec were obliged to take a course in censorship and the Index of Prohibited Books. The course was taught entirely by priests. During this period, the Catholic Church controlled many of the social and educational institutions in the province and instead of public libraries, it sponsored a network of small parish libraries. In this, the Church remained true to the spirit of the cardinal archbishop who in 1901 had opposed an approach for support from Andrew Carnegie for a new public library, on the grounds that such institutions were 'more dangerous than the most malevolent smallpox virus'.[29] It will be no surprise that apartheid South Africa carefully controlled its publishing industry but here too, as in East Germany, the gatekeepers, many of them writers or academics, regarded themselves more as critics than as censors. They lived up to this ideal by treating literature as separate privileged space; what was permitted to literary authors such as J. M. Coetzee and Mafika Gwala was not permitted to those who wrote for a mass audience.[30] It is rather more surprising to know of the troubles British publishers had exporting books to the Republic of Ireland or Australia, a surprisingly puritan culture in the Cold War era.

Attempts to control reality were not always successful, however, and in the Soviet scientific world, the Lysenko fiasco rumbled on.[31] The publication of his *Heredity and Its Variability* in 1943 inspired some critical articles in British and American scientific journals, and, in 1946, an English-language translation: one of the few occasions on which a scholarly translation was undertaken purely for the sake of humiliation, of its author, Lysenko, but also Soviet science more generally.[32] But Stalin was unconcerned. In 1948 works by leading geneticists were removed from libraries, and in 1951, the names of famous geneticists were inked over in the library of the Geographical Society of the USSR. Soviet science was increasingly detached from the international mainstream. In 1947, the Academy of Sciences ceased translating their abstracts into English. A regular feature in the Academy bulletin, 'On the Pages of Foreign Scientific Publications', was discontinued.[33]

Not surprisingly, Soviet science prospered mostly in fields where international competition replaced co-operation, such as nuclear physics and space exploration. By 1949, Russia had the atomic bomb, a development regarded in the West as inevitable, but substantially accelerated by the passing of critical nuclear information by Western fellow travellers. Far more alarming to the West was the launch in 1957 of the first satellite, Sputnik, compounded in 1961 by the first manned spaceflight. Yuri Gagarin became one of the best-known men on the planet, and American politicians talked ominously of Russia having pulled ahead in the development of nuclear weapons. Russia was now reaping the benefits of concentrating scientific research in academies and institutes largely separated from the mainstream universities.

In the last years of the Vietnam War, General Douglas Kinnard, himself a Vietnam veteran, asked 173 generals who had commanded in Vietnam to fill in a survey to assist his research. Of approximately two-thirds who responded, 70 per cent said they did not understand the war's overall objectives: and these were the commanders.[34] If a first goal of modern warfare is that those who risk their lives should be committed to the cause, then Vietnam was a catastrophe. It was not as if the United States did not recognise the importance of a propaganda offensive: it was just directed elsewhere. The Johnson administration devoted enormous efforts to persuading European allies to take part, yet Britain's Labour prime minister, Harold Wilson, resisted even Johnson's desperate appeal for a few Gurkhas, even a 'platoon of bagpipers', as a symbolic gesture of support.[35] The battle for hearts and minds in Vietnam itself was fought mostly with a cascade of dollars to prop up the South Vietnamese regime, much of which disappeared in the rampant corruption that to many in the South made the Viet Cong seem more attractive.

Where the US government did score was in the private briefings that kept the newspapers, weekly magazines and, crucially, television on side with government policy for far longer than we remember. The Vietnam War today seems like the ultimate folly: a war America could not win but could not stop fighting. So it is important to remind ourselves that at the time, Vietnam was a war overwhelmingly supported by American public opinion. Even in 1970, two years after Nixon had promised the American people peace with honour, when four students were killed in a demonstration against the war at Kent State University in Ohio, reporters who hurried to the scene were shocked by the reaction of the local inhabitants they interviewed. Some told the researchers they wished the National Guard had killed more of the demonstrators. When Nixon ran for re-election in 1972, with the war still raging, he was endorsed by 93 per cent of the nation's newspapers (753 dailies for Nixon, fifty-six for his Democratic opponent George McGovern) and was rewarded with a forty-nine-state landslide.[36]

The anti-war movement was far from negligible: it was simply not speaking to middle America. In 1967, more than 500 writers and editors made a public commitment not to pay a tax surcharge for the Vietnam War. Among the signatories were Betty Friedan, Gloria Steinem, Susan Sontag, Philip K. Dick, Allen Ginsberg,

Thomas Pynchon, Norman Mailer, Benjamin Spock, Hunter S. Thompson and Kurt Vonnegut. Mailer is perhaps the critical figure here, as his *The Naked and the Dead*, based on his service in the Philippines and a publishing sensation in 1948, has a reasonable claim to have refashioned the war novel; it remained on *The New York Times* bestseller charts for sixty-two weeks. But nothing he wrote on Vietnam had anything like this appeal. *Why Are We in Vietnam?* (1967) turns out to be entirely allegorical, an account of a hunting trip in Alaska that addresses Vietnam only obliquely. His non-fiction novel *Army of the Night* was a third-person account of Mailer's part in the anti-Vietnam March on the Pentagon in 1967. It was widely admired, won a National Book Award and the Pulitzer Prize, but did not resonate with a wider public.[37]

America was divided into two tribes, largely talking past each other. The TV networks and newspapers remained staunchly behind the administration, first Johnson, then Nixon. When the organisers of the War Tax Protest made up an advertisement to publish it, only three publications would run it, the *New York Post*, *New York Review of Books* and *Ramparts*, the radical magazine that had first broken the story about CIA involvement in *Encounter* and Radio Free Europe. Eyewitness accounts of the horrors being perpetrated in South-East Asia might have cut through, but embedded journalists had no incentive to make trouble. The most powerful journalistic accounts of Vietnam, such as Michael Herr's *Dispatches*, appeared after the war's sour and humiliating end, when public opinion had, in any case, finally turned against the war. Ultimately, the most important literary legacy of the Vietnam War, in an echo of the First World War, would be the wave of novels published after its conclusion.[38] But we need also to remind ourselves that the all-time bestselling novel of the war was Robin Moore's *The Green Berets*, published in 1965 and filmed, with extensive co-operation from the Department of Defense and the US Army, with John Wayne in the lead. Released in 1968, the year of the North Vietnamese Tet Offensive, it was panned by the critics, but proved a commercial success, as audiences sought some patriotic reassurance in America's *annus horribilis*.

The government's attention to television reflects a shrewd

recognition of the shift in where citizens got their news, and the potency of an opinion-shaping power still monopolised by three major networks. In 1964, 63 per cent of Americans told pollsters that they paid little or no attention to the Vietnam War.[39] This made Vietnam a tricky propaganda assignment for the Johnson administration, who had to promote support for the war while not calling too much attention to it. Newspaper reporters and TV personnel were carefully shepherded around Vietnam by up to 3,000 information liaison personnel. Since journalists relied wholly on the military for protection and transportation, and the troops with whom they were embedded were increasingly jittery, there was no incentive to denounce the war, or report disturbing treatment of civilians. American troops, mostly unwilling conscripts under the voting age (then twenty-one), found it difficult to distinguish the villagers they were trying to protect from Viet Cong, and were decreasingly inclined to try. The massacre of up to 500 men, women and children at the village of My Lai in March 1968 would cause worldwide outrage, but only became public, twenty months after the event, when the military authorities belatedly intervened. Although the action had been accompanied by both a reporter and a photographer, it was left to appalled troops to draw the army's attention to the massacre. Only one man, Lieutenant William Calley, was convicted of the crimes committed.[40]

At home, television companies agreed not to show pictures of dead or wounded Americans, and took an editorial line strongly supporting 'our boys'. Reporting demonstrations, TV cameras focused on the more colourful hippies, rather than the neatly dressed students who died at Kent State. The opponents of the war had many of the best lines, with the black activist Stokely Carmichael condemning Vietnam as 'white people sending black people to make war on yellow people in order to defend the land they stole from red people'. But in 1967, 83 per cent of the Americans reported feeling more pro-war after watching TV.[41]

These were difficult years for pleading the moral superiority of the West. The revelation of the CIA role at the heart of the Congress for Cultural Freedom and *Encounter* had seriously detrimental effects for the cultural programmes in developing countries. *Huar*, in Lebanon, closed in 1967, and in 1968, the offices of *Transition* in Uganda were raided and its editors imprisoned. *Quest*, in India, folded in the 1970s, its credibility destroyed by the revelations, as was the case with *Jiyu* in Japan.[42] The United States could no longer pose as the world's moral arbiter, as it did with the ill-judged Anglo-French response to Colonel Nasser's nationalisation of the Suez Canal in 1956, a crushing blow to the prestige of the stumbling European powers.

For France and the United Kingdom, decolonisation was an urgent necessity and a divisive domestic political issue. The colonial powers tried at first to fight nationalist liberation movements with traditional weapons, pamphlets and leafleting. These seem to have had as little effect as in the two world wars, often only contributing to the tragedy. In Vietnam, My Lai was leafleted before the massacre to warn non-combatants to flee, with predictable lack of response. Sometimes this air-dropped propaganda could prove counter-productive. The diplomat Christopher Mallaby tells the story of his father sent to Java in 1945 to disarm Japanese troops and prepare Indonesia for return to Dutch rule. Not surprisingly, this met with bitter resistance from Indonesian nationalists, who had declared Indonesia independent when Japan surrendered. Brigadier Mallaby successfully negotiated a ceasefire with the local nationalist leader, only to be undercut when a British plane dropped a printed proclamation over the city, threatening the death penalty for carrying arms. Three days later, Mallaby was murdered by a fifteen-year-old with a Japanese rifle. Within four years, the Dutch recognised Indonesian independence.[43]

In Kenya, during the Mau Mau rebellion (1952–60), the British also made use of air drops to distribute print to the insurgents; other persuasive literature was tacked onto trees. The capacity of the nationalists to build their movement was limited by the British near-monopoly of print, and the colonial government's propaganda played an effective role in preventing the movement attracting wider support from other groups in Kenyan society, or the international community. Print was also used to persuade local white settlers that they would not be abandoned, while at the same time preparing them for the inevitability of change: the settlers themselves used newsprint and journals to vent their anger and anxiety.[44] The British could also count on a degree of international solidarity in the West for their handling of the Malayan Emergency of 1948–60, not least, because the Malayan National Liberation Army (MLNA) was clearly and unapologetically aligned with the Communist Party. The British strategy in British Malaya, a collection of states on the Malay peninsula and Singapore, relied on containing the guerrillas while ensuring that they did not win general support from the ethnic Chinese, legitimately angry at their political and economic subordination by the dominant Malay population. Thus military activity was accompanied by an emphasis on propaganda and 'education', particularly in the new settlements into which rural villagers had been corralled to impede co-operation with the guerrillas. By 1952, half the new villages had schools, accompanied by improved healthcare provision. The colonial authority also established fortnightly Tamil and Malay newspapers, and some newspapers in Chinese, of which the most widely circulated was *Farmers' News*. In 1951, this sponsored reading material amounted to 5 million published items, weekly and monthly. Their impact was further amplified by coffeehouse culture, and the Chinese and Malay traditions of reading aloud.[45] Crucially, the MNLA found little support in the wider population, permitting the negotiation of a ceasefire in 1955.

In Algeria, the French government controlled print media, but was outflanked by the ubiquity of radio and the popularity of the Cairo-based channel Voice of the Arabs. By 1956, the National Liberation Front (FLN) also had its own radio station. The French authorities were placed in a rhetorical fix of their own making. Their determination to crush the insurgency by all means, including censorship, executions and torture, aligned poorly with their claims to be offering Algeria liberal values, modernity and diversity. The FLN, in contrast, played a canny hand with its propaganda.[46] *El Moudjahid*, the official newspaper of the FLN, presented their cause as a national struggle, rather than a clash of rival religious cultures. When French troops restored control in Algeria, the insurgents switched their focus to swaying world opinion. The

'Battle of New York', to win the support of the United Nations, saw both sides spending liberally on print propaganda. France distributed 166,000 copies of a single pamphlet in English, German and Spanish, and spent an eye-watering $450,000 on advertisements in thirty-one US newspapers. Nevertheless, with each passing year, the incongruity of the French 'civilising' mission was ever more apparent. General de Gaulle, called back into government at the height of the Algerian crisis, soon concluded that the fight was unwinnable. When he faced down a half-hearted military coup in 1961, Algeria's independence was assured.

As the Cold War wore on, an increasingly evident feature of Third World liberation movements was the appearance of alternative role models of freedom, such as that offered by Egypt's Gamal Abdel Nasser, and the tendency to look to China, rather than Russia, as the dynamic face of communism. To tell the story of this remarkable transformation in great power dynamics, we must cast our eye back to 1936, and eavesdrop on two men chatting in a cave. The host, Mao Zedong, had come a long way since we met him at the beginning of this book as a disgruntled library assistant. Now he was the guiding spirit behind the Chinese Communist Party, while his nationalist adversary, Chiang Kai-shek, prepared for what he promised his Western allies would be the final victory in the Chinese Civil War. But Mao, as ever, was playing the long game, hence his warm welcome to the young American journalist Edgar Snow. Snow's three months in the communist hideout would prove richly rewarding for both parties, as his account of his conversations, *Red Star over China*, became a worldwide bestseller. It did an enormous amount to alert the worldwide left to the appeal of Chinese communism, particularly when compared to the sclerotic Soviet alternative.

It is fair to say that for twenty years after its publication, *Red Star over China* was the most important vehicle by which first China, then the world, became acquainted with Mao's cause. In the late 1940s, British soldiers picking through the scattered remains of an abandoned rebel camp in Malaya found dozens of copies. During the Second World War, copies reached the Huk guerrillas in the Philippines and Russian partisans fighting the Nazis. Edgar Snow was especially delighted when in 1943 he came across three teenage women partisans in the Soviet Union and asked them how they had learned to fight: 'We bought a book called *Red Star over China*. Just about everyone in our squad had read it,' was the gratifying reply. Nelson Mandela, preparing to take up the armed struggle in 1961, took copious notes on Snow's 'brilliant' book. The voice he heard was not Snow, but Mao Zedong.[47]

Within China, the critical moment was the publication of *Red Star over China* in Chinese in late 1937. Fifty thousand copies were printed in Shanghai, despite the fierce battle ranging between the Japanese and Nationalist forces for control of the city. For the patriotic youth of the occupied city, Snow's text promised a route to national regeneration; student groups swiftly adopted it as their manifesto. As pirated versions spread Mao's renown over China, more and more recruits flocked to join Mao's forces in Yan'an. By 1949, the defeated remnant of the Nationalist armies had decamped to Taiwan; China was now a communist state.

For the first decade after the takeover of power, Mao proceeded with caution when it came to dealing with the intelligentsia. Chinese culture held intellectuals in high esteem, and Mao recognised the importance of a peaceful takeover of the universities if the new project were to succeed. A sweeping programme of reorganisation and renewal reshaped universities on the Soviet model; academics kept their counsel until encouraged by the Hundred Flowers campaign of 1956–7 to offer their criticisms. This proved naive, and many found themselves among the million 'rightists' despatched to rural villages to reform themselves through labour.[48]

The period of obeisance to the senior communist state was coming to its end. When, in 1960, the Soviet premier Nikita Khrushchev flirted with a policy of peaceful coexistence with the United States, Mao took a different road. A surge of pamphlets, widely distributed, set out China's alternative of global class struggle against 'US imperialists in Asia, Africa and Latin America'. This message of solidarity to anti-colonial movements throughout the world was eagerly received. The Soviet response, a pamphlet refuting these slanderous attacks, seems not to have had the same impact, despite being circulated in 3.2 million copies, in thirty-five languages, to eighty-five countries. China deluged sympathetic movements in all of these continents with printed and broadcast propaganda, while dramatically increasing its aid budget. At one point, it was supplying 20 per cent of Albania's grain needs; this while famine raged at home. The revolutionaries who attended the Chinese military academy set up at Nanjing to foment world revolution included the Peruvian professor of philosophy Abimael Guzmán, the guiding force behind the Maoist Shining Path guerrillas in their brutal battle again the Peruvian government. Publications and financial help were showered upon radical European groups identifying as Maoists – so generously, indeed, that the Dutch security forces set up such a group to gather intelligence on China.[49] By this point, the movement, chaotic and inchoate in its purposes, had at least a totem of identity in a small, cheap, vinyl-covered booklet, published in 1964 as *200 Quotations from Chairman Mao* and soon universally known as Mao's Little Red Book.

The *Quotations* were initially meant only for distribution in the People's Liberation Army, following from an initiative of an old comrade, Lin Biao, who had asked the army paper, *PLA Daily*, to provide a Mao quote of the day. In its final form it would comprise 427 excerpts from the chairman's writings and speeches, organised in thirty-three themes. It was only in 1966 that it began to be systematically distributed to citizens outside the army. It soon took on a life of its own, circulated in unofficial reprints (at least 500 by 1970) and translated into multiple languages. Between October 1966 and May 1967, the Chinese International Bookstore despatched copies to more than 100 countries worldwide, just in time for the student revolts of 1968: it became the symbol of youth rebellion. In Britain, a copy of the Little Red Book could be obtained free of charge in return for a polite letter to the Chinese Embassy.[50]

In China, the tradition of quotations and maxims was of long standing: Sun Tzu's *The Art of War*, which we met at the beginning of this book, is a similar collection of taut epigrams. The nature of the collection, a series of decontextualised references, eased memorising and group recitation and allowed for near-infinite rearrangement and study. Mao's maxims were also spread through a network of wired radio, with an estimated 140 million loudspeakers in streets, schools, train and bus stations, factories and even private homes. The loudspeakers had no off switch, so Mao's ruminations became literally inescapable, not least when set to music. The quotation song became a significant phenomenon between 1966 and 1969, using tunes from native folk songs. One can only assume that the song entitled 'Ensure that Literature and Art Operate as Powerful Weapons for Exterminating the Enemy' loses some of its power in translation, though the sentiment is certainly a neat encapsulation of Mao's faith in the power of the word. Mao's wife, Jiang Qing, was definitely not impressed, and denounced quotation songs at the party's ninth annual congress in 1969.[51]

By the time Jiang Qing issued her broadside, the Little Red Book had reached its peak of influence. Although it continued to exert a powerful appeal abroad, for instance in the Naxalite movement in India, in China the book had become almost an object of worship, and the communist hierarchy decided to rein in its influence. From 1971, it was essentially out of print, and in 1979, it was officially withdrawn from circulation. With Mao now dead, more than a hundred million copies stored in warehouses were destroyed. Despite its ignoble end, this was undoubtedly the most successful book of the twentieth century: more than a billion copies were distributed worldwide. Its infinite flexibility, as slogans, talking points and songs, chanted, read, sung or blared out on the radio, made it the perfect vehicle for a revolution touching parts of the world where literacy levels remained low.

CODA: THE END OF HISTORY AND
THE CONTINUATION OF WAR

At the beginning of 1989, Francis Fukuyama was a valued but not particularly well-known official in the United States State Department. Three years later he was one of the most widely discussed thinkers of the immediate post-Cold War era. The cause of this transformation was a brief, brave essay (published before the fall of the Berlin Wall) called 'The End of History'. This eye-catching piece was subsequently reworked as an influential book, *The End of History and the Last Man*, published in 1992.

Fukuyama's central thesis was that with the collapse of the Soviet bloc, the fundamental issues of historical conflict had been resolved:

> What we may be witnessing is not just the end of the Cold War, or the passing of a particular period of postwar history, but the end of history as such: that is, the end point of mankind's ideological evolution and the universalization of Western liberal democracy as the final form of human government.[1]

Capitalism had triumphed, and with it the political systems that underpinned the economies of the West, democracy and representative government. Fukuyama envisaged a future in which other nations now looking to join the consumer jamboree in an increasing connected global economy, would follow the Eastern European nations and adopt the values of the victorious West.

Fukuyama would spend the next thirty years explaining that it was all a little more complicated than that, albeit from the ever more luminous institutions to which his new fame had propelled him. In truth it was the label, the 'End of History', as much as the longer gloss, that fired the public imagination: a political scientist's contribution to the exhalation of relief and hubristic self-congratulation as the Soviet system crumbled before our astonished eyes.

There was indeed something deeply moving about the way in which proud nations like Poland, Hungary, Czechoslovakia and the newly freed Baltic republics embraced the opportunity to rejoin the wider European family, with free elections and ultimately membership of both NATO and the European Union. The rebirth of Baltic liberty has its monument in the new National Library of Latvia, an astonishing piece of modern architecture constructed between 2008 and 2014 in the heart of the capital, Riga. The movement of the books from the old library to their new home was dramatised by the construction of a symbolic human chain between the two buildings, passing the books from hand to hand. Thousands of Riga's inhabitants turned out on a freezing January day to take part in this ceremony of regeneration.

The transition from communist satellites to democratic countries was exhilarating, but also tough – particularly, as it turned out, for those whose life was bound up with the business of books. One of my own most vivid memories of this time was walking through the streets of Lutherstadt-Wittenberg, previously in communist East Germany, eighteen months after the breach of the Berlin Wall, and seeing much of the stock of the public library on the street in barrows. You could take away any text for a nominal fifty pfennigs. Schools and universities went through a similar cleansing process: existing textbooks were replaced and most university professors in the humanities were dismissed, along with many high-school teachers. The fall of the Berlin Wall had a very human cost. The dash to modern Western fiction doomed even editions of the English classics: editions of Dickens and Shakespeare published locally were no longer trusted, and took their place in the skips along with the collected speeches of the deposed leaders.

A transformation so rapid, so unexpected, inevitably witnessed some regrettable over-compensation and rough justice. Had this been the progenitor of the new era of harmony envisaged after the collapse of the Soviet Empire, this might have been quickly healed. But, as it turned out, this was neither the end of history, nor the end of war. Nor would the next two decades witness the universalisation of Western values: by some measures, commitment to democracy as the logical and ultimately only plausible system of government went backwards. As for war, the first decade of the post-Cold War peace dividend witnessed a series of bloody tragedies: the first Gulf War (1990–1) to liberate Kuwait after Iraq's invasion, and wars in Rwanda (1990–4), Croatia (1991–5), Sierra Leone (1991–2002), Somalia (1991–), Bosnia (1992–5), Chechnya (1994–6) and Kosovo (1998–9). The 'End of History' had turned into a maelstrom of ethnic conflict, leaving international bodies and concerned observers in the West with moral dilemmas for which they have no immediate answers.

All of this posed the Western powers difficult questions, leading to inconsistent leadership and bitterly divided public discussion. The extent to which we care about foreign wars is largely determined by what is covered in our newspapers or beamed from our television screens. On the one hand, it is impressive that we do care about the fate of peoples to whom we have no immediate or strategic connection: this sense that we have obligations to humans everywhere on the globe, to enforce their basic human rights, is a relatively new development in history. Nevertheless, there is no denying, in the neat encapsulation of Michael Ignatieff, that 'our moral engagements with faraway places are notoriously selective and partial. We are more likely to help people who look like us than those who don't; more likely to help people whose plight we can understand than people whose situation we cannot fathom.'[2]

So the conflicts of the post-Cold War are treated very differently by both policymakers and the media. There are those that the secretary-general of the UN Boutros Boutros-Ghali called the 'orphaned conflicts', those with which the West chose not to engage. Then there was a smaller number where great powers could claim a strategic interest, such as the two Gulf Wars and the ethnic tensions in the new post-Soviet Central Asian republics, where Russia was given a free hand. When intervention was attempted, television continued to set the terms of engagement: it had become 'the privileged medium through which moral relations between strangers are mediated in the modern world'.[3] But television has a short attention span, and its own conventions. In messy, often triangular conflicts, the search for a blameless victim was fruitless. To maintain public support, Western military engagement was generally limited to low-risk, low-gain strategies to be followed by a rapid withdrawal once these limited objectives had been realised. In countries where the institutions of civil society had broken down, this post-Cold War style of instant intervention and quick exit was never destined to succeed.

Even those wars in which the West became deeply involved had a profound moral ambiguity. During the second Gulf War, on the way to Baghdad under artillery fire, a marine lieutenant heard a corporal sing, 'One, two, three, four, what the fuck are we fighting for?' and decided on a bit of impromptu ideological training.

Marine lieutenant: 'You'll have to answer that for yourself.'

'Well sir, I guess I'm fighting for cheap gas and a world without ragheads blowing up our fucking buildings.'

'Good to know you're such an idealist.'

'That world sounds pretty ideal to me right about now.'[4]

With that the exchange concluded, though not, one might think, to the disadvantage of the soldier. In one respect he was the idealist: the US government had invested considerable effort in persuading the American people of the connection between Iraq and 9/11, and they had succeeded. By March 2003, polls showed that 53–70 per cent of the US population believed that Saddam Hussein had been involved in the attack on the Twin Towers: Lieutenant Fick's grunt interlocutor spoke for the American people and his fellow soldiers. According to one survey, 85 per cent of troops thought they were in Iraq to retaliate for Saddam's role in 9/11.[5]

When American and British troops overran jihadi training camps in Afghanistan in 2001, they found numerous notebooks abandoned by students being instructed in the use of the AK-47. This normally comprised the first week of training: in the absence of a printed manual, they made meticulous notes of their progress by hand. It is a reminder that even in this period of digital media not everything was high tech. There was still plenty of room for the legacy technologies that had shaped and chronicled the art of war for the last two millennia. In the Egyptian uprising of 2011, there was considerable resentment that this conflict was constantly described in Western media as the 'Facebook Revolution'. In fact, the uprising was saturated by a long literary tradition of freedom. The slogan 'the people want to topple the regime' was adapted from the poem 'The Will to Live' written in 1933 by Tunisian-born Aboul-Qacem Echebbi, which achieved iconic status in 1950s. In the years of military rule and repression under President Hosni Mubarak, the work of writers and artists remained largely outside the framework of state censorship that suffocated journalists. The trope of 'spontaneous, unforeseen and contagious' revolution, and an emphasis on social media, suggesting an abrupt transition from inertia to action, does little credit to this historical heritage, prioritising Western technology over Arab agency.[6]

The role of a long literary heritage in the ultimately frustrated Arab Spring is a reminder that the accrued intellectual capital of books will continue to play a part in our lives and conflicts, notwithstanding the domination of new technologies of war-making and information gathering. At one stage in the first years of the twenty-first century there were 400,000 American service personnel stationed abroad, and their need for reading matter was addressed along with all the other provisions of a modern army. This was a highly trained professional force made up of career soldiers, and there was no official attempt to revive the Armed Services Editions of the Second World War. This left a gap that would be filled by Andrew Carroll, co-founder of an initiative to promote a revival of poetry reading in America, and of the Legacy Project, gathering together correspondence from American wars.[7] With the help of American publishers, Carroll distributed more than 2 million copies of seven titles, all in the characteristic oblong format of the original Armed Services Editions. Unlike the wartime series, these were books that soldiers would be unlikely to choose for their own recreational reading, four with a martial theme: Shakespeare's *Henry V*, Sun Tzu's *Art of War*, Allen Mikaelian's *Medal of Honor*, profiles of American heroes from the Civil War onwards, and a

Afghanistan 2012. A British officer enjoys a little light reading
on a helicopter ride to inspect troops in Kunar Province.

condensed version of Carroll's own collection of war letters from
the American Civil War to Operation Desert Storm.

It would be interesting to know what impact the ancient
Chinese seer, or indeed King Henry at the gates of Harfleur, would
have on the officers and troops facing a more elusive enemy in
Afghanistan and Iraq. The experience of Elizabeth Samet, who has
spent her career teaching English literature at West Point, suggests
they might have been quite receptive. Samet records both the eager-
ness of cadets for reading and their search for lessons to guide them
in the responsibilities they would face. The poet Jorie Graham, who
gave a reading at West Point in 1996, found herself deeply moved by
the way cadets 'searched through the literature, from Shakespeare
to contemporary poets, in order to determine a right moral choice
in a situation where, increasingly, that is impossible'.[8] But history,
and literature, can also be a burden. In American popular culture,
the 'Good War', the Second World War, where America came to
Europe's rescue, sets an impossible standard for the messy wars
of today. An exaggerated, sanitised view of wars past makes it far
easier for military cultures to canonise their dead, with all deaths

gaining the lustre of patriotic sacrifice, than to care for their returning wounded, the physical manifestation of war's horror. This is a
particularly urgent issue when battlefield surgery has made such
astonishing strides. In Vietnam, 24 per cent of wounds were still
lethal; in the recent wars of Afghanistan and Iraq, 10 per cent.[9]

In the major military training academies every effort is made
to prepare officers for the multi-cultural realities they will encounter in global combat zones or peacekeeping. West Point is a leader
in matters of moral and ethical development: its Center for the
Professional Military Ethic generates material used throughout
the US Army. Dutch military cadets face a compulsory module on
war crimes, and reassuringly cannot proceed with their training
until they have passed it. Even the ancients have their continuing
relevance: the Athenian historian Thucydides has enjoyed a revival
since 9/11, his warning of the perils of empire and the responsibilities of democracy striking a particular chord. The learning of
ancient Greece and Rome had, we remember, a hallowed place
in the reading of the Western educational curriculum from the
Renaissance to the early twentieth century, also in the military
academies. It is interesting to see that the ancients' strategic notions
still have purchase today.

Libraries too, retain their salience, for the cadets in the military training academies and officers in the staff colleges, but also
for the 779 prisoners who have been detained in the camp established in the wake of the 9/11 attacks at Guantanamo Bay in Cuba.
From slow beginnings, this library grew to a collection of 18,000
books, divided between texts in Arabic and recent bestsellers. In
2010, the contents of the library took on evidential importance
in the sentencing hearing of Omar Khadr, who was detained in
Afghanistan at the age of fifteen. After testimony that Khadr was
an irredeemable jihadist who spent much of his time reading the
Qur'an, defence counsel were able to establish that he had also borrowed Nelson Mandela's *Long Road to Freedom*, Barack Obama's
Dreams from My Father, the *Twilight* series of Stephenie Meyer
and novels by John Grisham and Danielle Steel. Ishmael Beah's *A
Long Way Gone: Memoirs of a Boy Soldier* was the most poignant
item on his reading list.

*

Military training requires a mixture of certainty and mental flexibility, particularly in officers. But when the underlying certainties of the righteous cause unravel, it is easy for morale to disintegrate. In February 2022, as Russian troops advanced into Ukraine, many of them appeared to have been told they were on a training exercise, but they found, against their expectations, a population determined on resistance. The effect on troop morale was predictably dire. The reaction in the West was also confused and contradictory, not least because most political leaders thought the reigniting of a great power 'hot war' in Europe was inconceivable. The American political columnist Robert Reich bared his soul in a powerful article in the *Guardian*. Reich was a key figure in the Clinton administration in the last decade of the twentieth century, and was now professor of public policy at the University of California at Berkeley. In this article he openly acknowledged that his fundamental assumptions about the twenty-first century lay in tatters, destroyed by populism at home and a great power strike on a vulnerable neighbour.

Reich had assumed that nationalism would recede: 'Globalization would blur borders, create economic interdependence among nations and regions and extend a modern consumer and artistic culture worldwide.' Russia's invasion of Ukraine, warmly applauded by its state-dominated media and, to all appearances, the large majority of its people, gave the lie to that. Reich had thought that nations would no longer be able to control what their citizens knew: 'that emerging digital technologies, including the internet, would make it impossible to control worldwide flows of information and knowledge'. That hope had certainly taken a body blow, not least in the success of China's government in bending the digital media giants to its will. He thought that advanced nations would no longer war over geographic territory; that major nuclear powers would never risk war against each other because of the certainty of mutually assured destruction; that advances in warfare, such as cyber-warfare and precision weapons, would minimise civilian casualties. That too had proved naive: indeed twenty-first-century warfare seemed to produce far more civilian casualties than among troops of regular armies, more frequently employed as peacekeepers than combatants.

Most of all Reich had believed, in a sign of how far the Fukuyama delusion had spread across the political spectrum, that democracy was now inevitable:

> I formed this belief in the early 1990s, when the Soviet Union had imploded and China was still poor. It seemed to me that totalitarian regimes didn't stand a chance in the new technologically driven, globalized world. Sure, petty dictatorships would remain in some retrograde regions of the world. But modernity came with democracy, and democracy with modernity.[10]

Reich deserves every credit for setting this out in such self-lacerating detail: and many must have shared these hopes as we welcomed in the new millennium. Globalism and an almost unlimited appetite for consumer comforts have brought consequences that we could not have anticipated. In the first two months after the Russian attack on Ukraine, the West warmly applauded Ukraine's heroism, and condemned Russian aggression; and in the same two months the twenty-seven nations of the European Union, led by Germany, sent an eye-watering 43 billion euros to Russia, the condemned aggressor, in return for oil and gas.

The unfolding tragedy of Ukraine has taught us much, not least that the outdated nineteenth-century concept of spheres of influence can still have toxic consequences for nations like Ukraine struggling for independence. We were reminded that the climate emergency was always likely to be a major factor in future military conflict; and that the greatest weapon of any insurgent, terrorist or freedom fighter is the willingness to die for a cause. The widespread expectation of a swift Russian victory was predicated on overwhelming military force; it did not take into account the steely determination of Ukrainians to defend their homes and prove themselves a free nation.

The war in Ukraine has left us many moving images, not least a picture of one apartment, where a resident used their valuable personal library to block the window as blast protection. The printed word has performed many functions in this study, as comfort, instruction, the vector of poisonous ideologies, the source of essential technical knowledge or a handbook guide to the strange customs of unfamiliar peoples, such as *112 Gripes about the French*, issued to American troops in Europe in 1945.[11] We have not previously come across the book as sandbag, though we have seen books torn up to make cartridges in the French revolutionary wars, and propaganda leaflets fired in shell cases to arrive slightly singed and battered behind enemy lines.

The confusion of the world order in the thirty-five years since the end of the Cold War went beyond the false predictions of the 'End of History' and the hubris of the 'peace dividend'; it suggests that Fukuyama and other Western policymakers fundamentally misread the process of modernisation. Here the history of communication, which had played such an important part in the transformation of warfare, offers some useful lessons. The history of the book is a notable example of successful modernisation, an organic process over many centuries of incremental development, building new markets, introducing new products (the novel, the paperback) but essentially preserving the obvious benefits of the amalgamation of texts into light, portable volumes, bound for protection against the elements. Even the more explosive moments of growth, such as the introduction of printing with moveable type, left room for existing modes of discourse, such as song, conversation and manuscripts. In the same way, we have failed to recognise that countries outside the original heartland of print culture would take what they felt culturally appropriate from the technologies of the West, without necessarily adopting its political systems and social practices.

We started this book with military texts in the age before print and concluded with the dictums of Chairman Mao set to music. It is the perfect demonstration of the truth that the advance of new media does not necessarily render older means of communication redundant. The history of communication is cumulative rather than sequential. Humans developed language, but they did not stop talking when they started writing; they did not abandon writing when they invented print; and they will not stop printing because they have the internet. Such is the history of communication, in war as in peace. This is why the new technologies repeatedly predicted as harbingers of 'the death of the book' (microfilm, CD-ROMs and the e-reader) have mostly come and gone, or simply – like radio, television and the iPhone – taken their place alongside print in the ecology of communication. Forced modernisations, on the other hand, often predicated on a mass adoption of new communication technology, such as the loudspeakers in Mao's Cultural Revolution, have seldom realised their objectives.

This nuanced history of the development of communication is highly relevant to the relationship between print and warfare. In this book, we have experienced books as training manuals, as spiritual inspiration, as recreation and refuge. We have seen that books could often be victims of the conflict, targeted for their intellectual freight, from the Reformation to the fall of the Berlin Wall and beyond. We have seen the full variety of print in all its manifestations – leaflets, posters, pamphlets, newspapers, magazines, paperbacks and hardbacks – deployed in the task of informing the population, shifting opinions and influencing young minds. Yet the critical truth is that however brutal wars have been to books and libraries, the advance of print technologies meant that at every stage of history, books could be published in far greater numbers than could be destroyed.

This is unusual in the economy of war. The cost of destroying buildings and infrastructure is far lower than the cost of rebuilding, as every post-war settlement is obliged to recognise. The sheer ubiquity of print, and the low unit cost of books, is its greatest defence in war. A museum artefact or work of art may be irreplaceable. Yet a lost book may be replicated in copies held in hundreds of other institutional collections, or in thousands of private homes. Print, and the ideas to which it gives permanence, will outlive us, as the first printed books have outlived the twenty generations that have come and gone since the death of their first proud owners.

Print, in all its rich variety, will continue to play its part in human interactions throughout the globe, in war as in peacetime, not least through this enormous accrued archive of books, casually saved in many hundreds or thousands of copies. As we continue to look to books for inspiration and context on the problems that beset us, we can recognise that our hopes for a better world, the end of war, the construction of harmonious social relationships, were shared across the continuum of history. When books go to war, others stay behind, a reminder of the better times when conflict can be banished to the edge of our consciousness, if never wholly eradicated.

ACKNOWLEDGEMENTS

To write about books you need to have access to books, and that became more complicated during a global pandemic. I am grateful to the University of St Andrews Library for their smoothly efficient click and collect service, to the London Library for their million books on open stacks, and the Imperial War Museum research room for allocating me one of their precious workspaces at a critical stage of my research. Rachel Hart, the University of St Andrews archivist, called my attention to the university's run of the *Ruhleben Camp Magazine* from 1916–17. This was not a time for travel overseas, but I was able to reach into cupboards of materials accumulated in three decades of roving work in libraries, and, of course, my own book collection. Even so, the world's online bookshops were a crucial resource, and I am more than grateful for the booksellers and the courier services who delivered something to my door almost every day. I now have a neat little collection of wartime publishing. In the course of researching this book, I read many wartime diaries and biographies, as well as a range of superb interpretative work. I am grateful to the University of Sussex Special Collections for guidance on the use of the Mass Observation archive, and to Patricia and Robert Malcolmson for bringing so many of these wartime diaries to a wider public.

My personal debts are, as ever, numerous, most notably to Arthur der Weduwen, my co-author on our last four books. Arthur had to peel off to write his much-anticipated and ground-breaking monograph on state communication, but he has been the first reader of every chapter of this book, and I owe a great deal to his meticulous eye. We plan to get back together for a couple of projects in the pipeline. Other readers include Basil Bowdler, Jacob

Baxter, Jessica Dalton and Peter Truesdale. I was grateful to Professor Sir Hew Strachan for pointing me in some useful directions at the beginning of this project, and a later stage for making the acquaintance of Dr Simon Trew, of the Royal Military Academy Sandhurst, with whom I had several fascinating and illuminating conversations. I was especially delighted to be back with the excellent team at Profile, Andrew Franklin, Niamh Murray, Anna-Marie Fitzgerald and their talented colleagues in production and design. Cecily Gayford is the editor that every author would wish for; likewise Robert Davies, whose sensitive and rigorous copy-editing has measurably improved the final product. I am grateful also to Jon Petre for his help sourcing illustrations. My thanks to my agent Catherine Clarke for orchestrating this continuing partnership with an outstanding publisher.

My wife Jane and my daughters Megan and Sophie lived through the pandemic with me, at one point with three of us tapping away on our laptops around the dining-room table. Even though the girls are both now embarked on their own careers, I am greatly touched by their continuing interest in their father's activities. To write on books and warfare in the middle of a war was an unexpected twist of fate. It makes me ever more grateful for the love of family, while our heart goes out to all the families separated, broken and bereaved by the consequences of war. It is tragic that in the third decade of the twenty-first century this remains part of our current news agenda, rather than just our history.

St Andrews, *March 2023*

NOTES

Introduction

1 Most recently, Caroline Shenton, *National Treasures: Saving the Nation's Art in World War II* (London: John Murray, 2021).
2 See Chapters 14 and 17, below.
3 Anonymous, *A Woman in Berlin* (London: Virago, 2011), p. 37.
4 Patricia and Robert Malcolmson, *Dorset in Wartime: The Diary of Phyllis Walther 1941–1942* (Dorchester: Dorset Record Society, 2009), p. 111.
5 Richard Broad and Suzie Fleming, *Nella Last's War: A Mother's Diary, 1939–1945* (Bristol: Falling Wall, 1981); reprinted as *Nella Last's War: The Second World War Diaries of a Housewife, 49* (London: Profile, 2006). See also Patricia and Robert Malcolmson, *The Diaries of Nella Last: Writing in War and Peace* (London: Profile, 2012).
6 Duncan White, *Cold Warriors: Writers who Waged the Literary Cold War* (New York: HarperCollins, 2019), pp. 212–14, 216.
7 Timothy W. Ryback, *Hitler's Private Library: The Books that Shaped His Life* (London: Vintage, 2010).
8 Geoffrey Roberts, *Stalin's Library: A Dictator and His Books* (New Haven, CT: Yale University Press, 2022).
9 Julian Jackson, *A Certain Idea of France: The Life of Charles de Gaulle* (London: Allen Lane, 2019), pp. 72–4.
10 Philip Short, *Mao: A Life* (London: Hodder and Stoughton, 1999), p. 83.
11 Roberts, *Stalin's Library*, p. 11.
12 Philip Oltermann, *The Stasi Poetry Circle* (London: Faber, 2022), p. 39.
13 Message to the American Booksellers Association, 23 April 1942.

1. A Call to Arms

1 Gustavs Strenga and Andris Levans (eds), *Catalogue of the Riga Jesuit Book Collection (1583–1621): History and Reconstruction of the Collection* (Riga: National Library of Latvia, 2021).
2 Archibald MacLeish, 'The Library and the Nation', in Pierce Butler (ed.), *Books and Libraries in Warfare* (Chicago: University of Chicago Press, 1945), pp. 141–54, at pp. 143–4.
3 Catherine Merridale, *Lenin on the Train* (London: Allen Lane, 2016), pp. 72–3.
4 Geoffrey Roberts, *Stalin's Library: A Dictator and His Books* (New Haven, CT: Yale University Press, 2022), pp. 13–14.

5 Peter Englund, *The Beauty and the Sorrow* (London: Profile, 2011), p. 28; Geert Buelens, *Everything to Nothing: The Poetry of the Great War, Revolution and the Transformation of Europe* (London: Verso, 2015), p. 49.

6 Robert D. Kaplan, *Balkan Ghosts: A Journey through History* (New York: St Martin's Press, 1993).

7 Buelens, *Everything to Nothing*, pp. 19, 21, 25.

8 Simon Sebag Montefiore, *Young Stalin* (London: Weidenfeld & Nicolson, 2007), p. 65.

9 Roberts, *Stalin's Library*, p. 178.

10 Valerie Holman, 'Air-Borne Culture: Propaganda Leaflets over Occupied France in the Second World War', in James Raven (ed.), *Free Print and Non-Commercial Publishing since 1700* (Aldershot: Ashgate, 2000), pp. 194–221, at p. 207.

11 Philip Oltermann, *The Stasi Poetry Circle* (London: Faber, 2022), p. 31.

12 Barbara Diefendorf, *Beneath the Cross: Catholics and Huguenots in Sixteenth-Century Paris* (New York: Oxford University Press, 1991).

13 Luc Racault, 'Nicolas Chesneau, Catholic Printer in Paris during the French Wars of Religion', *Historical Journal*, 52 (2009), pp. 23–41.

14 William Beveridge, *Social Insurance and Allied Services* (London: HMSO, 1942).

15 Jose Harris, *William Beveridge*, 2nd ed. (Oxford: Oxford University Press, 1997), p. 415.

16 Donald V. Coers, *John Steinbeck Goes to War: The Moon is Down as Propaganda* (Tuscaloosa: University of Alabama Press, 1991).

17 James Fleming, *Bond: Behind the Iron Curtain* (Cheltenham: The Book Collector, 2021).

18 Oltermann, *Stasi Poetry Circle*, p. 87.

19 Adam Sisman, *John Le Carré* (London: Bloomsbury, 2015), p. 32.

20 Andreas Kramer and Ritchie Robertson (eds), *Pacifist and Anti-Militarist Writing in German, 1889–1926* (London: University of London Press, 2018).

21 Peter Brock, *Pacifism in Europe to 1914* (Princeton, NJ: Princeton University Press, 1972), pp. 407–41.

22 Martin Ceadel, *Pacifism in Britain, 1914–1945: The Defining of a Faith* (Oxford: Oxford University Press, 1980), pp. 44–5; Miranda Seymour, *Ottoline Morrell: Life on the Grand Scale* (London: Hodder & Stoughton, 1992).

23 Mrs Henry Hobhouse, *I Appeal unto Caesar: The Case of the Conscientious Objector* (London: George Allen and Unwin, 1917).

24 Stanley Unwin, *The Truth about a Publisher* (London: George Allen & Unwin, 1960), pp. 154–5; Adam Hochschild, *To End All Wars: How the First World War Divided Britain* (London: Macmillan, 2011), pp. 269–73.

25 Beverley Nicolas, *Cry Havoc!* (London: Jonathan Cape, 1933); Storm Jameson, *No Time Like the Present* (London: Cassell, 1933); A. A. Milne, *Peace with Honour: An Inquiry into the War Convention* (London: Methuen, 1934).

26 Mark Gilbert, 'Pacifist Attitudes to Nazi Germany, 1936–45', *Journal of Contemporary History*, 27 (1992), pp. 493–511.

27 Storm Jameson, *The End of this War* (London: George Allen & Unwin, 1941).

28 Frances Partridge, *A Pacifist's Diary* (London: Hogarth Press, 1978).

29 Ceadel, *Pacifism*, p. 301.

30 Patricia and Robert Malcolmson, *A Soldier in Bedfordshire, 1941–1942* (Woodford: Boydell, for the Bedfordshire Historical Record Society, 2009).

2. The Art of War

1 For an introduction to the huge literature on Clausewitz, see Hew Strachan, *Carl von Clausewitz's On War: A Biography* (London: Atlantic Books, 2007), and Peter Paret, *Clausewitz and the State* (Oxford: Oxford University Press, 1976).

2 For the discovery, see: https://thestrategybridge.org/the-bridge/2018/8/6/clausewitzs-library-strategy-politics-and-poetry. There is an inventory of the collection at https://static1.squarespace.com/static/5497331ae4b0148a6141bd47/t/5b60bd05562fa7ec2eba3 f0d/1533066502259/Clausewitz_Book_List_31Jul18.pdf.

3 Paret, *Clausewitz and the State*, p. 308.

4 Antoine Henri Jomini, *The Art of War*, tr. G. H. Mendel and W. P. Craighill (Rockville, MD: Arc Manor, 2006).

5 Sun Tzu, *The Art of War* (London: Collins, 2013).

6 John A. Wood, *Perspectives on War in the Bible* (Macon, GA: Mercer University Press, 1998).

7 Psalm 149: 4, 6–9 (New International Version).

8 The Universal Short Title Catalogue (ustc.ac.uk) lists almost 2,000 military texts and handbooks published between 1450 and 1650.

9 Nina Lamal, 'Publishing Military Books in the Low Countries and in Italy in the Early Seventeenth Century', in Sophie Mullins and Richard Kirwan (eds), *Specialist Markets in the Early Modern Book World* (Leiden: Brill, 2015), pp. 222–39.

10 Gabriel Naudé, *Syntagma de Studio Militari* (Rome: Giacomo Facciotti, 1637). The USTC lists twenty-four surviving copies (USTC 4014234).

11 Vegetius is represented by thirty editions in the USTC.

12 Ian C. Hope, *A Scientific Way of War: Antebellum Military Science, West Point and the Origins of American Military Thought* (Lincoln: University of Nebraska Press, 2015); Stephen Ambrose, *Duty, Honor, Country: A History of West Point* (Baltimore, MD: Johns Hopkins University Press, 1966).

13 Thayer's French purchases are prominently displayed in the first published list of the library's holdings from 1822: https://catalog.hathitrust.org/Record/009018731.

14 Marvin J. Anderson, 'The Architectural Education of Nineteenth-Century Engineers: Dennis Hart Mayan at West Point', *Journal of the Society of Architectural Historians*, 67 (2008), pp. 222–47.

15 *Catalogue of the Library of the US Military Academy, West Point NY* (New York: John F. Trow, 1853). By 1873 the collection had grown further to 13,765 titles, as revealed in a published catalogue from 1876: https://babel.hathitrust.org/cgi/pt?id=nyp.33433069262743&view=1up&seq=7.

16 James Robertson, *Stonewall Jackson: The Man, the Soldier, the Legend* (New York: Macmillan, 1997).

17 William B. Skelton, *West Point: Two Centuries and Beyond* (Abilene, TX: McWhiney Foundations, 2004), pp. 29–30.

18 Trevor N. Dupuy, *A Genius for War: The German Army and General Staff, 1807–1945* (London: MacDonald and Jane's, 1977), p. 17.

19 Christopher Bassford, *Clausewitz in English: The Reception of Clausewitz in Britain and America, 1815–1945* (New York: Oxford University Press, 1994).

20 See Chapter 4.

21 Helen Roche, *Sparta's German Children* (Swansea: Classical Press of Wales, 2013).

22 Hugh Thomas, *The Story of Sandhurst* (London: Hutchinson, 1961), p. 68.

23 Roche, *Sparta's German Children*, p. 63.

24 Helen Roche, *The Third Reich's Elite Schools: A History of the Napolas* (Oxford: Oxford University Press, 2021).

25 Robert M. Citino, *The German Way of War* (Lawrence: University Press of Kansas, 2005), pp. 142–90.

26 Citino, *The German Way of War*, p. 150.

27 Isabel V. Hull, *Absolute Destruction: Military Culture and the Practices of War in Imperial Germany* (Ithaca, NY: Cornell University Press, 2005), p. 116.

28 Bryce Sait, *The Indoctrination of the Wehrmacht: Nazi Ideology and the War Crimes of the German Military* (New York: Berghahn, 2019).

29 Hull, *Absolute Destruction*, p. 121.

30 Thomas, *Sandhurst*; John Smyth, *Sandhurst: The History of the Royal Military Academy, Woolwich, the Royal Military College, Sandhurst and the Royal Military Academy, Sandhurst, 1741–1961* (London: Weidenfeld & Nicolson, 1961).

31 Winston S. Churchill, *My Early Life: A Roving Commission* (London: Macmillan, 1941), p. 57.

32 Paul H. Vickers, *A Gift So Graciously Bestowed: The History of the Prince Consort's Library, Aldershot* (Aldershot: Friends of Aldershot Military Museum, 2010), p. 36.

33 Brian Bond, *The Victorian Army and the Staff College, 1854–1914* (London: Eyre Methuen, 1972).

34 Alfred Reade Godwin-Austen, *The Staff and the Staff College* (London: Constable, 1927), p. 133; Adam Dighton, 'Jomini versus Clausewitz: Hamley's *Operations of War* and Military Thought in the British Army, 1866–1933', *War in History*, 27 (2020), pp. 179–201.

35 Churchill, *Early Life*, p. 106.

36 Thomas, *Sandhurst*, p. 80.

37 Thomas, *Sandhurst*, p. 32.

38 Sharon Murphy, 'Imperial Reading? The East India Company's Lending Libraries for Soldiers, *c.* 1819–1834', *Book History*, 12 (2009), pp. 74–99, at p. 77. Cf. Sharon Murphy, *The British Soldier and His Libraries, c. 1822–1901* (London: Palgrave Macmillan, 2016).

39 Vickers, *Gift so Graciously Bestowed*, pp. 10–12.

40 Michael D. Calabria, 'Florence Nightingale and the Libraries of the British Army', *Libraries and Culture*, 29 (1994), pp. 367–88.

41 Vickers, *Gift so Graciously Bestowed*, p. 73.

42 Lefroy's report was published as *Report on the Regimental and Garrison Schools*

of the Army and on Military Libraries and Reading Rooms (London: Eyre and Spottiswoode, 1859).

43 John Lewis-Stempel, *Six Weeks: The Short and Gallant Life of the British Officer in the First World War* (London: Weidenfeld & Nicolson, 2010), pp. 98–101.

44 See below, Chapter 10.

45 Bond, *Victorian Army*, pp. 299–301.

46 Carl von Clausewitz, *On War*, ed. Michael Howard and Peter Paret (Princeton, NJ: Princeton University Press, 1984), p. 101 ('On Military Genius').

3. From *Uncle Tom's Cabin* to Stalingrad: Why Men Fight

1 Claire Parfait, *The Publishing History of Uncle's Tom's Cabin, 1852–2002* (Aldershot: Ashgate, 2007).

2 Harry Stone, 'Charles Dickens and Harriet Beecher Stowe', *Nineteenth-Century Fiction*, 12 (1957), pp. 188–202.

3 Frederick Douglass, *The Life and Times of Frederick Douglass* (1881; repr. Mineola, NY: Dover, 2003), p. 202.

4 Parfait, *Publishing History*, pp. 33–4.

5 Olivier Rolin, *Stalin's Meteorologist*, tr. Ros Schwartz (London: Harvill Secker, 2017), p. 94.

6 Daniel R. Vollaro, 'Lincoln, Stowe and the "Little Woman/Great War" Story: The Making and Breaking of a Great American Anecdote', *Journal of the Abraham Lincoln Association*, 30 (2009), pp. 18–34.

7 James M. McPherson, *For Cause and Comrades: Why Men Fought in the Civil War* (New York: Oxford University Press, 1997), p. 117.

8 Reid Mitchell, *Civil War Soldiers* (New York: Viking Penguin, 1988), p. 12.

9 Parfait, *Publishing History*, pp. 96, 98.

10 Richard N. Price, 'Society, Status and Jingoism: The Social Roots of Lower Middle-Class Patriotism, 1870–1900', in Geoffrey Crossick (ed.), *The Lower Middle Class in Britain, 1870–1914* (London: Croom Helm, 1977), pp. 89–112; Glenn R. Wilkinson, *Depictions and Images of War in Edwardian Newspapers, 1899–1914* (Basingstoke: Palgrave Macmillan, 2003).

11 Thomas Pakenham, *The Boer War* (London: Macdonald, 1979).

12 James Percy FitzPatrick, *The Transvaal from Within* (London: Heinemann, 1899).

13 *The Story of the Malakand Field Force* (London: Longman, 1898); *The River War* (London: Longman, 1899).

14 Winston S. Churchill, *My Early Life: A Roving Commission* (London: Macmillan, 1941), p. 347.

15 Richard Symonds, *Oxford and Empire: The Last Lost Cause?* (London: Macmillan, 1986), pp. 62–79.

16 John Buchan, *The African Colony: Studies in the Reconstruction* (Edinburgh and London: Blackwood, 1903).

17 Ursula Buchan, *Beyond the Thirty-Nine Steps: A Life of John Buchan* (London: Bloomsbury, 2019).

18 I. F. Clarke, *Voices Prophesying War: Future Wars, 1763–3749* (Oxford: Oxford University Press, 1992; rev. ed., 1996).

19 Andrew Boyle, *The Riddle of Erskine Childers* (London: Hutchinson, 1977), p. 111.

20 N. St. Barbe Sladen, *The Real Le Queux: The Official Biography of William Le Queux* (London: Nicholson & Watson, 1938).

21 John Ramsden, *Don't Mention the War: The British and the Germans since 1890* (London: Little, Brown, 2006), pp. 57–9.

22 E. S. Turner, *Boys Will Be Boys*, 3rd ed. (London: Michael Joseph, 1975), pp. 14, 191–5.

23 Turner, *Boys Will Be Boys*, p. 126.

24 *Boy's Own Paper*, March 1905; Jack Cox, *Take a Cold Tub, Sir! The Story of the Boy's Own Paper* (Guildford: Lutterworth, 1982), p. 73.

25 For a splendid compilation, see Karl Sabbagh, *Your Case is Hopeless: Bracing Advice from the Boy's Own Paper* (London: John Murray, 2007). Kelly Boyd, *Manliness and the Boys' Story Paper in Britain: A Cultural History, 1855–1940* (Basingstoke: Palgrave Macmillan, 2003); Ted Beardow, 'The Empire Hero', *Studies in Popular Culture*, 41 (2018), pp. 66–93.

26 Cox, *Take a Cold Tub*, p. 60.

27 Cox, *Take a Cold Tub*, p. 46.

28 Cox, *Take a Cold Tub*, p. 92.

29 Karel C. Berkhoff, *Motherland in Danger: Soviet Propaganda during World War II* (Cambridge, MA: Harvard University Press, 2012); Roger R. Reese, *Why Stalin's Soldiers Fought: The Red Army's Military Effectiveness in World War II* (Lawrence: University of Kansas Press, 2011).

30 Daniel J. Hughes and Richard L. Dinardo, *Imperial Germany and War, 1871–1918* (Lawrence: University of Kansas Press, 2018).

31 Wolfgang J. Mommsen, 'The Topos of Inevitable War in Germany in the Decades before 1914', in Volker R. Berghahn and Martin Kitchen (eds), *Germany in the Age of Total War* (London: Croom Helm, 1981), pp. 23–45.

32 Azar Gat, *The Development of Military Thought: The Nineteenth Century* (Oxford: Oxford University Press, 1992), pp. 59–60.

33 A. Michael Malin, '"The Hun is at the Gate!": Historicising Kipling's Militaristic Rhetoric from the Imperial Periphery to the National Center: Part Two: The French, Russian and German Threats to Great Britain', *Studies in the Novel*, 31 (1999), pp. 432–70; Clara Claiborne Park, 'Artist of Empire: Kipling and Kim', *Hudson Review*, 55 (2003), pp. 537–61.

34 John Philip Short, 'Everyman's Colonial Library: Imperialism and Working-Class Readers in Leipzig, 1890–1914', *German History*, 21 (2003), pp. 445–75.

35 Ian McDonald, *The Boer War in Postcards* (Stroud: Alan Sutton, 1990).

36 Mommsen, 'Topos of Inevitable War', p. 34.

37 Michael Grütter, 'German Universities under the Swastika', in John Connelly and Michael Grüttner (eds), *Universities under Dictatorship* (University Park, PA: Penn University State Press, 2005), pp. 75–112.

38 Helen Roche, *The Third Reich's Elite Schools: A History of the Napolas* (Oxford: Oxford University Press, 2021), p. 6.

39 Roche, *The Third Reich's Elite Schools*, p. 162.

40 Omer Bartov, *Hitler's Army. Soldiers, Nazis and War in the Third Reich* (New York: Oxford University Press, 1991), p. 150.

41 Robert M. Citino, *The German Way of War: From the Thirty Years' War to the Third Reich* (Lawrence: University of Kansas Press, 2005), p. 299.

42 Ursula Lange, *East Germany: What Happened to the Silesians in 1945?* (Lewes: Book Guild, 2000), p. 145.

43 H. W. Koch, *The Hitler Youth: Origins and Development, 1922–1945* (New York: Cooper Square, 2000), pp. 137–61.

44 Desmond Young, *Rommel* (London: Collins, 1950), p. 37.

45 Roche, *The Third Reich's Elite Schools*; Helen Roche, *Sparta's German Children* (Swansea: Classical Press of Wales, 2013).

46 Berkhoff, *Motherland*, p. 18.

47 Berkhoff, *Motherland*, p. 21.

48 Berkhoff, *Motherland*, pp. 276–7.

49 Alexander Solzhenitsyn, *The Gulag Archipelago* (London: Collins, 1975), vol. II, pp. 25–167. For the library, Rolin, *Stalin's Meteorologist*, pp. 72, 78

50 Reese, *Why Stalin's Soldiers Fought*, p. 96.

51 Reese, *Why Stalin's Soldiers Fought*, p. 106.

52 McPherson, *For Cause and Comrades*; Reese, *Why Stalin's Soldiers Fought*, p. 20.

53 Reese, *Why Stalin's Soldiers Fought*, p. 22.

54 Thomas Kühne, *The Rise and Fall of Comradeship: Hitler's Soldiers, Male Bonding and Mass Violence in the Twentieth Century* (Cambridge: Cambridge University Press, 2017).

55 Guy Sajer, *The Forgotten Soldier: War on the Russian Front: A True Story*, tr. Lily Emmet (London: Weidenfeld & Nicolson, 1971).

56 Koch, *Hitler Youth*, p. 249.

4. The Battle of Science

1 James Hinton, 'Ernest van Someren', in *Nine Wartime Lives: Mass Observation and the Making of the Modern Self* (Oxford: Oxford University Press, 2010), pp. 137–53. Excerpts from the diary are to be found in Simon Garfield, *Private Battles: How the War Almost Defeated Us* (London: Ebury, 2006).

2 Ernest H. S. van Someren, *Spectrochemical Abstracts* (London: Hilger, 1938–41).

3 Garfield, *Private Battles*, pp. 27–8, 70–91; William Manchester, *The Arms of Krupp* (New York: Little, Brown, 1964), p. 389.

4 Garfield, *Private Battles*, p. 308.

5 Garfield, *Private Battles*, p. 353.

6 Below, Chapter 5. R. V. Jones, *Most Secret War* (London: Hamish Hamilton, 1978), p. 121.

7 C. J. Chivers, *The Gun. The Story of the AK-47* (New York: Simon & Schuster, 2010).

8 Pamela Spence Richards, *Scientific Information in Wartime: The Allied–German Rivalry, 1939–1945* (Westport, CT: Greenwood, 1994), p. 6.

9 Isabel V. Hull, *Absolute Destruction: Military Culture and the Practices of War in Imperial Germany* (Ithaca, NY: Cornell University Press, 2005), p. 214.

10 Manchester, *Arms of Krupp*, pp. 258–9, 363–4.

11 Stephen Budiansky, *Blackett's War: The Men who Defeated the Nazi U-Boats and Brought Science to the Art of Warfare* (New York: Vintage, 2013), p. 108.

12 E. M. R. Ditmas, 'Special Libraries', *Royal Society Empire Scientific Conference 1946* (2 vols, London: Royal Society, 1948), vol. I, pp. 703–17, at p. 707.

13 Heinz Gomoll, 'Die Werkbücherei der Fried. Krupp AG in Essen', *Zentralbibliothek für Bibliothekswesen*, 54 (1937).

14 Richards, *Scientific Information*, pp. 23–6.

15 Pamela Spence Richards, 'German Libraries and Scientific and Technical Information in Nazi Germany', *Library Quarterly: Information, Community, Policy*, 55 (1985), pp. 151–73.

16 Alan D. Beyerchen, *Scientists under Hitler: Politics and the Physics Community in the Third Reich* (New Haven, CT: Yale University Press, 1977), pp. 33, 36.

17 Richards, *Scientific Information*, p. 60.

18 Steven P. Remy, *The Heidelberg Myth: The Nazification and Denazification of a German University* (Cambridge, MA: Harvard University Press, 2002), p. 86.

19 Michael B. Petersen, *Missiles for the Fatherland: Pennemünde, National Socialism and the V-2 Missile* (Cambridge: Cambridge University Press, 2009).

20 Richards, *Scientific Information*, p. 14; Simon Ings, *Stalin and the Scientists: A History of Triumph and Tragedy, 1905–1953* (New York: Atlantic Monthly, 2016), p. 329.

21 Richards, *Scientific Information*, p. 1.

22 Richards, *Scientific Information*, pp. 89–90.

23 Beyerchen, *Scientists under Hitler*, p. 43.

24 Richards, *Scientific Information*, p. 83; Joseph Borkin, *The Crime and Punishment of IG Farben* (London: Andre Deutsch, 1979).

25 Pamela Spence Richards, 'Scientific Information in Occupied France, 1940–1944', *Library Quarterly: Information, Community, Policy*, 62 (1992), pp. 295–305.

26 See further Chapter 14, below.

27 R. V. Jones, *Reflections on Intelligence* (London: Heinemann, 1989), pp. 174, 182–3.

28 Margaret Gowing, *Britain and Atomic Energy 1939–1945* (New York: St Martin's Press, 1964); Pamela Spence Richards, 'Aslib at War: The Brief but Intrepid Career of a Library Organization as a Hub of Allied Scientific Intelligence 1942–1945', *Journal of Education for Library and Information Science*, 29 (1989), pp. 279–96.

29 Pamela Spence Richards, 'Gathering Enemy Scientific Information in Wartime: The OSS and the Periodical Republication Programme', *Journal of Library History*, 16 (1981), pp. 253–64, at 256–7.

30 Olivier Rolin, *Stalin's Meteorologist* (London: Harvill Secker, 2017), pp. 44–5.

31 Ings, *Stalin and the Scientists*, pp. 247–50, 254.

32 Ings, *Stalin and the Scientists*, p. 56.

33 Ings, *Stalin and the Scientists*, p. 382.

34 Richards, *Scientific Information*, p. 125. Luther H. Evans, 'Research Libraries in the War Period, 1939–45', *Library Quarterly: Information, Community, Policy*, 17 (1947), pp. 241–62.

35 Richards, *Scientific Information*, p. 106.

36 And indeed for the Pettegree family, as my father had been transferred to India in preparation for the assault on mainland Japan.

5. The Spooks of Academe

1 Robin W. Winks, *Cloak and Gown: Scholars in the Secret War, 1939–1961*, 2nd ed. (New Haven, CT: Yale University Press, 1996), pp. 116–51. Winks tells a good tale, though as a Yale alumnus, his account privileges the contributions of fellow Yale men.

2 *Henry V*, Act 2, Scene 2.

3 Christopher Andrew, *Secret Service: The Making of the British Intelligence Community* (London: Heinemann, 1985), p. 1.

4 David Kahn, *The Codebreakers: The Story of Secret Writing* (London: Weidenfeld and Nicolson, 1966).

5 John Keegan, *Intelligence in War: Knowledge of the Enemy from Napoleon to al-Qaeda* (New York: Knopf, 2003), p. 18.

6 Mark Urban, *The Man Who Broke Napoleon's Codes: The Story of George Scovell* (London: Faber & Faber, 2001).

7 Hector C. Bywater and H. C. Ferraby, *Strange Intelligence: Memoirs of Naval Secret Service* (London: Frank Cass, 1998).

8 Sir Reginald Hall, *A Clear Case of Genius: Room 40's Code-Breaking Pioneer* (Stroud: History Press, 2017).

9 Christian Jennings, *The Third Reich Is Listening: Inside German Codebreaking, 1939–45* (Oxford: Osprey, 2018), pp. 23–5.

10 Winks, *Cloak and Gown*, p. 107.

11 Winks, *Cloak and Gown*, p. 79.

12 Barry M. Katz, *Foreign Intelligence: Research and Analysis in the Office of Strategic Services, 1942–1945* (Cambridge, MA: Harvard University Press, 1989), pp. 16–17, 50.

13 Katz, *Foreign Intelligence*, p. 27.

14 Adam Sissman, *Hugh Trevor-Roper* (London: Weidenfeld & Nicolson, 2010), p. 96.

15 Christopher Andrew, *Secret Service: The Making of the British Intelligence Community* (London: Heinemann, 1985), p. 459.

16 Max Hastings, *The Secret War: Spies, Codes and Guerillas, 1939–1945* (London: William Collins, 2015), p. 302.

17 Sönke Neitzel and Harald Welzer, *Soldaten: The Secret WWII Transcripts of German POWs* (New York: Knopf, 2012); Helen Fry, *The Walls Have Ears* (London: Yale University Press, 2019).

18 Jennings, *Third Reich Is Listening*, pp. 70–1.

19 Walter Schellenberg, *The Schellenberg Memoirs*, ed. Louis Hagen (London: Andre Deutsch, 1956), p. 119; Jennings, *Third Reich Is Listening*, p. 121.

20 Jennings, *Third Reich Is Listening*, pp. 60, 131, 165.

21 Richard Bassett, *Hitler's Spy Chief: The Wilhelm Canaris Mystery* (London: Cassell, 2005), p. 94.

22 Schellenberg, *Memoirs*, pp. 62, 120.

23 Bassett, *Hitler's Spy Chief*, p. 95.

24 Noël Coward, *Future Indefinite* (1954; repr. London: Bloomsbury, 2014), p. 92.
25 Below, Chapter 16. There is a modern translation based on the copy in the Imperial War Museum: John Erickson (ed.), *Invasion 1940: The Nazi Invasion Plan for Britain by SS General Walter Schellenberg* (London: St Ermin's Press, 2000).
26 Schellenberg, *Memoirs*, pp. 241, 318.
27 Chapter 16, below.
28 Andrews Hodges, *Alan Turing: The Enigma* (London: Vintage, 2014).
29 Michael Smith, *The Secrets of Station X: How Bletchley Park Helped Win the War* (London: Biteback, 2011), pp. 34–5.
30 Asa Briggs, *Secret Days: Code-Breaking in Bletchley House* (London: Frontline, 2011), pp. 7, 120.
31 Joan Thirsk was also the doctoral supervisor of the current author. She never mentioned her war work. James Thirsk, *Bletchley Park: An Inmate's Story* (Bromley: Galago, 2008).
32 Smith, *Secrets of Station X*, p. 35.
33 Erickson, *Invasion 1940*, p. xxvi; Colin B. Burke, *Information and Intrigue: From Index Cards to Dewey Decimals to Alger Hiss* (Cambridge, MA: MIT Press, 2014).
34 Alex Wright, *Cataloging the World: Paul Otlet and the Birth of the Information Age* (Oxford: Oxford University Press, 2014).
35 Stephen Budiansky, *Blackett's War: The Men Who Defeated the Nazi U-Boats and Brought Science to the Art of Warfare* (New York: Knopf Doubleday, 2013).
36 Edwin Black, *IBM and the Holocaust: The Strategic Alliance between Nazi Germany and America's Most Powerful Corporation,* 2nd paperback ed. (Washington, DC: Dialog Press, 2009). For a more critical view of Black's book see Michael Allen, 'Stranger than Science Fiction: Edwin Black, IBM and the Holocaust', *Technology and Culture*, 43 (2002), pp. 150–4.
37 Edward P. F. Rose, Jonathan C. Clatworthy and C. Paul Nathanail, 'Specialist Maps Prepared by British Military Geologists for the D-Day Landings and Operations in Normandy, 1944', *Cartographical Journal*, 43 (2006), pp. 117–43.
38 Hodges, *Turing*, p. 308. For a list of German intelligence failures see Jonathan Trigg, *To VE-Day through German Eyes* (Stroud: Amberley, 2020), p. 192.
39 Briggs, *Secret Days*, p. 127.
40 Hodges, *Turing*, p. 362.

6. Lines on a Map
1 John Tebbel, *A History of Book Publishing in the United States. IV: The Great Change, 1940–1980* (New York: Bowker, 1981), pp. 1, 15, 19.
2 *Bookseller*, no. 1836 (13 February 1941), pp. 108, 110, 130.
3 Simon Garfield, *We Are at War* (London: Ebury Press, 2005), p. 99.
4 *Library Association Record*, 42 (1940), pp. 231, 260. *Bookseller*, no. 1831 (9 January 1941), p. 26.
5 *Library Association Record*, 45 (1943), p. 3.
6 Edward Stebbing, *Diary of a Decade, 1939–1950* (Lewes: Book Guild, 1998), p. 176.

7 Peter Caddick-Adams, *Monte Cassino: Ten Armies in Hell* (London: Arrow, 2013), p. 137.

8 Quoted in Riaz Dean, *Mapping the Great Game: Explorers, Spies and Maps in 19th-century Asia* (Oxford: Casemate, 2019), p. 249

9 David Buisseret (ed.), *Monarchs, Ministers and Maps: The Emergence of Cartography as a Tool of Government in Early Modern Europe* (Chicago: University of Chicago Press, 1992).

10 Helmer Helmers, 'Cartography, War Correspondence and News Publishing: The Early Career of Nicolaes van Geelkercken, 1610–1630', in Joad Raymond and Noah Moxham (eds), *News Networks in Early Modern Europe* (Leiden: Brill, 2016), pp. 350–74, at p. 359.

11 Dean, *Mapping the Great Game*.

12 Dean, *Mapping the Great Game*, p. 133.

13 Ian Cameron, *To the Farthest Ends of the Earth: The History of the Royal Geographical Society, 1830–1980* (London: Macdonald and Jane's, 1980), p. 206.

14 Hugh Robert Mill, *Catalogue of the Library of the Royal Geographical Society* (London: Royal Geographical Society/John Murray, 1895).

15 Earle B. McElfresh, *Maps and Mapmakers of the Civil War* (New York: Abrams, 1999).

16 James I. Robertson, *Stonewall Jackson: The Man, the Soldier, the Legend* (New York: Macmillan, 1997); John Keegan, *Intelligence in War: Knowledge of the Enemy from Napoleon to Al-Qaeda* (London: Pimlico, 2004), Chapter 3.

17 McElfresh, *Maps and Mapmakers*, p. 30.

18 McElfresh, *Maps and Mapmakers*, p. 27.

19 Peter Chasseaud, *Rats' Alley: British Trench Names of the Western Front, 1914–1918* (Stroud: History Press, 2017).These examples are taken from the collection of the Imperial War Museum, https://www.iwm.org.uk/collections.

20 Michael Heffernan, 'Geography, Cartography and Military Intelligence: The Royal Geographical Society and the First World War', *Transactions of the Institute of British Geographers*, 21 (1996), pp. 504–33.

21 Hugh Clout and Cyril Gosme, 'The Naval Intelligence Handbooks: A Monument in Geographical Writing', *Progress in Human Geography*, 27 (2003), pp. 153–73, at pp. 154–5.

22 Heffernan, 'Geography', p. 520.

23 Guntram Henrik Herb, *Under the Map of Germany: Nationalism and Propaganda, 1918–1945* (London: Routledge, 1997), p. 16.

24 Herb, *Under the Map of Germany*, p. 79.

25 Herb, *Under the Map of Germany*, pp. 111, 133.

26 Herb, *Under the Map of Germany*, pp. 136, 138, 156.

27 Matthew D. Mingus, *Remapping Modern Germany after National Socialism, 1945–1961* (Syracuse, NY: Syracuse University Press, 2017).

28 Alice Hudson, 'The New York Public Library's Map Division Goes to War', *Bulletin, Special Libraries Association, Geography and Map Division*, 182 (1996), pp. 2–25.

29 Leonard S. Wilson, 'Lessons from the Experience of the Map Information Section, OSS', *Geographical Review*, 39 (1949), pp. 298–301.

30 Trevor J. Barnes, 'Geographical Intelligence: American Geographers and Research and Analysis in the Office of Strategic Services, 1941–1945', *Journal of Historical Geography*, 32 (2006), pp. 149–68.

31 Hudson, 'New York Public Library', p. 2

32 Wilson, 'Lessons', p. 306.

33 See below, Chapter 16.

34 Mary E. DeLong, 'Trailblazing and Pioneering Mapmakers: A Case Study of Women Cartographers and Geographers during World War II' (master's thesis, Harvard University, 2013).

35 Mary Murphy, 'History of the Army Map Service Collection', in Richard W. Stephenson (ed.), *Federal Government Map Collecting: A Brief History* (Washington, DC: Special Libraries Association, 1969).

36 Murphy, 'History of the Army Map Service Collection', pp. 165, 169.

37 Hugh Clout and Cyril Gosme, 'The Naval Intelligence Handbooks: A Monument in Geographical Writing', *Progress in Human Geography*, 27 (2003), pp. 153–73; W. G. V. Balchin, 'United Kingdom Geographers in the Second World War: A Report', *Geographical Journal*, 153 (1987), pp. 170–1.

38 Edward P. F. Rose, Jonathan C. Clatworthy and C. Paul Nathanail, 'Specialist Maps Prepared by British Military Geologists for the D-Day Landings and Operations in Normandy', *Cartographical Journal*, 43 (2006), pp. 117–43.

39 Barbara A. Bond, *Great Escapes: The Story of MI9's Second World War Escape and Evasion Maps* (Glasgow: HarperCollins, 2015)

40 Walter Kempowski, *Swansong: A Collective Diary of the Last Days of the Third Reich* (New York: Norton, 2015), p. 158.

7. Print for Victory

1 Winston Churchill, 'The Defence of Freedom and Peace' (speech, 1938), https://winstonchurchill.org/resources/speeches/1930-1938-the-wilderness/the-defence-of-freedom-and-peace/.

2 Robert O. Ballou, *A History of the Council on Books in Wartime* (New York: Country Life, 1946).

3 Jan-Pieter Barbian, *The Politics of Literature in Nazi Germany* (New York: Bloomsbury, 2013), p. 352.

4 See below, Chapter 11. M. L. Sanders 'Wellington House and British Propaganda during the First World War', *Historical Journal*, 18 (1975), pp. 119–46.

5 Georg Jäger and Minka Esterman, 'Geschichtliche Grundlagen und Entwicklung des Buchhandels im Deutschen Reich bis 1871', in Georg Jäger (ed.), *Geschichte des deutschen Buchhandels im 19. und 20. Jahrhundert: Das Kaiserreich 1871–1918* (Frankfurt: Buchhändler Vereinigung, 2001), I, 1:18; Reinhard Wittman, *Geschichte des deutschen Buchhandels: Ein Überblick* (Munich: Beck, 1991), p. 271.

6 Roger Chickering, *The Great War and Urban Life in Germany: Freiburg, 1914–1918* (Cambridge: Cambridge University Press, 2007).

7 Mary Hammond and Shafquat Towheed (eds), *Publishing in the First World War: Essays in Book History* (Basingstoke: Palgrave Macmillan, 2007), p. 4.

8 Stanley Unwin, *The Truth about a Publisher* (London: George Allen and Unwin, 1960), pp. 131, 143–4; Jane Potter, 'For Country, Conscience and Commerce:

Publishers and Publishing, 1914–8', in Hammond and Towheed, *Publishing in the First World War*, pp. 11–26.

9 Potter, 'For Country, Conscience and Commerce', p. 16; Unwin, *Truth*, 141.

10 Chickering, *Great War and Urban Life*, pp. 423, 435.

11 Chickering, *Great War and Urban Life*, pp. 384–8.

12 Unwin, *Truth*, pp. 154–5.

13 Chickering, *Great War and Urban Life*, pp. 98–110; Chris Williams, 'Wonders of Science! The German Air Campaign against Britain, 1915–1918', unpublished paper.

14 Peter Englund, *The Beauty and the Sorrow* (London: Profile, 2011), p. 485; Geert Buelens, *Everything to Nothing: The Poetry of the Great War, Revolution and the Transformation of Europe* (London: Verso, 2015), p. 298.

15 Stephen Colclough, '"No Such Bookselling Has Ever before Taken Place in this Country": Propaganda and the Wartime Distribution practices of W. H. Smith & Son', in Hammond and Towheed, *Publishing in the First World War*, pp. 27–45, at p. 42.

16 Colclough, '"No Such Bookselling"', p. 38.

17 Potter, 'For Country, Conscience and Commerce', p. 22.

18 John Tebbel, *A History of Book Publishing in the United States. II: The Expansion of an Industry, 1865–1919* (New York: Bowker, 1975), pp. 83–4.

19 Michael Korda, *Making the List: A Cultural History of the American Bestseller, 1900–1999* (New York: Barnes & Noble, 2001), pp. 33–53.

20 Andrew Pettegree and Arthur der Weduwen, *The Library: A Fragile History* (London: Profile, 2021), Chapter 17.

21 John Tebbel, *A History of Book Publishing in the United States. III: The Golden Age between Two Wars, 1920–1940* (New York: Bowker, 1978), pp. 43, 435–8.

22 Janice A. Radway, *A Feeling for Books: The Book-of-the-Month Club, Literary Taste and Middle-Class Desire* (Chapel Hill: University of North Carolina Press, 1997); James D. Hart, *The Popular Book: A History of America's Literary Taste* (New York: Oxford University Press, 1950), p. 273.

23 Barbian, *Politics of Literature*, p. 25.

24 Barbian, *Politics of Literature*, pp. 33–9.

25 Hans-Eugen Bühler with Edelgard Bühler, *Der Frontbuchhandel, 1939–1945* (Frankfurt am Main: De Gruyter Aaur, 2002). See Chapter 10 below.

26 Barbian, *Politics of Literature*, pp. 333, 376.

27 Barbian, *Politics of Literature*, p. 259.

28 Barbian, *Politics of Literature*, pp. 294–5.

29 Anonymous [Marta Hillers], *A Woman in Berlin* (London: Virago, 2011), p. 153.

30 Henry Irving, '"Propaganda Bestsellers": British Official War Books, 1941–1946', in Cynthia Johnston (ed.), *The Concept of the Book: The Production, Progression and Dissemination of Information* (London: Institute of English Studies, 2019), pp. 125–46.

31 Valerie Holman, *Book Publishing in England, 1939–1945* (London: British Library, 2008).

32 Jeremy Lewis, *Penguin Special: The Life and Times of Allen Lane* (London: Viking, 2005), p. 155.

33 E. Haldeman-Julius, *The First Hundred Million* (New York: Simon & Schuster, 1928); Tebbel, *Golden Age*, pp. 203–9.

34 Kenneth C. Davis, *Two-Bit Culture: The Paperbacking of America* (Boston: Houghton Mifflin, 1984), pp. 21–5; Alistair McCleery, 'Tauchnitz and Albatross: A "Community of Interests" in English-Language Paperback Publishing, 1934–51', *The Library*, 7th ser., 7 (2006), pp. 297–316.

35 Lewis, *Penguin Special*, p. 97.

36 J. P. Morpurgo, *Allen Lane: King Penguin* (London: Hutchinson, 1979), p. 131.

37 See Chapter 10, below.

38 Frederick Grisewood, *The Kitchen Front: 122 Wartime Recipes Specially Selected by the Ministry of Food* (London: Nicholson and Watson, 1942).

39 Christian Lamb, *Beyond the Sea: A Wren at War* (London: Mardle, 2021), p. 214.

40 Jessamyn Neuhaus, *Manly Meals and Mom's Home Cooking: Cookbooks and Gender in Modern America* (Baltimore, MD: Johns Hopkins University Press, 2003), p. 142.

41 Karina Urbach, *Alice's Book: How the Nazis Stole My Grandmother's Cookbook* (London: MacLehose Press, 2022), pp. 150–72.

8. Reading in Wartime

1 Richard Broad and Suzie Fleming, *Nella Last's War: A Mother's Diary, 1939–1945* (Bristol: Falling Wall, 1981); reprinted as *Nella Last's War: The Second World War Diaries of a Housewife, 49* (London: Profile, 2006). Patricia and Robert Malcolmson, *The Diaries of Nella Last. Writing in War and Peace* (London: Profile, 2012).

2 See Chapter 10, for books for the troops. See also Wayne A. Wiegand, *An Active Instrument for Propaganda: The American Public Library during World War I* (New York: Greenwood, 1989).

3 Dee Garrison, *Apostles of Culture: The Public Librarian and American Society, 1876–1920* (London: Free Press, 1979).

4 Alistair Black, *The Public Library in Britain, 1914–2000* (London: British Library, 2000), p. 29.

5 Black, *Public Library*, p. 24.

6 The correspondence was printed in the September 1939 issue of the *Library Association Record*.

7 Dale C. Russell, '"Our Special Providence": Providing a Library Service for London's Public Shelters, 1940–1942', *Library History*, 13 (1997), pp. 3–15; *Library Association Record*, February 1941, pp. 1–2.

8 *Library Association Record*, November 1941, p. 200, November 1943, p. 219.

9 University of Sussex, Mass Observation Archive (MOA), 'Books and the Public', June 1942. MOA FR 1332.

10 For a vivid testimony to the pressures on shop owners see Patricia and Robert Malcolmson, *The View from the Corner Shop: The Diary of a Wartime Shop Assistant* (New York: Simon & Schuster, 2016).

11 Robert James, '"Read for Victory": Public Libraries and Book Reading in a British Naval Port City during the Second World War', *Cultural and Social History*, 15 (2018), pp. 233–53, at p. 242.

12 MOA FR 1332, p. 156.

13 Robert James, "'Literature Acknowledges no Boundaries": Book Reading and Social Class in Britain, *c*. 1930–*c*. 1945', *Social History*, 51 (2017), pp. 80–100.

14 James, "'Read for Victory'", p. 345.

15 Patricia and Robert Malcolmson, *A Parson in Wartime: The Boston Diary of the Reverend Arthur Hopkins, 1942–1945* (Lincoln: Lincoln Record Society, 2017).

16 Patricia and Robert Malcolmson, *A Free-Spirited Woman: The London Diaries of Gladys Langford, 1936–1940* (London: London Record Society, 2014).

17 Robin Woolven (ed.), *The London Diary of Anthony Heap, 1931–1945* (London: London Record Society, 2017), pp. 190, 191, 193, 415.

18 Sandra Koa Wing (ed.), *Our Longest Day: A People's History of the Second World War* (London: Profile, 2008), pp. 133, 267.

19 Patricia and Robert Malcolmson, *Dorset in Wartime: The Diary of Phyllis Walther 1941–1942* (Dorset Record Society, 2009), p. 111.

20 Broad and Fleming, *Nella Last's War*, p. 103.

21 *Library Association Record*, 41 (1939), p. 37.

22 Patricia and Robert Malcolmson, *A Soldier in Bedfordshire 1941–1942: The Diary of Private Denis Argent, Royal Engineers* (Bedford: Bedfordshire Historical Record Society, 2009), p. 69.

23 *Bookseller*, no. 1783 (1 February 1940), p. 96.

24 Malcolmson, *View from the Corner Shop*, pp. 39, 54, 78.

25 Malcolmson, *A Parson in Wartime*, p. 70.

26 Henry Irving, "'Propaganda Bestsellers'".

27 Information on these and other new titles is drawn from the *Bookseller*, for 1939–42, which also contains most useful information on prices and print runs.

28 *Bookseller*, no. 1808 (25 July 1940), p. 142. The price was one shilling for the poster, mounted on board with cord for hanging.

29 Patrick Bishop, *Air Force Blue: The RAF in World War Two* (London: William Collins, 2017); Patrick Bishop, *Fighter Boys: Saving Britain 1940* (London: HarperCollins, 2003).

30 Charles de Gaulle, *The Army of the Future* (London: Hutchinson, 1940).

31 *Bookseller*, no. 1821 (24 October 1940), pp. 412, 414.

32 Robert Scott Kellner (ed.), *My Opposition: The Diary of Friedrich Kellner* (Cambridge: Cambridge University Press, 2018), pp. 221–2.

33 Margaret F. Stieg, *Public Libraries in Nazi Germany* (Tuscaloosa: University of Alabama Press, 1992). Gertrud E. Kallmann, 'German Public Libraries and Their Principles of Book Selection', *Library Association Record*, 36 (1934), pp. 169–72.

34 Muriel Green, 'Two Months in a German Library', *Library Association Record*, 38 (1936), pp. 614–15.

35 Robert F. Ashby, 'The German Public Library', *Library Association Record*, 39 (1937), pp. 379–84.

36 Margaret F. Stieg, 'The Second World War and the Public Libraries of Nazi Germany', *Journal of Contemporary History*, 27 (1992), pp. 23–40.

37 Stieg, 'Second World War', pp. 36–7.

38 Douglas Botting, *In the Ruins of the Reich* (London: George Allen and Unwin, 1985), pp. 15–20.

39 Michael Korda, *Making the List: A Cultural History of the American Bestseller, 1900–1999* (New York: Barnes and Noble, 2001).

40 James D. Hart, *The Popular Book: A History of America's Literary Taste* (New York: Oxford University Press, 1950), pp. 273–6.

41 Hart, *The Popular Book*, pp. 273, 276.

9. Blacklists

1 Molly Guptill Manning, *When Books Went to War: The Stories that Helped Us Win World War II* (New York: Houghton Mifflin Harcourt, 2014), p. 48.

2 Erik Kirschbaum, *Burning Beethoven: The Eradication of German Culture in the United States during World War I* (New York: Berlinica, 2015).

3 Wayne Wiegand, 'An Active Instrument for Propaganda': The American Public Library during World War I* (New York: Greenwood Press, 1989), pp. 7, 106.

4 Wiegand, 'An Active Instrument', p. 58.

5 Wiegand, 'An Active Instrument', pp. 107–8.

6 Wiegand, 'An Active Instrument', p. 111.

7 Stanley Unwin, *The Truth about a Publisher* (London: George Allen & Unwin, 1960), pp. 140–1.

8 Leonidas E. Hill, 'The Nazi Attack on "Un-German" Literature, 1933–1945', in Jonathan Rose (ed.), *The Holocaust and the Book* (Amherst: University of Massachusetts Press, 2001), pp. 9–46.

9 Jan-Pieter Barbian, *The Politics of Literature in Nazi Germany* (New York: Bloomsbury, 2013), p. 25.

10 Barbian, *Politics of Literature*, pp. 336–52.

11 From a typescript in the Bundesarchiv Koblenz, reprinted in Gerhard Sauder, *Die Bücherverbrennung: Zum 10. Mai 1933* (Munich: Hanser, 1983).

12 Barbian, *Politics of Literature*, pp. 193–7.

13 Barbian, *Politics of Literature*, pp. 236–7.

14 Jenny Williams, *More Lives than One: A Biography of Hans Fallada* (London: Libris, 1998).

15 Unwin, *Truth about a Publisher*, pp. 260–1.

16 Ruth Dudley Edwards, *Victor Gollancz: A Biography* (London: Victor Gollancz, 1987), pp. 246–8.

17 Valerie Holman, *Print for Victory: Book Publishing in England, 1939–1945* (London: British Library, 2008), p. 243.

18 Peter Berresford Ellis and Piers Williams, *By Jove, Biggles! The Life of Captain W. E. Johns* (London: W. H. Allen, 1981), pp. 144–73.

19 Richard Griffiths, 'The Reception of Bryant's *Unfinished Victory*: Insights into British Public Opinion in Early 1940', *Patterns of Prejudice*, 38 (2004), pp. 18–36; Pamela Street, *Arthur Bryant: Portrait of a Historian* (London: HarperCollins, 1979), pp. 104–11, attempts to place this episode in a more sympathetic context (Street was Bryant's former personal assistant). Andrew Roberts, *Eminent Churchillians* (London: Simon & Schuster, 1994), pp. 287–322, takes a far more critical perspective.

20 Adam Sissman, *Hugh Trevor-Roper* (London: Weidenfeld & Nicolson, 2010), p. 79.

21 *Diary of a Staff Officer* (6th ed., May 1941), pp. 29, 45.

22 Patricia and Robert Malcolmson, *A Soldier in Bedfordshire 1941–1942: The Diary of Private Denis Argent, Royal Engineers* (Bedford: Bedfordshire Historical Record Society, 2009), p. 3.

23 Simon Garfield, *We Are at War* (London: Ebury Press, 2005), p. 170.

24 *Library Association Record*, 42 (1940), pp. 180, 270.

25 Patricia and Robert Malcolmson, *The View from the Corner Shop: The Diary of a Wartime Shop Assistant* (New York: Simon & Schuster, 2016), pp. 42, 54 (16 August, 10 September 1941).

26 Robert McCrum, *Wodehouse: A Life* (London: Viking, 2004), pp. 267–358.

27 A selection is printed in Iain Sproat, *Wodehouse at War* (London: Milner, 1981), pp. 15–25.

28 William Neil Connor, *Cassandra at His Finest and Funniest* (London: Daily Mirror, 1967); Sproat, *Wodehouse at War*, pp. 13–15; McCrum, *Wodehouse*, pp. 318–19.

29 *Library Association Record*, 43 (1941), pp. 170, 186–7; 44 (1942), p. 5; 45 (1943), p. 191.

30 *Bookseller*, no. 1861 (7 August 1941), p. 172.

31 Patricia and Robert Malcolmson, *A Woman in Wartime London: The Diary of Kathleen Tipper 1941–1945* (London: London Record Society, 2006), p. 81 (1 February 1944).

32 *Library Association Record*, 44 (1942), p. 83.

33 Holman, *Print for Victory*, pp. 216–19.

34 Malcolmson, *Soldier in Bedfordshire*, pp. 142, 149.

35 James J. and Patience P. Barnes, *Hitler's Mein Kampf in Britain and America: A Publishing History, 1930–1939* (Cambridge: Cambridge University Press, 1980), p. 64.

36 *Library Association Record*, 41 (1939), p. 596; Holman, *Print for Victory*, p. 254.

37 Chris McCooey (ed.), *Despatches from the Home Front: The War Diaries of Joan Strange, 1939–1945* (Tunbridge Wells: JAK, 1994), p. 1.

38 A story told with customary panache in Owen Dudley Edwards, *British Children's Fiction in the Second World War* (Edinburgh: Edinburgh University Press, 2007), pp. 94–5. See also Stephanie Spencer, 'No "Fear of Flying"? Worrals of the WAAF, Fiction, and Girls' Informal Wartime Education', *Paedagogica Historica*, 52 (2016), pp. 137–53.

39 *Bookseller*, no. 1776 (14 December 1939), p. 865; no. 1816 (19 September 1940), p. 329; no. 1821 (24 October 1940), p. 417; no. 1829 (19 December 1940), p. 636.

10. Troops

1 Molly Guptill Manning, *When Books Went to War: The Stories that Helped Us Win World War II* (New York: Houghton Mifflin Harcourt, 2014), p. 102; Christopher P. Loss, 'Reading between Enemy Lines: Armed Services Editions and World War II', *Journal of Military History*, 67 (2003), pp. 811–34.

2 John Tebbel, *A History of Book Publishing in the United States. IV: The Great Change, 1940–1980* (New York: Bowker, 1981), p. 32.

3 Tebbel, *History of Book Publishing*, p. 32.

4 Patricia and Robert Malcolmson, *A Soldier in Bedfordshire 1941–1942: The Diary of Private Denis Argent, Royal Engineers* (Bedford: Bedfordshire Historical Record Society, 2009).

5 Arthur P. Young, *Books for Sammies: The American Library Association and World War I* (Pittsburgh, PA: Beta Phi Mu, 1981).

6 Wayne A. Wiegand, *'An Active Instrument for Propaganda': The American Public Library during World War I* (New York: Greenwood, 1989), p. 64.

7 Wiegand, *'An Active Instrument'*, p. 45.

8 Alistair Black, *The Public Library in Britain, 1914–2000* (London: British Library, 2000), pp. 13–48.

9 Mary Burgoyne, '"Writing Man to Fighting Man": Conrad Republished for the Armed Services during the World Wars', *The Conradian*, 38 (2013), pp. 99–127.

10 John Lewis-Stempel, *Six Weeks: The Short and Gallant Life of the British Officer in the First World War* (London: Weidenfeld & Nicolson, 2010).

11 J. G. Fuller, *Troop Morale and Popular Culture in the British and Dominion Armies, 1914–1918* (Oxford: Clarendon Press, 1990), p. 149.

12 This would still be the case in the 1940s, when Mass Observation conducted its surveys.

13 Lewis-Stempel, *Six Weeks*, pp. 98–101.

14 Malcolm Brown and Ian Hislop (eds), *The Wipers Times: The Complete Series of the Famous Wartime Trench Newspaper* (London: Little Books, 2013).

15 Fuller, *Troop Morale*, pp. 13–14. For a survey of surviving collections see John Pegum, 'British Trench Journals and a Geography of Identity', in Mary Hammond and Shafquat Towheed (eds), *Publishing in the First World War: Essays in Book History* (Basingstoke: Palgrave Macmillan, 2007), pp. 129–47.

16 *Library Association Record*, 42 (1940), pp. 94 (Derbyshire), 273 (Herts), 43 (1941), 39 (Liverpool), 44 (1942), 192 (Kent).

17 *Library Association Record*, 42 (1940), p. 154.

18 *Library Association Record*, 45 (1943), pp. 329–31.

19 *Library Association Record*, 45 (1943), p. 189; 47 (1945), pp. 24–30.

20 John Jamieson, *Books for the Army* (New York: Columbia University Press, 1950).

21 Quoted in Guptill Manning, *When Books Went to War*, p. 31.

22 Quoted in Guptill Manning, *When Books Went to War*, p. 53.

23 Jeremy Lewis, *Penguin Special: The Life and Times of Allen Lane* (London: Viking, 2005), pp. 164–5.

24 Lewis, *Penguin Special*, p. 162.

25 *Library Association Record*, 44 (1942), p. 89; 46 (1944), pp. 175–7.

26 Robert O. Ballou and Irene Rakosky, *History of the Council on Books in Wartime* (New York: Country Life Press, 1946).

27 Guptill Manning, *When Books Went to War*, pp. 88–9.

28 Guptill Manning, *When Books Went to War*, p. xi.

29 David Hajdu, *The Ten-Cent Plague: The Great Comic-Book Scare and How It Changed America* (New York: Farrar, Straus and Giroux, 2008), pp. 55, 70; Manning, *When Books Went to War*, pp. 55–7; Christopher Murray, *Champion of the Oppressed: Superhero Comics, Popular Culture and Propaganda in America during World War II* (Cresskill, NJ: Hampton Press, 2011).

30 Patrick Bishop, *Air Force Blue. The RAF in World War Two* (London: William Collins, 2017).

31 S. P. MacKenzie, 'Vox Populi: British Army Newspapers in the Second World War', *Journal of Contemporary History*, 24 (1989), pp. 665–81, at p. 666; Michael Anglo, *Service Newspapers of the Second World War* (London: Jupiter, 1977).

32 Egbert White, 'A Free Press in a Citizen's Army', *Journal of Educational Sociology*, 19 (1945), pp. 236–48, at p. 246.

33 Barrett McGurn, *Yank, the Army Weekly: Reporting the Greatest Generation* (Golden, CO: Fulcrum Publishing, 2004). A selection of articles from *Yank* is available in Steve Kluger, *Yank, the Army Weekly: World War II from the Guys Who Brought You Victory* (London: Arms and Armour, 1991).

34 Jan-Pieter Barbian, *The Politics of Literature in Nazi Germany* (New York: Bloomsbury, 2013), pp. 121, 281.

35 Barbian, *Politics of Literature*, pp. 144, 283.

36 Barbian, *Politics of Literature*, p. 375, citing Elke Fröhlich (ed.), *Die Tagebücher von Joseph Goebbels*, 29 vols (Munich: Saur, 1993–2008), III, 382 (27 February 1942).

37 *Tagebücher von Joseph Goebbels*, VI, 332 (25 November 1942).

38 Barbian, *Politics of Literature*, pp. 281–4.

39 Barbian, *Politics of Literature*, p. 285.

11. The Author at War

1 Peter Buitenhuis, *The Great War of Words: Literature as Propaganda 1914–1918 and After* (London: Batsford, 1989).

2 Wayne A. Wiegand, 'British Propaganda in American Public Libraries, 1914–1917', *Journal of Library History*, 18 (1983), pp. 237–54.

3 Buitenhuis, *Great War of Words*, p. 24.

4 Jessica Meyer, 'The Tuition of Manhood: "Sapper's" War Stories and the Literature of War', in Mary Hammond and Shafquat Towheed (eds), *Publishing in the First World War: Essays in Book History* (Basingstoke: Palgrave Macmillan, 2007), pp. 113–28.

5 Ursula Buchan, *Beyond the Thirty-Nine Steps: A Life of John Buchan* (London: Bloomsbury, 2019), p. 180. By 1965, it had sold 1.5 million copies.

6 John Buchan, *The Battle of the Somme* (London: Nelson, 1916), p. 31; Hew Strachan, 'John Buchan and the First World War: Fact into Fiction', *War and History*, 16 (2009), pp. 298–324; Buitenhuis, *Great War of Words*, pp. 93–8.

7 Quoted in Buitenhuis, *Great War of Words*, p. 110.

8 Buitenhuis, *Great War of Words*, p. 171.

9 Robert Hewison, *Under Siege: Literary Life in London, 1939–1945* (New York: Oxford University Press, 1977).

10 Valerie Holman, *Print for Victory: Book Publishing in England, 1939–1945* (London: British Library, 2008), p. 57.

11 Holman, *Print for Victory*, p. 127; Henry Irving, '"Propaganda Bestsellers": British Official War Books, 1941–1946', in Cynthia Johnston (ed.), *The Concept of the Book: The Production, Progression and Dissemination of Information* (London: Institute of English Studies, 2019), pp. 125–46.

12 Dorothy Sheridan, *Among You Taking Notes: The Wartime Diary of Naomi Mitchison, 1939–1945* (London: Gollancz, 1985).

13 Owen Dudley Edwards, *British Children's Fiction in the Second World War* (Edinburgh: Edinburgh University Press, 2007); Peter Berresford Ellis and Piers Williams, *By Jove, Biggles! The Life of Captain W. E. Johns* (London: W. H. Allen, 1981).

14 James Lansdale Hodson, *Through the Dark Night* (London: Victor Gollancz, 1941).

15 Holman, *Print for Victory*, p. 98.

16 Michael Strobel, 'Writings of History: Authenticity and Self-Censorship in William L. Shirer's *Berlin Diary*, *German Life and Letters*, 66 (2013), pp. 308–25.

17 Richard Hillary, *The Last Enemy* (London: Macmillan, 1942).

18 Sebastian Faulks, *The Fatal Englishman* (London: Hutchinson, 1996).

19 Michael Harrison, *Peter Cheyney: Prince of Hokum* (London: N. Spearman, 1954).

20 Constance Miles, *Mrs Miles's Diary: The Wartime Journal of a Housewife on the Home Front*, ed. S. V. Partington (New York: Simon & Schuster, 2013).

21 Steve Hare, *Penguin Portrait* (London: Penguin, 1995), pp. 89–90.

22 *The Life of Florence L. Barclay, by One of Her Daughters* (London: Putnam, 1921).

23 Hare, *Penguin Portrait*, p. 114.

24 Betty Smith, 'Who Died?', *New York Times Magazine*, 9 July 1944; Molly Guptill Manning, *When Books Went to War: The Stories that Helped Us Win World War II* (New York: Mariner, 2014), pp. 105–9.

25 Joseph Goebbels, *Die Tagebücher: Diktate 1941–1945. 9: Juli–September 1943* (Munich: Saur, 1987).

26 Selena Hastings, *Evelyn Waugh: A Biography* (London: Sinclair-Stevenson, 1994), pp. 451–2.

27 Hastings, *Evelyn Waugh*, pp. 456–62.

28 John Sutherland, *Reading the Decades: Fifty Years of the Nation's Bestselling Books* (London: BBC Worldwide, 2002).

29 See above, Chapter 7.

30 Jan-Pieter Barbian, *The Politics of Literature in Nazi Germany: Books in the Media Dictatorship* (New York: Bloomsbury, 2013), p. 15.

31 Barbian, *Politics of Literature*, pp. 73–9.

32 Joseph Goebbels, *Vom Kaiserhof zur Reichskanzlei: Eine historische Darstellung in Tagebuchblättern* (Munich: Eher, 1934), translated into English as *My Part in Germany's Fight* (London: Hurst & Blackett, 1935).

33 Anson Rabinbach, 'The Reader, the Popular Novel and the Imperative to Participate: Reflections on Public and Private Experience in the Third Reich', *History and Memory*, 3 (1991), pp. 5–44; George L. Mosse, 'What Germans Really Read', in his *Mass and Man: Nationalist and Fascist Perceptions of Reality* (New York: Howard Fertig, 1980). A pirate edition in Japanese also sold 200,000 copies, for which Margaret Mitchell received no royalty, but the gift of a doll.

34 Albert Speer, *Spandau: The Secret Diaries* (London: Macmillan, 1976), p. 347; Barbian, *Politics of Literature*, pp. 341, 365–6.

35 Gisèle Shapiro, *The French Writers' War, 1940–1953* (Durham, NC: Duke

University Press, 1994); Philip Short, *Mitterrand: A Study in Ambiguity* (London: Bodley Head, 2013), pp. 61–111.

36 Julian Jackson, *A Certain Idea of France: The Life of Charles de Gaulle* (London: Allen Lane, 2019), p. 757; Alice Kaplan, *The Collaborator: The Trial and Execution of Robert Brasillach* (Chicago: University of Chicago Press, 2001).

37 André Gide, *Journals 1889–1949*, ed. Justin O'Brien (London: Penguin, 1978), pp. 646, 649.

38 There were 1,200 in Poland, 1,000 in France, 800 in Denmark, 800 in Norway, 1,200 in the Netherlands and 500 in Belgium. Halik Kochanski, *Resistance: The Underground War in Europe, 1939–1945* (London: Allen Lane, 2022), p. 40.

39 Harry Stone, *Writing in the Shadows: Resistance Publications in Occupied Europe* (London: Frank Cass, 1996), pp. 50, 56.

40 Jeroen Dewulf, *Spirit of Resistance: Dutch Clandestine Literature during the Nazi Occupation* (Rochester, NY: Camden House, 2010), pp. 47, 49.

41 Dewulf, *Spirit of Resistance*, p. 6.

42 Anne Frank, *The Diary of a Young Girl, Anne Frank*, ed. Otto Frank and Mirjam Pressler, tr. Susan Massotty (London: Viking, 1997). The first English translation was published in 1952.

43 Carol Ann Lee, *The Hidden Life of Otto Frank* (London: Viking, 2002), pp. 169, 172–3; Dewulf, *Spirit of Resistance*, p. 192. The classic survey of this clandestine literature is Dirk de Jong, *Het Vrije Boek in onvrije tijd. Bibliografie van illegale en clandestiene Bellettrie* (Leiden: Sijthoff, 1958).

12. The Great Escape

1   Imperial War Museum 88/20/1.

2   Robert Kee, *A Crowd Is not Company*, 2nd ed. (London: Jonathan Cape, 1982), p. 115.

3   R. P. L. Mogg, *For this Alone* (Oxford: Blackwell, 1943); Rita Ricketts, *Scholars, Poets and Radicals: Discovering Forgotten Lives in the Blackwell Collection* (Oxford: Bodleian Library, 2015), p. 218.

4   Francis Stewart, diary entry, 10 March 1945, Imperial War Museum 88/20/1. Quoted in Clare Makepeace, *Captives of War: British Prisoners of War in Europe in the Second World War* (Cambridge: Cambridge University Press, 2017), p. 70.

5   Midge Gillies, *The Barbed-Wire University: The Real Lives of Allied Prisoners of War in the Second World War* (London: Aurum, 2011), p. 260.

6   Letter printed in *The Prisoner of War*, 3, 31 (November 1944), p. 5.

7   Rainer Pöppinghege, 'The Battle of the Books: Supplying Prisoners of War', in Mary Hammond and Shafquat Towheed (eds), *Publishing in the First World War: Essays in Book History* (Basingstoke: Palgrave Macmillan, 2007), pp. 78–92, at p. 78.

8   Pöppinghege, 'Battle of the Books', p. 79. On the Second World War see Simon Parkin, *The Island of Extraordinary Captives* (London: Sceptre, 2022).

9   Michael Foley, *Prisoners of the British: Internees and Prisoners of War during the First World War* (Stroud: Fonthill, 2015), p. 40; Robert Jackson, *The Prisoners, 1914–18* (London: Routledge, 1989).

10 Pöppinghege, 'Battle of the Books', pp. 78–9.

11 Edmund G. C. King, '"Books Are More to Me Than Food": British Prisoners of War as Readers, 1914–1918', *Book History*, 16 (2013), pp. 246–71; Oliver Wilkinson, *British Prisoners of War in First World War Germany* (Cambridge: Cambridge University Press, 2019).

12 King, '"Books Are More to Me Than Food"', pp. 251–2.

13 Alfred T. Davies, *Student Captives: An Account of the Work of the British Prisoner of Work Book Scheme (Educational)* (Leicester: Stevens, 1917), p. 17, quoted in King, '"Books Are More to Me Than Food"', p. 253.

14 King, '"Books Are More to Me Than Food"', p. 256.

15 *Ruhleben Camp Magazine*, 1916–17. Consulted in St Andrews University Special Collections: rD627.G3A15.

16 P. G. Cambray and G. C. B. Briggs, *Red Cross & St John: The Official Record of Humanitarians Services of the War Organisation of the British Red Cross and Order of St John of Jerusalem, 1939–1947* (London: Aurum, 1949).

17 Patricia and Robert Malcolmson, *A Parson in Wartime: The Boston Diary of the Reverend Arthur Hopkins, 1942–1945* (Lincoln: Lincoln Record Society, 2017), p. 52.

18 Gillies, *Barbed-Wire University*, p. 229.

19 Steve Hare, *Penguin Portrait: Allen Lane and the Penguin Editors, 1935–1970* (London: Penguin, 1995), p. 116.

20 Hare, *Penguin Portrait*, p. 117.

21 Adrian Gilbert, POW. *Allies Prisoners in Europe, 1939–1945* (London: John Murray, 2006), pp. 184–5.

22 Valerie Holman, 'Captive Readers in the Second World War', *Publishing History*, 52 (2002), pp. 83–94 at p. 93 n. 16.

23 David Shavit, '"The Greatest Morale Factor next to the Red Army": Books and Libraries in American and British Prisoner of War Camps in Germany during World War II', *Libraries & Culture*, 34 (1999), pp. 113–34.

24 Gillies, *Barbed-Wire University*, pp. 275–80; David Rolf, 'The Education of British Prisoners of War in German Captivity, 1939–1945', *History of Education*, 18 (1989), pp. 257–65.

25 Cambray and Briggs, *Red Cross & St John*.

26 Bruce R. Johnson, 'The Efforts of C. S. Lewis to Aid British prisoners of War during World War II', *C. S. Lewis Journal*, 12 (2018), pp. 41–76.

27 Montgomery Belgion, *Reading for Profit* (Harmondsworth: Penguin, 1945).

28 Robert Holland, *Adversis Major: A Short History of the Educational Books Scheme of the Prisoners of War Department of the British Red Cross Society and Order of St John of Jerusalem* (London: Staples, 1949).

29 Gillies, *Barbed-Wire University*, pp. 277, 279.

30 David J. Carter, *POW behind Canadian Barbed Wire: Alien, Refugee and Prisoner of War Camps in Canada, 1914–1946* (Elkwater, Alberta: Eagle Butt Press, 1998).

31 Matthew Barry Sullivan, *Thresholds of Peace: German Prisoners and the People of Britain, 1944–1948* (London: Hamish Hamilton, 1979).

32 Ron Robin, *The Barbed-Wire College: Re-Educating German POWs in the United States during World War II* (Princeton, NJ: Princeton University Press, 1995).

On Axis prisoners in the United States see also Arnold Kramer, *Nazi Prisoners of War in America* (Lanham, MD: Scarborough House, 1996); David Fieldler, *The Enemy among Us: POWs in Missouri during World War II* (St Louis: Missouri Historical Society Press, 2003); Louis E. Keefer, *Italian Prisoners of War in America, 1942–1946* (New York: Praeger, 1992).

33 Bob Moore and Kent Fedorowich, *The British Empire and Its Italian Prisoners of War, 1940–1947* (Basingstoke: Palgrave, 2002).

34 Sullivan, *Thresholds of Peace*, p. 209.

35 Valerie Campbell, *Camp 165 Watten* (Dunbeath: Whittles, 2008). See also the same author's *Camp 21 Combrie: POWs and Post-War Stories from Cultybraggan* (Dunbeath: Whittles, 2017).

36 Basil Liddell-Hart, *The Other Side of the Hill* (London: Cassell, 1948), adapted for publication in America as *The Generals Talk* (New York: Morrow, 1948).

37 Russell Braddon, *The Naked Island* (London: Bodley Head, 1952) offers a graphic view of the horrors of POW life from the perspective of an Australian soldier. See also Eric Lomax, *The Railway Man* (London: Jonathan Cape, 1995).

38 Gillies, *Barbed-Wire University*, pp. 204–5.

39 Hare, *Penguin Portrait*, pp. 118–19.

40 Kee, *A Crowd Is not Company*, pp. 193–206.

13. Sanctuary

1 Thomas Cairns Livingstone, *Tommy's War: A First World War Diary*, ed. Ronnie Scott (London: Harper Press, 2008), p. 138.

2 John H. Morrow, *The Great War in the Air: Military Aviation from 1909 to 1921* (Washington, DC: Smithsonian Institution, 1993); Christopher Cole and E. F. Cheesman, *The Air Defence of Great Britain 1914–1918* (London: Putnam, 1984); Raymond H. Fredette, *The Sky on Fire: The First Battle of Britain 1917–1918* (New York: Harvest, 1976).

3 Peter Englund, *The Beauty and the Sorrow* (London: Profile, 2011), p. 440; Susan R. Grayzel, '"The Souls of Soldiers": Civilians under Fire in First World War France', *Journal of Modern History*, 78 (2006), pp. 588–622.

4 Flavia Bruni, 'All Is not Lost: Italian Archives and Libraries in the Second World War', in Flavia Bruni and Andrew Pettegree (eds), *Lost Books: Reconstructing the Print World of Pre-Industrial Europe* (Leiden: Brill, 2016), pp. 469–87.

5 Quoted by Matthew Parker, *Monte Cassino* (London: Headline, 2003), p. 170.

6 *Libraries Guests of the Vaticana during the Second World War* (Rome: Apostolic Vatican Library, 1945).

7 G. K. Barker, *The History of Public Libraries in France from Revolution to 1939* (Ann Arbor, MI: UMI, 1977); G. K. Barker, 'La léthargie des bibliothèques municipales', in Martine Poulain (ed.), *Histoire des bibliothèques françaises: Les bibliothèques aux xxe siècle, 1914–1990* (Lyon: Promodis, 1992), pp. 65–103.

8 Marie Kühlmann, 'Les bibliothèques dans la tourmente', in Poulain (ed.), *Histoire des bibliothèques*, pp. 298–9.

9 Kühlmann, 'Les bibliothèques dans la tourmente', p. 153.

10 Marta L. Dosa, *Libraries in the Political Scene* (Westport, CT: Greenwood, 1974), p. 94.

11 Jan L. Alessandrini, 'Lost Books of "Operation Gomorrah": Rescue, Reconstruction and Restitution at Hamburg's Library in the Second World War', in Bruni and Pettegree (eds), *Lost Books*, pp. 441–61.

12 Nicola Schneider, 'The Loss of the Music Collection of the Hessiche Landesbibliothek in Darmstadt in 1944', in Anna-Silvia Goeing, Anthony T. Grafton and Paul Michel (eds), *Collectors' Knowledge: What Is Kept, What Is Discarded* (Leiden: Brill, 2013), pp. 381–412.

13 Dosa, *Libraries in the Political Scene*, pp. 100–3; Werner Schochow, *Bücherschicksale: Die Verlagerungsgeschichte der Preussischen Staastbibliothek; Auslagerung, Zerstörung, Rückführung* (Berlin: De Gruyter, 2003).

14 P. R. Harris, 'Acquisitions in the Department of Printed Books, 1935–50, and the Effects of the War', in his *History of the British Museum Library 1753–1973* (London: British Library, 1998), pp. 119–44.

15 *Short Title Catalogue of Books Printed in the Netherlands and Belgium from 1470 to 1600 now in the British Museum* (London: British Museum, 1965), pp. 215–18; *Short-Title Catalogue of Books Printed in Italy and of Italian Books Printed in Other Countries from 1465 to 1600 now in the British Museum* (London: British Museum, 1958), pp. 746–52.

16 M. L. Caygill, 'The Protection of National Treasures at the British Museum During the First and Second World Wars', *MRS Online Proceedings Library*, 267 (1992), pp. 29–99.

17 Caroline Shenton, *National Treasures: Saving the Nation's Art in World War II* (London: John Murray, 2021), p. 180.

18 Bruni, 'All Is not Lost', p. 476.

19 Brian Dyson, 'In the Line of Fire: The Library of University College Hull during World War II', *Library History*, 15 (1999), pp. 113–24.

20 Robert C. Mikesh, *Japan's World War II Bomb Attacks on North America* (Washington, DC: Smithsonian Institution, 1973), p. 67.

21 Brett Spencer, 'Preparing for an Air Attack: Libraries and American Air Raid Defence during World War II', *Libraries and the Cultural Record*, 43 (2008), pp. 125–47.

22 For example, see Conrad Borchling and Bruno Claussen, *Niederdeutsche Bibliographie: Gesamtverzeichnis der niederdeutschen Drucke bis zum Jahre 1800*, 2 vols (Neumünster: Karl Wachholtz, 1931–6).

14. Plunder

1   Seth A. Givens, 'Liberating the Germans: The US Army and Looting in Germany during the Second World War', *War in History*, 21 (2014), pp. 33–54.

2   Cynthia Saltzman, *Napoleon's Plunder and the Theft of Veronese's Feast* (London: Thames & Hudson, 2021).

3   Kristian Jensen, *Revolution and the Antiquarian Book: Reshaping the Past, 1780–1815* (Cambridge: Cambridge University Press, 2011), p. 8.

4   Jensen, *Revolution and the Antiquarian Book*, p. 10.

5   J. Bepler, '*Vicissitudo Temporum*: Some Sidelights on Book Collecting in the Thirty Years' War', *Sixteenth Century Journal*, 32 (2001), pp. 953–68.

6   Emma Hagström Molin, 'To Place in a Chest: On the Cultural Looting of

Gustavus Adolphus and the Creation of Uppsala University Library in the Seventeenth Century', *Barok*, 44 (2016), pp. 135–48; Emma Hagström Molin, 'Spoils of Knowledge: Looted Books in Uppsala University Library in the Seventeenth Century', in Gerhild Williams et al. (eds), *Rethinking Europe: War and Peace in the Early Modern German Lands* (Leiden: Brill, 2019).

7 Jonathan Petropoulos, *Göring's Man in Paris: The Story of a Nazi Art Plunderer and His World* (London: Yale University Press, 2021).

8 Petropoulos, *Göring's Man in Paris*, p. 166.

9 Timothy W. Ryback, *Hitler's Private Library: The Books that Shaped His Life* (London: Bodley Head, 2009), pp. 142–62.

10 Petropoulos, *Göring's Man in Paris*, p. 128.

11 Jacqueline Borin, 'Embers of the Soul: The Destruction of Jewish Books and Libraries during World War II', *Libraries and Culture*, 28 (1993), pp. 445–60; Marek Sroka, 'The Destruction of Jewish Libraries and Archives in Cracow during World War II', *Libraries and Culture*, 38 (2003), pp. 147–65. Marek Sroka, 'The University of Cracow Library under Nazi Occupation: 1939–1945', *Libraries and Culture*, 34 (1999), pp. 1–16.

12 Rebecca Knuth, *Libricide: The Regime-Sponsored Destruction of Books and Libraries in the Twentieth Century* (Westport, CT: Praeger, 2003), pp. 98–9.

13 Anders Rydell, *The Book Thieves: The Nazi Looting of Europe's Libraries and the Race to Return a Literary Inheritance* (New York: Viking, 2015), p. 96.

14 Patricia Kennedy Grimsted, *The Odyssey of the Turgenev Library from Paris, 1940–2002: Books as Victims and Trophies of War* (Amsterdam: IISH, 2003).

15 Nancy Sinkoff, 'From the Archives: Lucy S. Dawidowicz and the Restitution of Jewish Cultural Property', *American Jewish History*, 100 (2016), pp. 95–126, at p. 102; Patricia Kennedy Grimsted, 'Roads to Ratibor: Library and Archival Plunder by the Einsatzstab Reichsleiter Rosenberg', *Holocaust Genocide Studies*, 19 (2005), pp. 390–458.

16 Rudolf Sment, 'Isaac Leo Seeligmann: Fascinated by the Septuagint', *Studia Rosenthaliana*, 38/9 (2005/6), pp. 100–6.

17 Rydell, *Book Thieves*, p. 108.

18 Sroka, 'University of Cracow Library'.

19 Dosa, *Libraries in the Political Scene*, pp. 87, 101.

20 Cornelia Briel, *Beschlagnahmt, Erpresst, Erbeutet: NS-Raubgut, Reichstauschstelle und Preussische Staatsbibliothek zwischen 1933 und 1945* (Berlin: Akademie Verlag, 2013).

21 Rydell, *Book Thieves*, p. 287.

22 *New York Times*, 14 June 1990. https://www.nytimes.com/1990/06/14/arts/a-trove-of-medieval-art-turns-up-in-texas.html.

23 Douglas Botting, *In the Ruins of the Reich* (London: George Allen & Unwin, 1985), p. 283.

24 Jonathan Trigg, *To VE-Day through German Eyes* (Stroud: Amberley, 2020), p. 240.

25 Konstantin Akinska, 'Stalin's Decrees and Soviet Trophy Brigades: Restitution in Kind or Trophies of War?', *International Journal of Cultural Property*, 17 (2010), pp. 195–216; Norman M. Naimark, *The Russians in Germany: A History of the*

Soviet Zone of Occupation, 1945–1949 (Cambridge, MA: Harvard University Press, 1995).

26 Botting, *Ruins of the Reich*, pp. 280–314; Patricia Meehan, *A Strange Enemy People: Germans under the British, 1945–1950* (London: Peter Owen, 2001), pp. 113–32.

27 Kenneth Alford, *Allied Looting in World War II: Thefts of Art, Manuscripts, Stamps and Jewellery in Europe* (Jefferson, NC: McFarland, 2011), p. 49.

28 Alford, *Allied Looting*, pp. 81–101, 162–5.

29 Alford, *Allied Looting*, pp. 166–9.

30 Alford, *Allied Looting*, p. 127.

31 Alford, *Allied Looting*, pp. 126–7.

32 Alford, *Allied Looting*, p. 145.

15. Pulp and Ashes

1 Walter Kempowski, *Swansong: A Collective Diary of the Last Days of the Third Reich* (New York: W. W. Norton, 2015), p. 138.

2 See above, Chapter 10.

3 Robert Malcolmson, *Love and War in London: The Mass Observation Wartime Diary of Olivia Crockett* (Stroud: History Press, 2008), p. 174.

4 Manuscript diary, Imperial War Museum, London, 93/14/1.

5 Malcolmson, *Love and War in London*, p. 175.

6 Hilda Urén Stubbings, *Blitzkrieg and Books: British and European Libraries as Casualties of World War II* (Bloomington, IN: Rubena Press, 1993), pp. 146–55; Richard Ovenden, *Burning the Books: A History of Knowledge under Attack* (London: John Murray, 2020), pp. 107–17.

7 Marie Kühlmann, 'Les bibliothèques dans la tourmente', in Martine Poulain (ed.), *Histoire des bibliothèques*, p. 316.

8 Rebecca Knuth, *Libricide: The Regime-Sponsored Destruction of Books and Libraries in the Twentieth Century* (Westport, CT: Praeger, 2003), p. 98. For the Library of Congress, see Ovenden, *Burning the Books*, pp. 79–90.

9 Marek Sroka, 'The University of Cracow Library under Nazi Occupation: 1939–1945', *Libraries and Culture*, 34 (1999), pp. 1–16.

10 Jacqueline Borin, 'Embers of the Soul: The Destruction of Jewish Books and Libraries in Poland during World War II', *Libraries and Culture*, 28 (1993), pp. 445–60, at pp. 447–8.

11 Joshua Starr, 'Jewish Cultural Property under Nazi Control', *Jewish Social Studies*, 12 (1950), pp. 27–48.

12 David E. Fishman, *The Book Smugglers: Partisans, Poets and the Race to Save Jewish treasures from the Nazis* (Lebanon, NH: University Press of New England, 2017).

13 Herman Kruk, 'Library and Reading Room in the Vilna Ghetto, Strashun Street 6', in Jonathan Rose (ed.), *The Holocaust and the Book* (Amherst: University of Massachusetts Press, 2001), pp. 171–200.

14 Walter Kempowski, *All for Nothing* (London: Granta, 2015).

15 R. M. Douglas, *Orderly and Humane: The Expulsion of the Germans after the Second World War* (New Haven, CT: Yale University Press, 2012).

16 Marek Sroka, '"Forsaken and Abandoned": The Nationalization and Salvage of Deserted, Displaced, and Private Library Collections in Poland, 1945–1948', *Library and Information Studies*, 28 (2012), pp. 272–88.

17 Kempowski, *Swansong*, p. 104.

18 Jonathan Trigg, *To VE-Day through German Eyes* (Stroud: Amberley, 2020), p. 187.

19 Examples from the Alexander Turnbull Library, Wellington, New Zealand, can be found in the plate section of Matthew Parker, *Monte Cassino* (London: Headline, 2003), and at pp. 273–7.

20 London, National Archives, WO 204/986. Cited in Parker, *Monte Cassino*, p. 276.

21 This was the charmingly named 'Operation Sauerkraut'. Elizabeth P. McIntosh, *Sisterhood of Spies: The Women of the OSS* (Annapolis, MD: Naval Institute Press, 1998), pp. 60–71.

22 Henry Irving, 'Paper Salvage in Britain during the Second World War', *Historical Research*, 89 (2016), pp. 373–93.

23 *Library Association Record*, May 1943, p. 87; June 1943, p. 93.

24 Hans van der Hoeven and Joan van Albada, *Memory of the World: Lost Memory. Libraries and Archives Destroyed in the Twentieth Century* (Paris: UNESCO, 1996), p. 8.

25 Theodore F. Welch, *Libraries and Librarianship in Japan* (Westport, CT: Greenwood, 1997), p. 17.

26 Jan-Pieter Barbian, *The Politics of Literature in Nazi Germany* (New York: Bloomsbury, 2013), p. 333.

16. Cleansing

1 Ben Shephard, *The Long Road Home: The Aftermath of the Second World War* (London: Bodley Head, 2010).

2 Frederick Taylor, *Exorcising Hitler: The Occupation and Denazification of Germany* (London: Bloomsbury, 2011); James F. Tent, *Mission on the Rhine: Re-Education and Denazification in American-Occupied Germany* (Chicago: University of Chicago Press, 1982).

3 Stephen Remy, *The Heidelberg Myth: The Nazification and Denazification of a German University* (Cambridge, MA: Harvard University Press, 2002), Chapters 1–3.

4 Margaret F. Stieg, 'The Postwar Purge of German Public Libraries, Democracy and the American Reaction', *Libraries and Culture*, 28 (1993), pp. 143–64, at p. 147.

5 Stephen Spender, *European Witness* (London: Hamish Hamilton, 1946).

6 Remy, *Heidelberg Myth*; Dominik Rigoll, 'From Denazification to Renazification? West German Government Officials after 1945', in Camilo Erlichman and Christopher Knowles (eds), *Transforming Occupation in Western Zones of Germany* (London: Bloomsbury, 2018), pp. 251–69.

7 Spender, *European Witness*, p. 153.

8 Jonathan Trigg, *To VE-Day through German Eyes* (Stroud: Amberley, 2020), pp. 225–6, 243.

9 Urvashi Goutam, 'Pedagogical Nazi Propaganda, (1939–1945)', *Proceedings of the Indian History Congress*, 75 (2014), pp. 1018–26.

10 Stieg, 'Postwar Purge', p. 147; Matthew D. Mingus, *Remapping Modern Germany after National Socialism, 1945–1961* (Syracuse, NY: Syracuse University Press, 2017).

11 Edith Davies, 'British Policy and the Schools', in Arthur Hearnden (ed.), *The British in Germany: Educational Reconstruction after 1945* (London: Hamish Hamilton, 1978); Mingus, *Remapping*, p. 81.

12 Kathy Peiss, *Information Hunters: When Librarians, Soldiers and Spies Banded Together in World War II Europe* (Oxford: Oxford University Press, 2020), p. 156.

13 Peiss, *Information Hunters*, p. 147.

14 Stieg, 'Postwar Purge', p. 154.

15 'On censoring German Books', *ALA Bulletin*, 40 (June 1946), p. 218.

16 Above, Chapters 5 and 6.

17 Peiss, *Information Hunters*, p. 85.

18 Peiss, *Information Hunters*, p. 86.

19 Peiss, *Information Hunters*, p. 77.

20 https://www.loc.gov/rr/european/coll/germ.html (accessed 20 January 2023).

21 Timothy W. Ryback, *Hitler's Private Library: The Books that Shaped His Life* (London: Bodley Head, 2009), pp. xv–xvi; https://library.brown.edu/collatoz/info.php?id=145 (accessed 20 January 2023).

22 A. D. Harvey, 'Confiscated Nazi Books in the British Library', *Electronic British Library Journal* (2003), pp. 1–13.

23 See below, Chapter 17.

24 Elaine Feinstein, *Anna of all the Russias: A Life of Anna Akhmatova* (London: Weidenfeld & Nicolson, 2005).

25 P. J. P. Whitehead, 'The Lost Berlin Manuscripts', *Notes*, 33 (1976), pp. 7–15; Aleksandra Patalas, *Catalogue of Early Music Prints from the Collections of the Former Preußische Staatsbibliothek in Berlin, Kept at the Jagiellonian Library in Cracow* (Kraków: Musica Iagellonica, 1999); Jane Perlez, 'A Clash over a Trove of Original Scores', *New York Times*, 25 April 1995.

26 Marek Sroka, '"Forsaken and Abandoned": The Nationalization and Salvage of Deserted, Displaced, and Private Library Collections in Poland, 1945–1948', *Library and Information Studies*, 28 (2012), pp. 272–88.

27 Marek Sroka, '"Soldiers of the Cultural Revolution": The Stalinization of Libraries and Librarianship in Poland, 1945–1953', *Library History*, 16 (2000), pp. 105–25.

28 Andrew Pettegree and Arthur der Weduwen, *The Library: A Fragile History* (London: Profile, 2021), Chapter 15.

29 Sroka, '"Soldiers of the Cultural Revolution"', p. 117.

30 Jiřina Šmejkalova, *Cold War Books in the 'Other Europe' and What Came After* (Leiden: Brill, 2011), pp. 117, 151.

31 Norman M. Naimark, *The Russians in Germany: A History of the Soviet Zone of Occupation, 1945–1949* (Cambridge, MA: Harvard University Press, 1995); Filip Slavenski, *The Soviet Occupation of Germany: Hunger, Mass Violence and the Struggle for Peace, 1945–1947* (Cambridge: Cambridge University Press, 2013).

32 Jan L. Alessandrini, 'Bombs on Books: Allied Destruction of German Libraries during World War II', in Mel Collier (ed.), *What Do We Lose When We Lose a Library?* (Leuven: Leuven University Library, 2016), pp. 45–54, at p. 49.

33 Kathleen A. Smith, 'Collection Development in Public and University Libraries of the former Democratic Republic since German Unification', *Libraries and Culture*, 36 (2001), pp. 413–31.

17. Restitution

1 This story is beautifully told in Anders Rydell, *The Book Thieves: The Nazi Looting of Europe's Libraries and the Race to Return a Literary Inheritance* (New York: Viking, 2017), pp. 16, 292–6, 306–12.

2 Above, Chapter 16; John Cole, 'The Library of Congress Becomes a World Library, 1815–2005', *Libraries and Culture*, 40 (2005), pp. 385–98.

3 Patricia Kennedy Grimsted, 'Sudeten Crossroads for Europe's Displaced Books: The Mysterious twilight of the RSHA Amt VII Library and the Fate of a Million Victims of War', in Mecislav Borak (ed.), *Restitution of Confiscated Art Works: Wish or Reality?* (Prague: Tilia, 2008).

4 Patricia Kennedy Grimsted, 'Roads to Ratibor: Library and Archival Plunder by the Einsatzstab Reichsleiter Rosenberg', *Holocaust Genocide Studies*, 19 (2005), pp. 390–458.

5 Kathy Peiss, *Information Hunters: When Librarians, Soldiers and Spies Banded Together in World War II Europe* (Oxford: Oxford University Press, 2020), p. 177; Robert G. Waite, 'Returning Jewish Cultural Property: The Handling of Books Looted by the Nazis in the American Zone of Occupation, 1945 to 1952', *Libraries and Culture*, 37 (2002), pp. 213–28.

6 S. J. Pomrenze, 'Offenbach Reminiscences and the Restitution to the Netherlands', in F. J. Hoogewoud et al., *The Return of Looted Collections (1946–1996)* (Amsterdam, 1997), pp. 10–18.

7 Peiss, *Information Hunters*, pp. 191, 194.

8 Patricia Kennedy Grimsted, 'The Road to Minsk for Western "Trophy" Books: Twice Plundered but not yet "Home from the War"', *Libraries and Culture*, 39 (2004), pp. 351–404; Patricia Kennedy Grimsted, 'The Fate of Ukrainian Cultural Treasures During World War II: The Plunder of Archives, Libraries, and Museums under the Third Reich', *Jahrbücher für Geschichte Osteuropas*, 39 (1991), pp. 53–80, at p. 372.

9 Patricia Kennedy Grimsted, *Trophies of War and Empire: The Archival Heritage of Ukraine, World War II, and the International Politics of Restitution* (Cambridge, MA: Harvard University Press, 2001).

10 Grimsted, 'Road to Minsk', p. 360.

11 Konstantin Akinska, 'Stalin's Decrees and Soviet Trophy Brigades: Restitution in Kind or Trophies of War?', *International Journal of Cultural Property*, 17 (2010), pp. 195–216.

12 Norman M. Naimark, *The Russians in Germany: A History of the Soviet Zone of Occupation, 1945–1949* (Cambridge, MA: Harvard University Press, 1995), pp. 175–6; Grimsted, *Trophies of War*, p. 259.

13 Rydell, *Book Thieves*, pp. 19–22.

14 Grimsted, *Trophies of War*, p. 257.

15 Grimsted, 'Road to Minsk', pp. 355, 365.

16 Grimsted, 'Road to Minsk', pp. 381–2; Patricia Kennedy Grimsted, *The Odyssey of the Turgenev Library from Paris, 1940–2002: Books as Victims and Trophies of War* (Amsterdam: IISH, 2003).

17 Rydell, *Book Thieves*, p. 299.

18 Patricia Kennedy Grimsted, *Returned from Russia: Nazi Archival Plunder in Western Europe and Recent Restitution Issues* (Builth Wells: Institute of Art and Law, 2013); Patricia Kennedy Grimsted, 'Tracing Trophy Books in Russia', *Solanus*, 19 (2005), pp. 131–45.

19 Peiss, *Information Hunters*, p. 194.

20 Peiss, *Information Hunters*, p. 195.

21 Merav Mack and Benjamin Balint, *Jerusalem: City of the Book* (New Haven, CT: Yale University Press, 2019).

22 Nancy Sinkoff, 'From the Archives: Lucy S. Dawidowicz and the Restitution of Jewish Cultural Property', *American Jewish History*, 100 (2016), pp. 95–126.

23 Mack and Balint, *Jerusalem*, p. 169.

24 Mack and Balint, *Jerusalem*, p. 170; Peiss, *Information Hunters*, p. 196.

25 Mack and Balint, *Jerusalem*, pp. 113–32.

26 Mack and Balint, *Jerusalem*, pp. 185–91.

18. Hearts and Minds

1 Geert Buelens, *Everything to Nothing: The Poetry of the Great War, Revolution and the Transformation of Europe* (London: Verso, 2015), pp. 304, 310.

2 The author held such a scholarship in Hamburg between 1982 and 1984. The hospitality was generous, and the philanthropist's war record was never mentioned.

3 Anthony Beevor and Artemis Cooper, *Paris after the Liberation: 1944–1949* (London: Hamish Hamilton, 1994), p. 255.

4 Marek Sroka, '"A Book Never Dies": The American Library Association and the Cultural Reconstruction of Czechoslovak and Polish Libraries, 1945–1948', *Library and Information History*, 33 (2017), pp. 19–34; Marek Sroka, 'The American Library Association and the Post-World War II Rebuilding of Eastern European Libraries', *International Federation of Library Associations and Institutions*, 45 (2019), pp. 26–33.

5 Sroka, '"A Book Never Dies"', p. 22.

6 John B. Hench, *Books as Weapons: Propaganda, Publishing and the Battle for Global Markets in the Era of World War II* (Ithaca, NY: Cornell University Press, 2010), p. 94.

7 Hench, *Books as Weapons*, p. 245.

8 Frances Stonor Saunders, *Who Paid the Piper? The CIA and the Cultural Cold War* (London: Granta, 1999), pp. 45–56 (New York), 73–84 (Berlin).

9 Peter Coleman, *The Liberal Conspiracy: The Congress for Cultural Freedom and the Struggle for the Mind of Post-War Europe* (New York: Free Press, 1989).

10 Stonor Saunders, *Who Paid the Piper?*, pp. 176–7.

11 Stonor Saunders, *Who Paid the Piper?*, pp. 215–17, 331, 411–12.

12 Alfred A. Reich, *Hot Books in the Cold War. The CIA-Funded Secret Western Book Distribution Program Behind the Iron Curtain* (Budapest: Central European University Press, 2013).

13 Andrew Lycell, *Ian Fleming* (London: Weidenfeld and Nicolson, 1995); John Pearson, *The Life of Ian Fleming* (London: Jonathan Cape, 1966).

14 James Fleming, *Bond behind the Iron Curtain* (Cheltenham: Book Collector, 2021), p. 29.

15 Fleming, *Bond behind the Iron Curtain*, p. 46.

16 Fleming, *Bond behind the Iron Curtain*, pp. 58–90, at p. 78.

17 Nina Willner, *Forty Autumns* (London: Little, Brown, 2016).

18 Mary Fulbrook, *The People's State: East German Society from Hitler to Honecker* (New Haven, CT: Yale University Press, 2005).

19 Paul Lendvai, *Blacklisted: A Journalist's Life in Central Europe* (London: I. B. Tauris, 1998).

20 Philip Oltermann, *The Stasi Poetry Circle* (London: Faber, 2022).

21 Lendvai, *Blacklisted*, pp. 60, 131.

22 Geoffrey Roberts, *Stalin's Library: A Dictator and his Books* (New Haven, CT: Yale University Press, 2022), p. 202; *Falsifiers of History (Historical Survey)* (Moscow: Foreign Languages Publishing House, 1948).

23 John Connelly, *Captive University: The Sovietization of East German, Czech and Polish Higher Education, 1945–1956* (Chapel Hill: University of North Carolina Press, 2000); John Connelly and Michael Grüttner (eds), *Universities under Dictatorship* (University Park: Pennsylvania State University Press, 2005).

24 Connelly, *Captive University*, p. 292.

25 Robert Darnton, *Censors at Work* (London: British Library, 2014).

26 Stephen J. Whitfield, *The Culture of the Cold War*, 2nd ed. (Baltimore, MD: Johns Hopkins University Press, 1996), p. 102.

27 Duncan White, *Cold Warriors: Writers Who Waged the Literary Cold War* (New York: HarperCollins, 2019), p. 391.

28 Elizabeth D. Samet, *Looking for the Good War: American Amnesia and the Violent Pursuit of Happiness* (New York: Farrar, Straus and Giroux, 2021), p. 213; David Hajdu, *The Ten-Cent Plague: The Comic Book Scare and How It changed America* (New York: Farrar, Straus and Giroux, 2008), pp. 311–12.

29 Geoffrey Little, 'Teaching Librarians to Be Censors: Library Education for Francophones in Quebec, 1937–61', in Nicole Moore (ed.), *Censorship and the Limits of the Literary: A Global View* (London: Bloomsbury, 2015), pp. 93–103.

30 Peter D. McDonald, *The Literature Police: Apartheid Censorship and Its Cultural Consequences* (Oxford: Oxford University Press, 2009).

31 On Lysenko see Chapter 4, above.

32 Simon Ings, *Stalin and the Scientists: A History of Triumph and Tragedy, 1905–1953* (New York: Atlantic Monthly, 2016), p. 343.

33 Ings, *Stalin and the Scientists*, pp. 350, 368–9.

34 Susan A. Brewer, *Why America Fights: Patriotism and War Propaganda from the Philippines to Iraq* (New York: Oxford University Press, 2009), p. 182; Douglas Kinnard, *The War Managers* (Hanover, NH: University Press of New England, 1977).

35 John Dumbrell, 'The Johnson Administration and the British Labour Government: Vietnam, the Pound and East of Suez', *Journal of American Studies*, 30 (1996), pp. 211–31; Caroline Page, *US Official Propaganda during the Vietnam War, 1965–1973* (London: Leicester University Press, 1996).

36 Rich Perlstein, *Nixonland* (New York: Scribner, 2008), pp. 488–9. See also https://electionstudies.org/wp-content/uploads/2018/03/anes_timeseries_1972_newspaper_endorsements.pdf (accessed 23 January 2023).

37 J. Michael Lennon, *Norman Mailer: A Double Life* (New York: Simon & Schuster, 2013).

38 Michael Herr, *Dispatches* (New York: Knopf, 1977); Donald Ringnalda, 'Fighting and Writing: America's Vietnam War Literature', *Journal of American Studies*, 22 (1988), pp. 25–42.

39 Brewer, *Why America Fights*, p. 189.

40 Kendrick Oliver, *The My Lai Massacre in American History and Memory* (Manchester: Manchester Unversity Press, 2005); James Olson and Randy Roberts, *My Lai: A Brief History With Documents* (Boston: Bedford Books, 1998).

41 Brewer, *Why America Fights*, pp. 197, 202–3.

42 Duncan White, *Cold Warriors. Writers who Waged the Literary Cold War* (New York: Harper Collins, 2019), p. 532.

43 Christopher Mallaby, *Living the Cold War: Memoirs of a British Diplomat* (Stroud: Amberley, 2017), pp. 20–2.

44 Joanna Lewis, 'Mau Mau's War of Words: The Battle of the Pamphlets', in James Raven (ed.), *Free Print and Non-Commercial Publishing since 1700* (Aldershot: Ashgate, 2000), pp. 222–46.

45 Richard Stubbs, *Hearts and Minds in Guerrilla Warfare: The Malayan Emergency, 1948–1960* (Singapore: Oxford University Press, 1989), pp. 170, 181–2.

46 Matthew Connelly, *A Diplomatic Revolution: Algeria's Fight for Independence and the Origins of the Post-War Era* (Oxford: Oxford University Press, 2002); Daniel Lerner, *The Passing of Traditional Society: Modernizing the Middle East* (London: Collier-Macmillan, 1958).

47 Julia Lovell, *Maoism: A Global History* (London: Bodley Head, 2019), pp. 60–2, 83–4.

48 Douglas Stiffler, 'Resistance to the Sovietization of Higher Education in China', in Connelly and Grüttner (ed), *Universities under Dictatorship*, pp. 213–43.

49 Lovell, *Maoism*, pp. 147–8.

50 The author's own recollection of boarding school life in the late 1960s. See also Alexander C. Cook (ed.), *Mao's Little Red Book: A Global History* (Cambridge: Cambridge University Press, 2014), pp. 37–8, 45, 76.

51 Andrew F. Jones, 'Quotation Songs: Portable Media and the Maoist Pop Song', in Cook (ed.), *Mao's Little Red Book*, pp. 43–60.

Coda: The End of History and the Continuation of War

1 Francis Fukuyama, 'The End of History?', *National Interest*, 16 (1989), pp. 3–18, at p. 4.

2 Michael Ignatieff, *The Warrior's Honor: Ethnic War and the Modern Conscience* (London: Chatto & Windus, 1998), p. 97.

3 Ignatieff, *The Warrior's Honor*, pp. 10, 75.

4 Nathaniel Fick, *One Bullet Away: The Making of a Marine Officer* (Boston: Houghton Mifflin, 2005), p. 251.

5 Susan A. Brewer, *Why America Fights: Patriotism and War Propaganda from the Philippines to Iraq* (New York: Oxford University Press, 2009), pp. 245, 265.

6 Jumana Bayeh, 'Egypt's Facebook Revolution: Arab Diaspora Literature and Censorship in the Homeland', in Nicole Moore (ed.), *Censorship and the Limits of the Literary: A Global View* (London: Bloomsbury, 2015), pp. 219–31.

7 The Legacy Project is now the Center for American War Letters at Chapman University: https://www.chapman.edu/research/institutes-and-centers/cawl/index.aspx (accessed 23 January 2023).

8 Elizabeth D. Samet, *Soldier's Heart: Reading Literature through Peace and War at West Point* (New York: Farrar, Straus and Giroux, 2007), pp. 18, 70, 128.

9 Elizabeth D. Samet, *Looking for the Good War: American Amnesia and the Violent Pursuit of Happiness* (New York: Farrar, Straus and Giroux, 2021); Samet, *Soldier's Heart*, pp. 239, 241; Elizabeth D. Samet, *No Man's Land: Preparing for War and Peace in post-9/11 America* (New York: Farrar, Straus and Giroux, 2007).

10 Robert Reich, 'Putin and Trump Have Convinced Me: I Was Wrong about the 21st Century', *Guardian*, 13 March 2022, https://www.theguardian.com/commentisfree/2022/mar/13/putin-trump-ukraine-russia-invasion-war-21st-century (accessed 23 January 2023).

11 *112 Gripes about the French* (Paris: Information & Education Division of the US Occupation Forces, 1945). A facsimile edition was published by the Bodleian Library, Oxford, in 2013.

LIST OF ILLUSTRATIONS

Integrated

Plates

INDEX

Lviv 246
Lyon 269
Lysenko, Trofim 98–9, 398

M
Macaulay, Rose 31, 115
Macfarland, Lanning 'Packy' 102
Machiavelli, Niccolò 39, 387
MacLeish, Archibald 18, 99
Macmillan 188, 218
Macmillan, Harold 209, 240
Madge, Charles 170
Madrid 105, 391
    Prado 391
Mafeking 62, 69
magazines 4–5, 25, 27, 59, 64, 67–8, 73, 75,
    78, 141, 157, 178, 181, 224–5, 229–30, 232,
    235, 237, 239–40, 251, 255, 259, 280, 289,
    331, 333, 342, 386, 393, 399–400, 419
Magdeburg 390
Maginot Line 114
Magnes, Judah 376
Mahan, Dennis 41
Maida Vale 328
Mailer, Norman 196, 385, 400
Mainz 295, 310,
    Psalter 310, 323
Malaya 342, 403–4
Mallaby, Christopher 402
Malraux, André 385
Manchester 69, 175
Mandela, Nelson 405, 415
Mann, Heinrich 158
Mann, Thomas 288
Mao Zedong 3, 10, 25, 235, 274, 404–7,
    418–9
maps 2, 11, 17, 19–20, 29, 41, 54, 74, 103,
    118, 122, 124–45, 149, 230, 280, 304, 351,
    354–5
Marinetti, Filippo Tommaso 24
Marlow, James 186–7
Marshall Plan 381, 384
Marshall, Henrietta 28
Marx, Karl 393
Mass Observation (MO) 170, 175, 178–81,
    189, 210, 326–7, 333
Masterman, Charles 247
Masterman, J. C. 110
Mau Mau 402
Maugham, Somerset 235, 237

Mauriac, François 270
Maurois, André 156, 183, 187
Maximilian, Duke of Bavaria 312
May, Karl 191, 243, 264
Mayakovsky, Vladimir 25
Mayans 15
Mazaryk, Tomáš 136
McCarthy, Mary 385
McCarthy, Joseph 396
McCarthyism 390, 396
McGovern, George 399
McNeile, Herman Cyril 250
Meador, Joe 321, 323
Mediterranean 128, 242
Mein Kampf 3, 8, 59, 150, 160, 203–4, 211,
    216–7, 263–4, 274, 283, 290, 313, 333
Melville, Cecil F. 187
Mennonites 29
Merleau-Ponty, Maurice 386
Metcalf, Herbert J. 202
Methuen 218
Metz 41, 114
Mexico 106–7, 336
Meyer, Stephenie 415
Meynen, Emil 139
Michael, Jerome 374
Michel, Gaspard 311
Michelangelo 310
Michigan, University of 141
microfilm 93, 95, 141, 419
Middelburg 330
Midway, battle 306
Mikaelian, Allen 413
Milan 297, 311
Miller, Arthur 194, 385
Miller, Douglas 194
Milne, A.A. 30–1
Milner, Alfred 60–3
mines 296–7, 304, 321, 363, 366
Miniver, Mrs 261
Minsk 1, 369, 370, 373
Mitchell, Margaret 257
Mitchison, Naomi 255
Mitterrand, François 265
Moberly Pool 8, 215
Mogg, R.P.L. 275
Molotov, Vyacheslav 22
Moltke, Helmuth Graf von 43, 46–7,
    70–1
Monluc, Blaise de 38

Rauschenplat, Hellmut von 185
Rawlings, Charles 236
Reader's Digest 5, 180
Readers Union 180
Reading University 135
Red Cross 2, 171, 224, 227–8, 281, 283, 285, 290–1
Reed, Douglas 217
Reformation 26, 152, 302, 312, 419
Reich, Robert 416–7
Religious Tract Society 68
Remarque, Erich Maria 156, 158, 250, 288
resistance newspapers 267–70
Reuter, Professor 349
Reuters 186
Revere, Paul 237
Ribbentrop, Joachim von 313
Rice, Tilly 210
Rider Haggard, Henry 253–4
Riga 312, 318, 410
Roberts, Frederick Lord 61, 65
Rockefeller Foundation 382
Rocquancourt, Jean-Thomas 42
Romania, Rumania 113, 124, 392, 396
Rome 16, 246, 298, 339
   ancient 15, 38, 415
   Vatican 297–8, 310, 312
Romein, Jan 273
Rommel, Edwin 75, 121
Roosevelt, Eleanor 198
Roosevelt, Franklin Delano 11–2, 18, 76, 108, 149, 195, 198, 242, 256, 261, 347, 357, 381, 383
Rose, W.J. 165
Rosenberg, Alfred 204, 245, 264, 315–8, 333, 336, 355, 364, 368, 372
Rothermere, Harold Harmsworth, Lord 252
Rotterdam 326
Round Table 63
Rousseau 10
Rowohlt, Ernst 207
Rügen 79
Ruhleben 280–1
Rundstedt, Gerd von 290
Rundstedt, Hans Gerd von 290
Russell, Bertrand 30–1
Russia 7, 21–3, 27–9, 57, 67, 70, 75–9, 95–7, 100, 110–1, 129, 137, 150, 175, 187, 208,

254, 318, 357–8, 364, 369, 371, 373, 379–81, 383, 390, 398, 416–7
   see also Soviet Union
Rwanda 411
Ryle, Gilbert 110

S
Saarbrücken 323
Sacramento 200
St Andrews University 88, 299
Saint-Cyr 40
St George Saunders, Hilary 184, 255
St John, Order of 281
Saint-Nazaire 143
St Petersburg
   Imperial Library 376
salvage *see* paper
Samet, Elizabeth 414
San Jacinto 307
Sandhurst 45, 48–9, 54, 88, 422
Sarajevo 15
Sartre, Jean-Paul 383, 386
Savonarola, Girolamo 304
Sayers, Dorothy L. 103, 213
Scandinavia 19, 140, 267–9
Scapa Flow 114, 237
Schellenberg, Walter 112, 114–5, 119
Schiller, Friedrich 320
Schlesinger, Arthur 385
Schlieffen Plan 48, 133, 155
Schloss Lauenstein 303
Schocken, Salman 376
schools, schooling 2, 8, 9, 16, 24, 26, 34, 36, 40–1, 44–6, 51–2, 54, 67–8, 70, 73–5, 88, 95, 138–9, 152, 169, 186, 192, 201–2, 204, 226, 264, 274, 316–7, 334–5, 348, 350–1, 358, 396, 403, 407, 410
   English public 53–4
   Napoli 75, 79
Schuster, Wilhelm 203
Schwaneberg 390
Scovell, George 105–6
Seattle 200
Secker and Warburg 208–9
Seeligmann, Isaac Leo 319
Seyss-Inquart, Arthur 319
Shakespeare, William 104, 226, 275, 279, 410, 413–414
Shanghai 342, 405
Shap Wells 289

Andrew Pettegree is a professor of modern history at the University of St. Andrews. A leading expert on the history of book and media transformations, Pettegree is the award-winning author of several books on news and information culture, including *The Library: A Fragile History* (with Arthur der Weduwen). He lives in Scotland.